PETER THE HERMIT PREACHES THE FIRST CRUSADE

Frontispiece, Palestine.

PALESTINE

FROM THE

PATRIARCHAL AGE TO THE PRESENT TIME

WITH

INTRODUCTORY CHAPTERS ON THE GEOGRAPHY
AND NATURAL HISTORY OF THE COUNTRY,
AND ON THE CUSTOMS AND INSTITU-
TIONS OF THE HEBREWS

BY

JOHN KITTO, D.D.

ILLUSTRATED

NEW YORK
PETER FENELON COLLIER
MDCCCXCIX

ADVERTISEMENT.

THE present work was originally undertaken with the view of supplying what has been felt as a desideratum in schools—a History of Palestine, with accounts of the geography of the country, and of the customs and institutions of its ancient inhabitants; but it has been suggested to the Publishers, that the volume might be considered a valuable acquisition by readers of a more advanced class, on account of the information it contains, and the connected and compendious form in which it presents the history of the Hebrew nation from the time of Abraham, through the various political forms which it assumed till the dispersion of that peculiar people.

The HISTORY has been written expressly for its present use, and is in no respect an abridgment of the author's larger work, *The Pictorial History of Palestine.* In the Introductory Chapters much assistance has been obtained from the Biblical Archæology of Professor JAHN, and from a variety of other sources—the whole being illustrated by the results of such acquaintance with Oriental customs as the author's former residence in the East enabled him to acquire.

The present Edition has been carefully revised throughout ; considerable improvements have been made—particularly
in the Introduction ; and a greatly increased number of really
Illustrative Wood-cuts have been inserted.

                                                      J. K.

CONTENTS.

Part I. Historical and Physical Geography.—Names—Divisions—Bordering Nations—Mountains—Plains and Valleys—Rivers—Lakes—Climate and Seasons   Page 1

II. Agriculture and Pasturage.—Laws—Operations and Implements—Vines and Vineyards—Trees—Pastures—Flocks and Herds   25

III. Habits of Life.—Habitations and Utensils—Food and Dress—Women and Children—Etiquette—Travelling—Customs relating to the Dead 52

IV. Literature, Science, and Art.—Literature—Science and Art—Commerce and War 91

V. Institutions.—Religious—Political—Judicial . . 108

HISTORY OF PALESTINE.

Book I. From the Deluge till the Death of Joseph . . . 127

II. From the Birth till the Death of Moses . . . 157

III. From the Death of Moses till the Accession of Saul   191

IV. From the Reign of Saul till the Death of Solomon . 225

V. From the Revolt of the Ten Tribes till the Captivity of the Jews under Nebuchadnezzar 270

VI. From the Captivity till the Rise of the Maccabees . 316

VII. From the Rise of the Maccabees till the End of the Asamonean Dynasty 349

VIII. From the Reign of Herod the Great till the Restoration of Syria to the Dominion of the Porte . . 378

LIST OF ILLUSTRATIONS

PALESTINE

Frontispiece—Peter the Hermit Preaches the First Crusade . . .

The Hospitaler Castle of Krag in the Holy Land . . . .

The Battle of Azotus . . . .

Interior of the Church of the Holy Sepulchre . . . . .

TABLES OF SCRIPTURE MEASURES, WEIGHTS, AND COINS.

MEASURES OF LENGTH.

	Feet. Dec.
A Fathom, equal to 4 cubits, or	7·296

	Inches. Dec.
A Cubit, equal to	21·888
A Span the longer, equal to half a cubit, or	10·944
A Span the less, equal to a third of a cubit, or	7·296
A Hand's-breadth, equal to a sixth of a cubit, or . . .	3·684
A Finger's-breadth, equal to a twenty-fourth of a cubit, or	0·912

MEASURES OF CAPACITY.

	Wine Gall.	Pints
Chomer or Homer, equal to	75	5½
Ephah or Bath, equal to	7	5
Seah, one-third of ephah, equal to	2	4
Hin, one-sixth of ephah, equal to	1	2
Omer, one-tenth of ephah, equal to	0	6
Cab, one-eighteenth of ephah, equal to	0	3½

WEIGHTS AND COINS.

	Grains.			£.	s.	D.
Shekel, equal to . . .	219	silver, equal to	. .		2	4½
Bekah, half shekel . .	109·5	,, ,,	. .		1	2¼
Gerah, one-tenth of bekah,	10·95	,, ,,	. .		0	1⅛
Manen, equal to 100 shekel-weight.						
Maneh in coin, equal to 60 shekels				£7	1	5
Talent of Silver, equal to 3000 shekels				353	11	10
Talent of Gold, the same weight				5075	15	7

ROMAN MONEY MENTIONED IN NEW TESTAMENT.

	Pence.	Farth.
Denarius, silver, equal to	7	3
Assis, copper ,, ...	0	3
Assarium . . ,, ...	0	1½
Quadrans . . ,, ...	0	0¼
A Mite . . . ,, ...	0	0½

INTRODUCTION

PART I.—HISTORICAL AND PHYSICAL GEOGRAPHY

SECTION I.—HISTORICAL GEOGRAPHY

NAMES.

PALESTINE has, in different ages, been known by various names :—

1. In Scripture it is called, by way of pre-eminence, THE LAND ;* every region being pre-eminently the land or country of its inhabitants.   It is also called, distinctively, THE LAND of the successive proprietors or occupants of the whole country, or of particular parts of it:—as, 1. The LAND OF CANAAN ; from Canaan, the youngest son of Ham, and grandson of Noah, among whose eleven sons the country was divided, after the Confusion at Babel (Gen. x. 6, 15):—2. The LAND OF ISRAEL ; from the Israelites, the posterity of Israel (Jacob), who drove out the Canaanites, and settled therein :—3. The LAND OF JUDAH ; a name which was at first restricted to the domains of the tribe of Judah ; but was afterwards applied to the separate kingdom formed by the tribes of Judah and

* Often translated " The Earth," in English versions.

Benjamin (Psalm lxxvi. 1); and at last, under the form of JUDÆA, to the whole country.

2. The name the LORD'S (or JEHOVAH'S) LAND, or the LAND OF GOD, occurs frequently in the Old Testament, and bears a peculiar force when understood with reference to the fact that, under the Hebrew constitution, God Himself was the king of the land, and the sovereign proprietor of the soil (Lev. xxv. 23). The name HOLY LAND, does not seem to have been employed by the Jews until after the Captivity (Zech. ii. 12). They used it with reference to the fact, that the land was chosen by God to be the inheritance of His people, and the seat of His worship. Christians, among whom also the name is in common use, have, at the same time, regard to its being the scene of the acts and sufferings of Christ and His Apostles. THE LAND OF PROMISE (Heb. xi. 9), is a name given with reference to the promise which God made to Abraham, that He would bestow this land on his children.

3. PALESTINE may now, from general use, be regarded as the proper geographical name of the country. It is derived from the *Philistines ;* who obtained possession of a very important part of the land, and appear to have given their name to the whole of it in the time of Moses (Exod. xv. 14).

DIVISIONS.

1. The divisions of Palestine were different in different ages.—*In the time of the Patriarchs*, the country was divided among the tribes or nations descended from the sons of Canaan. The precise locality of each nation is not, in every case, distinctly known; but the map exhibits the most probable arrangement. Here it is sufficient to mention that the KENITES, the KENIZZITES, and the KADMONITES, lived on the east of the Jordan (Gen. xv. 18–21); and that, on the west of that river, or in Palestine Proper, the HITTITES, the PERIZZITES, the JEBUSITES, and the AMORITES, abode in the hill country of the south (afterwards belonging to Judah); the CANAANITES—properly so called—in the middle, across the country, from the sea-coast to the river Jordan; the

GIRGASHITES, along the eastern border of the lake of Gennesareth; and the HIVITES in the north, among the southern branches of the Lebanon mountains. The southern part of the coast was occupied by the PHILISTINES, and the northern part by the PHŒNICIANS.

2. *In the time of Moses*, when the Israelites prepared to enter Canaan, the distribution of the nations on the west of the Jordan had undergone very little change; but, on the east of that river, we find the three principal territories to have been BASHAN, in the north,—that is to say, east and north-east of the lake Gennesareth; GILEAD, in the middle; and, in the south, on the east of the Dead Sea, the LAND OF MOAB, so called from one of the sons of Lot, who settled there. There are traces of the name of Gilead in the time of Jacob.

3. *After the Conquest*, the land was distributed by lot among the tribes. The particulars of this distribution will be best seen by reference to the map. JUDAH, BENJAMIN, SIMEON, and DAN, occupied the south; EPHRAIM, half of MANASSEH, and ISSACHAR, the middle; and ZEBULON, NAPHTALI, and ASHER, the north. REUBEN, GAD, and the other half of MANASSEH, were settled beyond Jordan, in Bashan and Gilead. This distribution was in no way affected by the division of the country into two kingdoms, which took place after the death of Solomon. The boundary line between them was the northern limit of the tribe of Benjamin.

4. *After the Captivity*, we hear very little of the territories of the tribes, for ten of them never returned to occupy their ancient domains.

5. *In the time of Christ*, the country on the west of the Jordan was divided into the provinces of Galilee, Samaria, and Judæa. GALILEE is a name which occurs repeatedly in the book of Joshua (xxi. 32); and very often in the later history. It was applied to that part of Palestine north of the plain of Esdraelon or Jezreel. This province was divided into Lower or Southern, and Upper or Northern Galilee. The latter section was also denominated Galilee of the Gentiles (Matt. iv. 15). SAMARIA occupied nearly the middle of Palestine; but, although it extended across the country, it did not come down to the sea-shore. JUDÆA, as a province,

corresponded to the northern and western parts of the ancient kingdom of that name; but the south-eastern portion formed the territory of IDUMÆA. On the other side of the Jordan the divisions were, at this time, more numerous and less distinct. The whole country, generally, was called PERÆA, and was divided into eight districts or cantons, namely:—
1. PERÆA, in the more limited sense, which was the southernmost canton, extending from the river Arnon to the river Jabbok.—2. GILEAD, north of the Jabbok, and highly populous.—3. DECAPOLIS, or the district of ten cities, which were Scythopolis or Bethshan (on the west side of the Jordan), Hippos, Gadara, Pella, Philadelphia (formerly Rabbath), Dium, Canatha, Gerasa, Raphana, and, perhaps, Damascus; but there is not much certainty with regard to the ten cities from which the region had its name.—4. GAULONITIS, extending to the north-east of the Upper Jordan and of the lake Gennesareth.—5. BATANÆA, the ancient Bashan, but less extensive, east of the lake Gennesareth.—6. AURANITIS, also called ITURÆA, and known to this day by the old name of Hauran (Ezek. xlvii. 16–18), to the north of Batanæa and the east of Gaulonitis.—7. TRACHONITIS, extending to the north of Gaulonitis, and east from Paneas (Cæsarea Philippi) and the sources of the Jordan, where it was separated from Galilee (Luke iii. 1).—8. ABILENE, in the extreme north, among the mountains of Anti-Libanus, between Baalbec and Damascus.

BORDERING NATIONS.

The bordering nations mentioned in Scripture, are the PHILISTINES, PHŒNICIANS, MOABITES, AMMONITES, MIDIANITES, EDOMITES, and AMALEKITES.

1. The PHILISTINES, although they were settled in Palestine in the time of the Patriarchs, were not Canaanites, but strangers, who had probably migrated, or had been expelled, from Egypt. They drove out the Avites, a Canaanitish tribe, and established themselves in their room, in the small strip of territory on the south-west coast, from a point below Joppa to Gaza. Here they maintained themselves for many gene-

rations, and, at, times, made their power felt in the interior and in the south, long after the land of Canaan had been conquered by the Israelites. Their chief towns, each the seat of a distinct state or republic, were Gath, Ekron, Ashdod, Ascalon, and Gaza.

2. The PHŒNICIANS although Canaanites by origin, were not among the doomed nations whom the Israelites were ordered to expel. In fact, their presence was rather useful than otherwise to the Hebrew nation; and very friendly relations subsisted between them,

1. Gaza.

which were much to the temporal advantage of both nations. The Phœnicians needed the products of the soil, which the Israelites raised in abundance ; and the Israelites wanted the various commodities which the traffic of the Phœnicians afforded, and for which they were glad to exchange their corn, wine, and oil. This intercourse was chiefly with the southern states of Tyre and Sidon, the more northern states being little noticed in the history of the Jews. As a nation, the Phœnicians occupied the northern portion of that extended plain along the coast, the southern portion of which was in the hands of the Philistines.

3. MOAB and AMMON were the descendants of the two sons of Lot, the nephew of Abraham. They established themselves in the country to the east of the river Jordon, in territories from which they expelled the aboriginal inhabitants, the gigantic races of the Emim and Zamzummim. The Moabites had their territory to the east of the Dead Sea and the lower Jordan ; and the Ammonites lived to the northeast of Moab. The chief town of the Moabites was Ar, or Rabbath-Ammon, or Areopolis, as it was afterwards called.

situated upon the south bank of the Arnon, some ruins of which may still be traced.

4. The MIDIANITES were descended from Midian, the fourth son of Abraham, by his second wife, Keturah (Gen. xxv. 1-2). Their territory lay to the east and south-east of that of the Moabites. They seem to have been a more pastoral and less settled people than the Moabites, in alliance with whom we usually find them acting. By the time that history introduces us to them, they appear to have become wholly adolatrous (Num. xxii. 2-7; xxxi.) Another tribe of Midianites was established about the head of the eastern arm (Elanitic Gulf) of the Red Sea; among whom Moses found refuge when he fled from Egypt. They appear to have been a branch of the same stock, although it has been thought that the name of Cushites, which is sometimes given to them (Num. xii. 1; Hab. iii. 7), indicated a descent from Midian, the son of Cush. This, however, might be ascribed to their occupation of a territory usually considered as belonging to Cush or Ethiopia; and it is an argument in favour of their descent from Abraham, that these Midianites still retained, in the time of Moses, the knowledge of the true God, which the world in general had lost. These distant Midianites had little connection with the Jewish history after the time of Moses.

5. The EDOMITES were descended from Edom, or Esau, the son of Isaac and brother of Jacob. They were settled in the mountains of Seir, which extend along the eastern side of the great valley of Arabah, between the Dead Sea and the Elanitic Gulf. In a valley among these mountains, the remains of Petra, the chief city of Edom, have only lately been discovered, and have been viewed with much wonder on account of the beautiful tombs and other monuments hewn in the surrounding cliffs

2. Interior of a Tomb.

While the land was comparatively depopulated, during the Captivity of the Jews in Babylon, the Edomites established themselves in the south-eastern parts of Judæa, whence, as already mentioned, that quarter came to be called Idumæa, or the country of the Idumæans or Edomites.

6. The AMALEKITES were descended from Amalek, the son of Ham and grandson of Noah. They were the most bitter enemies of the Israelites, by whom they were eventually exterminated. We find them first in the fertile valleys near the foot of Mount Sinai (Exod. xvii. 8-16); and afterwards on the southern borders of Palestine. They seem to have been a pastoral people; and

3. Ravine in Idumæa.

in that quarter there is a much larger extent of fine pasture grounds than was, until lately, supposed.

All these nations have long been extinct; some before and others very soon after the final dispersion of the Jews.

SECTION II.—LAND.

───◆───

MOUNTAINS.

1. PALESTINE may be regarded as a mountainous country. The mountains are the most lofty and imposing in the north, where the ridges branch off from Lebanon. To the north of the great central plain of Esdraelon, the eminences take the form of rounded hills, except towards the valley of the Jordan and its lakes, where the scenery has a stern and abrupt character, with deep ravines, tall cliffs, and numerous caverns.—The principal mountains are Lebanon, Hermon, Tabor, Carmel, Ebal, and Gerizim.

2. *Lebanon.* The Labanon mountains consist of two ranges, which come down, parallel to each other, from the north, and extend their southern branches into Palestine. They enclose between them an extensive valley, called in Scripture "the valley of Lebanon" (Josh. xi. 17), and in other books, Cœle-Syria (the enclosed, or hollow Syria).

The outer or western ridge, fronting the sea, into which it projects several promontories, was called Libanus by ancient writers; while to the inner, or eastern range, fronting the plains of Damascus, they gave the name of Anti-Libanus. But these distinctions are not found in the Bible, where the name Lebanon is applied to both ranges. Of the two ridges, Libanus is the loftiest; and on its highest points, and in the fissures facing the north, snow may be found all the year round. Hence the ancient inhabitants obtained the snow with which they cooled their drinks in summer (Prov. xxv. 13). This snow is not, however, in sufficient quantity, nor does it give a sufficiently marked appearance, to account for the name of the White Mountain, which is, in Hebrew, the meaning of Lebanon. The name must rather be ascribed to the general appearance of the mountains; for they are composed of whitish limestone; and the surface, as it reflects the light, exhibits everywhere a whitish aspect. The mountains of the western Lebanon are cultivated in terraces; and this region is now, as it was formerly, full of villages and people.

3. *Mount Hermon* was the northern limit of the territory of Israel beyond Jordan (Deut. iii. 8; iv. 48; Josh. xi. 3-17; xiii. 11), and the Psalmist speaks of it and Tabor as the representatives of all the mountains of Israel (Psalm lxxxix. 12; see also cxxxiii. 3; Sol. Song, iv. 8). This mountain is properly a prolongation of Anti-Libanus, and now bears, in Arabic, the name of Jebel-es-Sheikh, *the Sheikh's Mountain.* Its top is usually stated to be 10,000 feet above the Mediterranean, and during the whole year is partially crowned with snow, or rather ice, which, as it lies in the ravines, presents the appearance of radiant stripes, around and below the summit of the mountain. This range must not be confounded with another Mount Hermon (distinguished as Little Hermon), in the plain of Esdraelon.

4. *Tabor* is, in many respects, the most remarkable mountain in Palestine. It stands apart and alone on the north-east border of the plain of Esdraelon, with all its fine proportions, from base to summit, displayed at one view. Seen from the south-west, it presents a semi-globular appearance; but from the north-west, it more resembles a truncated cone. Its height has been greatly over-estimated. Dr. Robinson thinks that it does not exceed 1000 feet above the level of the plain. By an ancient path, which winds considerably, one may *ride* to the summit, where is a small oblong plain, with the foundations of ancient buildings. The view of the country from this place is very beautiful and extensive. The mountain is of limestone, which is the general rock of Palestine. The sides of the mountain are mostly covered with bushes, and woods of oak trees (ilex and ægilops), with occasionally pistachio, presenting a beautiful appearance, and affording a fine shade. This mountain is several times mentioned in the Old Testament (Josh. xix. 12, 22; Judges iv. 6, 12, 14); but not in the New. It has, indeed, been said that it was the mountain on which our Lord was transfigured (Matt. xvii.); but this appears more than doubtful, from the fact, that the summit of Mount Tabor was then occupied by a fortified town.

5. *Carmel* is a mountain ridge, six or eight miles long stretching nearly north and south from the plain of Esdraelon into the sea, where it forms the high promontory which

encloses, on the south, the bay of Acre. It is composed of a whitish stone, in which flints, sometimes curiously shaped, are embedded. The height has been variously stated, but, from comparison, it appears that the elevation of the highest points is nearly equal to

4. Mount Carmel.

that of Mount Tabor. On the east is the river Kishon and the plain of Esdraelon; on the west, a small plain descending to the sea. Oaks and other trees grow abundantly on the mountain; and various wild fruits evince its ancient fertility and cultivation. Indeed, the name of *Carmel* means *The Garden of God*, or a very pleasant region. Mount Carmel is renowned in the Jewish history; and is often alluded to in the imagery of the Prophets (1 Kings xviii. 19; 2 Kings ii. 25; iv. 25; Isa. xxix. 17; xxxii. 15; xxxv. 2; Micah vii. 14; Jer. xlviii. 43).

6. *Mounts Ebal and Gerizim*, from which the solemn blessings and curses of the Law were declared to the assembled hosts of Israel, are mountains of Samaria, in the valley between which is the city of Shechem, now called Nabulus (Deut. xxvii.; Josh. viii. 30-35). These mountains rise, in steep rocky precipices, from the valley on each side, apparently to the height of 800 feet. They both appear to be equally naked and sterile, although some travellers have chosen to describe Gerizim, the mountain of blessings, as fair and fruitful, and Ebal, the mountain of curses, as bare and desolate. Gerizim is on the south east and Ebal on the north-west, side of the valley.

PLAINS AND VALLEYS.

The principal plains of Palestine, are those of Lebanon, of the Jordan, of Jericho, of Esdraelon, and of the Coast.

1. *The Plain of Lebanon* may be described as a valley, being enclosed between the parallel mountain ranges of Libanus and Anti-Libanus. Although the greater part of it must have been in Solomon's dominion, it can scarcely be deemed to belong to Palestine Proper, but its geographical and historical connection with that country requires its introduction. This enclosed plain is the Cœle-Syria of the ancients, and now bears the name of el-Bekka (the valley). It is about ninety miles in length, from north to south, by a breadth of eleven miles, nearly equal throughout, except that it widens at the northern end and narrows at the southern. This plain is, perhaps, the most rich and beautiful part of Syria. The soil is good, and the water abundant from the numerous mountain springs on each side; but the concentration of the sun's rays renders the summer heat excessive. These are the sources of that fertility for which the valley has, in all ages, been renowned; but only a small portion is now cultivated, the rest being left in pasture to the Arab tribes.

2. *The Plain of the Jordan.* By this name we understand the margin of the lakes, as well as the valley watered by the river. Here the heat is still greater than in the valley of Lebanon, and, in consequence, palm trees and the fruits of more southern climes than Palestine, will grow freely wherever there is soil and water. But the latter is usually wanting, and, therefore, except on the immediate borders of the river, of the lake of Gennesareth, and of the lesser streams, the whole plain is barren and desolate; for the intense heat which causes exuberant fertility wherever is water, consumes the plain wherever water is wanting.

3. *The Plain of Jericho* is but an opening or expansion in the plain of the Jordan, towards the Dead Sea. The whole expansion takes in the plains of Moab on the east side of the river, and the plains of Jericho on the west, and the breadth across is from ten to twelve miles. In fact, the plain

of the Jordan is in no other part so wide. The large plain
of Jericho is partly desert, but, from the abundance of water
and the heat of the climate, it might be rendered highly productive; indeed, the fertility of this plain has been celebrated
in every age.   Josephus describes it as the most fertile tract
of Judæa, and calls it a "divine region."   He speaks also of
its beautiful gardens, and its groves of palm trees; and his
description is borne out by Scripture, in which Jericho is described as "The City of Palm Trees" (Deut. xxxiv. 3 ;
Judges i. 16). This region also produced honey, opobalsam,
the cyproso tree, (or *el-henna*), and myrobalanum, as well as
the common fruits of the earth in prolific abundance.   The
Scripture adds the sycamore tree to the number of its products
(Luke xix. 4).   Of all these productions which so distinguished the climate of Jericho, and the greater part of which
it enjoyed in common with Egypt, very few now remain.
Only one solitary palm tree lingers in the plain; the syca-
mores have altogether disappeared; the celebrated opobalsam
is not known; and the myrobalanum alone appears to thrive,
being probably the thorny shrub, growing wild in the plain,
to which the name of *zukkum* is given by the present inhabitants—the modern "Balsam of Jericho" is an oil, extracted
from the kernels of the green nut which it bears.

4. *The Plain of Esdraelon* is often mentioned in sacred
history (Judges iv. 13-15, 16 ; v. 19 ; 2 Kings xxiii. 29 ;
Zech. xii. 11 ; Judith i. 8) as the great battle-field of the
Jewish and other nations, under the names of the
Valley of Megiddo and the *Valley of Jezreel ;* and by Josephus as the *Great Plain.* The convenience of its extent and
situation for military action and display has, from the earliest
periods of history down to our own day, caused its surface, at
certain intervals, to be moistened with the blood, and covered
with the bodies, of conflicting warriors of almost every nation
under heaven.   This great plain, exclusive of three great
arms which stretch eastward towards the valley of the Jordan,
may be said to be in the form of an acute triangle, having
the measure of thirteen or fourteen miles on the north, about
eighteen on the east, and above twenty on the south-west.
In the western portion this plain seems perfectly level, with
a general declivity towards the Mediterranean ; but in the

east it is somewhat undulated by slight spurs and swells from the roots of the mountains : from the eastern side three great valleys go off to the valley of the Jordan. These valleys are separated by the ridges of Gilboa and Little Hermon, and that which lies between these two ridges, is the *proper* valley of Jezreel, which name seems to be sometimes given to the whole plain of Esdraelon. The valley of Jezreel is a deep plain, and about three miles across. Before the verdure of spring and early summer has been parched up by the heat and drought of the late summer and autumn, the view of the Great Plain is, from its fertility and beauty, very delightful. In June, yellow fields of grain, with green patches of millet and cotton interspersed, chequer the landscape like a carpet. The plain itself is almost without villages, but there are several on the slopes of the enclosing hills, especially on the side of Mount Carmel.

5. *The Plain of the Coast* is that tract of land which extends along the coast, between the sea and the mountains. In some places, where the mountains approach the sea, this tract is interrupted by promontories and rising grounds ; but, taken generally, the whole coast of Palestine may be described as an extensive plain of various breadth. Sometimes it expands into broad plains, at others it is contracted into narrow valleys. With the exception of some sandy tracts, the soil is throughout rich, and exceedingly productive. The climate is everywhere very warm, and is considered rather insalubrious as compared with the upland country. It is not mentioned by any one collective name in Scripture. The part fronting Samaria, and between Mount Carmel and Jaffa, near a rich pasture ground, was called the *Valley of Sharon ;* and the continuation southward, between Jaffa and Gaza, was called *The Plain*, as distinguished from the hill-country of Judah.

SECTION III.—WATERS.

RIVERS.

1. THE Jordan is the only river of any note in Palestine, and besides it there are only two or three perennial streams. The greater number of the streams which figure in the history, and find place in the maps, are merely torrents or water-courses, which carry off the waters in the season of rain, or if they have their origin in springs, are spent, in the season of drought, soon after they quit their source.

2. *The Jordan.* The remotest origin of this river lies among the mountains, not much less than forty miles north of the Sea of Galilee. The source is a large fountain, just above a place called Hasbeiya, whence the stream which flows from it takes the name of Hasbany. This is about twenty miles north of Banias, or Cæsarea Philippi, and the ancient city of Dan, where again are large fountains, which have been from ancient times regarded as the sources of the Jordan, to the neglect of the more important and remoter source. The streams from these latter fountains there unite and form a small river, which, after running a short distance further, unites with the Hasbany, and the streams, thus joined into one to form the true Jordan, then proceeds to the lake Huleh, from which the fountain is about twenty-five miles distant. This fountain, which has an undoubted title to stand at the head of the springs and fountains and lakes of this renowned river, hails up from the bottom of a shallow pool some eight or ten rods in circumference. It at once, even in the dry season, forms a considerable stream, which meanders for the first three miles through a narrow, but very lovely, and highly cultivated valley, and then sinks rapidly down a constantly deepening gorge of dark basalt for about six miles, until it reaches the level of the great volcanic plain, extending to the marsh above the Lake Huleh. Through this plain it

proceeds eight or ten miles, receiving the other streams in its way, and enters the lake not far from its north-west corner. The other stream which joins the Hasbany, and whose

5. Ford of the Jordan.

sources have been so long regarded as those of the Jordan, has distinct sources, at Banias and at Tel-el-Kâdi. At Banias (anciently *Paneas*, from the worship of Pan) a stream issues from a spacious cavern, under a wall of rock, at the base of the Heish mountains. Directly over the cavern and in other parts, in the face of the perpendicular rock, niches have been cut to receive statues. Here Herod built a temple in honour of Augustus; and there was a town somewhat below, traces of which still remain. This is, undoubtedly, that place and cavern, at the foot of a mountain, which Josephus describes as the main source of the Jordan (Joseph. Ant. xv. 10, 3 ; Bell. Jud. i. 21-3). Yet, in another place (Joseph. Bell. Jud. iii. 10, 7), this writer refers the source to a remoter quarter. He relates that the Tetrarch Philip cast some chaff into the lake Phiala, and as it came out at the Paneas cavern, the lake was deemed the true source of the river. This lake lay 120 stadia eastward, and was deep and round, like a bowl or cup—whence its name Phiala. Such a lake, about a mile in circumference, and perfectly round, was discovered by Captains Irby and Mangles, as they journeyed from Damascus to Banias, not more than twelve miles from the latter place.*

A second source of the Jordan, as described by ancient writers, is at the place now called Tel-el-Kâdi, which is about three miles to the west of the cavern at Banias. The *Tel* (hill) is a small elevation in the plain, with a flat space on the top; here are two springs, one of which is very large. The united waters immediately form a stream, twelve or fifteen yards across, which rushes rapidly over a stony bed into a lower plain. After a course of about four miles the stream unites with that from Banias, forming the reputed Jordan, which then continues its course to join the Hasbany, and so to the lake Huleh.

Between the two lakes lies a tract of high uneven table-land, through which flows the Jordan for about ten miles, in

a narrow and somewhat tortuous valley —the upper part a rapid stream, the lower slow and turbid. Nearly two miles below the lake is a bridge, called Jacob's Bridge; and here the river is about eighty feet wide and four feet deep. It is said that, in

6. Jacob's Bridge.

passing through, the Jordan does not mingle its waters with those of the lake of Gennesareth; this is also reported of other rivers that pass through lakes. It is certain that the course of the river may be traced through the middle of the lake by a line of smoother water.

The portion of the Jordan which is historically and geo-

* It has been more lately visited by Mr. Tipping, who has given an interesting representation and description of it in the new translation of Josephus by Dr. Traill.

graphically the most interesting and important, is that which runs between the Lake of Tiberias and the Dead Sea. This portion was formerly but little known, but has of late been thoroughly explored (together with the Dead Sea) by an American expedition under the command of Lieut. Lynch of the United States naval service. It had been ascertained that the Dead Sea was more than a thousand feet below the level of the lake of Tiberias; but it was difficult to understand this, seeing that the distance was but sixty miles, and this would give a fall of twenty per mile* to a river which was not known to be tortuous or to have any falls or rapids. From this explanation we, however, know that the river is full of rapids; and that although the direct distance is but sixty miles, the course of the river is made at least 200 miles by the exceedingly tortuous course of the stream. This reduces the fall to not more than six feet in the mile, and for this the numerous rapids sufficiently account.

On leaving the lake of Gennesareth the river enters into a very broad valley, or *Ghor*, which name the natives apply to a depressed tract or plain between mountains. This name is applied to the plain of the Jordan, not only between the lake of Gennesareth and the Dead Sea, but quite across the Dead Sea, and to some distance beyond. The valley varies in width from five to ten miles between the mountains on each side. The river does not make its way straight through the midst of the Ghor; it flows first near the western hills, then near the eastern, but advances to the Dead Sea through the middle of the valley. Within this valley there is a lower one, and within that, another still lower, through which the river flows; the inner valley is about half a mile wide, and is generally green and beautiful, with trees and bushes, whereas the upper or large valley is, for the most part, sandy or barren; and the mountains, or rather cliffs, and slopes of the river uplands, present, for the most part, a wild and cheerless aspect. The mountains on the west are the most precipitous, while those on the east rise in a gradual slope to a much greater elevation. The water of the river is clear and transparent, and abounds in fish. It is wholesome, al-

---

* This was then thought to be without example: but it is now known that the Sacramento River of California has an average fall of 100 feet per mile.

ways cool, and nearly tasteless. It is turbid only in the vicinity of the falls and rapids, and on advancing to the Dead Sea, where it probably passes over beds of clay. The breadth and depth of the river varies much in different places and at different times of the year. Dr. Shaw calculates the average breadth at thirty yards, and the depth at nine feet. In the season of flood, in April and early in May, the river is full, and sometimes overflows its lower bank, to which fact there are several illusions in Scripture (Josh. iii. 15; 1 Chron. xii. 15; Jer. xii. 5; xlix. 19; l. 44; Ecclus. xxiv. 26).

3. *The Kishon*, that "ancient river," by whose wide and rapid stream the hosts of Sisera were swept away (Judges iv. 13; v. 21), is, in winter and spring, a mighty river, flowing from Mount Tabor, and collecting the waters of a large part of the plain of Esdraelon and its bordering hills; but in summer all the part which passes over the plain is quite dried up, and only water from perennial springs in Carmel is then found in the last seven miles of its bed. It enters the bay of Acre near the foot of Mount Carmel.

4. *The Belus*, now called *Nahr Kardanus*, enters the bay of Acre higher up than the Kishon. It is a small stream, fordable even at its mouth in summer. It is not mentioned in the Bible, and is chiefly celebrated for the tradition, that the accidental vitrification of its sands taught man the art of making glass.

5. The other streams of note enter the Jordan from the east; these are the Jarmuch, the Jabbok, and the Arnon.— *The Jarmuch*, called also *Sheriatel-Mandhur*, anciently *Hieromax*, joins the Jordan five miles below the lake of Gennesareth. Its source is ascribed to a small lake, almost a mile in circumference, at Mezareib, which is thirty miles east of the Jordan. It is a beautiful stream, and yields a considerable body of water to the Jordan.

6. *The Jabbok*, now called *Zerka*, is a small stream, winding prettily through a deep valley or ravine, which is not so well wooded as its neighbourhood. The water is very clear; and, although narrow, the stream is deep and its course rapid.

7. *The Arnon*, now called *Wady Modjeb*, enters the Dead Sea. It was the river of Moab, and as such is often men-

tioned in Scripture. This stream also flows through an
exceedingly deep valley, which is less shrubby than the river
valleys of this country usually are. It is almost exhausted
by the end of summer, but at all times there are clear indications of the furious rapidity with which the full stream rushes
to the Dead Sea during the season of rain.

LAKES.

The river Jordan in its course forms three remarkable
lakes, in the last of which, called the Dead Sea, it is lost :—

1. *The Lake Merom* (Josh. xi. 5-7), or *Samochonitis*
(Joseph. Antiq. v. 5, 1) now called *Huleh*, the first of these
serves as a kind of reservoir to collect the waters which form
the Jordan, and again to send them forth in a single stream.
The lake is of a triangular or funnel shape, five or six miles
broad at its base, and tapers down to an apex at its outlet,
at a distance of six or eight miles from the northern base.
This is in spring, when the waters are highest ; but in summer it becomes a mere marsh. In some parts it is sown with
rice, and its reeds and rushes afford shelter to wild hogs.

2. *The Lake of Gennesareth*, called also the *Sea of
Galilee*, and the *Lake of Tiberias*. After quitting the lake
Huleh, the river Jordan proceeds for about thirteen miles
southward, and then enters the great lake of Gennesareth.
This lake lies very deep, among fruitful hills and mountains,
from which, in the season, many rivulets descend ; its shape
will be seen from the map. The extent has been greatly over-
rated : Dr. Robinson considers that the length, in a straight
line, does not exceed eleven or twelve geographical miles,
and that the breadth is from five to six miles. From numerous indications, it is judged that the bed of this lake was
formed by some ancient volcanic eruption, which history has
not recorded ; the waters are very clear and sweet, and contain various kinds of excellent fish in great abundance. It
will be remembered that several of the Apostles were fishermen of this lake, and that it was also the scene of several
transactions in the life of Christ ; it is thus frequently mentioned in the New Testament, but very rarely in the Old,

where it is called the *Sea of Chinnereth*, of which *Gennesareth* is a corruption. The borders of the lake were in the time of Christ well peopled, having been covered with numerous towns and villages ; but now they are almost desolate, and the fish and water-fowl are but little disturbed.

3. *The Dead Sea*, called also the *Salt Sea*, the *Sea of Sodom*, and the *Asphaltic Lake* (*Lacus Asphaltitis*), is from its size the most important, and from its history and qualities the most remarkable, of all the lakes of Palestine. It has been assumed that this lake did not exist before the destruction of Sodom and the other "cities of the plain" (Gen. xix.); and that before that time the present bed of the lake was a fertile plain, in which those cities stood. It was also concluded that the river Jordan then flowed through this plain, and afterwards pursued its course through the great valley, of Arabah, to the eastern arm of the Red Sea. These conclusions seem to be substantially correct. The results of the recent complete survey and soundings of the whole lake by the American Expedition under Lieut. Lynch, are in conformity with the inference one would draw from the Scriptural account, that the entire chasm was a plain, sunk and "overwhelmed" by the wrath of God. The *bottom* of the sea consists of two submerged plains, an elevated and a depressed one ; the former averaging *thirteen*, and the latter about *thirteen hundred* feet below the surface. In the northern, and largest and deepest one, in a line corresponding with the bed of the Jordan, is a ravine which corresponds with another at the south bed of the lake. In the Jordan itself, between the Jabbok and this lake, there is a sudden break down in the bed of the river; and if there be a similar break in the water courses to the south of the Dead Sea, accompanied with like volcanic characters, there can scarcely be a doubt that the whole Ghor has sunk from some extraordinary convulsion, preceded most probably by an irruption of fire ; and a general conflagration of the bitumen which abounded in the plain.

The Dead Sea is about thirty-nine or forty geographical miles long from north to south, and nine or ten miles wide from east to west ; and it lies embedded very deep between lofty cliffs on the western side, which are about 1500 feet high, and mountains on the eastern shore, the highest ridges

of which are reckoned to be from 2000 to 2500 feet above the
water. The water of the lake is much salter than that of the
sea. From the quantity of salt which it holds in solution,
it is thick and heavy, and no fish can live or marine plants
grow in it. Even when subjected to a powerful microscope
the water exhibits no trace of animalculæ or of any animal
matter. The old stories respecting the pestiferous qualities of
the Dead Sea and its waters, are mere fables or delusions; and
actual appearances are the natural and obvious effects of the
confined and deep situation, the intense heat, and the uncommon saltness of the waters. Lying in its deep cauldron, surrounded by lofty cliffs of naked limestone rock, exposed for
seven or eight months in the year to the unclouded beams of
a burning sun, nothing but sterility and solitude can be looked
for upon its shores; and nothing else is actually found, except
in those parts where there are fountains or streams of fresh
water; in all such places there is a fertile soil and abundant
vegetation. Birds also abound, and they are observed to fly
over and across the sea without being, as old stories tell, injured or killed by its exhalations. The water, although unpleasant, acrid, and greasy, is entirely inodorous. The
noxious smells which pervade the shores are to be ascribed to
the fœtid springs and marshes along the shore, increased by
exhalations from stagnant pools. Indeed, the saline and
inodorous exhalations from the lake itself are probably rather
wholesome than otherwise; and as there is but little verdure
upon the shores, there can be no vegetable exhalations to
render the air impure. The evil to which the human frame
is here subject, arises from the dangerous and depressing influence of the intense concentrated heat, and from the acrid
and clammy quality of the waters, producing a most irritated
state of the skin, and eventually febrile symptoms, and great
prostration of strength.

On the borders of this lake is found much sulphur, in
pieces as large as walnuts, and even larger. There is also a
black shining stone, which will partly burn in the fire, and
which then emits a bituminous smell: this is the "stink-
stone" of Burckhardt. At Jerusalem it is made into rosaries
and toys, of which great quantities are sold to the pilgrims
visit the sacred places. Another remarkable production.

from which, indeed, the lake takes one of its names, is the
asphaltum, or bitumen.   Josephus says, that " the sea in
many places sends up black masses of asphaltum, which float
upon the surface, having the size and shape of headless oxen"
(Joseph. Bell. Jud. iv. 8, 4).   From recent information, it
appears that large masses are rarely found, and then generally
after earthquakes.   The substance is doubtless produced from
the bottom of the sea, in which it coagulates, and rises to the
surface ; or possibly the coagulation may have been ancient,
and the substance adheres to the bottom until detached by
earthquakes and other convulsions, when its buoyancy brings
it to the surface.   We know that " the vale of Siddim "
(Gen. xiv. 10), was anciently " full of slime-pits" or sources
of bitumen ; and these, now under the water, probably supply
the asphaltum which is found on such

SECTION IV.—CLIMATE AND SEASONS.

1. The variations of sunshine and rain which, with us, extend throughout the year, are in Palestine confined chiefly to the latter part of autumn and the winter. During all the rest of the year the sky is almost uninterruptedly cloudless, and rain very rarely falls.

The autumnal rains usually commence at the latter end of October, or beginning of November; not suddenly, but by degrees, which gives opportunity to the husbandman to sow his wheat and barley. The rains come mostly from the west (Luke xii. 54) and south-west, and continue for two or three days at a time, falling chiefly in the night; the wind then changes to the north or east, and several days of fine weather succeed. During the months of November and December the rains continue to fall heavily; afterwards they return at longer intervals, and are not so heavy; but at no period during the winter do they entirely cease to occur. Rain continues to fall more or less during the month of March, but is afterwards very rare. Morning mists occur as late as May, but rain almost never. Rain in the time of harvest was as incomprehensible to an ancient Jew as snow in summer (Prov. xxvi. 1; 1 Sam. xii. 17; Amos iv. 7). The "early" and the "latter" rains, for which the Jewish husbandmen awaited with longing (Prov. xvi. 15; James v. 7), seem to have been the first showers of autumn, which revived the parched and thirsty soil, and prepared it for the seed; and the later showers of spring which continued to refresh and forward the ripening crops and the vernal products of the fields.

2. The cold of winter is not severe, and the ground is never frozen. Snow falls more or less. In the low-lying plains but little falls, and it disappears early in the day; in the higher lands, as at Jerusalem, it often falls, chiefly in January and February, to the depth of a foot or more; but even there it does not lie long on the ground. Thunder and lightning are frequent in the winter.

3 In the plains and valleys the heat of summer is op-

pressive, but not in the more elevated tracts, as at Jerusalem, except when the south wind (*Sirocco*) blows (Luke xii. 55). In such high grounds the nights are cool, often with heavy dew.   The total absence of rain in summer soon destroys the verdure of the fields, and gives to the general landscape, even in the high country, an aspect of drought and barrenness. No green thing remains but the foliage of the scattered fruit trees, and occasional vineyards and fields of millet.   In autumn the whole land becomes dry and parched; the cisterns are nearly empty, and all nature, animate and inanimate, looks forward with longing for the return of the rainy season.

4. In the hill-country the season of harvest is later than in the plains of the Jordan and of the sea-coast.   The barley harvest is about a fortnight earlier than that of wheat.   In the plain of the Jordan the wheat harvest is early in May; in the plains of the Coast and of Esdraelon it is towards the latter end of that month, and in the hills, not until June. The general vintage is in September, but the first grapes ripen in July, and from that time the towns are well supplied with this fruit.

5. The climate of Palestine has always been considered healthy, and the inhabitants have generally enjoyed a high average duration of life.   Jerusalem, in particular, from its great elevation, clear sky, and bracing atmosphere, should be a healthy spot, and is usually so esteemed.

PART II.—AGRICULTURE AND PASTURAGE.

SECTION I.—LAWS AND OPERATIONS.

LAWS.

1 IT appeared to the Divine Wisdom, that the agricultural
life was best suited to maintain the Israelites in that particular position in which it was designed that they should be
placed.   A country well adapted to agriculture was, therefore, given to them; and laws were framed to encourage and
to render necessary the culture of the ground, and, in some
degree, to discourage other pursuits.   That all might find an
interest in the culture of the soil, every one had some land
to cultivate.   A plot of ground was given to every head of a
family, which he had full power to cultivate as he pleased,
and to transmit to his heirs.   The difficulty was not in acquiring, but in alienating a possession in land.   No one could
dispossess himself of his lands for a longer time than to the
next ensuing jubilee, which occurred every fifty years; and
if he disposed of his land for this limited period, himself, or
his nearest relative, always retained the right of resuming
possession, by paying the calculated value of the unexpired term
up to the year of jubilee.   As, by the original constitution, God
himself was the political head of the state, and the sovereign
proprietor of the soil, the land, thus secured to the heirs of
the first proprietors, was exempt from any other rent-charges
than the tithes and first-fruits which were offered to Him,
and used by His servants—the priests and Levites (Lev.
xxvii. 30 ; Deut. xii. 17-19 ; xiv. 22-29).   As fields are
not divided by hedges in the east, the stones which marked

B

the boundaries of lands (land-marks) were rendered inviolable by a solemn curse against whoever should remove them (Deut. xix. 14). All the inhabitants, except the priests and Levites, were considered by the laws, and were, for the most part, in fact, agriculturists, whether they dwelt in the country or in towns. This legislation had due effect; for agriculture was long held in high honour, and persons of condition did not disdain to put their hand to the plough (1 Sam. xi. 5, 7; 1 Kings xix. 19; 2 Chron. xxvi. 10). As luxury increased, this esteem for agriculture declined; especially after the Captivity, when many turned their attention towards merchandise and the mechanic arts.

2. *The Fallow Year.*—That the Israelites might exercise trust in their Divine King; that they might be trained to habits of economy and foresight; and that the soil might not be exhausted, it was ordered that every seventh year should be a sabbath of rest to the land. There was to be no sowing nor reaping, no pruning of vines nor olives, no vintage nor gathering of fruits; and whatever grew of itself was to be left to the poor, the stranger, and the beasts of the field (Lev. xxv. 1-7; Deut. xv. 1-10). But such an observance required more faith than the Israelites were prepared to exercise; it was for a long time utterly neglected (Lev. xxvi. 34, 35; 2 Chron. xxxvi. 21), but after the Captivity was more observed.

3. *Fertilization.*—The soil of Palestine is, for the most part, very fertile, when the rains and dews of autumn and spring are not withheld. Water is the great fertilizing agent; and therefore the ancient inhabitants were able, in some parts, to avert the aridity which the summer droughts occasioned, and to keep up a garden-like verdure, by means of aqueducts communicating with the brooks and rivers (Psalm i. 3; lxv. 10; Prov. xxi. 1; Isaiah xxx. 25; xxxii. 2, 20; Hosea xii. 11). Hence springs, fountains, and rivulets, were as much esteemed by husbandmen as by shepherds (Josh. xv. 19; Judges i. 15) The soil was also cleared of stones, and carefully cultivated; and its fertility was increased by the ashes to which the dry stubble and herbage were occasionally reduced by burning over the surface of the ground (Prov. xxiv. 31; Isaiah vii. 23; xxxii. 13). The dung and, in

the neighbourhood of Jerusalem, the blood of animals, were also used to enrich the soil (2 Kings ix. 37; Psalm lxxxiii. 10; Isaiah xxv. 10 Jer. ix. 22; Luke xiv. 34, 35).

4. *Fields.*—Under the term *dagan*, which we translate "grain," and "corn," the Hebrews comprehended almost every object of *field*-culture. Syria, including Palestine, was regarded by the ancients as one of the first countries for corn. *Wheat* was abundant and excellent; and there is still one bearded sort, the ear of which is three times as heavy, and contains twice as many grains, as our common English wheat. *Barley* was also much cultivated, not only for bread, but because it was the only kind of corn which was given to beasts; for oats and rye do not thrive in warm climates. Hay was not in use, and therefore the barley was mixed with chopped straw to form the food of beasts: this is what is called "provender" in Scripture. Other objects of field-culture were millet, spelt, various kinds of beans and peas, pepperwort, cummin, cucumbers, melons, flax, and perhaps cotton. Many other articles might be mentioned as being now cultivated in Palestine, but, as their names do not occur in Scripture, it is difficult to know whether they were grown there in ancient times.

7. Garden House.

5. *Gardens.*—The Israelites appear to have been fond of gardens, which, in the East, are chiefly planted with trees, with little regard to order or effect. As, however, the Egyptians were skilful florists, and laid out their gardens with care, introducing beds and borders of flowers, it is likely that the Israelites had some similar practices. Shade was chiefly sought; and, that

a double benefit might be realised, the shade of fruit trees was preferred. The more important gardens were named from the prevalence of certain trees in them; as " the garden of nuts," " the garden of pomegranates," &c. (Sol. Song vi. 11). The gardens owed all their freshness to the waters, of which they were never destitute (Num. xxiv. 6; Deut. xi. 10; Sol. Song iv. 15; Isaiah i. 30; lxvi. 17; Jer. xxxi. 12). So attached were the Israelites to their gardens, that they often had their sepulchres in them (2 Kings ix. 37; xxi. 18; Mark xv. 46). Trees were multiplied by seeds and shoots; they were transplanted, dug around, manured, and pruned (Job viii. 16; Isaiah xvii. 10); and the operation of grafting was well known (Rom. xi. 17).

OPERATIONS AND IMPLEMENTS.

1. Of late years much light has been thrown upon the agricultural operations and implements of ancient times by the

discovery of various representations on the sculptured monuments and painted tombs of Egypt. As these agree surprisingly with the notices in the Bible, and, indeed, differ little from

8. Syrian Plough.

the existing usages in Syria and Egypt, it is very safe to receive the instruction which they offer.

2. *Ploughing.*—This has always been a light and superficial operation in the East. At first the ground was opened with pointed sticks; then a kind of hoe was employed, and this, in many parts of the world, is still the substitute for a plough. But the plough was known in Egypt and Syria

9. Hoeing.

before the Hebrews became cultivators (Job i. 14). In the

East, however, it has always been a light and inartificial implement. At first it was little more than a stout branch of a tree, from which projected another limb, shortened and pointed; this being turned into the ground made the furrows, while at the further end of the larger branch was fastened a transverse yoke, to which the oxen were harnessed.

10. Ancient Egyptian Plough.

Afterwards a handle to guide the plough was added: thus the plough consisted of—1, the pole; 2, the point or share; 3, the handle; 4, the yoke. The Syrian plough is, and doubtless was, light enough for a man to carry with one hand; it was drawn by oxen, which were sometimes urged by a scourge (Isaiah x. 26; Nahum iii. 2), but oftener by

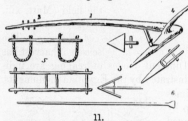

11.

1. The plough. 2. The pole. 3. Shares (various).
4. Handle.   5. Yokes   6. Ox-goad.

a long staff, furnished at one end with a flat piece of metal for clearing the plough, and at the other with a spike for goading the oxen: this ox-goad might be easily used as a spear (Judges iii. 31; 1 Sam. xiii. 21). Sometimes men followed the plough with hoes to break the clods (Isaiah xxviii. 24); but in later times a kind of hammer was employed, which appears to have been then, as now, merely a thick block of wood pressed down by a weight, or by a man sitting on it, and drawn over the ploughed field.

3. *Sowing.*—The ground, having been ploughed as soon as the autumnal rains had mollified the soil, was fit, by the end of October, to receive the seed; and the sowing of wheat continued, in different situations, through November and into December. Barley was not generally sown till January and February. The seed appears to have been sown and harrowed at the same time; although sometimes it was ploughed

in by a cross furrow. The Egyptian paintings illustrate the Scriptures by shewing that the sower held the seed in

a basket, with one hand, and scattered it with the other; while another person filled a fresh basket. We also see that the mode of sowing was what we call "broad-cast," in which the seed is thrown loosely over the field (Matt. xiii. 3-8).

12. Sowing.

4. *Reaping.*—The season of harvest has been noticed (p. 23). Different modes of reaping are indicated in Scripture, and illustrated by the Egyptian monuments.

In the most ancient times the corn was plucked up by the roots, which continued to be the practice with particular kinds of grain after the sickle was known; in Egypt, at this day, barley and dourra are pulled up by the roots. When the sickle

13. Plucking Corn.

was used, the wheat was either cropped off under the ear, or cut close to the ground; in the former case the straw was

afterwards plucked up for use, in the latter the stubble was left and burnt in the ground for manure. As the Egyptians needed not such manure, and were economical of straw, they generally followed the former method; while the

14. Reaping.

Israelites, whose lands derived benefit from the burnt stubble, used the latter, although the practice of cutting off the ears was also known to them (Job xxiv. 24). Cropping the ears short, the Egyptians did not generally bind them into sheaves, but removed them in baskets. Sometimes they bound them into *double* sheaves; and such as they plucked up were bound into long sheaves. The

15. Binding Corn.

Israelites appear always to have made up their corn into sheaves (Gen. xxxvii. 7; Lev. xxiii. 10-15; Ruth ii. 7, 15;

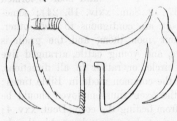

16. Reaping Hooks.

Job xxiv. 10; Jer. ix. 22; Mic. iv. 12), which were collected into a heap, or removed in a cart (Amos ii. 13) to the threshing-floor. The reapers were the owners and their children, men and women-servants, and hired day-labourers, (Ruth ii. 4, 8, 21, 23; John iv. 36; James v. 4). Refreshments were provided for them, especially drink, of which the gleaners were often allowed to partake (Ruth ii. 9); so, in the Egyptian scenes, we see reapers drinking, and the gleaners applying to share the draught. Among the

17. Reapers Drinking.

Israelites, gleaning was one of the stated provisions for the poor; and for their benefit the corners of the fields were left unreaped, and the reapers might not return for a forgotten sheaf. Gleaners could not, however, force themselves upon a particular field, without the consent of the owner (Lev. xix. 9, 10; Deut. xxiv. 19; Ruth ii. 2).

5. *Threshing.* — The ancient mode of threshing, as described in Scripture, and figured on the Egyptian monuments, is still preserved in Palestine. Formerly the sheaves were conveyed from the field to the threshing-floor in carts, but now they are borne generally on the backs of camels and

18. Threshing.

asses. The threshing-floor is a level plot of ground, of a circular shape, generally about fifty feet in diameter, prepared for use by beating down the earth till a hard floor is formed (Gen. l. 10; Judges vi. 37; 2 Sam. xxiv. 16, 24); sometimes several of these floors are contiguous to each other. The sheaves are spread out upon them, and the grain is trodden out by oxen, cows, and young cattle, arranged five abreast, and driven in a circle, or rather in all directions, over the floor. This was the common mode in Bible times; and Moses forbade that the oxen thus employed should be muzzled to prevent them from tasting the corn (Deut. xxv. 4; Isaiah xxviii. 28). *Flails*, or sticks, were only used in threshing small quantities, or for the lighter kinds of grain (Ruth ii. 17; Isaiah xxviii. 27). There were, however, some kinds of threshing-machines, which are still employed in Palestine and Egypt. One of them, represented in the annexed figure, is very much used in Palestine. It is composed of two thick planks, fastened together side by side, and bent upward in

19. Corn-Drag.

front; sharp fragments of stone are fixed into holes bored in the bottom. This machine is drawn over the corn by oxen, a man or boy sometimes sitting on it to increase the weight; it not only separates the grain, but cuts the straw and makes it fit for fodder (2 Kings xiii. 7). This is most probably the *corn-drag* which is mentioned in Scripture (Isaiah xxviii. 27; xli. 15; Amos i. 3, rendered "threshing-instrument"), and would seem to have been sometimes furnished with iron points instead of stones. The Bible also notices a machine called a *moreg* (2 Sam. xxi. 22; 1 Chron. xxi. 23; Isaiah xli. 15), which is unquestion- ably the same which still in Arabic bears the name of *noreg;* and which, although not now seen in Pales- tine, is common in Egypt. It is a sort of frame of wood, in which are inserted

20. Noreg.

three wooden rollers, armed with iron teeth, &c.; it bears a sort of seat or chair, in which the driver sits to give the benefit of his weight; it is generally drawn over the corn by two oxen, and separates the grain and breaks up the straw even more effectually than the drag. In all these processes the corn is occasionally turned by a fork, and when sufficiently threshed is thrown up by the same fork against the wind to separate the grain, which is then gathered up and winnowed.

6. *Winnowing.*—This was generally accomplished by repeating the process of tossing up the grain against the wind

with a fork (Jer. iv. 11, 12), by which the broken straw and chaff were dispersed and the grain fell to the ground. The grain after- wards passed through a sieve, to separate the bits of earth and other impurities; after this it underwent a still further purifi- cation, by being tossed up with wooden scoops, or short-handled shovels, such as we see in Egyp-

21.

tian paintings (Isaiah xxx. 24).

7. *Corn-stores.*—The unwinnowed grain was originally kept in subterranean storehouses, and even in caverns; but, in process of time, granaries were built both in Egypt and Palestine (Gen. xli. 35; Exod. i. 11; 1 Chron. xxvii. 25).

SECTION II.-- PRINCIPAL VEGETABLE PRODUCTS.

—— ◆ ——

VINES AND VINEYARDS.

1. PALESTINE was very much celebrated for its vines, and for the wine which they afforded; they still grow exceedingly well, from one end of the country to the other; and both the clusters and the grapes are often of very large size (Num. xiii. 23). Clusters weighing ten or twelve pounds, and grapes as large as prunes, are mentioned by travellers. The varieties differ, of course, in size, as well as in quality, and the largest are not necessarily the best. A small white grape is, indeed, considered the best that grows in that quarter, and may be the celebrated "vine of Sorek." The grapes of Palestine are mostly black and red varieties; hence the wine was generally red, whence arose the phrase "blood of grapes" (Gen. xlix. 11; Deut. xxxii. 14; Isaiah xxvii. 2).

2. *Vineyards.*—The modes of cultivation were, and still are, various. In general the sides of hills were preferred; and Lebanon was particularly famous for its vines and wines (Hosea xiv. 7). The hill-side vineyards often rose in successive terraces, faced with stone, which collected and retained the soil brought down from the higher parts by the rains; this continues to be the prevalent mode for all kinds of cultivation in Lebanon, and there are still large traces of it in the hills of Palestine (Isaiah v. 1; Jer. xxxi. 5; Joel iii. 18; Amos ix. 13; Micah i. 6). In Lebanon, and some other parts, the vine is allowed to run along the ground, like the cucumber (Ezek. xvii. 6, 7). Sometimes several vines are so planted as to support one another, by being fastened together at the top, so as to form a kind of cone. In other cases they grow without support, having stout stems and extensive branches, which the Israelites used often to prop and train, so as to form a pleasant shade. Hence, "sitting under one's own vine," is a frequent phrase for a state of repose and comfort (1 Kings iv. 25; Hosea ii. 12; Mic. iv

4, Zech. iii. 10). In many of the vineyards there are still watch-towers of stone, round or square, from ten to fifteen or twenty feet high, in which keepers are stationed, during the season of the grape, to protect the fruit from injury or pillage (Isaiah v. 2 ; Matt. xxi. 33). The passing traveller was allowed to pluck and eat grapes from the way-side vineyards, but not to carry them away in his vessel (Deut. xxiii. 24). Many minute allusions to processes in the culture of the vine manifest the very great attention which was paid to it by the ancient Hebrews. There are fine allegories based upon this culture in Psalm lxxx. 8-15; Isaiah v. 1-7 ; xxvii. 2-6 ; Matt. xxi. 33-41.

3. *Vintage.*—Grapes may always be had after June, but the regular vintage does not begin until the middle of September, and is not over everywhere until the middle of November. The gleanings of the vineyard, as well as of the corn-field, were left to the poor (Lev. xix. 10). The vintage was a season of gladness (Judges ix. 27 ; Isaiah xvi. 10 ; Jer. xxv. 30; xlviii. 33) ; and, with loud shouts and other signs of rejoicing, the grapes were plucked off and carried to the wine-press, which was generally in the vineyard (Isaiah v. 2; Hag. ii. 16; Zech. xiv. 10 ; Matt. xxi. 33; Rev. xiv. 19, 20).

22. Wine-Press.

The Wine-presses were either formed with stones, and covered with an insoluble cement, or were, in certain situations, hewn out of the rock, forming an elevated reservoir, into which the grapes were thrown, and were trodden upon by men to press out the juice. The expressed juice flowed through gratings or apertures into a lower receptacle outside, or into large vessels of stone or earthenware. From the Egyptian paintings, we see that a beam was temporarily erected over the press, from which thongs were suspended, by which the men held on as they trod the grapes, and which must have been a great support to them in their work. Although laborious, this work was performed with great animation—with songs, and with a shout or cry, peculiar to the occasion; and was sometimes accompanied by instrumental music (Isaiah xvi. 9, 10; Jer. xxv. 30; xlviii. 32, 33).

4. *The Olive Tree.*—The olive rarely becomes a large tree, and its dull whitish foliage does not deserve the name

of verdure; but there was no tree more honoured by the Israelites, or more truly valuable to them. It was an object of special culture in plantations or "olive yards," for the sake of the valuable oil obtained from the fruit. This oil is drawn, not from the kernel, as with most other vegetable oils, but from the fleshy part (pericarp) of the fruit. Vast quantities were obtained; and it was not only used profusely, with

23. Olive Tree.

food, for light, and for anointings, but large quantities remained for traffic with the Tyrians and others (Ezek. xxvii. 17). The oil, like the juice of the grape, appears to have been extracted by treading (Mic. vi. 15). The fruit itself does not seem to have been commonly eaten. The olive is an evergreen tree, and although small, singly, two or three trunks frequently rise from the same root. It is from **twenty** to thirty feet high, and the branches are numerous and very widely extended. The Mount of Olives, near Jerusalem, was so named from the numerous olive trees that once grew there ; and some remarkable old olive trees are still found thereon.

5. *The Fig Tree.*—Fig trees were common in Palestine. They are tall but irregular trees, whose expanded shade was deemed very pleasant (1 Kings iv. 25 ; Mic. iv. 4). The fig tree sprouts at the vernal equinox, and affords three crops of fruit, the first of which (called the *Untimely Fig*) appears before the leaves in spring, and ripens about the end of June (Matt. xxi. 19 ; Mark xi. 13) ; this has the best flavour (Jer. xxiv. 2), and is eaten green. The others are dried in the sun, and preserved in masses, or, as they are called in the Bible, "cakes" of figs (1 Sam. xxv. 18 ; xxx. 12 ; 2 Kings xx. 7 ; 1 Chron. xii. 40).

6. *The Sycamore,* or rather the *Sycamore Fig Tree,* is not the common sycamore. It is a large tree, with **leaves** like the mulberry, and fruit not unlike the fig, to which joint resemblance it owes its name. It is more common, and grows larger, in Egypt than in Palestine. The trunk is often very thick, and the branches spread out widely, affording a most ample shade. The wood is light and unsubstantial, but lasts a long while, and was much used in building by the Hebrews (as by the Egyptians) till they found means

24. Sycamore Fig.

of getting cedar wood from Lebanon (1 Kings x. 21). **The** fruit grows out of the trunk of the tree, in clusters, and chiefly differs from a fig in the absence of seeds, and in a cloying sweetness not much relished by Europeans; the tree yields several successive crops during the year, but the fruit will not ripen without being wounded by the cultivators; this was an employment of the prophet Amos (chap. vii. 14). We learn from 1 Chron. xxvii. 28, that the tree was largely cultivated in Palestine, doubtless for the fruit.

7. *The Almond Tree* grows extensively in Palestine, and forms a handsome and picturesque tree. It blossoms in

winter; which fact, together with the whiteness of the blossoms, furnished the Hebrew poets with a beautiful emblem of old age (Eccles. xii. 5). The nut of the almond, and the oil of that nut, are well known to us; the former is the kernel of a fruit unfit to be eaten. The almond was considered one of the distinguishing products of Palestine (Gen. xliii. 11); and the branches of the tree furnished rods of office (Num. xvii. 8).

25. Almond Tree.

8. *The Palm.*— This famous tree is now but rarely seen in Palestine, although in former times it was so abundant as to be made the symbol of that country. It was, however, confined to the plains and valleys, and was most frequent in the valley of the Jordan, and the plain of the Coast (Lev. xxiii. 40; Deut. xxxiv. 3; Judges i. 16; iii. 13; iv. 5). This tree, with its straight and lofty stem without branches, but crowned by a splendid tuft of evergreen foliage, was justly admired by the Hebrews, who carved it in ornamental work (1 Kings vi. 32), made it the symbol of a beautiful person (Sol. Song vii. 8), and

also of a religious upright man (Psalm i. 3; xcii 12). It was also the symbol of victory (Rev. vii. 9). At the Feast of Tabernacles the Jews bore palm-branches in their hands (Lev. xxiii. 40); and they strewed them in the path of kings, as they publicly entered their cities (Matt. xxi. 8). The palm produces large clusters of dates, which become ripe in autumn, and which are consumed in various ways—fresh, preserved, or dried; and form no small part of man's food in southwestern Asia. In 2 Chron. xxxi. 5 [margin], "dates" are mentioned along with

26. Palm Tree.

"corn, wine, and oil," as among the principal products of Palestine.

9. *The Terebinth Tree* is one of the most common forest trees of Palestine. Its name does not appear in our Bibles; but it is supposed to be intended in words which are translated "a plain" and "an oak." It is a long-lived but moderately-sized tree, with branches very extensive, and head very large in proportion to the trunk. It is an ever-green; the leaves, like those of the olive, being of a green colour intermixed with red and purple. The name of Terebinth tree, or Turpentine tree, is from the turpentine which exudes from the trunk when the bark is wounded. There was, formerly, a very large and very old terebinth tree in the valley of Mamre, near Hebron, around which a great fair was held, in the belief that the angels were entertained beneath its shade by Abraham (Gen. xviii. 4). A noble old oak is now found near the same place

10 *The Pistachio Tree* which is allied to the terebinth, afforded the "nuts" which Jacob sent to Egypt, as one of

the most valued products of the land of Canaan (Gen. xliii. 11). This smooth-shelled nut, with its green kernel, grows in clusters, and is nowhere finer than in Syria. The tree which yields them is from twenty to thirty feet high, and is by no means remarkable for its beauty. But it interests the traveller from being found in such places as on Mount Tabor, and on the very top of the mountain (Attarus,

27. Terebinth Tree.

probably the same as Nebo), supposed to be that from which Moses surveyed the Promised Land (Deut. xxxiv. 1).

11. *The Mulberry Tree* was evidently very common in Palestine formerly, as it is still (2 Sam. v. 23, 24; 1 Chron xiv. 14, 15), although all parts of the country are not equally favourable to its growth. In and under Lebanon the mulberry tree is largely cultivated for the sake of its leaves, as the food of silk-worms, and is cropped and dressed so as to afford the greatest quantity; but in the *gardens* of Palestine it is allowed to grow after its own fashion. In the East it is very common to have trees growing in the courts of houses, and in Palestine these are often mulberry trees.

12. *The Pomegranate Tree.*—This is a thick and bushy fruit tree, with thorny twigs, rising twenty feet high. The fruit is about the size of an orange, and contains within its hard, leathery, and reddish-brown rind, many orderly rows of seeds or grains, invested with a red and lustrous pulp, which gives them the appearance of rubies. This pulp affords the

pleasant juice for the sake of which the grains are eaten; and of which various pleasant and refreshing summer drinks are made (Num. xx. 5; Deut. viii. 8; Sol. Song iv. 13; vi. 11; vii. 12.) The fruit was much esteemed by the Jews, and was imitated by them in their ornamental works (Exod. xxviii. 33, 34; 1 Kings vii. 18).

13. *The Cedar Tree* which is so often mentioned in the Bible, is rather a tree of the Lebanon mountains than of Palestine generally. In those mountains many groves of cedars, of all sizes and ages, have, of late years, been discovered. Formerly, one grove, which lies high up, not far from the northern and, perhaps, highest summit of the mountains, was regarded as the only remnant of the ancient cedars of Lebanon, and was, as such, visited and described by various travellers. It still contains the largest and most ancient

28. Cedar Tree.

trees which have been found, together with many of inferior age and size. Altogether there are some hundreds of trees in this famous grove, and the number seems rather to increase than diminish. The largest of the trees is about forty feet in circumference, and several others are nearly as large. In some instances several trees have grown together, and now form one. The Israelites being but poorly furnished with timber trees, were glad to get cedar wood, for building, from Lebanon, through the Phœnicians of Tyre, who brought it along the coast in floats, and landed it at Joppa (1 Kings v. 6, 10; ix. 11; 2 Chron. i. 15; ii. 8; Ezra iii. 7).

SECTION III.—PASTORAL LIFE AND ANIMALS

PASTURES.

1. In the first period of their history the Hebrews led an unsettled pastoral life, such as we still find among many Oriental tribes.   One great object of the Mosaical polity was to turn them from this condition into that of fixed cultivators of the soil.   Pasturage was, however, only discouraged as a *condition of life*, unfriendly to settled habits and institutions, and not as a pursuit connected with agriculture.   Hence, although in later times the principal attention of the Hebrews was given to agriculture, the tending of sheep and cattle was not at any time neglected.

2. The shepherds who move about with their flocks from one pasture-ground to another according to the demands of the season, the state of the herbage, and the supply of water, are called *nomads*—that is, not merely *shepherds*, but *wandering shepherds*.   They feed their flocks in the "commons," or the deserts and wildernesses, which no settled or cultivating people have appropriated.   At first, no pastoral tribe can have any particular property in such tracts of ground in preference to another tribe; but, in the end, a particular tract becomes appropriated to some one tribe, or section of a tribe, either from long occupation, or from digging wells therein.   According to the ideas of the East, the digging of a well is so meritorious an act, that he who performs it acquires a property in the waste-lands around.   In the time of the patriarchs, Palestine was but thinly peopled by the Canaanites, and offered many such tracts of unappropriated grounds fit for pasturage. In these they fed their flocks, without establishing any exclusive claims to the soil, until they proceeded to dig wells, which, being considered as an act of appropriation, was opposed by some of the inhabitants (Gen. xxi. 25, 26).   After the conquest of Canaan, those Israelites who possessed large flocks

and herds, sent them out, under the care of shepherds, into the "wildernesses," or commons, of the east and south, where there are rich and juicy pasturages during the moist seasons of the year (1 Sam. xvii. 28 ; xxv. 4, 15 ; 1 Chron. xxvii. 29-31 ; Isaiah lxv. 10 ; Jer. l. 39). The nomads occupy, successively, the same stations in the deserts every year. In summer, when the plains are parched with drought, and every green herb is dried up, they proceed northwards, or into the mountains, or to the banks of rivers ; and in winter and spring, when the rains have re-clothed the plains with verdure, and filled the water-courses, they return. When these pastors remove, they strike their tents, pack them up, ard convey them on camels to the next station. Nearly all the pastoral usages were the same, anciently, as now. The sheep were constantly kept in the open air, and guarded by hired servants, and by the sons and daughters of the owners. Even the daughters of emirs, or chiefs, did not disdain to tend the sheep (Gen. xxiv. 17-20 ; xxix. 9 ; Exod. ii. 16).

The principal shepherd was responsible for the sheep intrusted to his care, and if any were lost he had to make them good, except in certain cases (Gen. xxxi. 39 ; Exod. xxii. 12 ; Amos iii. 12). Their services were often paid by a certain proportion of the young of the flock (Gen. xxx. 30). On the more dangerous stations, towers were erected, from which the approach of enemies might be discovered. These were

29. Tower.

called the Towers of the Flock (Gen. xxxv. 21 ; 2 Chron xxvi. 10 ; Micah iv. 8).

3. *Waters.*—Water is even more than usually necessary in warm regions, especially to those who have many cattle : and, being very scarce, especially in the plains and deserts, it is highly valued, and very frugally used (Num. xx. 17-19; Deut. ii. 6, 28 ; Job xxii. 7). Hence, wells and cisterns are dug by the nomads, at the places which they frequent ; and these wells being formed with great labour, by a rude people, are objects of much solicitude and care. We have already alluded to the property in the land which is thus acquired. A well is invariably the property of the party by

whom, or at whose cost, it was dug; and is inherited by his descendants. No stranger has any right to draw water from it, without the permission of the owner; and for this he generally expects payment (Num. xx. 17-19). It appears that sometimes the wells were owned by a number of pastors in common, and that the flocks were brought to them on appointed days, in an order previously arranged. A well was often covered with a great stone, which being removed, the person descended some steps to the surface of the water, and, on his return, poured into a trough that which he had brought up (Gen. xxiv. 11-15; xxix. 3-10; Exod. ii. 16; Judges v. 11). But as this process was only applicable where the well was not deep, and we must assume that the Israelites had the use of the same contrivances for raising water which we still find in operation in the East, and the antiquity of most of which is evinced by the Egyptian paintings and sculptures. From the deeper kind of well, the water is usually drawn by hand in a leathern bucket—sometimes by the aid of a windlass, but oftener, where the well is only of moderate depth, by the *shadoof,* which is the most common

30. Well and Bucket at Jaffa.

and simple of all the machines used in the East for raising water, whether from wells, reservoirs, or rivers. This is a tapering lever unequally balanced upon an upright stem, and to the smaller end of which the bucket is attached by the rope. The weight of the larger end balancing the laden bucket, it is drawn up with ease, the only care being to regulate its ascent. The water of wells, as well as of fountains, was called by the Hebrews "living water" (translated "running water"), and was highly esteemed (Lev. xiv. 5; Num. xix. 17). This epithet was not applied to the waters preserved in cisterns and other reservoirs.

4. *Cisterns.*—These were large reservoirs, in which the waters from rain and melted snows were collected, and reserved for use in the season of drought. They sometimes

occur as large subterraneous vaults, perhaps an acre in extent, but with a very small mouth, or entrance. In cities, they were very elaborate works, being often hewn out of the solid rock, or lined with masonry, covered with a firm incrustation, on which water had no effect. Remains of such cisterns are still found in Palestine, especially in the country beyond Jordan. The cisterns of the open country, intended for the pastors and their flocks, when they have received their supply of water, have often the mouth covered with large flat stones, over which sand is spread, so that strangers may pass without being aware of the treasure beneath their feet. Sometimes, however, the owners, on returning from distant stations, find their cisterns without water, either from their having been broken by earthquakes or other causes, or from their having been discovered and rifled of their precious contents. In such cases, the shepherd and his flocks are in a situation of great danger; and hence, a failure of this description is used as an image of any great calamity (Isaiah xli. 17, 18; xliv. 3). As there is often a large deposit of mud at the bottom of these cisterns, a miserable death awaits any who fall into them (Gen. xxxvii. 22, &c.; Psalm xl. 2; lxix. 15; Jer. xxxviii. 6; Lam. iii. 53). Cisterns, when empty of water, were very often used as prisons, and as such were very secure.

FLOCKS AND HERDS.

A brief view of the flocks and herds of the Israelites, will shew the kinds of animals most common among them, before, as well as after, they ceased to be a nomad people.

5. *Sheep.*—In Scripture mention is made of different species and varieties of sheep. At present, the chief breeds in the country are the broad-tailed and the common horned white. The latter resembles the horned breed of continental Europe, but with a somewhat thicker and larger tail. It is often black and white about the face and feet, but is seldom otherwise black, and sheep wholly black of any breed are and were uncommon (Psalm cxlvii. 16; Isaiah i. 18; Daniel vii. 9). The other breed is chiefly valued for the fat of their broad tails, which tastes very much like marrow. The flesh

of neither breed is remarkably delicate, nor is the wool of peculiar fineness. Mutton is, and always has been, the principal animal food used in the East, on which account, as well

as for the milk and the wool, sheep were held in high estimation. Sometimes one person owned many thousands of them (Job i. 3; 1 Sam. xxv. 2; 1 Chron. v. 21). Sheepshearings were great festivals (1 Sam. xxv. 2, 4, 8; 2 Sam. xiii. 23). On such occasions, the sheep

31. Syrian Sheep.

were collected within uncovered enclosures, which are the "sheepfolds" mentioned in Scripture; for there are no other sheepfolds in the East (Num. xxxii. 16, 24, 36 ; 2 Sam. vii. 8; Zeph. ii. 6).

6. *Goats* were comprehended with sheep under the general term of "flock," both being commonly pastured together, as is still the case in Palestine. There are two varieties or species of the goat in Palestine:—one of them differs little from the common goat; the other is distinguished by its larger size, and still more by its very long, hanging ears (Amos iii. 12), and by the ram-like appearance of its horns and head. The hair is long, and almost inva-

32. Syrian Goat.

riably black. The "wild goats," mentioned in Scripture, were, probably, the ibex and the kebsch, both of which are still found in the mountains in or near Palestine. The first is well known ; the latter is remarkable for the long pendant mane with which its front is furnished. The milk of goats was more esteemed than that of any other animal (Prov. xxvii. 27), and the flesh was much liked, especially that of the kids. The hair was woven into tent-coverings; and the entire skins formed vessels, or "skin bottles," in which water was carried. Smaller vessels, made of kid-skins, were in very common use. When the vessel was intended for water, the side on which the hair grew was turned inward; when for wine, that side was turned out-ward.

33. Water-Skins.

7. *Oxen.*—Animals of this kind belong rather to the agricultural than the pastoral condition of life; and do not, therefore, figure in the possessions of the modern nomads of Western Asia. In this respect, the patriarchal fathers more resembled the Eastern Tartars, for they had large possessions of black cattle (Gen. xxiv. 35; Job i. 3). In after-times, oxen are more frequently mentioned in connexion with agri-cultural life. The richest pastures were those of Bashan, Sharon, and Achor; and the well-fed bulls of Bashan were particularly strong and ferocious (Deut. xxxiii. 17; Psalm xxii. 12; lxviii. 30; Prov. xiv. 4; Isaiah xxxiv. 7). Oxen were employed in carrying burdens, as well as in drawing ploughs and carts. Beef is now but little used in the East; but considerable quantities appear to have been consumed by the Israelites. Veal also was more in use than now, and "the fatted calf" was often slaughtered for a feast (Gen. xviii. 7; Luke xv. 23). Cheese was made from the milk of cows (2 Sam. xvii. 29); but for drinking, goat's milk was preferred. At present there are two principal breeds of oxen in Syria; both short-horned, but one larger, and having longer legs than the other. There are also buffaloes, and the wild ox is still found in the bordering deserts.

8. *Camels.*—There are two species of camels; one with a single hump, and the other with two. The camel so often mentioned in Scripture, is that with the single hump; the other was, probably, scarcely known to the Israelites, as it belongs rather to central than to western Asia. The *Drome*

dary is merely a finer and swifter breed of the camel, used exclusively for riding (Isaiah lx. 6; lxvi. 20; Jer. ii. 23). The camel can endure much abstinence from food and water,

by which, and by its other habits, it is adapted, as by the special destination of Providence, to traverse the deserts, in which much privation must be sustained. Its broad and well-cushioned foot is also peculiarly suited to tread the hard, dry, gravelly soil of the desert. Hence, this animal

34. Arabian Camel: baggage.

is the favourite and the most valued beast of the nomads, who now, as in the times of Scripture, possess large numbers of them (Gen. xxiv. 10; xxxi. 17; 1 Sam. xxx. 17; 1 Kings x. 2; Isaiah xxx. 6; Ezek. xxv. 4). The milk is much used, chiefly in a sour or thickened state, and the flesh is eaten by

the Arabs, though it was forbidden to the Jews (Lev. xi. 4). The hair, which is shed yearly, is made into a kind of coarse cloth, of which robes are made, such as John the Baptist wore (Matt. iii. 4). Camels were used to carry all kinds of burthens (Gen. xxxvii. 25; Judges

35. Arabian Camel: saddle.

vi. 5; 2 Kings viii. 9; 1 Chron. xii. 40; 2 Chron. xiv. 15), and also for riding (Gen. xxiv. 61; xxxi. 17; 1 Sam. xxx. 17). The travellers sit astride, on a proper riding camel, as on

norseback; or squat in a peculiar fashion on the luggage.
Great persons, the sick, and women, sometimes journey at
ease in a covered litter,
or sort of tent, which
is secured upon the
camel's back; or else
two persons balance
each other in covered
cribs, or cradles, slung
over the camel's back,
after the manner of

36. Double Camel Litter.

panniers.   The camels on which wealthy persons ride, are
often garnished with chains and other rich ornaments of metal
(Judges viii. 21, 26).

9. *Horses* were not much used among the more ancient
Israelites; and, as they were then employed chiefly in war
like enterprises, the rearing
of them was discouraged by
the law (Deut. xvii. 16). The
horses of Egypt are the earliest mentioned (Gen. xlvii.
17), and that country was
always noted for its horses.
Joshua encountered chariots
and horses in northern Palestine (Josh. xi. 4-9); and not
long after we find them in

37. Single Camel Litter.

use among the Philistines (Judges i. 19; 1 Sam. xiii. 5).
David reserved some of the horses and chariots which he
captured in his wars (2 Sam. viii. 4; 1 Chron. xviii. 4);
and there are frequent allusions to these animals, and to
equestrian troops, in the book of Psalms.   Solomon established
a large trade with Egypt for chariots and horses (1 Kings x.
28; 2 Chron. i. 16, 17); and after his time horses are often
mentioned, but chiefly as connected with the state and the
army, for they were never much in use by private persons.
A piece of cloth served instead of a saddle, and stirrups were
not known; but a bridle and curb were in use (Psalm xxxii.
3). As horses were not shod, a hard hoof was much esteemed
(Isaiah v. 28; Amos vi. 12)

c

10. *Asses.*—In the East, when properly trained and cared for, the ass is a fine and even elegant animal, while it is still patient and diligent.   Hence, its name is applied in Scripture

not, as with us, to characterise doltish or obstinate, but industrious and active men (Gen. xlix. 14). Before horses were used by the Israelites, and while they were employed chiefly in war, all peaceful operations were carried on by means of asses.   Persons of the first consequence rode on them (Gen.

38. Domestic Ass.

xxii. 3, 5 ; Num. xxii. 21, 30 ; Josh. xv. 18 ; Judges i. 14, v. 10 ; x. 4 ; xii. 14 ; 1 Sam. xxv. 20, 42 ; 2 Sam. xvii. 23, xix. 26 ; 1 Kings ii. 40 ; xiii. 13 ; 2 Kings iv. 22, 24 ; Zech. ix. 9 ; Matt. xxi. 1-7).   When the Jews returned from the Babylonish captivity, there were in their caravan no fewer

than 6720 asses, but not more than 736 horses and 245 mules, and only 435 camels (Ezra ii. 66, 67). White asses, which are less uncommon in the East than with us, were much admired (Judges v. 10). When a person of consequence, or a lady, rode forth, a servant followed to

39. Wild Ass.

urge the beast occasionally with his staff (Judges xix. 3 : 2 Kings iv. 24 ; Prov. xxvi. 3).   Asses were also employed to carry burthens, and in the labours of the field ; but Moses relieved the ass from ploughing in the same yoke with the ox (Deut. xxii. 10). *Wild asses* are often named in Scripture. They are still found in Mesopotamia and further east, but not now in the Syrian deserts. They are of a fine figure and great swiftness, and roam in desert places, far from the abodes of men. They go in herds, and by their acute scent discover water at a great distance (Psalm civ. 11; Isaiah xxxii. 14; Jer. xiv. 6). Asses and mules are still much used for riding in Palestine, as they afford a species of locomotion well suited to the nature of the country.

11. *Mules* are first mentioned in the time of David; but were, probably, known much earlier. They were used for riding and burthen; but do not seem to have become very common (2 Sam. xiii. 29; xviii. 9, 10; 1 Kings i. 33; 1 Chron. xii. 40; Psalm xxxii. 9; Ezek. xxvii. 14). Litters were sometimes borne by mules, as is still the case in those parts of Western Asia where camels are not common.

PART III.—HABITS OF LIFE.

SECTION I.—HABITATIONS

1. THE patriarchal fathers of the Israelites were a tent-dwelling people; and their descendants proceeded at once from tents to houses. We therefore read but little of *huts* among them; and never as the fixed habitations of any people with whom they were conversant. By huts we understand small

dwellings, made of the green or dry branches of trees intertwined, and sometimes plastered with mud. In Scripture they are called *booths*. Such were made by Jacob to shelter his cattle in

41. Hut.

the first winter of his return from Mesopotamia (Gen. xxxiii. 17). In after times we more frequently read of them as being erected in the vineyards and orchards, to shelter the man who guarded the ripened produce (Job xxvii. 18; Isaiah i. 8; xxiv. 20). It was one of the Mosaical institutions that, during the Feast of Tabernacles, the people should live for a week in booths made of green boughs (Lev. xxiii. 42).

2. With *tents* the Scriptures make us more familiar than with huts. They were invented before the Deluge, and appear from the first to have been associated with the pastoral life, to which a moveable habitation was necessary (Gen. iv. 20). The practice of the pastoral fathers was to have their tents near wells of water, and, if possible, under some shady tree (Gen. xviii. 4; Judges iv. 5). The first tents were unloubtedly covered with skins, of which there are traces in the Pentateuch (Exodus xxvi. 14); but nearly all the tents mentioned in Scripture were, doubtless, of goat's hair, spun and woven by the women Exodus xxxv. 26; xxxvi. 14); such as are now in Western Asia, used by all who dwell in tents; hence their black colour (Sol. Song i. 5). Tents of linen were, and are, only used occasionally,

42. Tent.

for holiday or travelling purposes, by those who do not habitually live in them. The patriarchal tents were probably such as we see now in Arabia, of an oblong shape, and eight or ten feet high in the middle. They vary in size, and have, accordingly, a greater or less number of poles to support them—from three to nine. An encampment is generally arranged circularly, forming an enclosure, within which the cattle are driven at night, and the centre of which is occupied by the tent or tents of the Emir or Sheikh. If he is a person of much consequence, he may have three or four tents, for himself, for his wives, for his servants, and for strangers, respectively. The two first are of the most importance, and we know that Abraham's wife had a separate tent (Gen. xxiv. 12). It is more usual, however, for one very large tent to be divided into two or more apartments by curtains. The Holy Tabernacle was framed on this model (Exodus xxvi. 31-37).

3. The Israelites may have seen good houses in Egypt; but, on entering Palestine they had to occupy the dwellings which the previous inhabitants had built, and their own were afterwards constructed on the same model. These appear for a long time to have been poor and low, and built either of sun-dried mud, or of unhewn stones; timber for building being scarce in that country; and hence the employment of it in large quantities, as in some of Solomon's buildings, was a sign of costliness and magnificence. Domestic architecture made considerable progress during the monarchical period. Solomon's palace, built by the aid of the Phœnicians, must have

suggested many improvements (1 Kings vii. 1-12). Jeremiah (xxii. 13, 14) indicates some magnificence of building:
he speaks of upper storeys, of spacious apartments, of many

windows, of cedar ceil-
ings, and of vermillion
painting. By the time
of Christ the buildings
of the upper classes had
become much improved
by some attention to the
rules of Grecian archi-
tecture. It would seem
that the mass of the
houses in Palestine were
such as we now see in
Syria and Mesopotamia.
They were generally
only one storey high,
and when they consist-
ed of more, the upper
storey was inhabited by
the family, the ground-

43. Eastern Palace.

floor being laid out in stores, kitchens, and servants' rooms
and offices. But what such houses wanted in elevation was
made up in extent, as they occupied two, three, or four sides
of an enclosed court; and in great houses, there were two or

three such courts
communicating with
each other. All the
buildings fronted in-
to these quadrangles,
and had no front to
the street, unless a
high wall with the
principal entrance,
and perhaps a lattice
above, may be so

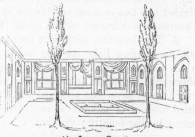

44. Inner Court.

called. The enclosed courts had generally a reservoir or
fountain in the centre, and were often planted with a few
trees. A gallery, or verandah, screened the principal front

of building, and sometimes two, or all the fronts. This gallery was broad and substantial, and had a balustrade, and the covering was upheld by pillars of wood. Hence the many allusions to columns (Psalm lxxv. 3; Prov. ix. 1; Gal. ii. 9). The roofs of the houses were, and are, flat, and covered with mould or a prepared compost. They were fenced by a parapet or balustrade (Deut. xxii. 8). In fine weather the people resorted much to these roofs, to which there was a stair, to breathe the fresh air, to enjoy a prospect, or to witness any event that occurred in the neighbourhood (2 Sam xi. 2; Isaiah xxii. 1; Matt. xxiv. 17; Mark xiii. 15). For the cool air, they slept on the housetop in summer; and to enjoy the air and prospect in the day-time, without inconvenience from the sun, sheds, booths, and tents were sometimes erected there (2 Sam xvi. 22). The Hebrew kings had winter and summer palaces, and in good houses there were sitting-rooms for both seasons. In the one the situation, the exposure, the form, were designed to promote coolness; in the other to preserve warmth (Judges iii. 20; 1 Kings vii. 2-6; Jer. xxii. 14; xxxvi. 22; Amos iii. 15).

45. Basement of an Eastern House.

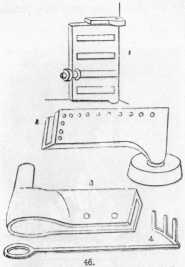

46.

1. Ancient Egyptian Door.   2, 3. Door Pins (in lieu of hinges).   4. Key.

4. Doors were double, or folding, and moved on pivots inserted into holes in the threshold below and the lintel above.

47. Door of Private House.

They were secured by bars (Deut. iii. 5; Judges xvi. 3; Job xxxviii. 10), which were of wood; only those to the gates of fortresses and valuable stores being of metal (Isaiah xlv. 2). There were also locks, which were merely wooden slides which entered a hole in the door-post, and were there secured by teeth or catches (Sol. Song v. 4). The street-doors, as well as the gates of towns, among the Jews, were adorned with inscriptions taken from the Law of Moses (Deut. vi. 9; xi. 20.)

5. The windows had no glass; they were only latticed, and thus gave free passage to the air and admitted light, while they excluded birds and bats. In winter, the cold was kept out by thin veils over the windows, or by shutters with holes in them sufficient to admit light (1 Kings vii. 17; Sol. Song ii. 9).

6. No ancient houses had chimneys. The word so translated in Hosea (xiii. 3) means a hole through which the smoke escaped. This was only in the lower class dwellings, where raw

48. Interior of Private Room.

wood was employed for fuel or cooking, and where there was

an opening immediately over the hearth, to let out the smoke. In better houses, the rooms were warmed in winter by charcoal in braziers, as is still very generally the practice in Western Asia (Jer. xxxvi. 22 ; Mark xiv. 54 ; John xviii. 18).

7. In the East, where the climate allows the people to spend much of their time out of doors, the articles of household furniture and the domestic utensils have always been few and simple : in the sitting-rooms, almost nothing but seats appear. These seats are now low mattresses or couches at the upper end, and sometimes along the sides of the room, with bolsters against the wall to support the back. On these the people sit cross-legged or with their knees bent under them: they sit in the same manner upon the ground, or on rugs and mats.

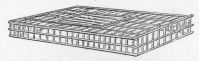

49. Bedstead of Palm-sticks.

Although it would seem that the Hebrews had these customs, yet not so exclusively as the modern Orientals ; as it is clear

50. Royal Bed.

that they had also raised seats, such as chairs and stools, like their Egyptian neighbours, among whom both modes of sitting prevailed (1 Sam. i. 9 ; iv. 13, 18 ; 1 Kings ii.19 ; Prov. ix. 14 ; Matt. xxi. 12). The beds consisted of mattresses and quilted coverlets, laid upon the floor at night, and stowed away in a recess by day. Sheets, blankets, and bedsteads, are not known in the East ; but in Persia and Mesopotamia there is a kind of raised frame, or settee of wood, or of palm branches, on which the

C

beds are sometimes placed at night for sleeping on the housetop. The Jews seem to have had something of the same
kind (Psalm xli. 3 ; cxxxii. 3 ; Amos vi. 4).   A bed with a
tester is mentioned in Judith (xvi. 23) which, with other
indications, and the frequent mention of rich tapestries hung
about and upon a bed for luxuriousness and ornament, seems
to prove that such beds as may yet be found in Eastern
palaces were not unknown under the Hebrew monarchies.
See Esth. i. 6 ; Prov. vii. 16 ; Ezek. xxiii. 41.

8. As every family ground its own corn, a hand-mill is
often named among the domestic utensils.   This consisted of
two circular stones,
placed horizontally
one upon another ;
and the upper being
made to revolve
upon the lower,
reduced to flour the
corn which was in-
troduced through a
hole in the topmost
stone (called *the
rider*). This work
was performed by
women, and was
their first morning
labour, which they
often cheered by
singing (Exodus xi.
5; Num. xi. 8; Deut.
xxiv. 6; Isaiah xlvii.
2 ; Matt. xxiv. 41 ;
Rev. xviii. 22).

51. Grinding Corn.

9. The common domestic vessels were of earthenware, or
of copper (perhaps tinned), and a few were of leather—such
as pots, kettles, leather bottles (made of the whole skins of
goats or kids), plates, cups, and pitchers They all seem to
have been such as are still used in the East. Lamps, fed
with oil of olives, were used for giving light at night. They
were of earthenware or metal, according to circumstances ;

and in the houses of the rich were raised on stands, which are called "candlesticks" in our Bible, and which, judging from that made for the Tabernacle, must sometimes have been costly and elegant, with branches for several lamps (Gen. xv. 17; Exodus xxv. 31-40; xxvii. 20, 21; Zech. iv. 2; Matt. xxv. 1-9). A lamp was, and is, always kept burning at night, which explains an allusion contained in many passages of Scripture (2 Sam. xxi. 17; Job xviii. 6; Prov. xx.

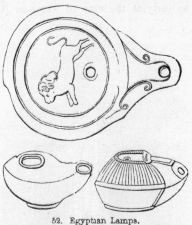

52. Egyptian Lamps.

20). Candles were not in use, and when the word "candle" occurs in our Bibles it means a lamp.

10. The towns of Palestine do not appear to have been considerable for size or population; but this was compensated by their great numbers. We are surprised at the number of towns mentioned even so early as the time of Joshua. They, of course, grew larger and more populous as the country became more densely inhabited; but the only cities that we should be disposed to rank with our first-rate towns were Jerusalem, Samaria, and, eventually, Cæsarea. We know not the ordinary population of Jerusalem; but, from a calculation founded on the number of lambs slain at the Passover, it would seem that the concourse at that great festival must have amounted to between two and three millions. The houses of Jerusalem, which were of many storeys, were then full of people, and many lodged outside in tents. In the time of Christ, Josephus describes Galilee, in particular, as exceedingly populous: the towns lay near each other, and the population of the least important exceeded fifteen thousand. Towns had high walls in the time of Moses, which seemed very formidable to the Israelites (Num. xiii. 25-33); and

afterwards the defences of towns were greatly improved. Indeed, the gates of towns, which imply walls, are mentioned as early as the time of Abraham (Gen. xix. 1; xxiii. 10).

Villages, being un-walled, or surrounded only by a hedge, were abandoned in times of war and trouble, and the inhabitants removed into caves or walled towns (Judges v. 7). At the gates of towns, most of the public business was transacted(Gen. xxiii. 10,18; Deut. xxi. 19; xxii. 24; xxv. 7; Ruth iv. 1). At the gates also the markets were held, as long as the transactions of the Israelites were almost confined to the sale or interchange of the

53. Gate of Konieh (Iconium).

produce of their fields and flocks (2 Chron. xviii. 9; xxxii. 6; Neh. viii. 1, 3; 2 Kings vii. 18; Job xxix. 7); but after-wards they had, in their large towns, as Josephus testifies, such covered bazaars, or streets of shops, for the sale of manu-factured goods, as are now usual in the East. The streets in Eastern towns are always exceedingly narrow, that the shadow of the houses may keep them cool; and the appear-ance of these streets is dull and uninviting, as the houses do not front the road. The streets are always unpaved; but some streets in Jerusalem, and in the new cities, were paved in the time of the Herods, who had witnessed the benefits of this practice in Rome and Italy. The Jewish towns must have had rather a mean appearance in the distance, from the want of temples and public buildings (except at Jerusalem), as well as of such elegant minarets and domes as enliven and embellish the towns of the modern East.

SECTION II.—FOOD AND DRESS.

1. LIKE most Eastern people, the Israelites were plain and simple in their food, which consisted chiefly of bread, vegetables, fruits (green and preserved), honey, milk, curds, cream, butter, and cheese. Meat could hardly be called an ordinary article of food, except among the higher class of the people dwelling in towns. The use of animal food was, indeed, restricted in some degree by the law, which allowed the flesh of no beasts to be eaten but such as chewed the cud and parted the hoof, nor any fish but such as had both fins and scales (Lev. xi. 1-28). Blood and fat were also interdicted, as well as the large lobe of the liver, and the kidneys (Lev. iii. 15, 17). These restrictions rendered it difficult for a strict Jew to eat with a heathen : and this was probably the motive ; as it was one great object of the Mosaical law to keep the Israelites separate from all other nations. The hog was not forbidden more especially than many other animals; but being the only unclean beast the flesh of which was usually and commonly eaten, its absence from the diet of the Jews attracted more attention than any other prohibition. Poultry was but sparingly used. The only domestic birds kept were pigeons and the common fowl ; and the Scripture gives no instance of their being used for food, except the "fatted fowl," provided for the regal and vice-regal tables of Solomon and Nehemiah (1 Kings iv. 23 ; Neh. v. 18). The quails eaten in the wilderness furnish the only other instance of birds used for food (Exod. xvi. 12, 13; Num. xi. 31). Eggs are only twice mentioned as articles of food (Job vi. 6; Luke xi. 12). Although fish with fins and scales were allowed to the Israelites for food, it does not seem that much use was made of this indulgence until the later days of the Jewish history. In the Old Testament, the only direct reference to the consumption of fish is where we learn that Mediterranean fish were brought across the country by the Phœnicians for sale at Jerusalem (Neh. xiii. 16). The fish brought to the city were sold at a particular gate, called the Fish-Gate (2 Chron. xxxiii. 14 ; Neh. iii. 3 ; xii. 39). Fish-ponds are mentioned (Sol. Song

vii. 4) ; and there are such allusions to fishing with nets (Job xix. 6 ; Isaiah li. 20), with hooks (Job xli. 1 ; Isaian xix. 8 ; Amos iv. 2), and with spears (Job xli. 7), as shew that these operations were well known. In the New Testament we read oftener of fish and fishing. Several of the Apostles were fishermen of the lake of Gennesareth, which abounded in fish ; and the Gospels frequently notice their proceedings in that character, with which some of the most signal miracles of Christ were connected. The eating of fish is also often mentioned, and it would seem to have been generally broiled (Matt. vii. 10 ; Luke xxiv. 42 ; John xxi. 9, 10, 13).

2. Bread was not baked in loaves, as with us, but in cakes, in rolls, and in large and thin plats, like pancakes. Every family generally baked its own bread, and that daily, after the flour had been ground. The modes of baking were various, and on these the shape of the bread depended. There was the heated hearth for the thicker cakes and rolls ; and the thin bread was baked either on a metal plate over hot embers, or by being stuck against the heated sides of a large earthenware vessel, or of a pit in the floor (Gen. xviii. 6 ; xix. 3 ; Lev. ii. 4 ; vi. 21 ; xi. 35 ; 1 Kings xix. 6). This work of baking bread, like that of grinding corn, was at first performed by the wives and daughters, however high their station (Gen. xviii. 6 ; Lev. xxvi. 26 ; 2 Sam. xiii. 6, 8 ; Jer. vii. 18, 19) ; but was in time abandoned, in families of consequence, to female servants (1 Sam. viii. 13). There were, however, in large towns, as at present, public ovens and bakers by trade (Jer. xxxvii. 21 ; Hos. vii. 4) ; and from the former text which mentions " the bakers' street," it appears that, as is still the case, the bakers, as well as other trades, had a particular part of the market or bazaar set apart to their own use, instead of being, as with us, dispersed through the towns in which they lived. The customers of the bakers were chiefly the small households, the poor, and the unsettled part of the population. For their more extensive operations, the bakers have ovens of brick, not unlike our own ; and in very large households similar ovens are used. Bread, such as has been mentioned, needed not to be cut; it was always broken (Isaiah lviii. 7 ; Lam. iv. 4 ; Matt. xiv. 19 ; &c.) In eating, generally, no knives, and much less forks, were used, but each

morsel of food was conveyed from the dish to the mouth by the right hand (Ruth ii. 14; Prov. xxvi. 15; John xiii. 26). Meat was dressed so as to be easily separated by the fingers; and if a morsel was too large, it was transferred to the cake of bread which was placed before each person; for the use of plates was unknown. This mode of feeding made it necessary that the hands should be washed before and after meals (Matt. xv. 2; Mark vii. 3); which was done by a servant pouring water over the hands from an ewer, and receiving it in a basin held below, as it fell from them (2 Kings iii. 11).

3. A kind of lunch, consisting of bread, milk, cheese, &c., was taken in the forenoon; but the principal meal was in the evening after the labours of the day were over, and when the coolness of the air allowed enjoyment and created appetite. Hence it is called a supper (Mark vi. 21; Luke xiv. 24; John xii. 2). A short prayer was said before and after meals (Matt. xiv. 9; xv. 36; xxvi. 27; &c.) We have supposed before that the Hebrews had two modes of sitting; when they used seats they ate from a table, but when they sat on the ground, the meal was laid out on a cloth spread on the floor, with a large piece of leather under it, to prevent the mats or carpets from being soiled. Or a kind of table, raised only a few inches, may have been occasionally employed, as at present. During the Captivity, the Jews learned (as did afterwards the Romans) the Persian practice of reclining at meals upon mats or cushions, around the

54. Modern Syrians at Meat.

table, in such a way that the head of every person approached the bosom of the one who reclined next above him (John xiii. 23). In ancient times, every person seems to have had his separate portion of meat, and honour was shewn to a distinguished or favoured guest, by the quantity or quality of that which was set before him (Gen. xliii. 34; 1 Sam. i. 4, 5; ix. 23, 24); but in later times every one helped himself from

55. Ancient Dinner-Bed.

the dish nearest to him, or from one dish if the party was small enough for one dish to be within the reach of all (Matt. xxvi. 23; John xiii. 26). The Orientals do not drink during meals, but afterwards water or wine is handed round in vessels of tinned copper (Matt. xxvi. 27). Wine was used freely among the Jews, whose country was, indeed, noted for wine and oil : all their wines appear to have been red (Prov. xxiii. 31; Isaiah xxvii. 2). The kind most commonly drunk was weak, or much diluted with water, and was used much as we use table ale or beer. Strong and generous wines were necessarily confined to the rich, and were sparingly used. Wine was also sometimes strengthened or flavoured with spices, especially myrrh (Num. xv. 10; Psalm lxxv. 8; Prov. xxiii. 30; Hos. xiv. 7). That which was called "strong drink," included the higher kinds of wine, but more particularly denoted a very inebriating liquor made of dates and of various seeds and roots (Lev. x. 9; Deut. xxix. 6; 1 Sam. i. 15; &c.) From this and pure wine was made another drink, which appears to have been much used for common purposes (Num. vi. 3; Ruth ii. 14; Matt. xxvii. 48).

4. At feasts or entertainments, the guests were anointed with precious and perfumed oils (Psalm xxiii. 5; xlv. 7; Amos vi. 6; Luke vii. 37, 38; &c.) It was not uncommon for the carousal to be prolonged through the night, with much excess of drinking (Rom. xiii. 13; Gal. v. 21; 1 Peter iv. 3). Jests, riddles, singing, music, dancing, were not wanting on these festive occasions (Judges xiv. 12; Prov. ix. 2-4; Isaiah v. 12; xxiv. 7, 9; Amos vi. 4, 5; Luke xv. 25). The Jews do not appear to have been addicted to gaming, for there is no allusion to it in the Scriptures. Neither is story-telling, that great pastime of the modern East, directly mentioned; but as they were in the habit of producing apologues, or

short stories, on particular occasions, we may safely number this among their amusements.

5. We know how the ancient Egyptians, Persians, Babylonians, Greeks, and Romans were dressed, for their costumes are represented in sculptures and paintings which still exist; but it is not so with respect to the Jews, who did not consider it lawful to carve or paint the human figure. This want is, however, well supplied by the existing costumes of the East Dress does not change there as with us; and it is clear, that the habits now worn by the people, as well as the common usages of life, are, for the most part, the same as in the times of the Bible. The patriarchs dressed somewhat differently, probably, from their settled descendants; and the difference was in all likelihood such as we now see between the pastoral Bedouin Arabs and the inhabitants of settled countries. The dresses of the great Arabian family, in its various conditions, appear to have been transmitted with little alteration from very ancient times, and may be taken as affording the nearest approximation which can now be obtained to the raiment worn by the ancient Israelites. The Arabian costumes may be deemed to agree with the dresses worn in the patriarchal and pastoral periods of the Hebrew history. The garb conventionally assigned by painters and sculptors to Scripture characters seems to have been founded partly on tradition, and partly derived from actual observation of Oriental dress

56. Arabian Dress.

in early pilgrimages to the Holy Land.   It is, upon the whole,
a noble costume, and makes a nearer approach to the truth
than has been of late usually supposed.   Long garments were

worn by the Israel-
ites, as they were,
indeed, by most an-
cient nations, and
are by the modern
Orientals. Such gar-
ments were also wide
and loose; and thus,
although easy and
dignified, they rather
impeded active and
vigorous exertion;
for which reason, in
manual action, the
sleeves were drawn

57. Sculptural Scripture Costumes.

up, or, as the Scripture describes it, "the arm made bare"
(Isaiah lii. 10; Ezek. iv. 7); and in travelling on foot, or
running, the skirts were gathered up, and confined by the

girdle; this was called
"girding the loins" (1
Kings xviii. 46; 2 Kings
v. 29; Luke xii. 35; 1
Peter i. 13). We may con-
ceive the figure of a Jew,
viewed externally, as that
of a full-bearded man, clad
in a long and loose gar-
ment with large sleeves,
which was confined to the
person by a girdle about
the loins; the neck bare,
the feet protected by a

58. Arms Bared.

piece of leather strapped to the sole, and the head either bare
(as it seems very often to have been), or covered, among
the higher classes, by a kind of turban, and among the
common people by a piece of cloth thrown over the head,
and confined by a fillet around the brows.   The ordinary

appearance of the Jew, however, was varied by circumstances; as when a large, loose, and ample cast garment was the dress after a cloak over the dress which has been described. This was worn with slitted sides by the upper classes, who had a row of fine materials as to the number of such service that it was fashionable, and long trains over high. (Read xxii. 35; 2C; 2 x 20; Job xxiii. 17.) This dress became soiled in winter, as well as in it when the slept at night, when then worn by the poorer, when nothing more suitable at his hands. It may have been worn day to day for ... (see Exod. xxii. 37.) It is generally

59. Common Dress: Shirts or Frocks without Outer Mantles
and with or without Girdles.

Matt. xix. 20. Luke.

VII. (v. 14.) In a tomb discovered by Ibhdani in the valley of Bubeh-Melhol, near Hebron, there are, among other figures,

60. Full Dress: with different sorts of Outer Mantles.

appearance of the Jew, however, was varied by circumstances; as when a large, loose, and shapeless garment was thrown, like a cloak, over the dress which has been described. This was worn with studied grace by the upper classes, who had it of finer materials; and to the poor it was of such service that it was forbidden by law to keep it in pledge over-night (Exod. xxii. 25, 26; see also Job xxii. 6; xxiv. 7). This was because such persons wrapped themselves up in it when they slept; it also served them to carry burthens in, when nothing more suitable was at hand; and this use of it may be seen every day in the East (Exod. xii. 34; 2 Kings iv. 39). It was

61. Captive Jews.

peculiar to the Jews to have a fringe with a piece of blue tape upon the four corners of this garment, to remind them that they were a peculiar people and under peculiar laws (Num. xv. 38, 39; Matt. ix. 20; Luke viii. 44). In a tomb discovered by Belzoni in the valley of Babel-Melook, near Thebes, there are, among other figures, four supposed to be of captive Jews of the time of Josiah, where the fringe is conspicuously represented—perhaps with some exaggeration. It was also peculiar to them, in later days, to wear 'frontlets,' or 'phylacteries,' which were little boxes of hard calf-skin, bound by thongs to the forehead, and

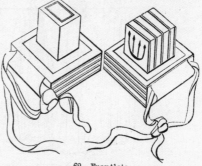

62. Frontlets.

folded up slips of parchment, on which were written out the texts of the law which were supposed to prescribe this curious observance (Exod. xiii. 16; Deut. vi. 8).

6. All these dresses of the Israelites were of linen or cotton, excepting the capacious outer garment which was of wool, or of wool and hair interwoven. The Egyptians were famous for the manufacture of various kinds of cloth; and that the Israelites had learnt this art from them, is evinced by their producing in the wilderness the various rich cloths required for the coverings and curtains of the tabernacle, and for the dress of the high-priest (Exod. xxvi. xxviii.). From various passages of Scripture we infer that the art of embroidery was carried to some degree of perfection (Exod. xxxv. 35; xxxviii. 23; Judges v. 30). There was a family of Judah particularly celebrated for its skill in the manufacture of fine linen (1 Chron. iv. 21). White, blue, and various shades of red and purple, seem to have been the favourite colours among the Israelites. No other colours of clothes are named in Scripture.

7. From Oriental analogies, we should suppose that the Israelites wore shirts under their tunics; but there is no positive evidence of this, unless, as some suppose, such were the "thirty sheets" (margin "shirts") which, with thirty changes of raiment, formed the forfeit of Samson's riddle (Judges xiv. 12). Loose linen drawers or trowsers, such as are still used in the East, were worn by the priests, and probably by others (Exod. xxviii. 42). These were at first very short, not reaching to the knees, but were at length extended to the middle of the leg, or to the ankle.

63. Shirt.

8. The girdle which confined the tunic was of two kinds. One was a broad band of leather, fastened with clasps (2 Kings i. 8; Matt. iii. 4), and the other was of fine linen or cotton, long and narrow, and wound in many folds around the waist (Jer. xiii. 1). The girdle answered the purpose of a pocket to carry money and other valuables, hence the word rendered "purse" in some passages literally means "a girdle" (2 Sam. xviii. 11; Matt.

x. 9 ; Mark vi. 8). It might be inferred from 2 Sam. xx. 8, that the Israelites wore daggers in their girdles, like the modern Orientals; but this is not very clear; and Joab, as the commander of the forces, might carry arms not generally worn.

9. Stockings and socks were not in use, and the mass of the people went altogether barefoot, except in winter, or upon a journey; but the wealthier classes always wore sandals out of doors, except during mourning. These sandals are called

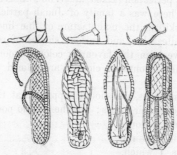

64. Sandals.

"shoes" in our Bible. They were pieces of hide or tanned leather, shaped to the sole of the foot, and bound to it with thongs of leather (Gen. xiv. 23; Exod. xii. 11; Isaiah v. 27; Matt. iii. 11; x. 10; &c.) When a person entered a house, or the presence of a superior, he took

off his sandals, as the modern Orientals do their shoes (Exod. iii. 5; Deut. xxv. 9; Ruth iv. 7, 8; Isaiah xx. 4; Ezek. xxiv. 17). It was the office of the lowest class of servants to take off and carry the master's sandals (Matt. iii. 11; Mark i. 7). Servants of that class also washed the soiled feet of the guests who came to an entertainment; although the master himself sometimes stooped to perform this office for a much-honoured visitant (Gen. xviii. 4; Luke vii. 44).

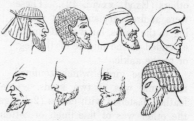

65. Beards of Syrian and other Foreign Nations, from Egyptian Monuments.

10. The Israelites allowed the hair of the head and beard to grow. The former was shorn occasionally; and the partial use of the razor in trimming the

beard was not unlawful to any but the Nazarites (Num. vi. 5; Judges xiii. 7; xvi. 17). A full head of hair seems to have been much admired (2 Sam. xiv. 26; Sol. Song v. 11). The hair was dressed and anointed with much care, especially at festivals (2 Sam. xiv. 2; Isaiah iii. 24; Matt. vi. 17; Luke vii. 46). Baldness in men not old was rare, and was despised (2 Kings ii. 23; Isaiah iii. 24; Jer. xlvii. 5). The beard, as the characteristic sign of manhood, was much respected by the Israelites; to shave it, to spit upon it, to pull it, and even to touch it, except for the purpose of salutation, were

66. Modern Oriental Beards.

the grossest insults which men could inflict upon one another (2 Sam. x. 4-6; 1 Chron. xix. 3-6; Isaiah vii. 20); and hence, for a man to neglect or maltreat his own beard was a sign of madness or of extreme grief (1 Sam. xxi. 13; 2 Sam. xix. 24; Isaiah xv. 2).

11. It appears to have been the custom to use walking-staves, even when not upon a journey (Gen. xxxii. 10; xxxviii. 18; Exod. xii. 11; 2 Kings iv. 29; Mark vi. 8; &c.) Rings were worn on the fingers: these were generally signet-rings bearing the name of the owner, and the impression from which was equivalent to his signature. This explains the high powers and dignities which a monarch conferred by the delivery of his own signet-ring (Gen. xli. 42; Est. iii. 10, 12; viii 2, Dan. vi. 9, 13, 17).

SECTION III.—WOMEN AND CHILDREN.

1. WOMEN appear to have enjoyed considerably more freedom among the Jews than is now allowed them in Western Asia, although in other respects their condition and employments seem to have been not dissimilar. At present, women of all ranks are much confined to their own houses, and never

see the men who visit their husbands or fathers; and in towns they never go abroad without their persons and faces being completely shrouded; they also take their meals apart from the males, even of their own family. But in the rural districts they enjoy more freedom, and often go about unveiled. Among the Jews, women were somewhat less restrained in their intercourse with men, and did not generally conceal their faces when they went abroad. Only one instance occurs in Scripture of women eating with men (Ruth ii. 14); but that was at a simple refection, and only illustrates the greater freedom of rural manners.

67. Matron in Full Dress.

2. The employments of the women were very various, and sufficiently engrossing. In the earlier or patriarchal state of society, the daughters of men of substance tended their father's flocks (Gen. xxix 9; Exod. ii. 16). In ordinary circumstances, the first labour of the day was to grind corn and bake bread, as already noticed. The other cares of the family occupied the rest of the day. The women of the

68. In-door Veils.

69. Dress Veils, &c. In-door.

peasantry and of the poor consumed much time in collecting
fuel, and in going to the wells for water. The wells were
usually outside the towns, and the labour of drawing water
from them was by no means confined to poor women. This
was usually, but not always, the labour of the evening; and
the water was carried in earthen vessels, borne upon the
shoulder (Gen. xxiv. 15-20; John iv. 7, 28). Working with
the needle also occupied much of their time, as it would seem
that not only their own clothes but those of the men were
made by the females. Some of the needlework was very fine,
and much valued (Exod. xxvi. 36; xxviii. 39; Judges v. 30;
Psalm xlv. 14). The women appear to have spun the yarn
for all the cloth that was in use (Exod. xxxv. 25; Prov.
xxxi. 19); and much of the weaving seems also to have been
executed by them (Judges xvi. 13, 14; Prov. xxxi. 22). The
tapestries for bed-coverings, mentioned in the last-cited text,
were probably produced in the loom, and appear to have been
much valued (Prov. vii. 16).

3. We have no certain information regarding the dress of
the women among the poorer classes; but it was probably
coarse and simple, and not materially different from that which

we now see among the Be-
douin women, and the female
peasantry of Syria. This
consists of drawers, and a
long and loose gown of coarse
blue linen, with some ornamental bordering wrought
with the needle, in another
colour, about the neck and
bosom. The head is covered
with a kind of turban, connected with which, behind, is
a veil which covers the neck,
back, and bosom. We may
presume, with still greater
certainty, that women of superior condition wore, over

76. Young Lady in Full Dress.

their inner dress, a frock or tunic like that of the men, but
more closely fitting the person, with a girdle formed by an

71. Out-door Veils.

72. Nose Jewel.

unfolded kerchief. Their head-dress was a kind of **turban**, with different sorts of veils and wrappers worn under **various** circumstances. The hair was worn long, **and**, as at present, was braided into numerous tresses, with **trinkets** and **ribands** (1 Cor. xi. 15; 1 Tim. ii. 9; 1 Peter iii. 3). With the head-dress the principal ornaments appear to have been connected, such as a jewel for the forehead, and rows of pearls (Sol. Song i. 10; Ezek. xvi. 12). Ear-rings were also worn (Isaiah iii. 20; Ezek. xvi. 12), as well as a nose-jewel, consisting, no doubt, as now, either of a ring inserted in the cartilage of the nose, or an ornament like a button attached

to it. The nose-jewel was of gold or silver, and sometimes set with jewels (Gen. xxiv. 47; Isaiah iii. 21). Bracelets were also generally worn (Isaiah iii. 19; Ezek. xvi. 11), some on the wrists, and some

73. Bracelets.

on the upper arm. They were worn both by men and women, but chiefly by the latter; and, for a man, the bracelet on the upper arms, seems to have been, as it is now in the East, a mark of royalty (2 Sam. i. 10). Anklets were also worn by females, and were, as at present, probably more like fetters than ornaments (Isaiah iii. 16, 20). The Jewish women had the art of staining their eyelids black, for effect and expression (2 Kings ix. 30; Jer. iv. 30; Ezek. xxiii. 40); and it is

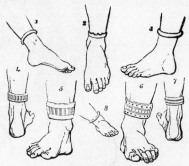

74. **Anklets.**

1, 2, 5, 6, 7, Ancient Oriental.   3, 4, 8, Modern Oriental.

more than probable that they had the present practice of staining the nails, and the palms of their hands and soles of their feet, of an iron-rust colour, by means of a paste made from the plant called *henna* (*Lawsonia inermis*). This plant appears to be mentioned in Sol. Song i. 14, and its present use is probably referred to in Deut. xxi. 12 ; 2 Sam. xix. 24.

4. Fathers claimed the absolute disposal of their sons and daughters in marriage (Gen. xxi. 21 ; Exod. xxi. 9 ; Deut. xxii. 16 ; Judges xiv. 1-4) ; but in a family where the children were from different mothers, the full brothers of a young woman expected also to be consulted (Gen. xxxiv. 11, 27 ; 2 Sam. xiii. 20-29). If a young man saw a damsel whom he liked, he might ask his own father to apply to her father on his behalf (Gen. xxxiv. 4 ; Judges xiv. 1, 2). To prevent the contamination of idolatry, all marriages with foreigners were forbidden to the Israelites (Exod. xxxiv. 15, 16 ; Neh. xiii. 23). If it happened that, for want of male heirs, daughters inherited an estate, it was expected that they should marry near kinsmen, or at least in their own tribe, that the property might be kept in the family or tribe to which it was first allotted (Num. xxvii. 1-11 ; xxxvi. 1-12). For a somewhat similar reason, if a man died without sons, his next brother was expected to marry his widow, and the first-born son of this union was considered as the son of the deceased, and inherited his estate (Deut. xxv. 5-10 ; Ruth iv. 1-5).

5. A father did not, as with us, give a fortune with his daughter, but expected to receive a consideration or dowry for giving her in marriage ; the amount of which was settled in the contract of marriage which was formed by the fathers of the respective parties (Gen. xxix. 18, 27 ; xxxiv. 11, 12 ; Josh. xv. 6 ; 1 Sam. xviii. 23-26). This covenant, which was, in fact, the essential act of marriage, was in earlier times rendered valid by the presence of witnesses ; but in later days it was reduced to writing, and appears to have been confirmed by oaths (Prov. ii. 17 ; Mal. ii. 14). In Jacob's case we have an instance of the husband's personal services to the father being accepted in lieu of money. Sometimes, however, a daughter was freely given by a father, without the exaction of what was called her " price," and such wives were the more highly honoured (Gen. xi. 15). In particular cases, it also occurred that a dowry was given by the father with his daughter (Josh. xv. 18, 19 ; Judges i. 12-15 ; 1 Kings ix. 16).

6. An interval of ten or twelve months, or even longer, usually passed between the contract of marriage and the actual nuptials. During this time the affianced pair saw little of each other; but were nevertheless accounted as man and wife,—so much so, that the engagement could not be broken off without a regular divorce; and the woman was stoned as an adulteress, if, in the meantime, she proved unchaste (Gen. xxiv. 55; Judges xiv. 8; Matt. i. 18-20). When the nuptial day arrived, the bridegroom went, in the evening with his friends and associates, in holiday attire, to take home his bride from her father's house. She, splendidly arrayed, and with the bridal crown upon her head, came forth attended by her young companions; and, walking under a canopy, was escorted to her future home with songs, and dances, and instrumental music. On their arrival there, the men and women feasted in separate apartments; and if the parties were wealthy, the feast was prolonged for a week (Judges xiv. 17). We know not of any ceremony attending this actual marriage, unless it were that the nuptial blessing —a prayer for a numerous offspring—was invoked on the newly-married pair.

7. For a man to have more than one wife was an abuse which existed at a very early date (Gen. iv. 19), and, in the course of time, became very prevalent. It was common among the Hebrews in the time of Moses, when it was deemed advisable to discourage rather than absolutely to interdict so rooted a practice. Afterwards, however, it became very unusual for a man to have more than one wife; as is, in fact, the case at present in countries where polygamy is allowed.

8. In like manner, Moses imposed some restrictions on the practice of divorce, which appears to have been before his time merely an oral act on the part of the man, but which he required to be effected by a written document. The repudiation might afterwards be retracted, if the woman had not, in the meanwhile, married another man; but if she had, it could not be recalled (Deut. xxiv. 1-4). It was disputed in later times, what the law intended to be a sufficient ground of divorce. One party contended that the man might divorce his wife for any cause, however trifling; the other, that he could do so for adultery only. Our Lord, in whose time the

practice of divorce had become frightfully common, decided the latter to be the just alternative (Matt. v. 31, 32). Even before the time of Moses, the punishment for adultery in a woman was death (Gen. xxxviii. 24; Lev. xx. 10), but we meet with no instance of its actual infliction. If a man suspected the chastity of his wife, without having legal evidence of the fact, it was in his power to subject her to the ordeal of " the water of jealousy," which, through the agency of a very awful oath, was to be instrumental in making her guilt or innocence appear (Num. v. 11-31).

9. The Israelites eagerly desired children, and especially sons. Hence the messenger who first brought to the father the news that a son was born, was well rewarded (Job iii. 3; Jer. xx. 15). The event was celebrated with music; and the father, when the child was presented to him, pressed it to his bosom, by which act he was understood to acknowledge it as his own (Gen. l. 23; Job iii. 12; Psalm xxii. 10). On the eighth day from the birth the child was circumcised (Gen. xvii. 10); at which time also, a name was given to it (Luke i. 59). The first-born son was highly esteemed, and had many distinguishing privileges. He had a double portion of the estate (Deut. xxi. 17); he exercised a sort of parental authority over his younger brothers (Gen. xxv. 23, &c.; xxvii. 29; Exod. xii. 29; 2 Chron. xxi. 3); and before the institution of the Levitical priesthood, he acted as the priest of the family (Num. iii. 12, 13; viii. 18). The patriarchs exercised the power of taking these privileges from the first-born, and giving them to any other son, or of distributing them among different sons; but this practice was overruled by the Mosaical law (Deut. xxi. 15-17).

10. The child continued about three years at the breast of the mother, and a great festival was given at the weaning (Gen. xxi. 8; 1 Sam. i. 22-24; 2 Chron. xxxi. 6; Matt. xxi. 16). He remained two years longer in charge of the women; after which he was taken under the especial care of the father with a view to his proper training (Deut. vi. 20-25; xi. 19). It appears that those who wished for their sons better instruction than they were themselves able or willing to give, employed a private teacher, or else sent them to a priest or Levite, who had perhaps several others under

his care. The principal object was, that they should be well acquainted with the law of Moses; and reading and writing were taught in subservience to this leading object.

11. The authority of a father was very great among the Israelites, and extended not only to his sons, but to his grandsons,—indeed, to all who were descended from him. His power had no recognised limit, and even if he put his son or grandson to death, there was, at first, no law by which he could be brought to account (Gen. xxi. 14; xxxviii. 24). But Moses circumscribed this power, by ordering that when a father judged his son worthy of death, he should bring him before the public tribunals. If, however, he had struck or cursed his father or mother, or was refractory or disobedient, he was still liable to capital punishment (Exod. xxi. 15, 17; Lev. xx. 9; Deut. xxi. 18-21).

SECTION IV.—ETIQUETTE.

1. THE Israelites, like other Orientals, gave stronger manifestations of their feelings of respect or dislike, than has ever been usual among western nations. In most cases their manner would express more, and ours less, than the real feeling; and, in general, the etiquette of Orientals is more refined than might be expected from their condition in life. Domestic servants who, in families of consideration, were foreign slaves, behaved with great submission and respect, and, when in actual attendance, stood at a distance with crossed arms, watching the slightest motion of the master's hand (Psalm cxxiii. 2). When equals, being friends, met they kissed each other's beards, as do the Arabians, placing the hand underneath (2 Sam. xx. 9). Sometimes, the cheeks were merely placed together, and this also is described as a kiss or salutation. The kisses of affection, were on the lips and cheeks in women, and the beard and cheeks in men; the kiss of respect and homage was upon the brow (Gen. xxvii. 26; Exod. iv. 27; 1 Sam. x. 1; 2 Sam. xv. 5; xix. 39; Psalm ii. 12; Prov. xxiv. 26; Matt. xxvi. 49; Acts xx. 37). In meeting, they asked each other of their health, and the health of their connections, which, with other ceremonies, consumed so much time that persons charged with urgent messages were enjoined to salute no one by the way (2 Kings iv. 29; Luke x. 4). Various forms of bowing and prostration are mentioned in Scripture. The most usual, as now, were to bow or incline the head, in doing which the Orientals lay the right hand upon the heart (Gen. xxiv. 26;

75. Eastern Forms of Bowing.

1 Kings i. 16, 31, &c.); to bow the body very low "with the face towards the ground," without bending the knees (1 Sam. xxv. 23; xxviii. 14; 2 Sam. xiv. 33; 1 Kings i. 23; 2 Chron.

vii. 3, &c.); to bend the knees (Num. xxiv. 9 ; Judges vii. 6;
1 Kings xix. 18); to kneel, in worship (2 Chron. vi. 13 ; Psalm
xcv. 6; Dan. vi. 11) ; and to prostrate one's-self upon the
ground, which was done either as an act of worship to God,
or in reverence, homage, or humiliation before man (Gen.
xxii. 5 ; 1 Sam. i. 3 ; 2 Sam. ix. 8 ; Psalm xlv. 12 ; Acts x.

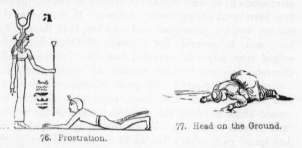

76. Prostration.

77. Head on the Ground.

25, 26 ; Rev. xix. 20 ; xxii. 9). This last posture consisted
sometimes in grovelling flat upon the ground ; but more

usually with the knees
bent, and the forehead
rested on the earth.
Other marks of reve-
rence were, kissing
the feet of the person
reverenced, or the hem
of his garment (Matt.
ix. 20 ; Luke vii. 38),

78. Kissing the Feet.

which acts were usually connected with some of the postures
of respect which have been mentioned. In their greetings

79. Kissing the Hand.

nearly the same verbal salutations were in use as we now find
among the Arabians and other
Moslems. The most usual were,
"Peace be with thee" (Judges
xix. 20; 1 Sam. xxv. 6; 1 Chron.
xii. 18 ; Luke xxiv. 36); "The
blessing of the Lord be upon
thee" (Psalm cxxix. 8); " Bles-
sed be thou of the Lord" (Ruth iii. 10 ; 1 Sam. xxiii. 21)

There is a pleas⎯ ⎯nstance of the interchange of salutations
in the case of Boaz, who said to his reapers, " The Lord be
with you," and was answered, " The Lord bless thee"
(Ruth ii. 4).

2. It has always been the custom in the East for an inferior to make a present to a superior, when paying him a
visit, or seeking any favour from him; and this custom was
very prevalent among the Jews (Prov. xviii. 16). It was
considered a mark of respect which it would be uncivil to
omit, even when the present was merely complimentary, and
of no intrinsic value; and it might consist of money, different
articles of food, clothes, arms, or anything which could, according to his means, evince the respect of the party making
the offering (Gen. xliii. 11; 1 Sam. ix. 7; xvi. 20; Job xlii.
11). Kings and princes were in the habit of making presents
as marks of distinction and favour to those whom they wished
to honour. These were generally dresses of more or less
value (Gen. xlv. 22, 23; Est. viii. 15); and there was a
royal wardrobe in which such garments were kept (2 Chron.
ix. 24). The most distinguished honour of this kind, was to
receive a robe which the prince had himself worn (1 Sam.
xviii. 4); and it was a great affront if the garment thus presented was not imm diately and publicly worn (Matt. xxii.
11, 12).

3. When kings and princes entered their cities in state, it
was usual to lay the dust by sprinkling the streets, to strew
the road with flowers and branches of trees, and even to spread
the ground with cloth, or with garments; while the spectators, crowding on the house-tops, and at the opened lattices
fronting the street, clapped their hands and shouted for joy :
at other times they performed their obeisance in silence as the
great one passed (2 Sam. xvi. 16; 1 Kings i. 40; 2 Kings
ix. 13; Isa. xlii. 11; Zech. ix. 9; Matthew xxi. 7-9).

4. The modes of shewing insult and inflicting disgrace,
among the Israelites, were very significant, although they appear to us childish. They consisted of maltreating the beard,
as formerly mentioned; of plucking off the hair (Isa. l. 6),
and of spitting in the face (Isa. l. 6; Mark xiv. 65). To
put men to the employments of women was a dreadful degra-
dation (Judges xvi. 21; Lam. v. 13); and clapping the

hands, hissing, thrusting out the tongue and making a wide mouth, crunching the teeth, and wagging the head, are described as modes in which the populace testified their hatred, or shewed malignant exultation or contempt (Job xxvii. 23; Jer. lvii. 4; ii. 15; Ezek. xxv. 6). But perhaps the greatest and most intolerable insult, was to cast contempt upon a man's mother: thus Saul, to insult his son, spoke contemptuously of his own wife (1 Sam. xx. 30); and more than once David speaks slightingly of his own sister Zeruiah, to humble her sons (2 Sam. iii. 39; xvi. 10; xix. 22). In popular tumults the people testified the vehemence of their rage by casting dust into the air (Acts xxii. 23). The dead were dishonoured by denying them the rites of sepulture (Rev. xi. 8, 9); by casting the great into the graves of the common people (Jer. xxvi. 23); by disinterring them after burial (Jer. viii. 1); or by exposing them to be devoured by ravenous beasts, and forbidding them to be publicly lamented (Jer. xvi. 5..7; xix 7; xxii. 18, 19).

SECTION V.—TRAVELLING.

1. When a person travelled on foot, he tucked up his skirts with his girdle, so as to leave free action to the leg and knee; he had a staff, wore sandals, and had a small "scrip" or bag suspended from the neck for provisions. If he was going to a distance he took a change of clothes, and sometimes a jar or kid-skin bottle of water (Gen. xxi. 14; Luke ix. 3). The cool of the morning or evening, or of the night, was the usual time for travelling; in the heat of the day travellers sought refreshment and rest (Gen. xviii. 1-5). The customary salutations on the road were neglected by hurried travellers (2 Kings iv. 29).

2. There were no inns like ours. In the early periods of Scripture history, if a traveller had no friends to whom he could repair in the place to which he came, he waited in the street, or at the gate, till some hospitable person invited him to his house (Gen. xix. 2; Judges xix. 15-21). In the time of Christ there appear to have been, in the towns, such places of public accommodation as we now find
in the East, namely,
khans, where strangers
are provided with lodg-
ing for themselves and

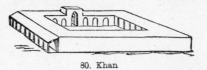

80. Khan

beasts, but have to provide provisions, fuel, and beds for themselves. In the stable of such a place, there being no room for his parents in the lodging apartments, the Saviour of the world was born (Luke ii. 7). Places of the same kind upon the road, for the accommodation of travellers, are called *caravanserais:* these are of more ancient date, being the "inns" of Gen. xlii. 27; xliii. 21; Exod. iv. 24; and Luke x. 34. Under such circumstances, persons making a journey are obliged to make preparation not required among us. This varies with the length and circumstances of the way; a long journey through a thinly peopled country, requiring more preparation than a short one where market

towns frequently occur But all preparations may be comprehended under the heads of,—1. Provender for the cattle,
consisting of barley and chopped straw :—2. Provisions and
water; the provisions being meal to make bread, or else a
kind of hard-baked bread or biscuit, rice, dried dates and
other fruits, cheese, and sometimes, but rarely, potted meat;
the water is carried in skin bags or bottles, of a size and number proportioned to the journey :—3. Conveniences; which
are more extensive now since the use of coffee and tobacco
has been introduced than formerly; but which may be said
to consist of a rug and quilted coverlet for a bed, a copper
pot for cooking, a few bowls of wood or of tinned copper, and a
ewer for ablutions. Few long journeys are described in Scripture; but in such as are mentioned, preparations like these
must be more or less understood, according to the exigencies
of the case (Gen. xlii. 25, 27; xliii. 11, 21; xlv. 21, 23;
Josh. ix. 11-15).

SECTION VI.—CUSTOMS RELATING TO THE DEAD.

1. WHEN a person died, his relations rent their upper garment from head to foot, and a smaller rent was made by the spectators. This rending of the clothes was also a common act of mourning on almost every occasion of distress (Gen. xxxvii. 29 ; Judges xi. 35 ; 2 Sam. i. 2 ; Esther iv. 1 ; &c.) In the case of death, a dismal cry was at the same time raised by the persons present; and if the parties were in good circumstances, the hired mourners and minstrels were soon in attendance to aggravate the ostensible mourning by their doleful la-

81. Wail with Tabrets, &c.

mentations and melancholy music (Jer. ix. 17, 18 ; Matt. ix. 23 ; Mark v. 38 ; Acts ix. 39). The eyes of the deceased were closed by one of his sons, or by the nearest present relative (Gen. xlvi. 4). The body was then laid out upon a cloth on the floor or on a table, and washed with warm water. It was next placed upon a table and embalmed. There were various ways of embalming; but except in the case of Jacob and Joseph, who were embalmed in Egypt (Gen. l. 2, 26), it is doubtful if this was ever done so elaborately as among the Egyptians. The most usual mode was to anoint the body with a solution of odoriferous drugs, and wrap it up in linen. Spices and perfumes were used in great abundance in preparing the bodies of the wealthy for the sepulchre. We may infer this from the large quantities provided by Joseph and Nicodemus for the body of Christ,

82. Grave-clothes.

which was wrapped up in linen, with a hundred-weight of

myrrh and lign aloes (John xix. 39, 40). Usually, after the
ordinary washing and anointing, the body was wrapped round
with many folds of linen, and the head enveloped in a napkin
(John xi. 44).

2. The funeral was seldom delayed above twenty-four
hours after death, as the process of decomposition commences
very soon in warm countries; and to enforce the salutary practice of speedy interment, the law extended to seven days the
ceremonial defilement communicated by the presence of a corpse
(Num. xix. 11-13; Acts v. 6, 10). The body was not put
into a coffin, but, closely wrapped up from head to foot, was
borne in an open bier to the place of burial (Luke vii. 14).

83. Ancient Jewish Funeral; Costume, Arabo-Syrian.

The bier was followed by the mourners, who expressed their
grief in loud lamentations; while the minstrels, with their
melancholy pipes, and the mourning women with doleful voices
and dishevelled hair, enhanced the effect of this public display
of sorrow (2 Sam. iii. 31, 32; Amos v. 31, 32; Matt. ix. 23;
xi. 17). The body was deposited in its last home without any
particular ceremony. As the funeral procession returned, there
were several pauses, to enable certain of the company to administer comfort to the afflicted relatives. The day was concluded by a funeral feast, in which they ate what was called
the "bread of mourning" and drank "the cup of consolation"
(2 Sam. iii. 35; Jer. xvi. 7; Hos. ix. 4). Rent clothes and
sackcloth formed the mourning attire of the Israelites (Gen.
xxxvii. 34; 2 Sam. iii. 31; Joel i. 8; &c.). Other acts of
mourning were, to go about with the face and head shrouded
(2 Sam. xix. 4), and to sprinkle dust upon the head (Job ii.
12; Lam. ii. 10; Rev. xviii. 19.)

3. Our own custom of burying the dead in towns would
not be endured in the East; nor did it exist among the

Israelites.   The burial-grounds are always at some distance
from the towns; they are unenclosed, and the highways often
pass through them.   This was also the case among the Jews,
as is evident from several passages of Scripture (Jer. xxvi.
23; Matt. xxvii. 52, 53), and from mention being made of
men walking over graves without being aware of them (Luke xi.
44).   Burial in these general cemeteries was for the mass of
the people, or those who had no private or family sepulchres.
The latter were commonly
in private fields and gardens, in the outskirts of
the towns; and, when pos-
sible, were caverns, some of
which, still remaining, are
extensive excavations, with
niches in the sides wherein
the corpses were deposited.
They were closed either by

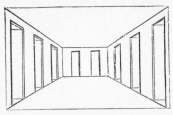

84. Interior of Sepulchre.

a stone door, or by a flat stone placed against the entrance
(Gen. xxiii. 17-20; 2 Kings xiii. 21; Isaiah xxii. 16; Matt.
xxiii. 27, 29; xxvii. 52, 53, 60).   Only the remains of kings
and very distinguished men were allowed to be deposited in
cities (1 Sam. xxviii. 3; 2 Kings xxi. 18; 2 Chron. xvi. 14;
xxiv. 16); and the sepulchre of the kings of the line of David
was upon Mount Zion (2 Kings xiv. 20; 2 Chron. xxi. 20;
&c.)   It was usual to whitewash the exterior of sepulchres
on the last day of the year, with the view of preventing the

85 Modern Syrian Tombs.

strangers who came
to Jerusalem from
defiling themselves
by inadvertent con-
tact therewith (Matt.
xxiii. 27); for con-
tact even with a bone
of a dead body was
counted a defilement
(2 Chron. xxxiv. 5).
By what kind of
monuments the Is-

raelites honoured the dead is not very clear.   In very early

D

times Jacob erected a stone (called a " pillar ") over the grave
of his beloved Rachel (Gen. xxxv. 20); and Absalom in his
lifetime erected a monument (also called a " pillar ") to keep
his name in remembrance (2 Sam. xviii. 18). The sepulchral
stones appear to have been engraved with inscriptions declaring the name and quality of the dead (2 Kings xxiii. 17).
That there were tombstones in the common cemeteries is not
altogether clear from Scripture, but may be inferred from
various circumstances, and from the analogy of existing
usages.

Garden Tomb.

PART IV.—LITERATURE, SCIENCE, AND ART.

SECTION I.—LITERATURE.

1. WITHOUT inquiring into the origin of the Hebrew language, we may observe that it was spoken both in Mesopotamia and Canaan in the time of Abraham; for that patriarch, who came from beyond the Euphrates, conversed freely with the inhabitants of Canaan; and when Jacob, who had been brought up in the land of Canaan, went into Mesopotamia, his speech was readily understood (Gen. xxiii. 3, &c.; xxix. 4-8). A more certain evidence of this is found in the fact, that the names of places and persons existing in Palestine when Abraham migrated to that country, have all a meaning in the language which Abraham spoke. That language is entirely unlike those of Europe, but it has a strong resemblance to the other original languages of Asia west of the Tigris,—the Arabic, the Syriac, and the Chaldean. As it is now known, the Hebrew language is very simple and significant, but it wants flexibility and copiousness. It should be observed, however, that only a part of the ancient language is known to us,—that which is contained in the Bible: and no one book, however large or various, can ever exemplify all the forms, or embrace the whole vocabulary, of any language.

2. Like all the languages of western Asia, Hebrew is read from right to left. The character in which it is written is the Chaldean, which the Jews adopted during the Captivity; and which, although not altogether different from that which they previously employed, is more neat and elegant. The older character is now known as the Samaritan, because it was retained by the Samaritans after it had been abandoned

by the Jews. The Hebrew alphabet consists of twenty-*five*, or, as some count them, twenty-two consonants :—

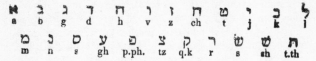

There are thirteen vowel sounds, which are now usually expressed by points set above or below the respective consonants with which they are joined. The antiquity of these points is a matter which has been much controverted.

3. The older alphabet of the Hebrews, and their mode of writing, were, like their language, the same as those of the Canaanites and Phœnicians. Their early knowledge of alphabetic writing is implied in the fact, that there were public genealogists (Deut. xvii. 18, 19 ; xxiv. 1-3) ; and is evinced by the writings of Moses, by the stone tables of the law, and by the frequent references which Moses makes to books and writings as to things well known (Exod. xvii. 14 ; xxiv. 4 ; xxviii. 9–11 ; xxxii. 32 ; xxxiv. 27, 28 ; Num. xxxiii. 2 ; Deut. xxvii. 8). In the course of time, many of the Israelites were able to read and write ; but the great mass of the people were content with oral instruction in the law of God, which was the only kind of learning in general deemed necessary. When occasion required, those who could, wrote for those who could not write ; and persons in the habit of thus acting as *scribes*, who were usually Levites, always went with inkhorns in their girdles, as

86. Arabian Writing Case.

is still done by the learned in the East. This implement was then, as now, provided not only with a receptacle for ink, but with a case for reed pens and a pen-knife (Jer. xxxvi. 23 ; Ezek. ix. 2, 3, 11). The materials for writing were very various at different times of the long period over which the Hebrew history extends. New inventions were introduced, and the purpose of the writing often dictated the character of the material. The most ancient which we *know* to have been actually used, were the stone tables on which the Decalogue was engraved, and the great stones which were set up on Mount Ebal (Deut. xxvii. 1-3). From the latter instance, it would seem that the engraved letters were sometimes filled up with plaster. In the book of Job, which is supposed to be of still earlier date, the practice of writing on rocks and tablets of lead, as well as in books, is mentioned (Job. xix. 23, 24). It is presumed that laws, treaties, and the history of great public events, were carved on the rocks and stones as well as on lead, for which brass, as being more durable, was afterwards substituted (1 Macc. viii. 22; xiv. 20-27). It is more difficult to determine the early material of books among the Hebrews. As we do not read of books being in use among them till they were in Egypt, it is probable that they would use the materials employed in that country. Now it is known that leather was among the materials on which the Egyptians wrote; and a few leathern rolls of the most remote antiquity have been found. As, therefore, the Hebrews, when they first had books, were a pastoral people, and had the art of preparing the skins of animals, it seems likely that their first books, or rolls, were of this material. Linen, also, was so prepared as to bear writing, and may have been employed to some extent by the Israelites. The invention of paper made from the papyrus reed (*Cyperus papyrus*) was of very ancient date ; and hence it also may have been in use

among the Jews. But as it was much dearer than leather, it may be assumed that the latter was the material chiefly used. Josephus affirms, that the copies of the sacred books were written on skins (Antiq. xii. 2); and that Jeremiah's roll of prophecy consisted of skin seems to be indicated by the

87. Ancient Writing Materials.

fact that the king cut it with a knife before throwing it into the fire (Jer. xxxvi. 23). Parchment was not invented until

250 B. C., and it soon came into general use among the Israelites, for their sacred writings. For common uses, tablets of wood were employed: these were not in the East, as among the Romans, covered with wax, but with a glazed composition capable of receiving ink. Such tablets were used by the Egyptians long after they had papyri, and are still used in the common schools of Egypt (Isaiah viii. 1; Ezek. xxxvii. 16; Luke i. 63).

4. Books of skin and parchment, and even of papyrus, were in the form of rolls, written in small columns, the beginning being at the open end. They were sometimes, but

88. Ancient Roll.

very rarely, written on both sides (Ezek. ii. 9, 10; Zech. v. 1). They were rolled round a stick or roller, like a map; or, if long, round two rollers, one at each end. The reader unrolled the book as he perused it, and rolled it up again when he had done; and hence a book was called a "volume," or a thing rolled up (2 Kings xix. 14; Ezra vi. 2; Isaiah xxxiv. 4). Books which were thus rolled up, and tied round with a string, could be easily sealed (Isaiah xxix. 11; Dan. xii. 4; Rev. v. 1, 5, 7).

5. No mention of letters or epistles occurs earlier than the time of David (2 Sam. xi. 14, &c.); but they are frequently spoken of afterwards. In the East, letters are usually sent unsealed; but when addressed to persons of consequence, they are enclosed in a valuable purse or bag, which is tied, sealed, and stamped with a signet. This seems also to have been the practice of the Jews (Neh. vi. 5; Isaiah xxix. 11). It has already been observed, that the common use of the signet in the East is not to seal letters, but to stamp with ink the name engraved thereon, instead of a manual signature.

6. In writing on hard materials, such as tables of stone or metal, use was made of a stylus or bodkin, made of iron, and sometimes tipped with diamond (Jer. xvii. 1). But the ordinary pen for writing with ink was a reed, cut and split much like our pen, but with a more blunt point. The ink used by the Orientals is most intensely black, and much less fluid than ours, more resembling

89. Persian Writing Case.

printers' ink (Num. v. 23; Jer. xxxvi. 18). The ink-horn, in which it is carried, consists of a small brass vessel at the end of a hollow shaft, which, as already mentioned, also contains the reeds and a knife for sharpening them (Jer. xxxvi. 23; Ezek. ix. 2, 3, 11).

SECTION II.—SCIENCE AND ART.

1. THE sciences were very little cultivated among the Hebrews, except for some of the ordinary purposes of life. They understood so much of arithmetic as to be able to state and compute large numbers; and they appear to have known the application of geometry to the measurement and demarcation of land. Astronomy was chiefly studied, in ancient times, for the sake of the vain science of astrology; and as the Israelites were interdicted from practising the latter (Deut. xviii. 10), they paid little attention to the former, except for the purpose of reckoning time.

2. The days and nights among the Hebrews were divided according to the natural periods of light and darkness; and the civil or calendar day was counted, not from morning to morning, but from evening to evening. Hence, their seventh day, or sabbath, began on the evening of our Friday, and ended on the evening of our Saturday. The natural day was divided into three parts, morning, noon, and evening (Psalm lv. 17); and there was also a more minute division of it into six unequal parts :—1, the break of day; 2, the morning, or sunrise; 3, the heat of the day; 4, mid-day; 5, the cool of the day; 6, evening. The natural night was also divided originally into three parts, or "watches;" the first watch (Lam. ii. 19); the middle watch (Judges vii. 19); and the morning watch (Exod. xiv. 24). In later times a fourth watch was added, when the divisions of the night were reckoned thus :—*Eventide*, from sunset to the third hour of the night (Mark xi. 11); *midnight*, from the third hour till midnight; *cock-crowing*, from midnight to the third hour after, or the ninth hour of the night; *morning-tide*, or "the early watch," from the ninth to the twelfth hour of the night, or sunrise (John xviii. 28).

3. *Hours* are not mentioned until the time of the Babylonish Captivity (Dan. iii. 6, 15; v. 5); after which the division of the day into twelve hours gradually came into common use. But as it was the natural day which was thus

divided, and as every hour was the twelfth portion of that day, the length of the hours was continually changing. The hours of chief note were the third, the sixth, and the ninth, which were the hours of prayer (Dan. vi. 10; Acts ii. 15; iii. 1; x. 9).

4. The division of time into *Weeks* was first made at the Creation, which it was designed to commemorate (Gen. ii. 2, 3). It continued to be observed till the Deluge (Gen. vii. 10; viii. 10, 12; xxix. 27), and was afterwards extended into the various nations descended from Noah, although the object of it was eventually forgotten. The Jews distinguished the days of the week by their numerical order; as, " first day of the week," " second day of the week," &c.

5. The septenary period was applied more extensively by the Jews, than by any other people. Not only was every seventh day a day of rest, but every seventh year was a year of rest, called " the Sabbatic year;" and every seventh recurrence of the latter period was still more eminently celebrated as the " year of Jubilee." During the whole of the Sabbatical year, the land lay fallow, the vine and the olives were not pruned, nor was any game taken or destroyed: whatever grew was the common right of all (Lev. xxv. 1–7). The fiftieth year, or the Jubilee, which was ushered in by the blowing of trumpets, was a year of general release; debtors and prisoners obtained their freedom, and property which had been sold, reverted to the original owner or his heirs (Lev. xxv. 8–17).

6. *Months* were originally regarded as the intervals of time between one new moon and another. The Israelites computed each of these intervals at thirty days; as did also the ancient patriarchs; for, at the Deluge, Noah reckoned one hundred and fifty days equal to five months. But twelve of such months made only three hundred and sixty days, a period which was soon found to be shorter than the natural year; and, therefore, a thirteenth month was occasionally intercalated after the month Adar. Originally the months had no names, but, like the days, were distinguished by their numerical order, with the exception of the first month, which was called Abib, or, " the month of young ears of corn " (Exod. xiii. 4, &c.) During the Captivity the Babylonish names of the months were adopted.

F

7. There were two kinds of *Years* in use among the Jews. The first was the civil year, which commenced in September, and by which they computed their jubilees, and all their civil and rural affairs. The other was the sacred year, which appears to have been first introduced by Moses, and by which the public feasts and all religious matters were computed: it commenced in March. The following are the Hebrew months, with the corresponding English months.

1. Nisan, or Abib, corresponding to part of March and April.
2. Zif, or Jyar .... April and May.
3. Sivan .... May and June.
4. Thammuz .... June and July.
5. Ab .... July and August.
6. Elul .... August and September.
7. Tisri .... September and October.
8. Marchesvan .... October and November.
9. Chisleu .... November and December.
10. Thebet .... December and January.
11. Sebat .... January and February.
12. Adar .... February and March.

There was also a sort of agricultural division of the year into six portions of two months each, under the names of seed-time, winter, the cold season, harvest, summer, and the hot season; or "seed-time and harvest, cold and heat, summer and winter" (Gen. viii. 22).

8. The Israelites were so much devoted to agriculture that the arts received little attention from them. After the extinction of the generation which came from Egypt, we find but faint traces of the arts which they had learned in that country. Every family furnished for itself whatever it required in the way of food and clothing, so that the only regular mechanics were masons, carpenters, smiths, and potters. For the first two there appears to have been little employment till the time of the kings; the fabrication of arms and ornaments afforded more occupation for the workers in metals; and the fragile wares of the potter were always in demand. That the Israelites did not attain superior skill in any manufacture is shewn by the fact, that they took only agricultural produce to the markets of Tyre (Ezek. xxvii. 17). Solomon was obliged to obtain assistance from the Phœnicians to enable him to build and furnish his temple and palaces, and even the humbler works of David required similar assis-

tance (1 Chron. xiv. 1; xxii. 15; 2 Chron. ii. 3, &c.) After the impulse given by the public works of these two kings, and as the population and luxury increased, artisans of various kinds became more numerous (2 Kings xxiv. 14; Jer. xxiv. 1; xxix. 2). The employments and habits of the Israelites were greatly changed during the Captivity. In Babylonia, many of them finding but little encouragement in agricultural pursuits, turned their attention to the arts and trade, for which that country offered eminent advantages. After the restoration, agriculture continued to engage the chief attention of the Jews who actually lived in Palestine; but the great numbers who were dispersed throughout foreign lands, lived chiefly by trade and the useful arts. Indeed, a practical knowledge of these arts was at length so much esteemed, that it was held a duty of all parents to have their sons taught some manual craft; and the Jews mention many learned men of their nation who lived by such employments. Thus, many of the persons mentioned in the New Testament history practised some trade. Joseph, the husband of Mary, was a carpenter (Matt. xiii. 55); Simon was a tanner (Acts ix. 43); Alexander, a coppersmith (2 Tim. iv. 14); and Paul and Aquila were tent-makers (Acts xviii. 3).

9. Music and poetry were much cultivated among the Hebrews, and their best poets were sometimes their best musicians, singing their own compositions to the harp (1 Sam. xvi. 18). The harp (*kinnor*), or rather a kind of lyre, was the national musical instrument. Its shape and the number of its strings are not known with certainty, and appear to have varied in different ages; but it seems to have been small and portable (2 Sam. vi. 5, 14; Ps. cxxxvii. 2). There was another kind of harp called a psaltery (*nebel*); and there were also straight and bent trumpets, two or three kinds of pipes, tambourines or tabrets, cymbals, and probably sistrums. The Jews seldom neglected any opportunity of introducing music. It was used at their private entertainments and public festivals; and, by the arrangement of David, a splendid establishment for sacred music, performed by well-instructed Levites, was associated with the public worship (1 Chron. xxv.)

10. Dancing was frequently connected with music among the Jews. It was sometimes an act of religious exultation

(Exod. xv. 20 ; 2 Sam. vi. 16), and was common on all ordinary occasions of mirth and rejoicing (Ps. xxx. 11 ; Jer. xxxi.
4, 13 ; Luke xv. 25), as well as at the great festivals (Judges
xxi. 19, 21), and on triumphal occasions (Judges xi. 34 ; 1
Sam. xviii. 6). The precise character of the Hebrew dances
is not known, but no ideas of levity were connected with
them. The proud-spirited Michal despised David, not because
he danced, but because he danced with the common people
(2 Sam. vi. 16, 20-23).

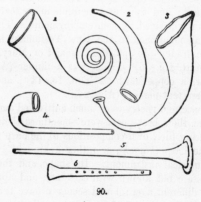

90.

1 2, 3 4, Ancient Horns and Curved Trumpets ; 5, Straight Trumpet ; 6, Pipe

91. Egyptian Figures of Lyres.

{1, 2, played without, and 3, 4, with the plectrum; 4, is the supposed Hebrew Lyra.}

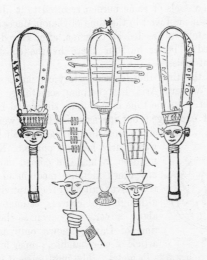

92. Sistra—various Egyptian specimens.

SECTION III.—COMMERCE AND WAR.

1. THE ancient Israelites were not a commercial people; nor did the Law of Moses afford much encouragement to what was calculated to promote that intercourse with other nations, which it was the object of so many of the Jewish institutions to prevent. They had no maritime traffic, and ships are rarely mentioned, except in connection with the spirited attempts of Solomon and Jehoshaphat to establish a commerce, through the Red Sea, with the shores of the Indian Ocean. The former, having the aid of Phœnician ships and mariners, was not unsuccessful; but the operations begun in his reign were broken off in the troubles which afterwards ensued, and Jehoshaphat's attempt to revive them proved abortive (1 Kings ix. 26; xxii. 48, 49; 2 Chron. ix. 21; xx. 36). Joppa, which was the only harbour in the Mediterranean belonging to the Jews, was the port of Jerusalem (2 Chron. ii. 16), and Phœnician vessels of some burden resorted to it (Jonah i. 3). It was much improved in the time of Simon Maccabæus; but was ultimately superseded by Cæsarea, after Herod the Great had formed a better harbour there by the construction of magnificent moles.

2. At the time the Jewish history commences, the land traffic of Western Asia had become something more than mere barter. In the time of Abraham silver had become the medium of exchange; but it was estimated by weight (Gen. xxiii. 16). The weight most in use was the shekel, which was nearly half an ounce. No distinct mention is made of coined money, or of any other metallic medium of exchange than silver, till after the Captivity. Gold, although of course estimated highly above silver, was, even so late as the time of David, known only as a costly article of merchandise, proper for trinkets, arms, and rich works in metal. The most ancient coin which

93. **Persian** Daric.

nistory makes known was the Persian *daric*, a gold coin somewhat heavier than a guinea; and this is also the first coin mentioned in the Bible (1 Chron. xxix. 7; Ezra ii. 69; viii. 27; Neh. vii. 70-72). During the Captivity, and for some time after it, the Jews used the coins of the nations to which they were subject. The first coinage by themselves was under Simon Maccabæus (1 Mac. xv. 6), who issued a currency under the name of shekels.

94. Shekel.

These coins were mostly silver, and were worth nearly half-a-crown; but some were of gold, and, in the proportion which gold now bears to silver, must have been worth nearly two pounds sterling. Greek and Roman coins also came into use, the latter of which are frequently mentioned in the New Testament. Their value

95. Quarter Shekel.

may be seen in the tables prefixed to this work. But it must be remembered, that the value affixed merely expresses the present English value of such a quantity of metal. Gold and silver were probably scarcer in ancient times than now, and therefore of higher relative value. It is possible that a given quantity of silver or gold may have purchased as much as ten times the same quantity will purchase now; and in that case a shekel of silver, equivalent to nearly half-a-crown, was really worth as much as five-and-twenty shillings in this country, at the present time. But all this is uncertain; and it is possible that the quantities of the precious metals existing in ancient times, from sources, the subsequent exhaustion of which, rendered them scarce until the discovery of America, has been greatly underrated in common opinion.

3. Prior to the introduction of coins among the Israelites, the use of weights and balances was necessary in all sales and purchases. Scales were commonly employed, but an instrument on the principle of the modern steel-yard also came into use. The weights were originally stones ; and hence the word for a *weight* denotes a *stone* in the Hebrew. Dealers were in the habit of carrying balances and weights about with them in a kind of pouch (Lev. xix. 35, 36; Deut. xxv. 13–15; Prov. xi. 1; xvi. 11; Mic. vi. 11); and the frequent injunction against the use of " divers weights," applies to those who carried in their bags two sets of weights, lighter and heavier, which they used fraudulently, as they had opportunity.

4. Among the Israelites, the soldiers were not a separate class, as in Europe, but every adult male was considered liable to bear arms, the priests and Levites not excepted. They were like a militia, and were called out in such proportion as the public service required, the whole body not being expected to take the field except on very extraordinary occasions. All the adult males, above the age of twenty, were enrolled, and from them the necessary levy was drawn by the genealogists. When a man was required to engage in military service, he might claim exemption on any of the following grounds; 1. If he had built a house, and had not occupied it; 2. If he had planted a vineyard or oliveyard, and had not yet eaten of the produce; 3. If he had espoused a wife, but had not yet taken her home; 4. If he were faint-hearted (Deut. xx. 5–8). All the Israelites being thus regarded as fighting-men, we perceive how it was that large armies were often raised in a very short time (Judges xx. 8–11, 17; 1 Sam. xi. 1–9). But they could be kept together only for a brief campaign, as every man served at his own expense (1 Sam. xvii. 13, 17). This inconvenience, and others of a similar kind, made the kings desirous of having a body of troops always at command. Hence Saul, instead of disbanding the whole army after his first campaign, retained three thousand in arms (1 Sam. xiii. 1, 2). David kept up a much larger number; but still they were only militia, in twelve legions of twenty-four thousand men each, which relieved one another in monthly rotation, so that each legion was one month

in service and eleven at home (1 Chron. xxvii). Later kings appear to have followed this example more or less ; but we do not find that there were ever soldiers *by profession* among the Israelites. The mercenary soldiers of the Herods were foreigners.

5. The armies of the Israelites were composed entirely of infantry till the time of the kings. Cavalry was of little use in a mountainous country, and was discouraged by the law (Deut. xvii. 16). David had a hundred horses, more for shew than use (2 Sam. viii. 4) ; but Solomon maintained a large number of horses and chariots of war (2 Chron. ix. 25). After him, however, the kings appear to have had no considerable force in cavalry, except when they obtained succours from Egypt. The infantry were divided into light-armed troops and spearmen : the former were furnished with slings, darts, bows and arrows, quivers, and in later times, bucklers ; the spearmen had spears, swords, and shields (1 Chron. xii. 24, 34 ; 2 Chron. xiv. 8 ; xvii. 17). We can collect little from Scripture respecting the order of battle ; but there can be little doubt that, as among other nations, the light-armed troops made the onset ; and that the main body following, with extended spears, made a rapid and impetuous rush upon the enemy. If the enemy's front remained unbroken they withdrew, and again came on in like manner. They advanced to the charge with a shout (Josh. vi. 20 ; Judges vii. 20 ; 1 Sam. xvii. 52). Battles were very sanguinary, and the slaughter immense, because quarter was seldom expected or given ; and the soldiers being often engaged hand to hand, the animosity and passions of the combatants were furiously excited. The barbarities committed by the conquerors upon the conquered were generally very revolting. Prisoners of distinction were often grievously maltreated (Josh. x. 24 ; Judges i. 6, 7 ; 2 Kings xxv. 7) ; and the captured soldiers were either kept in hard bondage, or sold as slaves (2 Sam. xii. 31 ; 2 Chron. xviii. 10 ; Psalm xliv. 12). When a town was taken by assault, all the men were slain, and the women and children sold into slavery.

6. Like all Orientals, the Israelites were averse to undertake sieges, in which they had but little skill. Sudden and violent onsets, stratagem, treachery, or famine, were the means

employed for taking towns. When the siege was much protracted, an extended ditch was sometimes dug between the camp and the city, and another parallel to it, behind the camp, for the purpose of protecting it in front and rear, and of cutting off from the town all assistance and supplies (Deut. xx. 19, 20; 2 Sam. xx. 15). The earth thrown up formed a wall on which towers were sometimes erected; or else it formed a mound against the city wall on which the besiegers might plant their engines, if they had any, project their missiles, and assail the wall (2 Sam. xx. 15; 2 Kings xix. 32). In later times battering-rams were used in the assault of towns (Ezek. iv. 1, 2; xxi. 22; xxvi. 9); and engines of defence, for casting large stones and other missiles, were introduced in the reign of King Uzziah (2 Chron. xxvi. 15).

96. Battering Ram.

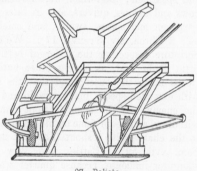

97. Balista.

7. The commander-in-chief of the army was called the captain of the host. Joshua was the first who held this office. After him the command was taken by the "Judges," who were successively raised up to deliver the nation. Under the kings, the command of the army was maintained as a distinct office, the possessor of which was of the highest rank and influence; although, in action, the kings themselves often took the chief command (Josh. v. 14; Judges iv. 2; 1 Sam. xiv. 50; 2 Sam. xx. 23; 2 Kings iv. 13). The whole army appears to have been formed into three grand divisions, each commanded

by a general, but the whole under the commander-in-chief
(Judges vii. 16, 20; 1 Sam. xi. 11; 2 Sam. xviii. 2); and
these were subdivided into bodies of ten thousand, a thousand,
a hundred, and fifty, each under its appropriate commander.
These commanders were generally the paternal chiefs of the
clans and families from which the troops were levied (1 Sam.
viii. 12; 2 Kings i. 9; 1 Chron. xii. 14; 2 Chron. xxv. 5).

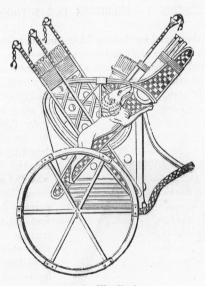

98. Egyptian War Chariot

PART V.—INSTITUTIONS.

SECTION I.—RELIGIOUS INSTITUTIONS.

1. The Tabernacle, erected by Moses in the wilderness, was not only the temple of God, but his palace—the place of his presence and residence as king of the Hebrew nation; and this two-fold character was preserved in its furniture, utensils, and ministers. It was of an oblong rectangular figure, 55 feet in length, 18 in breadth, and 18 in height. The inside was divided into two rooms by a veil or curtain hung upon four pillars. This curtain was made of rich stuff, curiously embroidered with figures of cherubim, and other ornaments. In the inner and smaller room, called the " Holy of Holies," was placed the ark, which was an oblong chest of wood, over-

99. The Tabernacle.

laid with gold, and surmounted by two golden figures of cherubim with outstretched wings. Above them appeared a mysterious resplendence, which symbolised the presence of

100.

101.

Different Representations of the Ark.

the Divine King. In the ark were kept the tables of stone on which the ten commandments were written. Beside the

102. Golden Altar.

ark were laid up for memorial a quantity of manna in a vase of gold, the rod of Aaron that budded, and a copy of the book of the law (Exod. xxv. 1-22; Deut. xxxi. 26; Heb. ix. 4). In the anteroom were placed, 1, The golden altar on which incense was burnt daily (Ex. xxx. 1-10); 2, The massive and highly ornamented seven - branched golden " candlestick" or lamp stand (Exod. xxv. 31-39); 3, The table of wood, overlaid with gold, called the table of shew-bread, from the bread which was always kept upon it, and renewed every week (Exod. xxv. 23-30).

2. Around the Tabernacle was an extensive area or court, formed by curtains of fine twined linen, hung upon pillars, which were set in bases of brass, and filleted with silver. Of these pillars there were twenty on each side, and ten at each end, five cubits apart (Exod. xxvii. 9-19). In this court all the public services of religion were performed, all sacrifices were offered, and all offerings made. It contained the great brazen altar for burnt-offerings, which was five cubits square, and three in height, with prominences at the corners, called " horns" (Exod. xxvii. 1-8; Psalm cxviii. 27). On this altar the sacrifices were consumed by fire which was miraculously kindled at first, and was always preserved afterwards (Lev. ix. 24). In the court of the Tabernacle also stood the large brazen laver, at which the priests were to perform their ablutions before they approached the altar (Exod. xxx. 15-21).

3. The Temple of Solomon was built on the same plan as the Tabernacle, and contained the same furniture and uten-

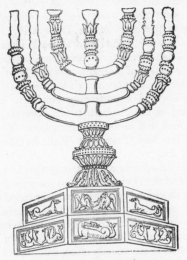

103. Golden Candlestick.

From the arch of Titus at Rome, in which the spoils of the Temple are represented. The base is supposed to have been added, or ornamented with the figures it is here seen to bear.

104. Brazen Altar.

sils; but it was much larger, the materials were more costly and durable, and the workmanship was more elaborate. Instead of one court there were three, the innermost of which corresponded to the court of the Tabernacle; and the curtained enclosure was supplied by walls and colonnades.

4. It does not appear that there were in the towns any synagogues, or places of religious meeting, before the Captivity; but under the Asamonean princes they became common. They were plain and unpretending buildings, in which the Jews assembled on the Sabbath to offer prayers, to hear the sacred books read, and to receive instruction. They are often mentioned in the New Testament (Matt. iv. 23; Acts vi. 9; ix. 2; xiii. 5, &c.)

5. As the Tabernacle was not only the Temple of God, but the palace of the Divine King; so the priests and Levites were not only sacerdotal ministers, but were at the same time his officers of state and the guards of his palace. The circumstances under which the tribe of Levi was set apart to this service, and one family of that tribe, the family of Aaron, specially consecrated to the priestly office, will claim to be noticed in the ensuing history. Aaron was consecrated by Moses as the first high priest, and his sons officiated as priests under him (Lev. viii.) Their duties were to offer sacrifices, to burn incense, and to bless the people; and it was death for any others to perform these offices (Num. xvi. 10; 2 Chron. xxvi. 16–21); although we read of some of the prophets in distant places, and on extraordinary occasions, offering sacrifices (1 Sam. xiii. 8–14; xvi. 1–5; 1 Kings xviii. 21–40). The inner chamber of the Tabernacle, containing the ark, was never entered but by the high priest, and even by him only once in the year, when he made a ceremonial atonement for the sins of the nation. This was called the "day of atonement" (Lev. xvi.)

6. The priests, when not engaged in their sacerdotal duties, dressed like other men; but when they were so employed, their tunics, drawers, girdles, and turbans, were all of white linen (Exod. xxxix. 27, 28). The high priest wore this dress only on the day he entered the most holy place; but his regular official dress was very splendid. Over the white tunic he wore a blue woollen robe, affixed to the hem

of which were small golden bells, separated by artificial pomegranates (Exod. xxviii. 31–34). Over this was a short
sleeveless garment, called an "ephod," of fine twisted linen,
inwrought with purple and gold, and having on each shoulder-
strap a precious stone, engraven with the names of the twelve
tribes (Exod. xxviii. 5–12). The "breast-plate of judgment"
was the greatest ornament of the dress. It was a span square,
and was composed of twelve precious stones, set in a doubled
piece of the same rich cloth which composed the ephod. On

105. The High Priest.

each stone was graven the name of one of the twelve tribes
(Exod. xxviii. 15–21). On his head the high priest wore a
kind of mitre, to the front of which was fastened a plate of
gold, inscribed with Hebrew words, meaning, "Holiness unto
the Lord" (Exod. xxviii. 36–38). To the breast-plate belonged the Urim and Thummim, by which the priest was
enabled to ascertain the will of the Divine King on any
matter submitted to him; but in what manner the response
was given has not been very satisfactorily determined. Some

think that when the high priest, wearing the breast-plate, appeared in the holy place with his face turned towards the ark, he became officially qualified to receive an oral answer to such questions as he uttered. Others presume that, as the twelve stones of the breast-plate bore the names of the twelve tribes, the letters composing the response were in some way or other supernaturally distinguished from the rest.

7. The priests had become so numerous in the time of David, that they could not all be employed at the same time in their sacred duties; and therefore the king divided the whole body into twenty-four companies or courses, which served in weekly rotation (1 Chron. xxiv.) Each course had its own head or chief; and these are supposed to be the "chief priests" so often mentioned in the New Testament. The tribe of Levi had originally been divided into three classes, according to their descent from Gershon, Kohath, and Merari, the three sons of Levi. The office of the Levites was to assist the priests, by slaughtering the victims, and by providing and preparing whatever was necessary for the sacred services. They commenced their service at the age of twenty-five, and retired at fifty (Numbers viii. 5–26). In the wilderness they encamped with the priests around the Tabernacle, and formed its guard. They also set it up, took it down, and conveyed it from place to place (Num. iv. 1–20). In later times, David divided the whole body into three classes, each of which was subdivided into twenty-four courses, which attended in weekly rotation. The first class attended upon the priests in their services; the second formed the choir of singers in the Temple; and the third acted as porters and guards in the Temple, and at its gates (1 Chron. xxiv. 20–30; xxv. xxvi.)

8. As the tribe of Levi, in order that it might be more completely detached from secular employments, received no share in the distribution of the land, it was necessary to pro vide in some other way for its maintenance. In addition, therefore, to the produce of the belt of land around the forty-eight cities assigned for their residence, the Levites received from the other tribes the tenth, or tithe, of all the produce of the country, including live stock (Lev. xxvii. 30; Num. xviii. 20–24; xxxv. 1–8). A tenth of this tithe was the share of the priests, who had also thirteen of the forty-eight cities.

There was another tithe, the produce of which the people were themselves to expend in feast-offerings, to which the Levites were to be invited (Deut. xiv. 22–27).

9. The sacrifices which the law required the Israelites to offer to God, were divided into four kinds :—1. *The Burnt-offering*, which was wholly consumed upon the altar (Lev. i.) ; 2. *The Sin-offering*, which was a sacrifice offered in ceremonial expiation of sins of ignorance, and of legal pollution. Of this class of offerings, only certain fat portions were consumed on the altar, the rest belonging to the priests (Lev. iv.) ; 3 *The Trespass-offering*, which is not clearly distinguishable from the former, but is supposed by some to refer to sins of omission ; the sin-offering referring to sins of commission (Lev. v.) ; 4. *The Peace (or Feast)-offering* which was eaten by the offerer and his friends, after the fat parts had been burnt on the altar, and a small portion given to the priests (Lev. iii.) All these sacrifices were only occasional : but there were others regular and national ; such as the daily sacrifice of two lambs. as burnt-offerings, one in the morning and the other in the evening, with each of which was offered a bread-offering, and a drink-offering of strong wine (Ex. xxix. 38, 41). This sacrifice was doubled on the Sabbath-day (Num. xxviii. 9, 10). There were also large and extraordinary sacrifices at the new moons, and at the annual recurrence of the great festivals.

10. Sacrifices were limited to three kinds of cattle,—oxen, sheep, and goats ; but all clean birds were allowed, although, practically, doves only appear to have been offered (Lev. xiv. 4–7). To ensure unity of worship, sacrifices could only be offered on the one altar at the Tabernacle, and afterwards at the Temple, whither all gifts and oblations were to be brought (Lev. xvii. 8, 9) ; but before the Captivity this regulation was much neglected, even in the best times.

11. The festivals of the Israelites were weekly, monthly, and annual. The weekly festival was the Sabbath, on which they rested from all labour, and double sacrifices were offered (Exod. xx. 8–11). After the Captivity, when Synagogues were built in the several towns, the people assembled in them on the Sabbath-day to hear the sacred books read and expounded (Luke iv. 16 ; Acts xiii. 15). The monthly festival was that of the new moon, which was proclaimed by the sound

of trumpets, and at which additional sacrifices were offered. The great annual festivals prescribed by the law were three, each of them of a week's continuance; and at their celebration all the adult males in Israel were required to appear at the place of the Sanctuary (Exod. xxiii. 14–17). 1. *The Passover* was kept in remembrance of the departure from Egypt. It began on the eve of the fourteenth day of the first month, with the eating of the Paschal Lamb, and was continued through the week, during which no leavened bread was to be eaten. On the sixteenth day, the first ripe ears of corn were offered, and till that was done the early harvest could not be commenced (Exod. xii. 1–27; Lev. xxiii. 9–14) 2. Seven weeks after the commencement of the Passover, when the labours of the harvest were usually completed, was the feast of *Pentecost*, which also continued for seven days. This was, properly, the harvest festival, in which the nation offered thanks to God for the bounties of the season, and presented the first-fruits, in bread baked of the new corn (Lev. xxiii. 15–21). 3. In autumn was the feast of *Tabernacles* or of *Booths*, which commenced on the fifteenth day of the seventh month. It celebrated the sojourn of the Israelites in the wilderness; and was also a festival of thanks for the fruits of autumn, whence it was called the *Feast of Ingathering*. During this festival the people dwelt in booths, formed of green boughs interwoven; they also carried green boughs in their hands, and the rejoicing was very great (Lev. xxiii. 34-43).

12. The only other periodical celebrations prescribed by the Mosaical Law, were the *Feast of Trumpets* and the *Day of Atonement*. The first was held on the first and second days of the month Tisri, and celebrated the commencement of the civil year, which was ushered in by the blowing of the sacerdotal trumpets with unusual solemnity; and hence the name of the feast (Lev. xxiii. 23-25). The *Day of Atonement* was the only periodical *fast* prescribed by the law. It occurred on the tenth day of the same month, between the feast of trumpets and that of tabernacles. It was a strict fast, when the people bewailed the sins of the past year, and a ceremonial expiation was made by the High Priest, who, on that day only, entered the most holy place, where he sprinkled the blood of a goat which had been sacrificed. This

goat was one of two, which were appointed by lot to their several destinations. The other, after the sins of the people had been confessed over it, and laid upon its head, was sent away alive to be lost in the wilderness (Lev. xvi. 7-10, 15, 20-22).

13. There were two other feasts, which, although not appointed by the law, or belonging to the more ancient times, became of considerable note. The *Feast of Purim*, which is still observed in two days of rejoicing, was instituted to celebrate the overthrow of Haman's plot for the extirpation of the Jews (Esther ix. 20-32). The other was the *Feast of Dedication*, instituted by Judas Maccabæus, to celebrate the re establishment of public worship at Jerusalem, after Antiochus Epiphanes had been vanquished and the Temple purified (1 Mac. iv. 59; John x. 22).

106. Altars.

[1, 2, 3, Greek. 4, Egyptian. 5, Babylonian. 6, Roman. 7, 8, Persian.]

SECTION II.—POLITICAL INSTITUTIONS.

1. THE theory of the Hebrew constitution supposed that God himself was the KING and General Governor of the nation; the high priest being his minister, and the interpreter of his will. From the time of Joshua to that of the kings, there was not a regular succession of human governors; for the authority of the "Judges" was by no means general, and was often intermitted. There were, however, an internal government and authority, in the several tribes, sufficient for domestic purposes. Each of the tribes was divided into "families," and these were again divided into "houses of fathers," and each section had its head or chief, called an "elder" (Josh. xxiii. 2; xxiv. 1). There appears also to have been a paternal chief, who represented the eldest branch of the whole tribe, and to whom the sectional chiefs were subordinate. We find these "princes" of tribes still subsisting in the time of David (1 Chron. xviii. 1); but their authority declined and passed away when a strong central government came to be established.

2. By the constitution, as originally established by Moses, the consent of all the tribes was required to give effect to public measures. As it was impossible to bring a matter efficiently before a whole nation at once, a certain number of persons must have been deputed to represent the tribes and families in the general convention or "assembly." These representatives are mentioned more than once (Num. i. 16; xvi. 2), and they appear to have been the heads of families and houses, already mentioned, together with the judges and officers (Deut. xxix. 10; Josh. xxiii. 2). By the advice of Jethro his father-in-law, Moses appointed judges of thousands, hundreds, and tens, allowing an appeal from one to another, and, in the last instance, to himself. As the judges of tens were in number sixty thousand, it is most likely that the judges of thousands only were called to the convention. This was in the wilderness. When settled in Canaan, they were to have magistrates in every city (Deut xvi. 18). The

persons named "officers," or scribes, existed among the Israelites in Egypt (Exod. v. 6-14), and appear to have had the duty of keeping the genealogical tables of the Israelites, and of apportioning to individuals their share of the services which were required of the nation. This class of men subsisted long afterwards, with modified duties, and seems to have been chiefly composed of members of the Levitical tribe.

3. The offices of Moses and Joshua were merely temporary; that of the one being to organise the nation, and that of the other to establish it in Canaan. These were different offices; and Joshua had no successor. But anticipating that the people would ultimately desire to have a king, like cther nations, Moses took care to provide for that contingency. He reserved the right of nomination to God, the supreme King, yet not so as to preclude the exercise of elective choice by the people; and he laid down certain general principles by which the conduct of the future monarchs should be guided. Among other things, the king was to be a native Israelite; he was not to maintain a numerous cavalry; and he was not to take many wives (Deut. xvii. 15-17). The first king, Saul, was accordingly nominated by God, through his prophet, then chosen by lot, and finally accepted by the people. After the rejection of Saul, the house or dynasty of David was established. He was accordingly nominated, by anointing, in Saul's lifetime, and was afterwards called to the throne by the people, who knew of this nomination. The king was far from being an absolute monarch. When Saul was made king, the prophet Samuel drew up certain rules and limitations according to which he was to govern (1 Sam. x. 25); the eleven tribes, in receiving David for their king, required and obtained his assent to a similar compact (2 Sam. v. 3); and the refusal of Rehoboam to submit to some further limitations, caused ten of the tribes to renounce their allegiance to the house of David (1 Kings xii. 1-20).

4. At his inauguration, the king went in state to some public place, or to the Temple, where he was anointed (1 Sam. x. 25; 2 Sam. ii. 4; v. 1-3; 2 Kings xi. 12-20; 2 Chron. xxiii.) crowned, took the sceptre (2 Sam. i. 10; Ps. xlv. 6; Ezek. xxi. 26), and received the kiss of homage (1 Sam. x. 1; Ps. ii. 12), after which he returned to the palace, amid the

acclamations of the people (1 Sam. x. 24; 1 Kings i. 39),
and seated himself upon the throne (1 Kings i. 35, 48; 2
Kings ix. 13; xi. 19).   On the same occasion, he took an
oath to govern according to the law of Moses, and accepted
the covenant which defined the principles on which the
government was to be conducted.   He was thus not only
bound to keep the law himself, but he had not the power of
making new laws, though he might promulgate temporary
edicts.   But, notwithstanding these limitations, the power of
the ancient Hebrew kings was very great.   They assumed
the power of life and death, without the forms of judicature
(2 Sam. i. 15; iv. 12), but appear to have exercised it only
where the guilt of the offender was manifest.   They also
levied taxes for the support of the government (1 Sam. xvii.
25; 1 Kings xii. 14).   The revenues of the Crown arose not
only from this source, from the spoils of successful wars, and
from the tribute of subject provinces, but also from the produce of arable lands and vineyards, of plantations, of olive
and fig trees, of herds of kine, camels and asses, and of flocks
of sheep (1 Chron. xxvii. 25-31).   The estates of traitors
lapsed to the Crown, by the accumulation of which forfeitures,
and by purchases, a valuable royal demesne seems to have
been ultimately formed.

5. Saul and David, and the kings of Israel, appear to
have lived with much plainness and simplicity, but Solomon
and the succeeding kings of Judah affected more state and
splendour.   When they appeared in public, they were attended
by guards and runners (2 Sam. xv. 1; 1 Kings i. 5), whose
duty it was not only to defend the palace and to protect the
sovereign himself, but to convey messages, edicts, and orders,
to execute the royal commands, and to inflict death when
awarded by the king.   When the culprit was a person of
rank, the captain of the guard executed the king's judgment
upon him with his own hand (1 Kings ii. 25, 34).

6. Several of the ministerial and household officers of the
Hebrew kings are named in Scripture, from which some
notion may be formed of the organisation of the government.
There was a body of royal councillors, apparently chosen for
their sagacity, and whose opinion was taken in public measures (2 Sam. xvi. 15-23; 1 Kings xii. 6-11; 1 Chron. xxvii

32, &c.) The officer of state, corresponding to our prime minister, seems to have been the personage who is called the next (or second) to the king (1 Sam. xxiii. 17; Esth. x. 3; 2 Chron. xxviii. 7). The *Mazkir*, or recorder, appears to have performed the duty of recording in the royal archives all the transactions of the court and government (2 Sam. viii. 16; 2 Kings xviii. 18, 37). The *Sopher*, or scribe, was the secretary of state, who prepared and issued the edicts and orders of the Crown (2 Sam. viii. 17; xx. 25; 2 Kings xviii. 18). The *Governor of the Palace* was the steward of the royal household, who is a very high and influential officer in the East (1 Kings iv. 6; xviii. 3; 2 Kings xviii. 18). The *King's Friend*, or companion, was the intimate and endeared associate, with whom the king conversed most freely and familiarly (2 Sam. xv. 37; xvi. 16; 1 Kings iv. 5). There was an "*Officer over the Taxes*" (tribute), who seems to have been the minister of finance, receiving and accounting for all the revenue of the Crown (2 Sam. xx. 24; 1 Kings iv. 6). The *Captain of the Guard* was another court officer, who has already been mentioned. There was also an officer in each of the provinces, called the *Prince of the Province*, whose duty it was to collect the provisions required for the royal establishment (1 Kings iv. 5, 7-19; xix. 22, 23; xx. 15; 1 Chron. xxvii. 25-31).

E

SECTION III.—JUDICIAL INSTITUTIONS.

1. THE arrangement which had been made in the wilderness for the administration of justice, by judges of thousands,
hundreds, fifties, and tens, ceased when the nation was settled
in Canaan; and, as Moses directed, judges and scribes were
appointed for every city, with jurisdiction over the surrounding villages. Cases of great importance and appeals were carried to the chief civil ruler, or to the high priest (Deut. xvi. 18;
xvii. 8, 9). This arrangement seems to have continued till
the time of the Maccabees, when a supreme tribunal of justice
was established at Jerusalem, composed of seventy members,
and denominated the Sanhedrim. This was the great
" council" of justice so often mentioned in the New Testament. It was composed of chief priests; of elders, or heads
of large family associations; and of scribes, or men of learning, who were mostly Levites. The Jewish writers speak
much of this institution. They state that its members sat in
a semicircle, of which the president and vice-president occupied the centre, and that it was attended by secretaries and
apparitors. This court tried appeals and other cases of
importance. It was by a hasty and irregular assembly of
its members, at the house of the high priest, that our Lord
was tried (Matt. xxvi. 3, 57; John xviii. 24); but they
could not themselves put him to death, as the power of capital
punishment had been taken from them by the Romans. In
later times, the district judicatures were so distributed, that,
as Josephus states, there were seven judges, with two Levites
as apparitors, in every city. This is that which is called
" the judgment" in the New Testament.

2. The courts of justice held their sittings in tne morning
(Psalm ci. 8; Jer. xxi. 12). As the gates of towns were the
places of the greatest public resort, justice was administered,
and civil business transacted there. This continued even
after the Captivity (Gen. xxiii. 10, &c.; Deut. xxi. 19; Ruth
iv. 1, &c.; Psalm cxxvii. 5; Prov. xxii. 22; Zech. viii. 16).

3 The form of trial appears to have been very simple.

The court consisted of a judge or judges, and, at least in later times, of a scribe, who wrote down the sentence, and the particulars of the trial or cause. Before them stood the accused, the accuser, and the witnesses. Two witnesses were necessary to establish any charge, and they were examined separately, in the presence of the accused (Num. xxxv. 30; Deut. xvii. 6; Matt. xxvi. 60). The sentence was pronounced soon after the examination, and, even when it decreed the punishment of death, was executed without delay (Joshua vii. 16-25; 1 Sam. xxii. 18; 1 Kings ii. 23-25). In the earlier periods of Jewish history imprisonment was not used as a punishment. When it was necessary to keep a person in custody, he was put under a guard (Lev. xxiv. 12), or confined in an empty cistern (Gen. xl. 15; Jer. xxxvii. 15-20), or in the house of the judge. In later times, however, prisons were better known, and imprisonment was more usual (Matt. v. 25; xviii. 30; Acts xii. 4-10). Prisoners often wore chains or fetters of iron or brass (Judges xvi. 21; Psalm cv. 18; cvii. 10; Jer. xl. 4; lii. 11). In the time of Christ, the Jews had borrowed from other nations the practice of imprisoning for debt; and the creditor seems to have had the power of demanding the application of stripes and torture (Matt. v. 26; xviii. 28-34). The vigilance and severity of the gaolers were sometimes enforced by their being subject to the punishment intended for their prisoners, if they allowed them to escape. Among the instruments of punishment, stocks for the feet are mentioned at a very early period (Job xiii. 27; xxxiii. 11).

4. With regard to punishments generally, the theory of the law was that life should be given for life, eye for eye, tooth for tooth, &c. (Exod. xxi. 23-25). But this was only done literally in the matter of life for life; in all other cases, indemnification equivalent to the damage sustained might be made by the offender to the sufferer (Exod. xxi. 30). Restitution, to twice the value of the property stolen, was the general punishment for theft; but, in some cases, the restitution was fourfold, or even fivefold (Exod. xxii. 1-6). If the thief was unable to make restitution, he was sold as a slave, and the price applied to that purpose; and if the full amount was not thus made up, his wife and children were also sold (Exod. xxii. 3; 2 Kings iv. 1).

5. There was only one kind of secondary corporal punishment—scourging. This was usually inflicted with a rod upon the back of the prostrate culprit. The blows could, in no case, exceed forty; and to prevent an inadvertent excess, the number was practically restricted to thirty-nine (Deut. xxv. 2, 3; Matt. x. 17; 2 Cor. xi. 24). A kind of scourge, called a scorpion—composed of thongs set with sharp iron points—appears to have been used for torture (1 Kings xii. 11). The punishment of scourging was chiefly applied to offences against the ceremonial law, and, in later times, it was usually inflicted in the synagogues. To such offences, also, was applicable the punishment of excommunication, which, in a theocratical state like that of the Hebrews, was as much a civil as an ecclesiastical punishment, and involved many afflictive privations (Num. xv. 30, 31). But if an offence liable to this punishment was committed inadvertently, the party might exonerate himself of the penalties, by confessing his error, and presenting a "trespass-offering" for sacrifice (Num. xv. 28, 29).

6. The crimes punished with death were murder, adultery, unnatural crimes, and gross misconduct to parents, also idolatry and Sabbath-breaking, which were acts of treason against the Supreme Head of the theocratical government. The common and national mode of inflicting the punishment of death was by casting stones at the culprit; but when the punishment was ordered by a king or military commander, it was usually inflicted by stabbing with a sword (Judges viii. 21; 1 Sam. xxii. 18; 2 Sam. i. 5; 1 Kings ii. 25, 29, 31, 34). Latterly decapitation came into use (Matt. xiv. 8-12: Acts xii. 2). The other modes of punishing with death, mentioned in Scripture, were inflicted by foreigners, not by Hebrews—such as crucifixion, which was a Roman punishment, introduced into Palestine after the power over life had been taken from the Jews by their conquerors.

7. There were also posthumous punishments, by which the memory of the deceased was rendered infamous. Of this kind was the hanging of the dead body on a tree or gallows; but the law required that it should be taken down and buried the same day (Num. xxv. 4, 5; Deut. xxi. 22, 23). Another was, to burn to ashes the body of a person who had been stoned (Lev. xx. 14; xxi. 9; Joshua vii. 15, 25); and a

third was, to raise a large heap of stones over the corpse (Josh. vii. 26 ; 2 Sam. xviii. 17).

8. Another institution remains to be mentioned, which engages much attention in the law and early history of the Israelites. In early pastoral life it had been the custom, when a person was slain, for his next of kin to take upon him the office of avenger (in Hebrew, *Goël*), who rested not until he had taken the life of the homicide. A practice so liable to gross abuse, and calculated to entail endless blood-feuds, could not be endured in an organised community. The law, therefore, provided for the mitigation of its evils. Six cities, in different parts of the country, were appointed as " cities of refuge," to any one of which the unintentional man-slayer might hasten ; and when he reached it, and while he remained in it, he was safe from the avenger. This protection he continued to enjoy till the death of the high priest, when he was at liberty to return home. But the shelter of these asylums was refused to actual murderers ; for although they might be received on their first arrival, yet, on their guilt being proved, they were delivered up to punishment (Num. xxxv. 9-34). The most laudable anxiety was manifested to secure to the homicide the just effect of this institution ; and, among other things, it was directed that the roads to the cities of refuge should be kept free from all obstruction (Deut. xix. 3).

HISTORY OF PALESTINE

BOOK I.

CHAPTER I.   B.C. 2348 TO 1909.

PATRIARCHS.		ASSYRIA.		EGYPT	
	B.C.		B.C.		B.C.
The Deluge . . .	2348	Empire founded by		Suphis I. . . .	2123
Confusion of Tongues	2230	Nimrod or Ashur	2204	Suphis II. . . .	2083
Birth of Terah . .	2126			Moscheris or Men heris	2043
Birth of Abraham .	1996			Musthis ?	2022
First Call of Abraham	1937			Pammus	2011
Second Call, and arrival				Aphoph or Apappus .	2001
in Canaan . . .	1921				
Defeat of Chedorlaomer	1912				

1. EARLY after the Flood, the country which we now call Palestine became the habitation of a portion of the tribes descended from Canaan, the youngest son of Ham. Hence the country acquired its earliest name, the Land of Canaan; and the inhabitants were, collectively, called Canaanites. At the time of Abraham the country was but thinly peopled, and the inhabitants were separated into the various nations, enumerated in the first section of the Introduction. These several nations were not united under a common head; but each was kept together by a common name and parentage, and by local connection. In all these nations every town, with its vicinage, appears to have formed a separate common-wealth under its own *Melek* or " king." These kings appear to have been no other than the chief magistrates of the place, who were also leaders in war, and sometimes priests. Their authority was small, and they seem to have been unable to transact any important matter without the direct consent of their citizens. As there was abundant room in the land, the

vacant pasturages were abandoned to the pastoral chiefs of other tribes or nations, with whom the Canaanites exchanged their goods and the produce of their fields for the products of the flocks and herds. Their language, with probably some difference of dialect, was the same with that which Abraham brought from Mesopotamia. Their moral practices had become very offensive, and their notions of God and his government were wild and uncertain; but there is no evidence that they were idolaters in the time of the Patriarchs.

2. Our only knowledge of the social condition of the Canaanites is to be gathered from the few intimations contained in the Book of Genesis. They lived in walled towns, at the gates of which public business was transacted; they cultivated the ground, and raised corn and wine. Silver by weight was their medium of exchange, and it would seem that every adult male was acquainted with the use of arms. Such were the people of Canaan, when their country was visited by the illustrious stranger whose descendants were to become its most celebrated inhabitants. The circumstances of that visit must now be explained.

3. One thousand six hundred and fifty-six years after the Creation, the race of Man had become so guilty before God, that he swept them from the earth by a flood of waters. Only one family, of which Noah was the father, was saved. Noah had three sons, Shem, Ham, and Japheth, through whom the vacant world was again replenished with inhabitants. In about 400 years after the flood, the new races of mankind had also forgotten God, and had only some vague remembrance of that ancient promise of a Deliverer, who should crush the head of the Serpent, by whose seducements sin and sorrow were brought into the world (Gen. iii.) The world then seemed fast ripening for a new desolation; but God had sworn not again to destroy the earth for man's iniquities (Gen. viii. 21, 22). He chose rather to take one of the numerous tribes of men, and commit to its care the great truths which it was needful to keep alive in the world, until the time should come in which he purposed to make his will more fully known. These truths were, the knowledge of himself as the Creator and Ruler of the Universe, and of his promise to provide a Redeemer for mankind.

4. The founder of this favoured tribe was Abraham (at first called Abram), a descendant of Shem, the son of Noah, in the line of Heber. He belonged to a wealthy pastoral family dwelling beyond the Euphrates, in that district in which the town of Ur (now Urfah) was situated. This family was not free from the general taint of idol-worship; for we are told that Terah, the father of Abraham, and probably also his sons, " served other gods" beyond the Euphrates. Nevertheless, the God of Noah does not appear to have been altogether unknown; and while the world at large lay in darkness, the last rays of departing truth still lingered upon the tents of Terah. Abraham was the youngest of three sons, the others being Haran and Nahor. Haran, the eldest, died early, leaving one son called Lot, and two daughters, Milcah and Sarah (at first called Sarai). Milcah became the wife of Nahor, and Sarah of Abraham. Nahor had children, but Abraham had none.

5. Before the flood, the life of man had been very long; after the flood, it gradually shortened; but in the times of which we write, it was not yet reduced to its present limit of three score and ten years. Abraham, therefore, although sixty years of age, was still in the prime of life when God made himself known to him in a vision, and required him to leave his own country for another which should be made known to him (Acts vii. 2-4). He must have disclosed this mandate to his family; for they all went with him from the land of their birth. But they proceeded no further than Haran, in another part of Mesopotamia. The cause we know not; but in that neighbourhood they remained sixteen years, when Terah died, at the age of 205 years. (Gen. xi. 27-32).

6. When Terah was dead, a second and more special call was received by Abraham, requiring him not only to quit his country, but his kindred, for a strange land. But this more strict requirement was accompanied with encouraging promises of blessedness and renown; and with the obscure intimation of some great distant blessing which the families of men should receive through him. With that undoubting faith and prompt and unquestioning obedience which he always exhibited, and for which he is much commended in the sacred books, Abraham separated himself from his brother

Nahor, and departed. He was accompanied by his nephew Lot, the son of his deceased brother Haran ; and as both had great possessions of flocks, and herds, and slaves, a large caravan was doubtless formed by their union. They crossed the river Euphrates, and, traversing the deserts to the west, at length entered the land of Canaan, and first pitched their tents in the beautiful valley of Moreh, lying between the mountains of Ebal and Gerizim, in which the city of Shechem was afterwards built.

7. In this early age there were no temples. Men worshipped their gods at altars erected in the open air, sometimes amid the shade of umbrageous groves. Their more solemn acts of worship consisted in the sacrifice of victims from their flocks or herds, or oblations of the fruits of the ground—corn, wine, and oil. So did the patriarchs worship God ; and many were the monuments of their piety, in the form of altars, which they erected in the land of their sojourning.

8. The year after Abraham's entrance into Canaan, a great scarcity arose in that land. This was no doubt occasioned by the absence of the customary rains. But Egypt, whose fertility depends upon the overflowing of the Nile, was not affected by this drought, and continued to afford its usual abundance of corn. To Egypt, therefore, the patriarch repaired. Fearing to be slain for the sake of his wife Sarah, who was very beautiful, Abraham desired her to declare that she was his sister. The consequence was, that the king, hearing of her great beauty, sent and took her to his own palace ; in return loading her alleged " brother" with valuable gifts, such as befitted his condition—camels, asses, sheep and oxen, and men and women slaves. But the truth was soon made known, through the grievous disorders with which the Lord afflicted the king and his household as soon as Sarah came under his roof. He therefore sent her back, and after reproving Abraham for his conduct, desired him to withdraw from the country, probably fearing what might happen through the presence of a man who so manifestly enjoyed the special protection of God.

9. So Abraham returned to Canaan very rich, not only in cattle, but in silver and gold. Proceeding northward, he came to his former station near Bethel, and encamped there.

The increased substance of Abraham and Lot, made it difficult to find sufficient pastures for the flocks of both in the same neighbourhood, and this led to frequent contentions between their shepherds.   They therefore separated ; and Lot removed to the fertile and well-watered plain which the waters of the Dead Sea now cover.   Here were the cities of Sodom, Gomorrah, Admah, Zeboim, and Bela (afterwards Zoar).   This enforced separation from the last of his kin was doubtless a great grief to Abraham.   But he was comforted by the renewed promises of God, who again assured him of a numerous posterity, and directed him to go forth and survey more largely the fine country which was to become their heritage.   He went first southward, and pitched his tent under the shade of a terebinth tree, in the pleasant valley of Mamre, near Hebron, where he remained a considerable time.

10. The Assyrian empire, beyond the Euphrates, appears already to have risen to some importance, by reducing many petty kings to the condition of tributaries.   The strength of these inferior chiefs appears to have been then employed in distinct and foreign expeditions, for the further aggrandizement of the empire to which they were subject.   About four years before Abraham entered the land of Canaan, one of these princes, Chedorlaomer, whose own kingdom was Elam (probably Elymais, a district of south-western Persia), was intrusted with a command to extend the empire in the country west of the Euphrates.   This he executed by rendering several nations tributary ; and he appears to have remained on this side the great river to keep his conquests in obedience.[*] After twelve years of subjection, and about eight years after the first arrival of Abraham in Canaan, some of the conquered nations revolted, and refused any longer to send their tribute. Among these were the petty " kings," or chiefs, in the five cities of the plain to which Lot had withdrawn.   This brought upon them the vengeance of Chedorlaomer, who, with his former confederates, invaded and ravaged all the

* It is right to apprise the reader that the above, as far as regards the Assyrian empire, and the position of Chedorlaomer and other kings under it, is not *certain* history; but it is supported by circumstances, and seems to us a better explanation of the obscure intimations in Genesis, than the supposition that the king of Elam and others, from very distinct quarters, were independent kings, acting for themselves, and allied for the occasion.

country east of the Jordan, defeated the five kings in a
pitched battle, and retired with numerous captives and abundant spoil. Lot was among the captives. No sooner was
intelligence of this brought to Abraham, who was still in the
valley of Mamre, than he called out all his servants who
were able to bear arms, in number three hundred and eighteen,
and being joined by a few friendly native chiefs, set forth in
pursuit. The invaders were overtaken near the source of the
Jordan, and Abraham falling upon them suddenly by night,
put them to utter rout, and pursued them to the neighbourhood of Damascus. Thus was Lot delivered, and with him
were recovered all the captives and spoil which had been
taken. According to the war-laws of the East, all this prey
had, by the act of recovery, become his own. This right
was cordially recognised by the king of Sodom; but with a
generous pride the patriarch declined to appropriate the
smallest portion of the spoil, lest it should be in the power
of any one of the native princes to say that he had made
Abraham rich.

11. His whole conduct on this occasion won the patriarch
the esteem of the well-disposed native princes. One of them,
Melchizedek (*the just king*), of whom we know nothing but
that he also was one of the remaining worshippers of the true
God, came forth from his town to meet the returning patriarch,
blessed him, and supplied his people with victuals;* and as
the priestly functions were then exercised by kings and chiefs,
he offered sacrifices for himself and Abraham to " the most
high God, the maker of heaven and earth." After this the
patriarch returned to his encampment at Mamre.

* All kinds of victuals are understood as comprehended under the terms " bread.
the chief article of food, and " wine," the chief article of drink.

CHAPTER II. B.C. 1909 TO 1893.

PATRIARCHS.	B.C.	EGYPT.	B.C.
Birth of Ishmael	1910	Achescus Ocaras	1901
Circumcision instituted }	1897	Nitocris	1900
Sodom destroyed }			
Isaac born	1896		
Hagar dismissed	1893		

1. ABRAHAM had been promised a numerous posterity. The promise was of some standing, but as yet there were no signs of its fulfilment: he had no child, nor seemed likely to have any. When he thought of this he was sometimes discouraged; but the Lord condescended to enter into a formal covenant with him, not only to assure him that a son of his own should inherit his substance, but that the posterity of that son should become a nation, which, after being afflicted many years in a strange land, should return to take possession of the beautiful country in which he himself lived as a stranger. But although Abraham was to be the father of this promised son, Sarah had not at any time been named as the mother. She had always been reputed barren; and now that she was advanced in years, had given over all hope of children. She therefore recommended a course which was sanctioned by the ideas and usages of the time. She proposed that the patriarch should receive her own handmaid, Hagar, as a secondary and inferior wife, and that any child which this bond-woman might have, should be counted as the child of the mistress. Abraham did not object to this course, and it soon became plain that Hagar would give birth to a child. This consideration appears to have made her behave unbecomingly towards Sarah, who, in return, treated her so harshly, that she fled, and wandered into the southern wilderness. But an angel met her there, and encouraged her to return to the tents of Abraham, where, in due season, she gave birth to a son, who was called Ishmael, and who became the founder of a large portion of the Arabian tribes.

2. Thirteen years after the birth of Ishmael, when Sarah

was ninety years old, and Abraham ninety and nine, the Lord again appeared to the patriarch, and solemnly renewed his covenant to be, in an especial manner, THE GOD of him and of his numerous race. And as a ratification of this covenant on their part, the ceremony of circumcision was instituted, that every male in that race should bear upon him a token of this covenant with God. And further, when Abraham so spoke as to shew that his hope of posterity was resting on Ishmael, he was assured that the heir of the covenant was not yet born, and that Sarah herself was his destined mother. Even the name (Isaac) by which he should be called was given; and it was on this occasion that the patriarch himself had his name changed from Abram to Abraham, and his wife's name was altered from Sarai to Sarah.

3. It was not long after this that three heavenly beings, in the guise of travellers, accepted the hospitality of Abraham. When they arose to depart, the patriarch went with them a little way. They directed their course towards Sodom; and as they proceeded, the Chief Person, as a mark of his confidence and favour, opened to Abraham the design of his present appearance in these parts. He declared that the iniquity of Sodom and of the other cities of the Plain, was very great; and that such enormous wickedness could be no longer allowed to pollute the earth, if their present conduct answered to the grievous cry which had come before His throne. The two avenging angels then went on, and Abraham, remaining alone with the Lord, and, touchingly describing himself as "but dust and ashes," deprecated his anger, while he took upon him to intercede for the devoted cities. This he did with reverential earnestness, until the Lord said, that if but ten upright men were found in Sodom, it should be saved for their sake. The same evening the two angels came to Sodom, and were invited by Lot to spend the night under his roof. They yielded to his hospitable importunity; and before the night was over, they had full reason to be satisfied that the wickedness of the inhabitants was fully answerable to the cry which had ascended unto God. The doom of these cities was therefore sealed; yet that the innocent might not perish with the guilty, the angels warned Lot of the impending destruction, and urged his immediate departure from the

place. Pressed and led by them, he left the town, with his wife and two daughters; and at his intercession, the small city of Bela, thenceforth called Zoar, was spared, that it might be a place of refuge to him. As they sped over the plain, Sodom and the other cities received their doom—" The Lord rained upon Sodom and upon Gomorrah brimstone and fire," whereby the cities and all their inhabitants were utterly consumed, and the waters of the Dead Sea came over the ground on which they had stood.* The family of Lot did not wholly escape; for as his wife lingered regretfully behind the rest, she was overwhelmed by the destroying shower, which encrusting her body, left it standing like " a pillar of salt." Lot went to Zoar, but withdrew to a cave in the neighbouring mountains, where he became the father of two sons, Moab and Ammon.†

4. Very soon after the destruction of Sodom, Abraham removed his encampment to the south-west, into that part of the country where the Philistines had already established themselves. Here an adventure happened very similar to that which had occurred in Egypt. Uninstructed by experience, Abraham pretended that Sarah was his sister. As such she was seen and admired by Abimelech, king of Gerar, who sent and took her to his own house; but being warned by God in a dream that she was another man's wife, he restored her to Abraham with valuable gifts, but not without a keen rebuke.

5. The time at length arrived when Sarah gave to her husband the long-promised blessing of a son. On the eighth day he was circumcised, and the name of Isaac was given to him. About three years the mother nourished him at her own breast, and then a great feast marked the day in which the child was weaned (B.C. 1893). The birth of Isaac, the great attention which was paid to him, and the consciousness that by him Ishmael was cut off from the heritage of Abraham, were matters very distasteful to Hagar and her son, and at this great feast they took no pains to hide their feelings. At this Sarah was highly provoked, and insisted with Abraham that they should be sent away from the camp. The patriarch

---

* See before, p. 20.   † See before, p. 5

was very reluctant to take so harsh a course; but on receiv
ing an intimation from Heaven that this was in accordance
with the divine intentions, and that the Lord would care for
the prosperity of Ishmael, he resisted no longer, but sent both
the mother and son away, with suitable provisions for the
journey.

6. They had not, however, travelled farther than the
wilderness of Beersheba when their supply of water failed,
and Ishmael, overcome with heat, thirst, and weariness,
declared himself unable to proceed any further. Hagar
assisted him to reach some shrubs, under the shade of which
he lay down; and his mother, not being able to endure the
anguish of seeing him die, withdrew to a distance. In her
grief, an angel of God called to her with words of comfort;
he made known to her that there was a well of fresh water
not far off, and encouraged her by renewed predictions of the
prosperity of Ishmael. Thus relieved, they remained among
the tribes of the Desert; and, in due time, Ishmael was married to a woman of Egypt, became a person of note, and was
the father of several sons, the founders of families and tribes,
which formed, and no doubt still form, a large portion of the
Arabian people.

CHAPTER III. B.C. 1893 TO 1796.

PATRIARCHS.		EGYPT.		GREECE.	
	B.C.		B.C.		B C
Isaac offered . . .	1871	Myrtæus	1890	Kingdom of Argos	
Sarah dies	1859	Thyosimares . . .	1880	founded	1856
Isaac marries . . .	1856	Thinillus	1866	Deluge of Ogyges, in	
Jacob and Esau born	1836	Semphucrates . .	1848	Attica . . .	1848
Abraham dies . . .	1821	Menmoph	1830		
Esau marries . . .	1796	The names and eras of			
		the kings that follow			
		to Osirtasen I. B.C.			
		1740, are uncertain.			

1. ABRAHAM still remained in the south country, near to Gerar, where his power and pastoral wealth had much increased; and, as he seemed to manifest no intention of removing, the king Abimelech thought it right to court a treaty of alliance with him, being the first which history records. To this he was probably the more induced, as some anxiety had been experienced on account of the wells which Abraham had digged—an act which, as we have already explained, gave to the party by whom such wells were made, a kind of appropriative right in lands not previously occupied. This matter being adjusted, and the rights of the patriarch being recognised by the king, the desired covenant was formed between them, and confirmed by an oath. It amounted to little more than that the contracting parties, and their heirs after them, should act with truth towards each other. In memory of this transaction, Abraham gave the name of Beersheba (*well of the oath*) to the well in question; and, the situation being agreeable and convenient, he remained there many years, and planted a grove of trees around the altar at which he worshipped God.

2. When Isaac had attained the age of twenty-five years, it pleased God to prove Abraham by one great trial of his faith and obedience. He was commanded to journey to a mountain in Canaan, and there to offer up his son Isaac in sacrifice to God. Firmly persuaded that since God had promised him a posterity through Isaac, he would even raise him again from the dead, rather than allow his promise to

fail (Heb. xi. 17-19), the "father of the faithful" prepared
to render full, however heart-rending, obedience to this extraordinary mandate.   He travelled to the appointed place; he
built an altar, and laid thereon the wood for the fire; he
bound his beloved son with cords; and his hand was uplifted
to give him the death-wound, when he was arrested by a
voice from heaven with words of commendation and encouragement, and by a more than ever solemn confirmation to
him and to his race of all the blessings that had before been
promised.   A ram, which was found entangled by the horns
in a thicket, was substituted for Isaac upon the altar, and the
father returned rejoicing to Beersheba with his son.

3. Twelve years after this Sarah died, in the 127th year
of her age.   Abraham had, before this, removed his camp
from Beersheba to his old station at Mamre, near Hebron, or
to some other spot in that neighbourhood; and as it had now
become necessary that he should have a family sepulchre in
which to lay his dead, he purchased for 400 shekels of silver
the field and cave of Machpelah, near Hebron.   Here Sarah
was buried; and thus a sepulchre became to the patriarchs
the earnest of their reversionary heritage.

4. Three years after this, when Isaac had reached the
age of forty years, Abraham bethought himself of seeking a
wife for his son.   The state of religion and morals in Canaan,
and the special nature of the promises made to his race, con-
curred with the usual habits and notions of a pastoral chief,
in leading his attention to his own family, which he had left
in Mesopotamia, of whose welfare he had, a few years before,
received intelligence.   He therefore gave it in solemn charge
to his old and confidential servant Eliezer to travel thither,
and, if possible, to obtain thence a wife for Isaac.   Eliezer
sped well on his journey.   On his first arrival at Haran, he
fell in with Rebekah, the grand-daughter of Abraham's
brother Nahor, and received kind attentions from her and
from the family, when he arrived at the house.   When he
made known the object of his journey, the proposed alliance
was accepted without hesitation.   Rebekah herself, on whom
the choice fell, made no objections; and she therefore, accompanied by her nurse Deborah, was soon on the road to Canaan
with Eliezer and his men   They arrived safely there; all

parties were well pleased; and Rebekah became the wife of Isaac.

5. Not long after, Abraham took to himself a second wife, named Keturah, by whom he had six sons, named Zimran, Jokshan, Medan, Midian, Ishbak, and Shuah, all of whom were provided for by their father during his lifetime, and sent to settle in Arabia Petræa, lest at his death they should interfere with his heir Isaac. They became the founders of Arabian tribes and nations—one of which, Midian, makes some figure in the early history of Isaac's descendants. Nothing more is recorded of Abraham until his death, which occurred at what was even then considered the advanced age of 175 years—just 100 years after his arrival in Canaan. His body was laid beside that of Sarah, in the sepulchral cave of Machpelah.

6. Rebekah, the wife of Isaac, presented her husband with two sons, twins, of whom the first-born was named Esau, and the other Jacob (B.C. 1836). They were fifteen years of age when their grandfather Abraham died. As they grew up, the brothers manifested very different dispositions; Esau was a rude and boisterous man, devoted to the sports of the field, while Jacob was of a sedate and quiet disposition, much employed in the cares and duties of pastoral life. Before their birth, it had been intimated to the mother, that the younger of the two was the destined heir of the promises; and this, together with his gentle disposition, rendered Jacob very dear to Rebekah; but the love of Isaac, although himself a quiet man, was more engaged by the first-born, Esau. Not knowing, or not rightly understanding, or not having much confidence in the intimation which had been given to his wife, Isaac was still disposed to consider Esau as the heir of the promises; and being aware of this, Rebekah was always contriving to bring about, by craft and management, the designs which the Lord would have accomplished without her aid. Jacob, in his early life, much resembled his mother in these respects; but time, trouble, and experience, made him a much better man in his later years.

7. The first object was to get from Esau a formal renun-ciation of his birthright, on which, in truth, Esau himself set so very little value, that he readily agreed to barter it for a

mess of savoury pottage which, one day, when he came home faint and hungry from hard hunting, he found Jacob preparing. It does not appear to us that he renounced, or that Jacob sought, the ordinary secular right of the first-born to a double portion of the father's goods, but rather the peculiar blessings and promises of the Abrahamic covenant, which all parties supposed must henceforth descend in the line of primogeniture, unless God otherwise specially determined, or unless the person most nearly interested abandoned his claim. All the parties appear to have laboured under some mistake in this matter; and Esau's light estimation of his supposed privilege was no less reprehensible than Jacob's over-anxiety to secure what he believed to be intended for him.

8. After this there was a famine in the land of Canaan, and Isaac would probably have withdrawn into Egypt, had he not been commanded by the Lord to remain in the land which was the destined inheritance of his race. On this occasion, the promise of that heritage, and of all the other blessings of the covenant with Abraham, was repeated to Isaac, who then removed into the territories of the Philistines, where another Abimelech than he who had entered into covenant with Abraham, reigned. During his residence in Gerar, Isaac denied his wife, as his father Abraham had done in the same country, and for the same reason, for which he also incurred the just rebuke of the reigning king. While in this quarter, Isaac paid some attention to the culture of the ground, which repaid him a hundred-fold; and in this and other ways, his wealth and power so rapidly increased, as to excite the alarm and jealousy of the Philistines, who filled up the wells which gave him a right to the soil, and whose king at length desired him to withdraw to a greater distance. The patriarch accordingly proceeded to the more open pastures which his father had occupied, and there digged again, without opposition, the wells of Abraham. But his attempts to dig *new* wells were vehemently resisted by the Philistine shepherds, until he did so at such a distance, that they no longer interfered. In this situation, his still growing prosperity suggested to Abimelech the propriety of renewing with the powerful nomad chief the convention which his own predecessor made with Abraham. The king, therefore, went

from Gerar to the camp of Isaac, whom he treated in all respects as an equal. He and his attendants were properly feasted by the patriarch, who, after a becoming remonstrance as to the treatment he had received, consented to renew the covenant of peace. At the age of forty, Esau married two women of Canaan, and thereby gave much pain to his parents, whose views in such matters were the same as those which Abraham had entertained.

CHAPTER IV.   B.C. 1796 TO 1739.

PATRIARCHS		EGYPT.	
	B.C.		B. C.
Ishmael dies	1773	Uncertain till Osirtasen I.	1746
Jacob leaves Palestine	1759		
Reuben born	1758		
Simeon born	1757		
Levi born	1756		
Judah born	1755		
Joseph born	1745		
Jacob returns	1739		

1. WHEN Jacob was 77 years old, and Isaac 137, we find the patriarchal family again at Beersheba. By that time Isaac's sight had failed him, and he concluded that he had not long to live. He therefore determined to bestow that blessing which the patriarchal fathers were wont to give to their sons in their last days, and to which much importance was attached, because on such occasions an influence from above enabled them to interpret the designs of the Almighty towards those whom they addressed. The blessings of the Abrahamic covenant, which God intended for Jacob, the fond Isaac now purposed to bestow on Esau. This he made known to him; but first sent him out into the fields to hunt, that, with the game, he might prepare one of those savoury messes with which he had been in the habit of gratifying the appetite of his aged father. All this was overheard by Rebekah, who instantly determined to frustrate the design by artifice. She dressed Jacob in his brother's clothes, and persuaded him to personate Esau: and he thus obtained from his blind father the important blessing—" Let people serve thee, and nations bow down to thee : be lord over thy brethren, and let thy mother's sons bow down to thee : cursed be every one that curseth thee, and blessed be every one that blesseth thee !" Jacob had scarcely withdrawn, when the entrance of Esau revealed the deception which had been practised. Isaac was seized with consternation when he discovered that his intention had been counteracted. But convinced that he had been rashly attempting to act in opposition to the divine will, and

that the whole matter had been overruled by a higher power, he made no attempt to recal the blessing he had bestowed on Jacob, but rather confirmed it by the emphatic declaration, " Yea, and he shall be blessed!"

2. The grief and rage of Esau at being thus circumvented by his brother were very great. He earnestly begged another blessing for himself, and obtained one which involved the promise, that although his posterity should for a while be subject to that of Jacob, yet in the end they should throw off the yoke, and establish their independence. All the parties in this transaction were much to blame; Rebekah and Jacob especially, were guilty of the sins of doing evil that good might come, and of promoting, by fraudulent means, the intentions of God, in effecting which their aid was not needful.

3. Esau cherished the most inexorable resentment against Jacob for what he had done. He vowed to be revenged by the death of his brother; but, out of regard for his father, purposed to wait till after his death. This came to the ears of Rebekah, who thereupon persuaded Jacob to withdraw for a time to her brother Laban in Mesopotamia. Not to trouble the mind of the aged Isaac, she forbore to tell him the principal reason for this course, but assigned another, which was also true, being her fear lest Jacob should follow the example of his brother, in marrying one of the women of the country in which they lived. Isaac therefore called Jacob, and charged him not to do this, but to go and obtain for a wife one of the daughters of Laban, his mother's brother.

4. Dismissed with his father's blessing, the heir of the promises set forth upon his journey. On his way, he was encouraged by an important vision at Bethel, and in due time arrived at Haran; and when he came to the well outside that city, he found a great number of persons of both sexes assembled there to water their flocks. Among them he discovered Rachel, the daughter of Laban, who had charge of the home flock. Having watered the flock for her, he told her who he was, and went with her to her father's house. He was well received by Laban, to whom he made his circumstances known. In a short time that person discovered that Jacob had a very superior knowledge of pastoral affairs, and became anxious to retain his services in the management

of his flocks.   He offered him wages; but Jacob, who had
much love for his cousin whom he had met at the well—but
had no means of paying the price which custom required a
man to give to the father of the woman he married—offered
Laban seven years of his services for Rachel.   Laban consented; and when the time came, made a great feast to
celebrate his daughter's marriage; but instead of giving
Jacob the youngest daughter, according to agreement, he
managed, by some deception, to substitute Leah, the eldest,
for whom Jacob had no regard.

5. Next day, when the fraud was discovered, Laban
excused himself by saying, that the custom of the country
would not permit the younger daughter to be given in mar
riage before the elder; and coolly added, that now the elder
was married, he might have the other also, if he chose to
serve other seven years for her.   Jacob, who saw no remedy,
and who greatly loved Rachel, agreed to this proposal, and,
after a proper interval, she was given to him.   He had now
two wives, as the custom of the time and country allowed.
As might be expected, Rachel was much dearer to him than
Leah, whom he treated with comparative neglect; but the
Lord, who hates injustice, restored the balance in this matter,
by giving Leah children, which were withheld from Rachel.
Leah bore successively four sons, whom she named Reuben,
Simeon, Levi, and Judah.   As children are greatly desired
by the Orientals, and were more especially desirable to him
whose posterity was to become a great nation, this gave to
Leah an advantage over her sister, which vexed Rachel
She therefore gave her handmaid Bilhah to Jacob, in the
same way, and with the same intention, as that with which
Sarah gave Hagar to Abraham, Rachel intending, that if
there were children, they should be considered her own.
Bilhah had two sons, whom Rachel named Dan and Naphtali.
On this, Leah would not be denied the right of giving also
her handmaid Zilpah to Jacob.   She bore two sons, Gad and
Asher, in addition to whom Leah herself had two more sons,
Issachar and Zebulun, and one daughter named Dinah.   At
last, after many years of repining, Rachel herself had a son,
who received the name of Joseph.

6. The fourteen years during which Jacob had agreed to

serve Laban for his two daughters were expired, and he now expressed an intention of returning to the land of Canaan. But Laban, convinced that the Lord had blessed him greatly for Jacob's sake, and that all his affairs had prospered in his hands, earnestly entreated him to remain, offering whatever recompense for his further services he might demand. As he was still poor, and felt it a duty to provide for his own house, Jacob found it prudent to accept this offer, and named the party-coloured sheep and goats which might henceforth be born in the flock as the reward of his cares. As pied animals are very rare in Syrian flocks, Laban eagerly agreed to this proposal. By forming into a separate flock, and removing to a distance all the animals which were already party-coloured, leaving all the rest under the care of Jacob, he took means to prevent the inordinate increase of such as were o become his nephew's share; but, on the other hand, Jacob, by an ingenious contrivance, endeavoured to promote their increase, and with such success, that a very few years sufficed to render his portion of the flocks greater than Laban's.

7. Annoyed at the discontent and envy, which Laban and his sons took no pains to conceal, longing to be at home, and deeming his present wealth sufficient, Jacob, after six years more of servitude, making twenty years in all, determined to return to Canaan. But fearing that Laban might oppose his departure, he took an occasion of removing clandestinely, with his wives and children, his flocks and herds. Three days passed before Laban heard of his departure, and with his relations and retainers he immediately set off in pursuit. In seven days he traversed the distance for which Jacob, encumbered with flocks and herds, had required ten days, and overtook him in the mountains of Gilead. It had, doubtless, been the intention of Laban either to compel Jacob to return, or to despoil him of his wealth; but the night before they met, he had been warned in a dream against committing any injurious or hostile act. Therefore, when they met the next day, he confined himself to reproofs, which Jacob retorted with great spirit, and much truth; and in the end they came to a good understanding, and entered into a covenant of peace; after which they parted, Laban returning home, and Jacob pursuing his journey.

8. Jacob's next anxiety was to ascertain the disposition towards him of his brother Esau, to evade whose wrath he had quitted the land of Canaan twenty years before. Meanwhile, Esau himself had become a person of consequence, and had established himself in great power as a military chief in the mountains of Seir. Thither Jacob sent messengers to announce his return, which they were instructed to do in terms of the utmost deference and respect. In due time the messengers returned with the alarming intelligence that Esau himself was advancing at the head of 400 men. Jacob much feared that the intentions of his brother were unfriendly; and he recommended himself, in an earnest prayer, to the protection of God. It was night: his caravan had already passed the river Jabbok, and he remained behind to renew his supplications in the solitude. While he was thus engaged, an angel of God appeared and struggled with him, in wrestling, for a long while, and refrained from overcoming the mortal man with whom he conflicted, until the morning broke; and then, to evince his power, he laid his hand upon the hollow of Jacob's thigh, when instantly the sinew shrank, and he halted with lameness. Yet Jacob left not his hold of the angel, but cried, " I will not let thee go except thou bless me !" The angel asked him, " What is thy name?" He answered, " Jacob." Then said the angel, " thy name shall be called no more Jacob, but ISRAEL *(prince of God)* ; for as a prince has thou power with God, and with men, and hast prevailed." He then received the blessing for which he strove, and derived all the intended encouragement from this mysterious interview. Israel then joined his family on the other side the Jabbok. The intentions of Esau may have been hostile; but his heart was so wrought upon by the sight of his long absent brother and his peaceful troop, that he ran to meet him, and fell upon his neck and kissed him, and they wept together.

CHAPTER V.   B. C. 1739 to 1708.

	B.C.		B.C.
Benjamin born	1734	Isaac dies	1716
Joseph sold	1728	Joseph Governor of Egypt	1715
Joseph imprisoned	1718	Famine begins	1708

1. ISRAEL made some stay at Succoth, after which he proceeded to the valley between Mounts Ebal and Gerizim, where Abraham first encamped on entering the Land of Promise. A city had since been built there, and the land appropriated, so that Jacob was obliged to purchase the ground on which he pitched his tents. Here a friendly understanding, and a mutually advantageous traffic, soon arose between this family of shepherds and the townspeople. The former could supply milk, and wool, and skins, and animals for use and slaughter, for which the latter could give the products of their fields and gardens, and the utensils, cloths, arms, and ornaments which towns usually produce. But it unfortunately happened that Shechem, the son of Hamor, the prince of the country, saw Dinah, Jacob's daughter, at a public festival in the town, and, becoming enamoured of her, allured her from her father's protection to his own house, where he detained her with the promise and intention of marriage. The young man opened the matter to his father, and persuaded him to go out to Jacob's camp, and make proposals of marriage to him.

2. Jacob was much grieved, and his sons were fired with indignation at the dishonour which the family had received, and at first refused to listen to the liberal offers which Hamor made. At last, however, they acceded to the proposed marriage, on condition that all the Shechemites should receive the rite of circumcision. To this the townspeople were induced by Hamor to consent; and on the third day, when they were least able to defend themselves, Simeon and Levi, full brothers of Dinah, entered the town, with some of their father's men, and slew all the male inhabitants, to avenge the indignity offered to their sister, whom they took away to the camp. After this the other sons of Jacob came and plun-

dered the place, bringing the women and children away as captives. Jacob was greatly distressed and alarmed at this atrocious action of his sons, and was glad to withdraw—in accordance with a divine intimation—from a neighbourhood stained by so great a crime, to Bethel.

3. From Bethel Jacob proceeded southward, probably with the intention of rejoining his aged father, who was still alive, and who abode in the plain of Mamre, near Hebron. When they were near Ephrath (afterwards Bethlehem), Rachel was delivered of a second son, named Benjamin; and she died in giving him birth. The bereaved husband honoured

the grave of his beloved wife with a sepulchral pillar, which long after stood there, but which is now replaced by a Mohammedan monumental tomb. Israel removed from Ephrath to a pasture ground in whic stood a tower, calle the Tower of th

107.   Rachel's Sepulchre.

Flock, and, after some stay there, at length joined his ol father in Mamre, and remained with him till his death.   Thi did not occur till sixteen years after, when Isaac had reache the advanced age of 180 years.   Esau was also present, an joined with Jacob in rendering the last offices of filial duty to their father, whose remains were deposited in the cave of Machpelah, with those of Sarah and Abraham.   After this Esau withdrew, with the portion of the property which fell to him, to his former residence in the mountains of Seir, where his posterity became a considerable nation.   At the time of Isaac's death, Jacob was 120 years old.   He continued still at Mamre, engaged with his sons in the usual pastoral employments.

4. The history now conducts us to Joseph, the eldest of Rachel's two sons.   His beauty, his engaging qualities, his early wisdom, and, more than all, his having been for many

years (before Benjamin was born) the only son of Rachel, had given him the first place in his father's love. This partiality may have been natural; but Jacob most unwisely displayed it before the eyes of his other sons, by clothing his favourite in a gaudy " coat of many colours." This and other things so moved the envy and jealousy of the brothers, that " they could not speak peaceably to him ;" and he especially offended the sons of Bilhah and Zilpah, by reporting to Jacob their misbehaviour when out with the flocks. The general ill-feeling of his brothers towards him was not a little strengthened by his account of certain dreams with which he was favoured, and which could only be interpreted to prefigure his own future greatness and their humiliation before him. At length their hatred rose to such a height, that they resolved to get rid of him by death as soon as a favourable opportunity should occur.

5. They had for some time been out with the flocks in distant pastures, when Israel sent Joseph from Mamre to enquire after their welfare. As soon as he came in sight they resolved to kill him; but were prevented by Reuben, who wished to deliver him out of their hands, and persuaded them to cast him into an empty pit. Afterwards, by the advice of Judah, they drew him out, and sold him for a slave to a caravan of Ishmaelitish and Midianitish merchants, who were going with costly drugs to Egypt. The brothers then took Joseph's coat—the coat of many colours—and dipped it in the blood of a kid, to induce the belief that he had been killed by a wild beast. They then sent it home to their father, who, receiving the impression they intended to convey, was overwhelmed with anguish. He rent his clothes, put on sackcloth, and mourned for his son many days. This was about three years after Jacob had joined his father Isaac at Mamre.

6. Meanwhile Joseph was taken to Egypt, and sold to Potiphar, captain of the guard to Pharaoh,* king of Egypt. By his abilities and excellent conduct he won the entire confidence of his master, who in the end left all his affairs in his

---

* *Pharaoh,* or *Phrah,* is not a name, but a title, meaning " king," which accounts for its being given in Scripture to nearly all the sovereigns of that country of whom it takes notice.

hands. But after serving Potiphar with great integrity and success for ten years, he was then thrown into prison, on account of a false accusation by his mistress, whose guilty enticements he had repelled. In the prison, his character and talents were soon appreciated by the governor, who committed all the other prisoners to his charge. Among these were the king's chief butler and chief baker—officers of some consequence in Eastern courts. These were both, in one night, troubled with remarkable dreams, which Joseph modestly undertook to interpret; and the event corresponded to his interpretations—the butler was restored to favour, and the baker was hanged.

7. Two years after this the king of Egypt himself had two very singular dreams in one night, which troubled him greatly, especially when he found that none of his diviners were able to discover their meaning. On this, the chief butler called to mind Joseph's most true interpretation of his own and his companion's dreams in prison, and spoke of this to the king. Pharaoh immediately sent to the prison for him, and related to him his dreams. Modestly disclaiming the wisdom which the king supposed him to possess, and ascribing all the honour to the God whom he served, Joseph told the king that the two dreams were to be received as a warning from God, that seven years of extreme plenty in Egypt would be succeeded by seven years of unexampled scarcity. He then proceeded to give such sound advice as to the mode in which the over-produce of the seven years of plenty might be husbanded for use during the seven years of famine, that Pharaoh at once determined to invest him with the power and station necessary for giving effect to the measures he had advised. By taking off his signet-ring, and placing it on Joseph's finger, he conveyed to him such high powers as made him next in authority to the king. He was then arrayed in the vestures of fine muslin and the chain of gold which belonged to his high place, and, standing in the royal chariot, he was conducted in grand procession through the metropolis, and proclaimed chief minister and governor of Egypt. Joseph was thirty years old when he attained this high advancement. Soon after Pharaoh—in order to strengthen Joseph's position, by connecting him with distinguished families—gave him in

marriage a lady of high rank, Asenath, daughter of Potipherah, high-priest of On, by whom in due time he had two sons, Manasseh and Ephraim.

8. During the seven years of plenty Joseph travelled through all the provinces, making surveys, building granaries, and filling them with corn. The effects of the years of scarcity which followed were felt not only in Egypt, but in all the adjacent countries, the inhabitants of which soon flocked to Egypt to purchase corn from the well-filled granaries of Joseph. The private stores of the Egyptians themselves were soon spent, and they became dependent upon the public stock, out of which they bought corn until they had nothing but their persons and their lands left to them. Then, at their own desire, Joseph bought their lands for the Crown, at the cost of supplying them with food during the scarcity; and for the convenience of distribution, he assembled the people of every district into the towns in which the corn was stored, and, when the famine was nearly ended, he gave them seed, and restored them their lands to farm, at the fixed Crown-rent of one-fifth of the produce. We have explained this procedure, because it appears to have been of late much misunderstood.

CHAPTER VI.   B.C. 1708 to 1635.

PATRIARCHS.		EGYPT.	
	B. C.		B. C.
Jacob sends his sons to Egypt for corn	1707	Amun-m-gori I.	1691
Jacob and his family go to Egypt .	1706	Amun-m-gori II.	1688
End of the Famine	1702	Osirtasen II.	1653
Jacob dies	1689		
Joseph dies	1635		

1. Among the foreigners who repaired to Egypt to buy corn in the first year of the famine, were the brethren of Joseph. As they stood " and bowed themselves before him, with their faces to the earth," and thus accomplished what was predicted by the dreams which they had so criminally endeavoured to frustrate, they little thought of their brother, but he knew them well. To try their present dispositions, he spoke roughly to them, and accused them of being spies, " come to spy the nakedness of the land." This was a most grave and dangerous charge, coming from such a quarter. This they felt ; and, in their anxiety to repel it, gave a particular account of their real condition, from which Joseph learned that his father still lived, and that his favourite son, their youngest brother, had remained at home with him. Joseph seized hold of this, and made the appearance of that younger brother before him the test of their sincerity, and decided that one of them should go for him, and the rest remain in custody till that one returned with Benjamin. Meanwhile they were cast into prison ; but on the third day he spoke more gently to them, and directed that they might all go home, except Simeon, who was to be detained as a hostage for their return. Their troubled consciences interpreted the difficulties into which they had fallen as a divine judgment upon them for the treatment of their brother ; and as they freely expressed this to one another—not supposing " the governor of the country" could understand them—Joseph was much moved, and turned from them and wept. He gave them provisions for the journey, and caused the money they had paid for corn to be privily restored in their sacks.

2. When they reached home they gave their father a full account of the strange behaviour of " the man, the governor of the land." He was much disconcerted at the demand for Benjamin, and refused to let him go. But, when the corn was all consumed, and Jacob desired his sons to go to Egypt for more, they absolutely refused again to appear before " the governor" without Benjamin. At length, with extreme difficulty, they extorted his consent—Judah making himself individually responsible for Benjamin's safe return. Anxious to make a favourable impression upon the much-dreaded " man" in Egypt, Jacob sent him a present of the choice products of the land of Canaan—balm and honey, spices and myrrh, nuts and almonds.

3. They arrived in Egypt, and again stood before Joseph, who no sooner saw Benjamin than he expressed his satisfaction, and set Simeon free. He asked them concerning that old man of whom they had spoken—their father—and was obliged to withdraw to indulge that burst of emotion which the sight of his brother inspired. He feasted them sumptuously that day, and the next morning allowed them to depart with the corn they required. But, to try their feeling towards Benjamin, he caused his own silver cup to be secretly introduced into the mouth of his corn-sack, that he might see whether, when Benjamin should be charged with the theft, they would leave him to his fate, and go home without him. Accordingly, after they had left the town, they were overtaken by a party of Joseph's servants, who ordered them to stop, and charged them with having stolen their master's silver cup. Alarmed at this accusation, but conscious of their innocence, they expressed their readiness to be searched, and declared that any one with whom the cup might be found deserved to die. When the cup was found in Benjamin's sack, they returned with the supposed culprit to the city, and once more stood before the governor of the land. They fell on their faces before him, and, in answer to his reproaches, declared themselves his bondsmen, without attempting to deny or vindicate the apparent guilt of their brother. But Joseph told them it was right that only the guilty should suffer. Benjamin, therefore, he would detain in bondage, but they might go home. Judah then interceded, and, in a

most eloquent and touching address, evinced the most tender affection towards his brother and his aged father; and, declaring the special trust he had incurred, entreated to be taken as a bondsman in the stead of Benjamin. The governor could contain himself no longer; he made himself known to them—" I am Joseph !—doth my father yet live ?" Perceiving them overwhelmed with apprehension and remorse, he endeavoured to comfort and reassure them, by directing their attention to the designs of Providence—" Be not grieved or angry with yourselves that ye sold me hither, for God did send me before you to preserve life." He then embraced them all, and opened to them his desire that they should return and bring their father and their families down to Egypt, where they would enjoy plenty during the remaining years of famine; and he would procure them a grant of the pastoral district of Goshen for their residence.

4. Joyful was their return, and rapturous their announcement to their father—" Joseph is yet alive, and is governor over all the land of Egypt !" Jacob's heart fainted, and he believed them not. Twenty years he had mourned his beloved Joseph as dead, and it was not easy at once to receive so great a joy. When at length their solemn assurance created belief, he said, " It is enough ; Joseph my son is yet alive—I will go down and see him before I die !" So Jacob left Canaan with all his family and possessions. On the way he paused to worship at the old family altar in Beersheba, and was there favoured with the intimation from God, that the purpose of His providence was, that his race should tarry in Egypt, to grow into a great nation there; and that, as such, they should then march forth to take possession of the land of Canaan, their promised inheritance. Jacob's family—consisting of his sons, with their wives and children— at the time it entered Egypt, consisted of seventy-five* per- sons (Acts vii. 14). On entering Egypt, Jacob sent Judah to give notice of his arrival to Joseph, who immediately rode

---

* In Gen. xlvi. 27, we read " seventy." The reason of the difference is this—Jacob 's eleven sons and a daughter, and their children and grandchildren, made sixty-six per sons, to whom the account in Acts adds the nine wives of Jacob's eleven sons. The account in Genesis omits these wives, but makes the number seventy, by adding to the sixty-six Jacob himself, and Joseph, with his two sons, already in Egypt.

rth in his chariot to meet his father, who, when he saw him, " fell upon his neck, and wept on his neck a good while ;" and, as soon as he could speak, he said, " Now, let me die since I have seen thy face, because thou art yet alive." Joseph conducted them into the land of Goshen, which they were to occupy. Having left their flocks and herds there, they proceeded to the metropolis, and were introduced by Joseph to the king, the father separately, and the sons together. Pharaoh was much struck by the venerable aspect of the patriarch, and asked him how old he was? He answered— " The days of the years of my pilgrimage are a hundred and thirty years : few and evil have the days of the years of my life been, and have not attained unto the days of the years of the life of my fathers, in the days of their pilgrimage."

5. Jacob and his family having taken possession of the district of Goshen, remained there, undisturbed, in their usual pastoral employments for seventeen years, at the end of which Jacob—being then 147 years old—felt that his last hour drew nigh. He therefore called his sons together, to tell them, in the spirit of prophecy, what should befall them and their tribes in the coming times. As they all stood around him, he gave utterance in the most beautiful language, replete with poetical images, to a wonderful series of predictions respecting the future character, circumstances, and situation of the tribes which were to spring from his several sons. To Judah was allotted the pre-eminence, and a more especial interest in the promises of the covenant ; nor was it obscurely intimated that in his tribe was to arise the promised Deliverer, whose coming was the main object of the Hebrew covenant, and of the Jewish polity, as established in after years. Joseph was eminently favoured with a double portion ; for Jacob adopted his two sons, Ephraim and Manasseh, as his own children, thereby making them heads of tribes, and entitling them, as such, to be counted as two tribes in the commonwealth of Israel ; but, at the same time, Jacob intimated that the tribe of the younger son Ephraim would take a leading part in the nation, and be greater and more renowned than the tribe of the elder Manasseh.

6. When he had finished blessing his sons, Israel gathered up his feet into the bed, and died. Joseph fell

upon the face of his dead father, kissed him, and closed his eyes. Egypt held a solemn mourning for him. His body was embalmed after the manner of the Egyptians, and carried with great state to the land of Canaan, to be laid in the family sepulchre. Such had been his own desire, in the unshaken conviction that the Lord would restore his race to the land which contained that sepulchre, and give it to them for a possession. In the same conviction Joseph himself, fifty-four years after, and just before his death—being then 110 years old—sent for his brethren, and required them, on behalf of the family, to swear to carry up his bones from Egypt, and bury them in the Land of Promise—thus, at once, evincing his faith, and taking his last place with the Israelites rather than with the Egyptians. He then died; and, as he had only charged them to remove his bones with them when the time of their final departure should arrive, his body was carefully preserved in a coffin against that time.

BOOK II.

CHAPTER I. B.C. 1571 TO 1491.

PATRIARCHS.		EGYPT.		EVENTS AND PERSONS.	
	B.C.		B.C.		B.C.
Levi dies	1619	Osirtasen III.	1636	Scamander leads a colony from Crete, and founds Troy	
The new king (dynasty) in Egypt	1575	Amun-m-gori III.	1621		1546
Aaron born	1574	Name unknown	1580		
Moses born	1571	Amosis	1575	Cecrops leads a colony from Sais in Egypt, and founds Athens	1556
Moses quits Egypt	1531	Amunoph I.	1550		
Moses returns to Egypt, and brings forth the Israelites	1491	Thothmes I.	1532		
		Thothmes II.	1505	Cadmus carries letters into Greece, and founds Thebes	1493
		Thothmes III.	1495		

1. THE posterity of Jacob's sons remained in the land of Goshen, increasing with prodigious rapidity, through the special blessing of Providence, who designed to multiply them soon into a nation. For many years we know little more of them; but it may be observed that Ephraim and Manasseh, the two sons of Joseph, instructed by their father to prefer the lot of God's chosen people, very early joined the Israelites in Goshen, and followed the same mode of life. All went on very well until the accession of a new dynasty to the throne of Lower Egypt—probably a foreign dynasty from Upper Egypt, which knew little and cared less for the memory and services of Joseph. The new government contemplated with alarm the position occupied by an active, closely united, and rapidly increasing body of foreigners in the land of Goshen. It was considered that, unless means were taken to reduce and keep down their numbers, their power would soon be too great for the Egyptians to control. While the troops were elsewhere employed they might get possession of the country, or might at any time ruin Egypt, by going over to its enemies in time of war.

2. Much of this alarm obviously arose from the fact of their living apart by themselves, in Goshen, so that their aggregate mass was so apparent as to inspire the Egyptians

with apprehension, and the Israelites with confidence. Had they been dispersed over Egypt, and intermixed with the native population, nothing of this could have been felt. Knowing how, under ordinary circumstances, a population may be kept in check by oppression and labour, the Egyptian government determined to reduce the free-born Israelites to the condition of serfs, requiring them to "serve with rigour" in the public works—to dig canals, to cultivate the ground, to build towns and granaries, and to make the sun dried bricks, compacted with straw, of which they were constructed. Task-masters were set over them to exact the full amount of labour; and those who failed were subjected to severe punishments. But although the yoke upon Israel was made very heavy, the population was not checked. The more they were oppressed, the more their numbers increased. Perceiving this, the king determined to resort to more decisive measures, and enjoined the Hebrew midwives to destroy every male infant in the birth. Fearing God more than they feared the king, the midwives disregarded this barbarous order. But, determined not to be balked in his politic design, Pharaoh no longer stooped to indirect and secret measures, but openly commanded that every male child thenceforth born should be thrown into the river Nile.

3. In those days, Jochebed, the wife of Amram, of the tribe of Levi, gave birth to a son. She had already two children, a son named Aaron, and a daughter called Miriam. For three months the mother managed to save her infant from its doom; and then, finding that she could hide him no longer, she placed him among the flags beside the river, in a basket which had been daubed with slime to keep the water out. In the good providence of God, who intended this infant for great deeds, it happened that he had not lain there long before the king's daughter came to the spot, attended by her maidens, to bathe. Perceiving the basket she sent for it, and was much struck by the extreme beauty of the child, and moved by its infant wail. She knew that it must be a Hebrew child, but resolved to save it; and sent Miriam—who had been watching the result—to find a nurse for him. She brought the mother, who joyfully received the charge of nursing her own infant for the king's daughter.

4. In due time the boy was taken home to the princess, who became attached to him, regarded him as her son, and gave him the name of MOSES *(from the water)*, because she had saved him from the water. He was duly instructed in the learning and science of the Egyptians—who were then, perhaps, the most cultivated people in the world; and it is said that in due time he rose to high employments, and rendered important services to the state.* At length, it seems to have been considered necessary that he should, by some legal form or ceremony, be recognised as "the son of Pharaoh's daughter," to qualify him for higher distinctions than he had yet attained. But when it came to this point, he refused the proposed adoption, and chose rather to take his part with the oppressed people to whom he by birth belonged. He repaired to the land of Goshen, and became an eye-witness of the misery which they still suffered. One day, seeing an Egyptian task-master beating an Israelite, he fell upon him, slew him, and hid his body in the sand. The next day, in endeavouring to pacify two quarrelling Israelites, he was treated with insult, and jeeringly reminded of what he had done the day before. Alarmed at finding that the deed was known, and fearing the vengeance of the Egyptians, Moses fled from the country without delay; being then forty years of age.

5. Moses travelled eastward, and came to a territory on the eastern arm of the Red Sea, occupied by a branch of the family descended from Midian, one of Abraham's sons by Keturah. Here, while resting beside a well, he interfered to protect seven young women of the country from some shepherds, and drew for them the water their flocks required. This led to his introduction to the father of these damsels, Jethro, the prince and priest of Midian, who persuaded the stranger from Egypt to take the charge of his flocks, and gave him in marriage Zipporah, one of his daughters. By her he had two sons, Gershom and Eliezer. Forty years Moses fed the flocks of Jethro, his father-in-law—at proper seasons leading them for pasture to the well-watered valleys of the

---

* This is not said in the Biblical narrative. But it is probable in itself, is affirmed by Josephus (Antiq. ii. 10), and is more than hinted at by St. Stephen, who, alluding to this period of Moses' life, says, he was "mighty in word and deed" (Acts vii.)

Sinai mountains.   At the end of that time, when he was in
this quarter, hard by the Mount Horeb, he was startled at
seeing a bush burning, and yet remaining unconsumed.   He
advanced to examine this wonder ; and as he drew near, the
voice of God called to him by name from out of the bush, forbidding him to come nearer, and admonishing him to take the
sandals from his feet in reverence of the Divine presence,
which rendered holy the ground on which he stood.   The
Voice then proceeded to announce that the cries of the oppressed Hebrews had entered heaven, and that the time was
now come to bring them forth from Egypt, and give them
possession of the Promised Land.

6. Moses himself was then required to become the agent
for working their deliverance ; but he shrunk from the responsibilities and care of this great commission.   He excused
himself by reason of his wanting that persuasive speech which
had power over men.   But, to meet this, his eloquent brother
Aaron was joined in the commission ; and when Moses persisted, on the ground that the Israelites were not likely to
listen to him, or to believe that he had been sent by the God
of their fathers, he was empowered to work miracles for their
conviction.   No longer able to refuse, Moses took leave of
Jethro, and returned to Egypt ; and as he approached the
land of Goshen, was met by Aaron, who had in a dream been
warned of his coming.   The brothers called together the
elders of Israel, and Moses opened to them his commission,
and confirmed it by the appointed miracles.   Having satisfied
them, they all repaired to the court of the reigning king, of
whom Moses demanded, in the name of JEHOVAH, the God of
the Hebrews, that the descendants of Israel should be allowed
to quit his dominions.   The Egyptians had, however, by this
time, found out the value of their forced services, and the
king flatly refused to listen to so extraordinary a proposal.
Indeed, affecting to consider such vain notions the effect of
idleness, he directed their labours to be increased, and their
bondage to be made more bitter.

7. Moses was then obliged to resort to " the plagues,"
which he was commissioned to inflict, in order to compel
Pharaoh to consent to their departure, and at the same time
to demonstrate the greatness and power of the God whom the

Hebrews worshipped. The heart of Pharaoh was **very hard,** and it required a succession of the most terrible inflictions to extort his consent. The waters were changed into blood; frogs, lice, and gnats, successively inundated the land; a murrain destroyed the cattle; the people were afflicted with painful and noisome ulcers; a tremendous hail-storm destroyed the fruits of the ground; clouds of locusts consumed all that the hail had left; and this was followed by a thick darkness which overspread all the land except that part which the Israelites occupied. By some cunning sleight, a few o these miracles were imitated by the Egyptian magicians, which much encouraged Pharaoh in his obstinacy. At times he wavered; but as at the end of all these plagues he still remained inexorable, one last and terrible infliction was threatened, and Moses was apprised that it would be effectual. This was no less than the sudden death of all the first-born in Egypt. Accordingly at midnight, the first-born, from the highest to the lowest, were smitten, and there was no house from which came not the wail for the dead. This calamity, like the others, touched not the Israelites, whose door-posts were sprinkled with the blood of a lamb offered up in sacrifice to God, according to his previous appointment. And that the memory of this signal distinction, when the Destroyer *passed over* the blood-sprinkled doors of the Israelites, and smote the first-born of the Egyptians only, might be preserved to all generations, the Lord instituted the feast of the PASS-OVER;* and as a further memorial, he directed that the first-born should henceforth be set apart for his service. Exod. vii. to xiii.

8. Although the king of Egypt had held out so long, his people had before this been anxious that the Israelites should be dismissed; and now they were no longer to be restrained. With their dead around them, and not knowing what might befall them next, they insisted on the instant departure of the Israelites. The king was not able to resist the popular impulse, and perhaps was not at the moment willing, for the first-born of the throne lay also dead. He gave his permission, and the people in every possible way urged and hastened their going forth. The Hebrews, however, took this opportunity

* This feast has been mentioned before, p. 116.

of universal consternation to demand* the wages of their long and laborious services; and the Egyptians in their eagerness to get them out of the country, were in no humour to contest the matter, but hastened to load them with "jewels of gold and jewels of silver," together with costly raiment. This, together with their numerous flocks and herds, caused the Israelites to go forth from Egypt a wealthy people. They had also become very numerous; for the men fit to bear arms amounted to six hundred thousand, which implies a total population of about two and a half millions;† besides these there was a large "mixed multitude," which chose rather to take their part with the Israelites than to remain in Egypt. Very probably a large proportion of these were foreigners who had, like the Israelites, been held in slavery by the Egyptians: the rest may have been Egyptians of the lower and more despised orders. At all events, this "mixed" body appears from the history to have formed the rabble of the immense multitude that quitted Egypt 215 years after Jacob and his family entered that country, and 430 years after the founder of the family went to the land of Canaan.

9. The ends for which that family had been sent into Egypt were now completely answered. Under the protection of the most powerful people in those parts, and in one of the most fertile countries of the world, they had rapidly multiplied into a great nation; so that, notwithstanding the ill feeling which ultimately prevailed, Egypt had been compelled to act as a nursing mother to Israel. During their residence in Egypt, the original character of the Israelites had been somewhat modified by intimacy with Egyptian habits and ideas, and by familiarity with Egyptian modes of life, though to a less degree than might have happened, had they not lived so much apart by themselves in the land of Goshen. Nevertheless, they must have acquired a knowledge of agriculture, and of the arts of settled and social life in which the Egyptians excelled, and so far they had undergone a useful training for their destined condition. And inasmuch as it was the divine intention that they should exchange the comparative

---

* Incorrectly rendered "borrow" in our version.

† Thus, the men fit to bear arms are seldom half the entire male population; and this again must be doubled for the females, who are never less, and generally more numerous than the males.

inertness of pastoral life for the cares and labours of agriculture, even the bitter bondage in Egypt may, in its real effect, have been a serviceable schooling of the nation into those habits of regular industry which their destined condition would require.   On the other hand, the iron of their bondage had entered into their soul; their religion had become tainted with the superstitions of Egypt; and their mind and character had acquired the hue which continued bondage never fails to impart.   They had become a timid, selfish, vain, idle, suspicious, unconfiding, mean, and ungenerous people.   It soon appeared that the generation which quitted Egypt was utterly unfit to enter Canaan; and several generations passed before the taint of the Egyptian bondage was wholly purged from the blood of Israel.

CHAPTER II. B. C. 1491.

	B. C.		B C
Passage of the Red Sea,	 1491	Defeat of Amalekites,	 1491
The first fall of Manna,	 1491	Arrival in Sinai,	 1491

1. WITH a view to the condition and character of the people, and their unfitness for immediate action, it was not the Divine intention that the emancipated Israelites should go directly and by the nearest way to the land of Canaan, entering it on the south-west, where the Philistines and other warlike tribes were stationed; but to go round by the desert and approach on the south-east, from which quarter they might get into the very heart of the country before any serious opposition could be encountered. But first they were to be led into the peninsula of Sinai, among the mountains where Moses had seen the burning bush, that they might there be properly organized, and receive the laws and institutions necessary to keep them as a peculiar people among the nations. In their march the Israelites could not be mistaken in their course; for a miraculous pillar, of cloud by day and of fire by night, went always before them to direct their way. They rested whenever it stood still, and whenever it moved they followed.

2. From Egypt the hosts of Israel marched towards the western arm* of the Red Sea, round the head of which lay the usual road to the peninsula of Sinai. On arriving at the sea, they encamped on its hither shore in such a manner that they had the sea before them and the mountains behind, and could only retreat by returning to Egypt by the way they came or by going round by the head of the gulf into the peninsula.

3. In the three days which had passed since the Israelites left Egypt, the alarm of the Egyptian king subsided into resentment for the calamities which Egypt had suffered for their sake; the loss of the services of so large a body of well-trained serfs, was also a matter of no small moment: and, therefore, when

* Now the Gulf of Suez.

he received information that they had encamped in so disadvantageous a position as that which has been described, he determined to follow them with his troops, and, by cutting off their retreat round the head of the gulf, either drive them back into Egypt by the way they came, or destroy them where they lay. Dreadful was the consternation of the Hebrews when the appearance of Pharaoh and his host made known to them their danger. Only a miracle could save them; and that miracle was wrought. At the command of God, Moses uplifted his rod over the waters, when immediately a strong wind arose, by which a broad track was opened through the sea for the passage of the chosen race, dryshod, to the other side, where, by the break of morning, they all arrived in safety. With marvellous temerity, Pharaoh, with his chariots and horsemen, entered in pursuit; when Moses,

108. Egyptian War Chariot.

from the further shore, again stretched forth his rod, and the waters suddenly returned and overwhelmed them all. This great event, which was celebrated by the daughters of Israel in triumphant hymns, had a most salutary effect upon the neighbouring nations, impressing them with a great dread of the mighty God by whom the Israelites were protected.

4. The now secure multitude tarried a short time at this place, and then marched southward for three days through the wilderness of Shur, where they began to be in want of water. This caused them to murmur greatly, especially when, on coming to Marah, they found water which was too bitter to be of any use. To pacify it Moses was instructed to cast a branch of a certain tree into it, and it then became sweet and drinkable. Their next resting-place was at Elim, where twelve wells, shaded by seventy palm trees, gave abundant water to the people and their flocks.

5. Journeying from Elim, the people having exhausted the provisions they had brought from Egypt, began to suffer hunger. On this they gave way to their usual unmanly wailings, and to the most ungenerous reflections upon their great leader. They forgot the miracles of God, and remembered only the "flesh pots" of Egypt. God rebuked them; but he promised that they should have meat in the evening, and in the morning bread to the full. This he made good by causing a vast flight of quails to rest that evening upon the camp; and of these large quantities were taken and dressed for food. And in the morning, when the dew was gone, the ground was found to be covered, as by hoar-frost, with small, round, white particles, like coriander seed for size and shape, and the taste of which was like fine bread sweetened with honey. The wondering inquiry *Man-hu?* (*what is this?*) which the Israelites addressed to one another on beholding it, caused this food to be called *Manna*. This proved to be the commencement of a supply of "bread from heaven," which was furnished daily, except on the Sabbaths, for forty years. Still advancing southward towards the upper region of Sinai, the Israelites passed over an arid tract of country and encamped at Rephidim. As no water was found at this place, the people broke forth into their usual murmurs; and on this occasion, so wild and fierce did their passions rise under the agonies of thirst, that Moses and Aaron were in danger of being stoned for having brought them to that wilderness, unless some immediate relief were given. Moses was instructed by God to take some of the elders as witnesses, and strike with his rod a rock in Horeb. He did so; and from that rock an abundant stream immediately broke forth and flowed to the Hebrew camp. Moses signalized this transaction by calling the place Massa (*temptation*), and Meribah (*strife*).

6. By this time the movements of the Israelites had attracted the attention of the inhabitants of the peninsula of Sinai; and that warlike tribe, the Amalekites, whose quarters the Hebrew host now approached, determined to assault them, stimulated, perhaps, by the hope of acquiring the Egyptian wealth with which they were laden. On this Moses directed a valiant young man named Joshua, who always attended him, to draw out a body of choice troops, and give the Amalekites battle on the morrow. The next morning when Joshua marched forth against the Amalekites, Moses, accompanied by his brother Aaron, and by Hur, ascended to the top of a mountain and prayed to God in view of the warriors and the people. It was soon discovered that while the hands of Moses were uplifted in prayer, Israel prevailed over Amalek; but that when his hands hung down in weariness, Amalek was the stronger; and, therefore, Aaron and Hur placed themselves beside the prophet and sustained his interceding hands until the evening, by which time the Amalekites were put to utter rout. This signal success in their first military enterprise greatly encouraged the Israelites; and by Divine authority and command, the race of Amalek was, for this first and most unprovoked act of hostility against the chosen people, devoted to utter extermination.

7. After this the Hebrews advanced to Mount Sinai, called also Mount Horeb, where the Lord had appeared to Moses in the burning bush. While the host remained encamped in the valleys below, Moses was frequently called up by the Lord into the mountain; and sometimes, by command, he took up Aaron, Nadab, Abihu, Joshua, and other principal persons, a part of the way with him; and they were permitted to behold that resplendence which is named "the glory of God." Never was the intercourse between God and a man made so obvious to the senses as it was at this time, with regard to Moses, upon this mountain; and the reason evidently was, that a weak-minded and suspicious people might be the more strongly convinced of his Divine mission, and the more readily obey him as their leader. An infant nation, circumstanced like the Israelites in leaving Egypt, required, more than an advanced people can well apprehend, that kind of evidence which may be seen and handled; and this consideration will be found to explain many circumstances in the history of the measures which God at this time took with the Israelites.

8. The first important act was to obtain from the assembled nation a distinct acknowledgment of the supreme authority of Jehovah, and the promise of implicit obedience to him. This was becomingly and cheerfully given by the people; and by that act they became a nation with the Lord himself for their King in a sense in which he never was the king of any other

people. **This it is** important to remember, as the clearness
of the history very much depends upon the recollection of the
fact, that the Lord was not only the God of the Israelites,
and of the whole world; and not only the King of the Israelites, in the same sense in which he was and is King and
Governor of the universe; but that he was, in a peculiar
sense, and for a peculiar purpose, their real political and
national King and Head, and as such entitled to direct the
affairs of the state, and to require political and civil obedience
from his people. His sovereign power being recognised, the
Lord appointed the third day after as that in which he would
appear with glory upon the mountain, to deliver the laws to
which he required obedience. Meanwhile the people were to
purify themselves against that day; and fences were placed
around the mountain, that none might trespass too near the
sacred presence.

9. On that day, being the fiftieth after the departure from
Egypt, the Lord descended upon the top of Mount Sinai, which
then trembled greatly, while the lightning flashed, and the
thunders rolled, and the summit was enveloped in a vast body
of flame, from which a great smoke arose. The awe-struck
multitude remained at the foot of the mountain; but Moses
and Aaron ascended, although only the former dared to enter
the cloud which veiled the presence of God. No *form* was
seen by the people or by Moses; but a VOICE was heard
giving utterance to the words of the Decalogue. So awful
was that voice, and so appalling were the circumstances, that
the people were struck with fear, and entreated that God
would henceforth make known to them his will through Moses,
and that they might thenceforth hear the VOICE and the
" mighty thunderings" no more. Accordingly, in successive
visits to the mountain, Moses received the great body of civil,
ceremonial, and political laws and institutions, which, on his
return, he wrote down as we now find them in the Pentateuch,
and read to the people. The greater number of these institutions were delivered to him on one occasion when he was
absent not less than forty days on the mountain, at the end
of which he received, written upon tables of stone, the ten
fundamental laws of the Decalogue, which had before been
orally delivered.

CHAPTER III.   B.C. 1491 to 1490

	B. C.		B. C.
The Law delivered . . .	1491	Aaron and his sons appointed	
Tabernacle completed . . .	1490	Priests	1490

1. During his absence, Moses left the charge of the people to Aaron and Hur. After long waiting, they gave him up for lost, and ceased to expect his return. The salutary restraint of his presence being thus withdrawn, the infatuated Israelites clamoured to Aaron for a sensible image or similitude of the God they worshipped, such as other nations had, that it might go before them, and be always among them. This was contrary to the very first law which the people had lately heard delivered from amidst the thunders of Sinai. From the prevalent danger of idolatry, they had been strictly enjoined not only not to worship other gods, but not to make any figure or similitude or symbol of the true God for the purpose of worship. But, heedless of this, the people persisted in their demand, and Aaron weakly yielded ; and of the ornaments which they

contributed, he caused to be made a golden calf—probably because under the form of a calf or young bull, the Egyptians worshipped their most popular god, Osiris. No sooner was the golden calf completed than Aaron proclaimed a feast to the Lord, which the people celebrated with

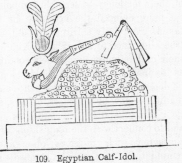

109. Egyptian Calf-Idol.

dances and heathenish sports, before the degrading symbol of his presence which they had set up.

2. Meanwhile, Moses was dismissed from his high conference with God on the clouded mountain top ; and in his descent, with the tables of the law in his hands, was joined

by the faithful Joshua, who had remained below. As they proceeded, they arrived at a point which commanded a view of the camp and the proceedings there. No sooner did the Prophet behold the people abandoning themselves to heathenish merriment before their idol, than he was seized with vehement indignation, and cast from him the tables of the law with such force that they were broken in pieces. He hastened forward, and his presence struck the crowd with dismay. He broke down and destroyed their image; and after reproving Aaron, called around him the men of his own tribe, the Levites, and ordered them to execute judgment on the revolters. Three thousand men fell in the slaughter which they made. After this, Moses was commanded to prepare two new tablets of stone, which he took up to the Mount, where they received the words which had been graven on the broken tables. When he came down from the Mount on this occasion, it was found that his countenance had become so radiant that the people were not able to look steadfastly at his face; and hence he covered his head with a veil.

3. Order being restored, Moses proceeded to execute the commands which he had received during his long stay in the Mount; and the recent exhibition which the people had made of their tendency to sensible symbols and material idols, only the more evinced the necessity for the measures which were taken. A purely spiritual worship of an invisible God, and a true allegiance to an invisible King, were beyond the reach of their understanding, and their condition. Therefore, in so far as his ineffable greatness could stoop to the littleness of man, he determined to make his presence among them felt by sensible manifestations, by ministers, officers, and ceremonies. He was their King; and he determined as such to dwell among them, and to connect with the requisitions of his peculiar and political character, such religious observances as would constantly remind them that he who stooped to be their King, was also their God, and the Lord of the universe.

4. In the first place, they were to provide for him a palace-temple, containing all things meet for the state of a Divine King; a throne, a table, an incense altar, a superb candelabrum,—all formed of, or overlaid with, the finest gold. The throne was the ark, the table that of shewbread. The

dwelling itself, the TABERNACLE, was necessarily so made as to be taken to pieces, and carried from place to place as occasion required. When standing it was an oblong structure fifty-five feet in length, by eighteen in breadth and in height, formed of acacia wood overlaid with plates of gold, and the whole overhung with rich palls and curtains. In the enclosure in front was erected a large but portable brazen-altar, on which were to be offered daily and occasional sacrifices; and here also was an immense basin or laver of the same metal, in which the ministers of the Divine King were to perform their ablutions. When the sacred edifice was completed and set up, the pillar of cloud, which has already been mentioned, moved from its previous station, and rested upon it; and a wondrous resplendence called the Shechinah, or "glory of God," filled the place, and ultimately concentrated over the ark, where it became the appropriate and abiding symbol of the Divine presence.

5. For the state of the Great King, ministers and officers were necessary. According to patriarchal usage, there was no distinct order of priesthood—such sacerdotal offices as their simple worship required being discharged by the first-born. In conformity with this, the first-born had, as we have seen, been set apart to the service of God on the departure from Egypt, with a further reference to a commemoration thereby of their preservation, when all the first-born of the Egyptians were destroyed. But now that the Israelites had evinced their need of a more ostensible system of worship, it was deemed proper, for the sake of better organization, that a whole tribe, instead of the first-born of all tribes, should be set apart for this service. The tribe of Levi, to which Moses and Aaron belonged, was therefore chosen for the general service of the theocratical government; and the family of Aaron was selected for the higher and more special services of the priesthood, Aaron himself being the high-priest. All these had peculiar dresses suitable to their service, which they were to use when they officiated: at other times they were dressed like the rest of the community. The dress of the high-priest was very splendid, especially by reason of a breast-plate of gold, in which were set twelve precious stones, on each of which was graven the name of a tribe in Israel. This was called the *Urim* and *Thummim*.

6. To support the court and ministers of the Great King, which involved also a provision for public worship, it was directed that the Levitical tribe should have one-tenth (tithe), and the first fruits of the produce of the fields and of the flocks. The tithe was what kings were in the habit of exacting for the support of the government, and as a sort of quit-rent for the soil, of which they were regarded the sovereign proprietors; and more than once does the Lord assert this right, as King, to the soil of Palestine. Besides, the tribe of Levi was to have no territorial inheritance; and as their exclusion left more for the other tribes, they had a claim of right to compensation from those tribes; for the few towns which were given to them for residence were no adequate compensation for their foregoing an equal heritage in the soil of the Promised Land.

7. The people worked with ardour, and contributed with liberality and zeal, in giving effect to all those designs and operations; for a gorgeous regality and theocracy, with a splendid court and imposing ritual, were exactly suited to their condition of mind, and gave them a feeling of importance and concentration, which they could not well have realized by any other means. Eight days after the solemn consecration of Aaron and his sons to the priesthood, their ministrations commenced by the first burnt-offering upon the altar. On that occasion the Lord was pleased to signify his complacency by the appearance of that "glory" or resplendence, of which we have so often spoken, and from which a fire now darted forth which consumed the burnt-offering that lay upon the altar. At this sign of favour and acceptance the people shouted and fell upon their faces in adoration (Lev. ix.) The fire thus kindled was commanded to be continually kept up (Lev. vi. 12, 13); nor was it lost until the Babylonish captivity. No fire but this was lawful in any ministerial service, as two of the sons of Aaron, called Nadab and Abihu, found to their cost; for when, through carelessness or wilful daring, they put common fire in their censers, and offered incense therewith, they were struck dead; a suffocating flame shot through and destroyed them, without injuring their bodies or their garments.

8. During the subsequent stay at Sinai, great pains were

taken to organise the vast body which now composed the
Hebrew nation. A census was taken, which exhibited nearly
the same result as the rough estimate given on quitting
Egypt, being rather more than 600,000 men fit to bear arms,
which, as we have shewn, is usually one-fourth of the entire
population (Num. i.)   A particular account of the order by
which the marchings and encampments of this vast host was
regulated is given in Num. ii.   This regulated movement
and orderly disposition must have been very imposing, whilst
nothing could be more effective for preventing confusion.
The tribes usually encamped so as to form a hollow square,
in the centre of which was the tabernacle, within a smaller
square formed by the tents of the sacerdotal tribe according
to the following order.

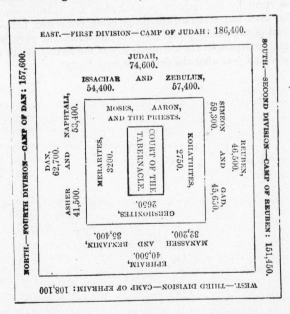

9. For the idea of another excellent arrangement, Moses
was indebted to Jethro, his father-in-law, who came from his
home, which was at no great distance, to congratulate the

Deliverer of Israel, and to bring to him his wife and two sons. During his stay this old man observed with concern the great labour which Moses had taken upon himself, in hearing the complaints and determining the differences of so great a people; and fearing that he would soon be utterly worn out by such incessant labour, he counselled him to commit the hearing of secondary causes to subordinate officers, some over thousands, some over hundreds, some over fifties, and some over tens—reserving for his own hearing only the weightier causes, and appeals from the inferior tribunals. This counsel being approved, was put into immediate execution, and the order thus established was long after preserved among the Israelites.

10. In the sequestered wilderness of Sinai, nearly a year was spent by the Hebrew people, when, the constitution of their civil and ecclesiastical polity being completed, the removal of the cloudy pillar from off the tabernacle, gave the signal to depart, in the twentieth day of the second month of the second year after the departure from Egyp

CHAPTER IV.   B.C. 1490 TO 1489.

	B.C.		B.C.
The Israelites leave Sinai	1490	Their ill report of the land discourages	
Supply of Quails	1490	the people	1490
Sedition of Miriam and Aaron	1490	Sentence to wander 40 years in the	
Arrival at Kadesh Barnea	1490	Desert	1490
Spies sent into Canaan	1490	Leave Kadesh Barnea	1489

1. IN the journey from Sinai to the frontiers of Canaan, several occurrences evinced the still intractable and unmanly character of the people, and their unfitness to receive the inheritance promised to their fathers. The renewed fatigues and privations of travel through the Desert soon raised their murmurs, which, at the third stage, became so outrageous, that their Divine King manifested his displeasure by causing a fire to rage in the outskirts of the camp, which was only stayed at the intercession of Moses, when the people recognised the hand of God. Hence the place was called Taberah (*the burning*).

2. The next offence commenced among the "mixed multitude" which accompanied the Hebrew host, but involved many of the Israelites. Whatever fortitude they had, soon gave way before the privations of the Desert. There was, indeed, plenty of manna; but they had grown dainty, and "their souls loathed that light food." They lamented that they had ever left Egypt, and remembered, with tender regret, the cooling melons, the leeks, the onions, the garlick, and the other fruits and vegetables which they had enjoyed in abundance; as well as the fish and the meat, which in that rich land they had "eaten to the full." All this greatly oppressed the spirit of Moses, and his address to God on that occasion marks his deep despondency. To comfort him, and to enable him the better to sustain his heavy charge, he was directed to choose seventy competent men from the elders of Israel, who should act as a council, and assist him in the government of the people. These being nominated by Moses, were to be brought to the door of the tabernacle, where the Divine King gave undoubted signs of their acceptance.

3. As to the murmuring people, it was promised—not in kindness, but in anger—that on the morrow, and for a month after, they should have "meat to the full." Accordingly, the miracle of the quails was repeated; and so abundant was the supply of these birds, that not only were the people able to glut themselves for the time, but to preserve a great quantity for future use. In the midst of their over-feeding on this meat, their incensed God caused a terrible plague to break out among them, whereby great numbers were destroyed. Excessive indulgence in a kind of food to which people have not been lately accustomed, produces a mortal fever well known to travellers; and this was probably the instrument employed in punishing the gluttonous people, who found a grave at Kibroth Hattaavah (*the graves of hungering*).

4. At Hazeroth, the spirit of opposition to Moses broke out in his own family, in consequence of his having married the foreign woman Zipporah, who had lately been brought among them. Miriam, the sister of Moses, who had previously held the chief place among the women in Israel, and who was now probably jealous of the respect paid to the wife of Moses, was the leader in this affair, and was soon joined by Aaron, who probably feared the influence which the newly arrived family were likely to acquire in prejudice to his own sons, on whom the priesthood had been conferred. At all events, their feeling was bad, and as the expression of it tended to undermine the authority of Moses, the Lord testified his displeasure by smiting Miriam with leprosy, and as a leper she was excluded from the camp. But in seven days she was restored at the intercession of Moses, after Aaron had humbled himself, and acknowledged their joint offence.

5. Nothing remarkable occurred in the march through the wilderness of Paran until the arrival at Kadesh Barnea, on the southern border of the Promised Land, when Moses encouraged the people to proceed boldly, and take possession of thei heritage. But they betrayed some diffidence, and resolved first to send twelve spies, one from each tribe, to traverse the country, and to bring them an account of the land and its inhabitants. After an absence of forty days, the spies came back with a large cluster of grapes, and other fruits of the country—many of which were new to men from

Egypt. Of the country itself, and of its productions, they gave a very glowing account; but the inhabitants they described as warlike and, in some places, gigantic, dwelling in high-walled and seemingly impregnable cities; and they declared it as their opinion, that however desirable the country, the Israelites were by no means equal to the conquest of it from the present inhabitants. This statement filled the timorous multitude with dismay; and they threatened to stone two of the spies, Joshua and Caleb, who proclaimed their conviction that, with the Divine aid, which was promised to them, they were fully equal to the enterprize. Breaking out into open mutiny, they even talked of appointing a leader to conduct them back to their bondage in Egypt.

6. For this last melancholy display of their utter unfitness for the promised inheritance, of their insensibility to the great things which had been done for them, and of their gross incapacity of comprehending his great designs, the Lord's anger was greatly kindled against them. The mysterious "glory" suddenly appeared in the cloud which rested upon the tabernacle; and that manifestation of the present God struck mute every clamorous tongue, and filled all hearts with fear. The Divine voice now threatened instant extinction to the revolters, and promised to make of Moses and his family a nation greater and mightier than they. This offer had been made on a former occasion, and was then, as now, reverently declined by the disinterested prophet; and he and his brother lay prostrate before the cloud, with their faces to the ground, interceding for the people. Their prayer had power with God, and the doom of instant death and disinheritance was averted. But it was pronounced that not one of the tainted generation—composed of those who were of full age on leaving Egypt—should enter the Promised Land; but that they should wander for forty years* to and fro in the wilderness, until they were all dead, and until their children had grown up into a generation fitter than they to receive the heritage of Abraham. From this doom only the two faithful spies, Joshua and Caleb, were exempted: the ten others were smitten with that instant death which their conduct deserved (Num. xiv.)

* Forty years from the departure from Egypt, nearly 38 from this point of time.

7. This awful denunciation had the remarkable, but not unnatural, effect of driving the Israelites from their childish timidity to the very opposite extreme of unauthorised and presumptuous rashness. The Canaanites and Amalekites had already taken alarm, and possessed themselves of the passes in the mountains which lay before the Hebrew host. Notwithstanding this advantage on the side of the enemy, and in spite of the earnest remonstrances of Moses, a large body of the Israelites determined to march forward and take possession of the country. They were driven back with great slaughter; and immediately after, in obedience to the Divine mandate, the camp at Kadesh Barnea was broken up, and the people conducted back into the desert towards the Red Sea.

8. Here, in the deserts between Palestine and Sinai, they wandered their appointed time, the generation which received the law in Horeb becoming gradually extinct. During all this time they continued to lead the same pastoral or Bedouin life as they had done before, living on manna and the produce of their flocks and herds; and removing from one station to another, as directed by the pillared cloud which rested upon the tabernacle.

CHAPTER V. B.C. 1489 to 1452.

PATRIARCHS.		EGYPT.		EVENTS AND PERSONS.	
	B. C.		B. C.		B. C
ebellion of Korah .	1471	Amunoph II. . .	1456	Danaus arrives (in a ship) from Egypt, and possesses himself of Argos . .	1481
Return to Kadesh Barnea	1453				
Death of Aaron .	1453			The Olympic games first celebrated at Elis	1453
The Fiery Serpents	1452				

1. DURING all this period, only one event of much importance is recorded. This was a very serious revolt against the theocratical government, by persons of high rank and consequence in some of the tribes. The rebels were heads of families and clans, who would have possessed high civil power, and would have exercised priestly functions under the patriarchal government: and their attempt must be regarded as a struggle of the old institutions against the new. In some shape or other, such a conflict almost always takes place between new forms of government and the ancient institutions which are altered or superseded. A settled and central government absorbs the power which, in a ruder state of society, is exercised by individuals over small sections of the general body; and these are commonly too fond of power to relinquish it without a struggle. Among the Hebrews, the supreme authority under which the new institutions had been framed, kept the great body of the natural heads of tribes and families quiet, whatever may have been their secret discontent; but there were some audacious spirits whom even this consideration could not restrain.

2. Korah, although himself a Levite, appears to have been the chief instigator of this revolt. His birth and station would have entitled him to a leading place in the tribe; and it is more than probable that another family being appointed to the priesthood, was the chief cause of his discontent. This, however, was not a ground on which he could expect much support from the chiefs of other tribes; and it was therefore pretended, that the liberties of the people

had been infringed by Moses and Aaron; and that the heads of families had been unjustly deprived of the sacerdotal and other powers, which naturally belonged to them. The manner in which the high-priesthood had been made a high political office in a theocracy, exposed the priesthood to the jealousy which it might have escaped had its duties been only sacerdotal.

3. Besides Korah, two chiefs of the tribe of Reuben, Dathan and Abiram, are named as the principal malcontents; and it will be remembered, that this tribe, descended from the first-born of Jacob, had, as regards the civil and sacerdotal rights of primogeniture, suffered more than any other by the existing institutions, which gave the civil pre-eminence to Judah, and the sacerdotal to Levi. Two hundred and fifty other chiefs, probably from the different tribes, joined in this conspiracy, the very grave character of which may be estimated from the description of these persons as " princes of the assembly, famous in the congregation, men of renown' (Num. xvi. 2).

4. The people appear to have been well disposed to listen to those who told them that they had cause to be discontented; that their liberties had been taken from them; and that the yoke of a central government was too heavy to be borne. The leaders, therefore, being supported by a large body of the " congregation," at length openly charged Moses and Aaron with the usurpation of civil and pontifical power, and required them to lay it down. It was admitted that the appointments of the Divine King were absolute; but it was denied that it was, or could be, his intention that such powers should be vested in their hands. This they could only dispute by indirectly doubting the testimony of Moses, who brought this institution with him on his return from the Mount; and it was clear that, if his legislative agency in this matter could be set aside, an opening was made for overturning the whole system which rested on the same foundation. This was, no doubt, secretly understood on all sides: hence Moses at once saw that a special manifestation that the Aaronic priesthood was a Divine appointment, had become necessary, not only to establish that institution, but for the confirmation of the whole system, of which that was an inte-

gral part : and, in the confidence that God would vindicate his own appointments, Moses was content to refer the matter to him. After some strong words of reproof, he therefore invited the leading conspirators to exercise on the morrow, by offering incense, the sacerdotal functions to which they laid claim, and then the Lord would doubtless make known his own decision. Awful was that decision! As they stood with their censers to offer incense, they were suddenly consumed by fire from His presence: and the Reubenites, Dathan and Abiram, who had refused to attend, did not escape; for the earth opened and engulphed them where they stood, with their tents and all that belonged to them.

5. The discontent which these unhappy men had encouraged among the people, was too widely spread, and too deeply rooted, for even this awful judgment to subdue. The turbulent mob were, indeed, struck with present horror and alarm at the destruction of their leaders; but the next day they rallied, and assembled in great numbers, clamouring against Moses and Aaron, as if they were the authors of that judgment which the wrath of God had inflicted. Now again was the Divine wrath kindled, and a consuming plague went forth among the people. They fell, like corn before the reaper, until Aaron, at the desire of Moses, took a censer, with burning incense, and rushing forth among the people, stood between the living and the dead, when the plague was stayed. On this occasion fourteen hundred people perished (Num. xvi.)

6. The destruction of those who unwarrantably pretended to sacerdotal functions, and the honour put upon Aaron by the plague being stayed at his intercession in his priestly character, were calculated to settle all real doubt regarding his appointment. But to place this matter beyond controversy, the Divine King was pleased to grant a special and abiding miracle. Moses was directed to take a rod from each of the tribes, and to engrave upon each rod the name of the tribe to which it belonged, but upon the rod of Levi to write Aaron's name. All these rods were laid up in the tabernacle, before the ark, God having signified that he would cause to blossom the dry rod of the man chosen and appointed by him. The next day the rods were brought

forth and delivered to those to whom they belonged, when it was found that the rod of Aaron had budded, blossomed, and borne ripe almonds. The rod which became the witness that Aaron had been divinely appointed to the priesthood, was directed to be laid up among the muniments of the tabernacle.

7. At length the forty years, during which the Israelites had been doomed to wander in the wilderness, were nearly expired, and the generation which, by their disobedience, had forfeited their title to the Promised Land, had perished. The new generation, although far from faultless, was, upon the whole, much superior to that which had passed away, and better fitted for the promised inheritance. As the time drew nigh, the host returned to the borders of Canaan, and we again find it encamped at Kadesh, whence it had formerly been sent back into the desert. Miriam, the sister of Moses and Aaron, died here; and here the brothers themselves forfeited their claim to enter the Promised Land. The want of water was experienced at Kadesh with so much severity, that the people became clamorous and reproachful. By this Moses and Aaron were so much disturbed, that, when instructed to smite a certain rock, from which water should then flow, they exhibited such impatience and distrust as, if left unpunished, might have had an injurious effect on the minds of the people. They were therefore interdicted from entering Canaan; but, at his earnest entreaty, Moses was promised a distant view of that "goodly land" which the Lord had promised to his people.

8. Considering the strength of the southern frontier of Canaan, and the warlike character of the inhabitants, it seemed much less desirable that the Israelites should invade the country on that side, and fight their way northward, than that they should at once enter a central and comparatively undefended part of the land. This could only be achieved by passing northward over into the country east of the Dead Sea, and crossing the Jordan into the heart of Palestine. From Kadesh, the nearest way to the east country was through a great valley in the mountains of Seir, which, however, could not be traversed with safety, if any resistance were made by its inhabitants the Edomites. An

embas.y was therefore sent to the king of Edom to remind him of the fraternity of the two nations, and request permission to pass through his country. This request, although couched in the most civil and respectful language, met with a direct and churlish refusal. It was therefore determined to return to the head of the eastern arm of the Red Sea, from which it was easy to pass to the other side of the Seir mountains. On the way they had to pass by Mount Hor, one of the loftiest of these mountains, at the base of which they encamped. Upon that mountain Aaron died, and was buried; and his tomb is still seen afar off by those who travel in that solitary region. He was succeeded in the pontificate by his eldest son Eleazer (Num. xx.)

9. Before the Israelites quitted this place, they were unexpectedly attacked by the Canaanitish king Arad, who took some of them prisoners. For this they in due season took ample vengeance, by the extermination of his tribe, and the desolation of the land in which it dwelt.

10. The hosts of Israel on reaching Kadesh had fully expected that they were immediately to enter the Promised Land. They were, therefore, much discouraged at having to take another troublesome journey through so unpleasant a wilderness as that which bordered the land of Edom; and, by the time they reached the vicinity of the Red Sea, they broke forth into loud complaints for bread and water, and expressed their distaste at the manner in which they had been fed for nearly forty years, saying, " our soul loatheth this light food." For this impatience, and for the contempt of God's merciful provision, without which they must long ago have perished, the serpents, which infested, and do still infest that region, were sent among them in unwonted numbers, and whoever was bitten by them died. On this the people confessed their sin, and sought the intercession of Moses, who was instructed to make a serpent of brass, and elevate it upon a pole in the midst of the camp; and those who looked upon it were instantly cured. The brazen serpent was preserved as a memorial of this miracle for about 900 years, when, because the people were disposed to render it idolatrous honours, it was destroyed by king Hezekiah.

CHAPTER VI.

	B.C.			B.C.
The Israelites cross the Arnon	1452	The Midianites smitten	.	1452
Sihon and Og defeated . .	1452	The people numbered	. .	1452
Balak and Balaam	. 1452	Moses dies .	.	1451

1. THE Israelites passed, without molestation, along the eastern border of Mount Seir, and through the country of Moab, and encamped by the river Arnon. Of the country immediately to the north of that river, the descendants of Lot had before this time been dispossessed, by a colony of the Amorites from the other side of the Jordan. As it was an early law of nations, of which we have had a previous instance, that a body of armed men could not pass through a country without permission from the sovereign, Moses sent ambassadors to Heshbon to ask that permission. This was not only refused by King Sihon, but he went forth with an army to fight against the Israelites, and to drive them back. Hearing this, the Hebrews did not await his attack, but advanced to meet im half way; and having routed him at Jahaz, they acquired possession of a very fine country, rich in pastures, and full of towns and cities. This acquisition brought them into the neighbourhood of Bashan, whose king, Og, was descended from the old gigantic race by whom the country was originally inhabited. To give an idea of his bulk and stature, the sacred historian informs us that his bedstead was of iron, and that its length was thirteen feet and a half, and its width six. This monarch prepared to resent the defeat and slaughter of his friend and neighbour; and the Israelites were somewhat dismayed when he appeared against them; but being encouraged by Moses with assurances of success, they fought bravely, and slew the monarch and dispersed his host. Thus the Israelites became possessed of the countries of Gilead and Bashan, east of the Jordan, although their views had in the first instance been confined to the region west of that river.

2. The Israelites now moved their encampment from the banks of the Arnon to the district of country near the northern extremity of the Dead Sea, called the Plains of Moab, as having once been in the territory of the Moabites. That nation was not at all pleased with these transactions. On entering the land of Moab, the Israelites had been cautioned to respect their descent from Lot, and offer them no molestation; and the Moabites, on their part, although they regarded the new-comers with no good will, were afraid to oppose them. Now, however, that the Hebrews had acquired such important possessions on that side of the river, a considerable portion of which had once belonged to the descendants of Lot, the wish to wound or crush this new power became very strong, and was only kept inoperative by a salutary dread of the consequences. At length Balak the king of Moab recollected a famous prophet who lived beyond the Euphrates, and fancied that if he could get him to come and lay a curse upon the Israelites, they might afterwards be attacked and destroyed with ease. He therefore sent an honourable embassy, with the promise of high distinctions and costly gifts, to tempt Balaam from his distant home. The covetous prophet was willing enough to earn the wages of iniquity; but being forbidden in a vision to go, he sent back the messengers with that intimation. Balak, however, believing that the objection was only urged with the view of extorting a higher bribe, again sent a more dignified embassy, with the offer of still greater rewards. Knowing already the Divine will, Balaam ought at once to have rejected these offers, and sent the messengers home; but, overcome by his avarice, he invited them to stay, and promised to make another effort to get leave to go with them. Displeased at this conduct, God left him to take his own course, and in the morning he joyfully mounted his ass to accompany the messengers of Balak.

3. On the way, however, he met with an unexpected check. In a narrow road, he was stopped by an angel with a drawn sword. The angel was at first only visible to the ass; and the obstinate refusal of the animal to proceed, so provoked Balaam, that he beat him most severely. On this

G

the beast was gifted for the moment with a human voice, in which he remonstrated against this treatment, and intimated that there was a cause for his obstinacy. That cause became instantly visible to the confounded prophet, who humbled himself before the angel, and offered to return home; but was allowed to proceed, with the strict caution that on his arrival he should speak and act only as directed (Num. xxii.) He was received with great honour by the king of Moab, who, intent upon his design, lost no time in taking Balaam, first, to the high places of Baal, then to the top of Pisgah, and the third time to the top of Mount Peor; from which, severally, he could view, first the whole, and then different parts of the Hebrew camp. At all these places altars were set up by Balaam's direction, and sacrifices offered. On each occasion the king wished the prophet to lay his curse upon the people before him; and Balaam was more than willing to gratify him; but he was constrained not only to abstain from cursing the Israelites, but to bless them altogether, and to utter the regretful but vain wish that his own portion were with them in life and in death. The king was displeased that he had brought a blessing upon those he intended to curse; and to pacify him, as well as to evince that he had acted contrary to his own will, Balaam proceeded to point out what he considered the most likely way to inflict a real injury upon the Israelites. He taught the king that none could injure that people while they remained faithful to their God, and had him for their defender; and that, therefore, the true way to weaken them was to endeavour to seduce them from their allegiance to him—in which seduction he intimated that the women of Moab and of Midian might be employed.

4. This atrocious counsel was eagerly followed by the princes of Moab and Midian. The latter nation were neighbours of the former, and took an active part with them in their underhand plots against the Israelites. A seemingly friendly intercourse was encouraged; and the women of Moab and Midian, the latter especially, succeeded in drawing very many of the Israelites into the worship of their own idols. But this could not last. Idolatry was now a capital crime

by the law, having been made an act of treason against the Divine head of the theocratical government. Moses, therefore, directed the judges to enforce the law, in consequence of which the chief of those who had followed Baal-Peor (the great idol of these parts) were "hanged up before the Lord." A mortal plague was also sent forth among the people to punish them for their idolatry and lust. Twenty-four thousand were destroyed by this pestilence, before its ravages were stayed through the Divine complacency at the zealous act of Phinehas, the son of the high-priest, in slaying with his own hand Zimri, a prince of Simeon, and one of the fair idolatresses of Midian, whom he brought to his tent at the very time that the people stood lamenting their sin and its punishment (Num. xxv.)

5. Moses was also commissioned to punish the Midianites by warring against them. A thousand men from each tribe were entrusted with this service, which they discharged with exemplary severity; for, being conquerors in battle, they made tremendous havoc among the Midianites, and took a large number of female captives, with an immense spoil in cattle and rich goods and ornaments. The Moabites were less severely punished; but for their conduct on this and other occasions, it was decreed that, for ten generations to come, they, notwithstanding their near relationship, should be counted as strangers to Israel.

6. The tribes of Reuben and Gad, and half the tribe of Manasseh, having large possessions in flocks and herds, and observing that the conquered country on the east of the Jordan was rich in pasturage, applied to Moses that it should be given to them for their portion of the promised inheritance. As they explained that they sought not this for the sake of an earlier provision, or with a view to abandon the general cause, but were willing that their own men should go and assist the other tribes in the conquest of Canaan, their est was granted.

7. Now that the host of Israel was composed of almost entirely new men, and that they were about to enter upon unwonted military actions, it was important that a fresh enumeration of the population should be taken. The comparison between it and the census taken thirty-nine years before in

Sinai affords some interesting information. The details are shewn in the table.

Tribes.	Chap. I.	Chap. XXVI.	Increase.	Decrease.
Reuben	46,500	43,730	...	2,770
Simeon	59,300	22,200	...	37,100
Gad	45,650	40,500	...	5,150
Judah	74,600	76,500	1,900	...
Issachar . . .	54,400	64,300	9,900	...
Zebulun . . .	57,400	60,500	3,100	...
Ephraim . . .	40,500	32,500	...	8,000
Manasseh . . .	32,200	52,700	20,500	...
Benjamin . . .	35,400	45,600	10,200	...
Dan	62,700	64,400	1,700	...
Asher . . .	41,500	53,400	11,900	...
Naphtali . . .	53,400	45,400	...	8,000
	603,550	601,730	59,200	61,020
			Decrease on the whole . .	} 1,820
Levites, from a } month old }	22,273	23,000	727	...

8. From this comparison it appears that the population which had increased so rapidly in Egypt, had rather decreased in the wilderness. This is clearly a result of the Divine determination to remove by death in forty years the whole of those who were past twenty on quitting Egypt, in consequence of which there could at this time be no old men in the congregation; and as the total population was nearly the same as when the Israelites commenced their journey, there must have been a great increase of the young, seeing there were none above sixty years old except Moses himself, who was soon to die, and Joshua and Caleb, who alone of the past generation were to enter the land of promise. The absence of aged and superannuated members exhibits a strange and singular social condition; and while their removal by death was intended in the first instance as a judgment, it at the same time gave a character of remarkably unencumbered physical efficiency to the generation on which the conquest of Canaan devolved. But although the full number is so nearly the same, it is surprising to notice the very great changes of proportion in the several tribes—such as the increase of 20,500 in Manasseh, 11,900 in Asher, and 10,200 in Benjamin; and the decrease of 37,100 in Simeon, and of

8000 in Ephraim and in Naphtali. On both occasions the number of Judah was the highest; but on the first occasion the lowest (omitting Levi) was Manasseh, and on the second, Simeon. At the first enumeration, the number of Judah more than doubled that of Manasseh, Benjamin, and Levi, and nearly doubled those of Reuben, Gad. Ephraim, and Asher. At the second, Judah more than doubled Simeon, Ephraim, and Levi, and nearly doubled Reuben, Benjamin, and Naphtali. Levi was the lowest in both accounts; much lower, indeed, than appears; for in that tribe all the males above a month old were counted, but in the other tribes only those fit to bear arms, or above twenty years of age. The enumeration being, as before, made only with reference to the adult male population, we must quadruple the amount to find the actual population, including women and children, and this, as before, we must necessarily estimate at about 2,500,000.

9. All this being accomplished, it only remained for Moses to die, and leave to other hands the task of conducting the children of Abraham into their promised inheritance. He therefore prepared for death by giving to the people who had so long been the objects of his solicitude, such directions and counsel as their circumstances appeared to require. After describing the boundaries of the Promised Land, he appointed the mode in which it should be divided among the several tribes, and directed that cities should be appropriated by each of them for the residence of the Levites who had no territorial inheritance, and that six of these cities should be regarded as places in which those who undesignedly or in self-defence slew others, might hold their lives safe from the avenger of blood (Num. xxxiv., xxxv.)

10. After this Moses repeated the law which had been given on Mount Sinai to the people, a great proportion of whom had been born since it was delivered, or were too young to hold it in remembrance. He also recapitulated the acts of Divine mercy towards them, and judgment upon them, since the departure from Egypt; and enjoined upon them the duty of destroying all the idols of Canaan, and of rooting out the doomed inhabitants. Then he renewed with the people, in the name of JEHOVAH, the covenant which had been made

in Sinai, and delivered the book of the law to the care of
the Levites, with directions to lay it up in the side of the ark.
These particulars form the contents of the book of Deutero-
nomy.

11. The official duties of this great and good man being
now terminated, he delivered to the assembled people an
address, in which he described, in the most vivid language,
the perverseness and disobedience of the nation, their punishment, repentance, and pardon. Lastly, he took leave of all
the tribes, together and severally, in an eloquent and pathetic
blessing, such as that which Jacob delivered to his sons before
he died. Then, as he had been commanded, Moses ascended
to the top of Pisgah, and took from thence a wide survey of
" the pleasant land," to whose borders he had led a nation.
And there he died unseen; and he was buried secretly, and
not by mortal hands; for it was feared that if the Israelites
knew the place of his sepulture, they might in the end be
tempted to pay divine honours to his remains. At the time
of his death Moses was 120 years of age, and we are told that
he was exempt from the usual infirmities of age—that " his
eye was not dim, nor his natural force abated."

BOOK III.

CHAPTER I.   B.C. 1451.

	B. C.		B. C
The Israelites cross the Jordan	1451	Jericho taken and destroyed	1451
Circumcision restored	1451	The offence of Achan	1451
The manna ceases	1451	Ai taken by stratagem	1451

1. AFTER the death of their great lawgiver, the Israelites remained encamped on the "plains of Moab," awaiting the order to advance to the arduous enterprise of dispossessing nations greater, mightier, and better armed and disciplined than themselves; more experienced in the art of war, and dwelling in fortified towns, with all the resources of the country at their command. So disproportionate seemed the situation of the invaders and the invaded, as to natural and acquired advantages, that the former, if they had looked to them only, might have been excused for regarding the result with some anxiety and apprehension. Certainly the Canaanites, regarded as a settled and valiant people, assailed by a comparatively undisciplined horde from the desert, may very well be spared the pity which some perverse understandings bestow upon them, as if they were so many sheep awaiting slaughter at the hands of the Israelites. The disproportion was indeed so much to the disadvantage of the Hebrews, that, to render the balance somewhat more equal, the Lord saw fit that the operations should commence by a series of special and signal acts of his own providence, to encourage the chosen people, and to dismay their enemies. Indeed the marvels which had attended their deliverance from Egypt, and their progress through the wilderness, were well known to the Canaanites, and had inspired them with dread—not of the Israelites themselves, whom they probably despised as enemies—but of the God, the mighty and terrible God, who fought on their behalf.

2. In the plain on the other side of the river stood the city of Jericho, which must evidently be the first object of attack after the passage of the river. Joshua, therefore, sent spies to that place to collect information, and to ascertain the sentiments of the people. The spies were lodged by a woman named Rahab, who also concealed them when they were inquired for by the authorities of the place; and from her they received the encouraging information that the Canaanites were already dispirited:—"Your terror is fallen upon us," she said, "and all the inhabitants of the land faint because of you.........As soon as we had heard these things, our hearts did melt; neither did there remain any more courage in any man because of you; for the Lord your God, he is God in heaven above, and in earth beneath." It was, in fact, thus to glorify his own great name, by forcing the conviction of His pre-eminence in power upon even those who did not serve him, that the Lord had wrought the wonders of which the Israelites were to reap the benefit.

3. The design of the Israelites to establish themselves in Palestine, and to root out the old inhabitants, was perfectly well known to the Canaanites; but they appear to have made no extraordinary preparations to repel the invaders,—trusting, probably, to the obstacle which at this time the river Jordan appeared to offer to their further progress; for it was the time of the barley harvest, when the river, swollen with the latter rains and the melted snows, overflowed its banks, and ran with the fullest stream to the Dead Sea. In this calculation they underrated the power of that Almighty arm which they had already learned to dread.

4. At length the order came to pass the river on a given day; and this order was accompanied with a distinct confirmation to Joshua of his high and glorious office, attended with the assurance that, while he adhered to the spirit and principles of the theocracy, none of those who opposed him should be able to stand before him. This appointment was recognised with acclamations by the people, who readily covenanted their obedience : and with them Joshua appears to have been at all times very popular; nor was his administration disturbed by such discontents and seditions as had disgraced the Israelites in the time of Moses.

5. The day appointed for the passage of the Jordan was the tenth day of the first month, only five days being wanting to complete forty years since the departure of the Hebrews from Egypt. On that day, the ark of the covenant was borne in solemn state by the priests, about one thousand yards before the people on their march to the river's brink. No sooner had the feet of the priests touched the water, than the course of the river at that point was stayed. The waters above suspended their course, while those below hastened into the Dead Sea, leaving the bed of the river dry for the hosts of Israel to pass over. The priests bearing the ark entered, and stood in the mid-channel, under the wall of waters, until all the hosts of Israel had gone over. Then the priests also left the river's bed ; and no sooner had they reached the bank, than the suspended waters resumed their course. As a standing memorial of this stupendous miracle, twelve large stones from the bed of the river were set up in the plain ; and twelve stones from the shore were deposited in the bed of the river.

6. At the place where the stones were set up, namely, at Gilgal in the plain of Jericho, the Israelites formed their first encampment in Canaan. Instead of proceeding to take advantage of the panic with which this event had inspired the inhabitants, as mere human policy would have dictated, by at once marching against them, the Israelites were directed to the observance of the details of that covenant under which they claimed their inheritance. Therefore, in the first place, the rite of circumcision, which had been intermitted during the sojourn in the wilderness, was renewed, and all the persons, forty years old and under, who had been born since the departure from Egypt, were taken into the Abrahamic covenant by being circumcised at Gilgal. They were then in a condition to observe the passover, the time for which had come round ; and this was the third celebration of that remarkable ordinance, as it had been entirely neglected since the second celebration in Sinai. The day after the passover they began to eat the corn, the fruits, and other products of the soil of Canaan ; and then the miraculous supply of manna, by which they had been so long fed, altogether ceased. It should be observed that the tabernacle was set up at Gilgal, and that it remained there during the seven years employed

in the conquest of Canaan.   Gilgal may, therefore, be regarded
as the head-quarters of the Israelites throughout that period.

7. When Joshua was one day surveying the strong defences
of Jericho, a person with a drawn sword in his hand appeared
suddenly before him.   He announced himself as the " Captain
of the Lord's host," and commanded Joshua to take the sandals
off his feet, because the ground was holy on which he stood
The prostration and worship rendered by the Hebrew chief on
this occasion indicates that this was the same mysterious
being who had spoken to Moses from the burning bush.   His
object was to encourage Joshua, by directing his attention to
the fact, that the success of the great enterprise before him
depended not upon his own skill and valour, or upon the endur-
ance and courage of his forces, but upon the assistance of the
Almighty, who had covenanted to bestow the land upon them,
and who would ensure the victory to his people in every contest which they undertook with a becoming confidence in their
Divine leader.   To evince this, in the first instance, means
were to be taken in the siege of Jericho which would be wholly
inoperative under ordinary circumstances, and which would,
therefore, refer the victory solely to that Almighty arm which
was made bare to fight for the chosen people.   Accordingly, the
army was directed to march round the city in solemn state
on six successive days, preceded by the ark, before which went
seven priests with rams'-horn trumpets in their hands.   This
seemingly idle parade probably occasioned nothing but wonder
to the people of Jericho, whom we may conceive crowding
the walls to behold the spectacle.   On the seventh day this
circumambulation was repeated seven times, and at the completion of the seventh circuit, the priests blew a long blast
with their trumpets, and the people raised a tremendous shout.
At that instant the strong walls of Jericho fell level with the
ground, and free ingress was offered on every side to the
Israelites, who, the place having before been put under a ban
of devotement to utter ruin, slew every living creature with
the sword, excepting only the family of the woman, Rahab
by whom the spies had been entertained.   Josh. vi.

8. Not only every living creature in Jericho had been
devoted to extinction, but all the effects were to be destroyed,
save articles of precious metal, which were to be consecrated

to the Lord, and laid up for the service of the Tabernacle. But a man named Achan, of the tribe of Judah, overcome by covetousness, appropriated to his own use, and concealed in his tent, a costly garment of Babylonish work, which should have been destroyed, and an ingot of gold, which should have been consecrated to the Lord. The disgraceful repulse and flight of a party which had been sent to take the neighbouring town of Ai, filled Joshua with anxiety and alarm,—such a circumstance being likely to impair that confidence of assured success which had thus far encouraged the Israelites and disheartened their enemies. He complained before the Lord, and was answered that the repulse was a punishment for the infraction of the vow of devotement, by the concealment in the camp of some of the spoil of Jericho.

9. On hearing this, the lot was resorted to for the detection of the offender. Achan was taken, and having confessed the crime, was stoned to death, and a tumulus of stones was raised over his body. After this expurgation, Ai was in another attempt easily taken by stratagem, in which one body, by a pretended flight, drew out the defenders in pursuit, on which, another body, which had lain in ambuscade, rushed into the town, and set it on fire. The pretended fugitives then turned upon their pursuers, who, being also attacked in the rear by the other body, and seeing their town in flames, were panic-struck, and easily cut in pieces. Twelve thousand, being the whole inhabitants, perished on this occasion; and the king, who was taken prisoner, was put to the sword, and his body hanged on a tree until the evening, when it was taken down, and buried at the gate of the place under a heap of stones. This and many similar acts of the Israelites in their warfare with the Canaanites were undoubtedly severe and cruel; but in those times all wars were carried on with great barbarity, as they still are in the countries of the East; and the conduct of the Hebrew invaders of Palestine was only in accordance with the war-practice of the time and country, and was not more harsh than would have been exercised towards themselves, had they been defeated and the Canaanites victorious. As the Lord was employing the sword of the Israelites for the extermination of a very guilty people, whose iniquities had at this time reached the highest point of aggra-

vation, he did not direct that the invaders of Palestine should
introduce any milder usages of war than those which then
ordinarily prevailed.   Josh. viii.

10. There can be no doubt that the success of the Hebrew
armies was much facilitated by the absence of any large or
central government, or of any one power strong enough to act
in opposition to the invaders.   The country was still, as in
the time of the Patriarchs, broken up into a vast number of
small independent states, which differed even in the form of
government,—some being monarchical, and others republican;
but the monarchical form was the most prevalent, and every
chief over one or more towns, with a few dependent villages
and a narrow tract of surrounding country, was dignified with
the title of king.   Among these kings there were a few who,
from their proportionately larger territories, their success in
war, or general character, had sufficient influence, on occasions
of great and general emergency, to induce a number of the
others to confederate with them for the common benefit; but
during the entire period of this war of life and death, no such
confederacy was ever formed by the Canaanites, as brought
all the military resources of the country to bear at one time
against the Hebrew host.

CHAPTER II.   B. C. 1451 to 1426.

Treaty with the Gibeonites . . . 1451
Defeat of the Five Amorite Kings . 1451
The solemnity at Ebal and Gerizim 1445
The Tabernacle established at Shiloh 1445
First Division of Lands 1445
Second Division of Lands 1440
Death of Joshua 1426

EGYPT.

Thothmes IV. 1444
Amunoph III. (Rathotis), the sup-
    posed Memnon of the vocal statue 1436

1. The inhabitants of the land appear to have trusted very much to the obstacle which their fortified towns would offer to the progress of the Israelites; but the capture of two such strong places as Jericho and Ai awoke them from this confidence, and shewed them the necessity of some decided course of action. Among the "kings" of that part of Palestine in which the invaders lay, five are named, who, headed by Adonizedek, king of Jerusalem, confederated together to resist them. Had the states in this quarter been disposed to make overtures of peace, or even of tribute, they would doubtless have been prevented by the knowledge that the Israelites were bent on dispossessing them altogether, and were under orders to enter into no treaties with them. The knowledge of this did not, however, hinder the inhabitants of Gibeon from attempting to obtain by stratagem what they knew would be refused to a direct application. Ambassadors were sent to the Hebrew camp at Gilgal, cunningly dressed up and disguised to appear as travel-worn men, whom the renown of the Lord's marvellous acts in behalf of Israel had drawn from a far country, to enter into engagements of friendship and peace with a people so highly favoured. Deceived by their appearance and by their professions, the Hebrews entered into the proposed engagements, without previously consulting their Divine King. For this neglect they were very soon punished by discovering how they had been outwitted; and then they sought counsel of the Lord as to the binding nature of an obligation incurred under such circumstances. They were told that a covenant so solemnly contracted, must be held binding; but that its terms did not prevent the Gibeonites being re-

duced to servitude. A tribute of labour, in hewing wood and drawing water, was therefore exacted from them. Josh. ix.

2. The kings, whose confederacy we have just mentioned, were much troubled at the defection of the Gibeonites and at the alliance they had formed. Determined to punish them first, the five kings made their appearance in arms before Gibeon. The inhabitants in this extremity sent to claim the protection of Joshua, who immediately went, at the head of a strong force, to their assistance. A rapid march by night brought him unexpectedly upon the besiegers, who were routed with great slaughter; those that fled were hotly pursued all the day. The fugitives were sorely distressed also by a shower of large stones, by which the Lord evinced that He fought for Israel; and when, under the covering of advancing night, many of them seemed likely to escape into the fortified towns, the light of day was prolonged at the request of Joshua, who, urged by the strong impulse of his faith, which taught him that even such a manifestation of the Divine power would not be refused, cried, "Sun, stand thou still upon Gibeon; and thou, moon, in the valley of Ajalon." Being ignorant of the true system of astronomy, Joshua described what appeared to him and those who heard him to be the only means of producing the desired result. His mandate was obeyed; the day was lengthened; or, in the sense in which Joshua and the people understood it, "the sun stood still, and the moon stayed," until the desired objects had been secured. As the worship of the Canaanites and other idolaters ultimately resolves itself into the worship of the heavenly bodies, of which the sun and moon are the chief, nothing could more strikingly evince the omnipotence of the God whom the Hebrews worshipped, than this proof, that the most glorious objects of the material world, of which men made to themselves gods, were but the creatures of his power.

3. The five kings were found hid in a cave near Makkedah, from which, when the pursuit was over, they were brought out, and the principal Hebrew officers set their feet upon their necks, which was a well-known act and symbol of victory in the East. They were then slain and hanged upon trees until the evening, as the king of Ai had been. At evening, as the law required (Deut. xx. 16, 17), they were taken down, and

their bodies were returned to the cave which had been their refuge. With his usual military skill, Joshua took advantage of the panic which his signal success and the attendant miracles had on this occasion inspired, and overran and reduced the greater part of the country from Gibeon southward to the desert frontier, including the cities of Makkedah, Libnah, Lachish, Eglon, Debir, and Hebron. The attack on Debir was commanded by Caleb, who, according to a romantic oriental usage, announced that he would give his daughter Achsah in marriage to the man who should first enter the town, or most distinguish himself in the assault. The prize of gallantry was won by Othniel, Caleb's own nephew, whom we shall hereafter recognise as the first "Judge" in Israel. After all these victories Joshua led back his army to Gilgal.

4. The success of this campaign gave great alarm to the princes of the north, who united in a very powerful league, headed by Jabin, king of Hazor. The allies took the field with such a vast force as seemed fully equal to the task of crushing the invaders by one stroke. Their army compre-hended a proportion of horses and chariots of war:—and this is the first occasion on which horses are men-tioned in Palestine, and the first time that they were brought in-to action against the Israelites, who them-selves had no cavalry

110. Persian Chariot.

till long after. In dealing with this very formidable host, the Hebrew general followed his usual course: he penetrated into Upper Galilee by rapid marches, and falling upon the enemy when least expected, defeated them with tremendous slaughter. This great loss so broke the power and spirits of the Canaan-ites, that, while Joshua lived, no other powerful combination could be formed against the Israelites, who occupied themselves in reducing in detail the petty kings and cities of the country. In the course of five years, thirty-one of these little states were subdued. This was the period of merciless and exterminating warfare, to avoid the horrors of which, it appears that some of these nations emigrated to foreign lands; and there are traditions which might lead us to trace some of them to the northern shores of Africa. The towns which the Israelites were unable to occupy or defend, they destroyed. These were chiefly such as were situated in the plains; for of those that stood on hills Hazor only was destroyed.

5. At the end of five years, Joshua had reduced the greater part of the country from the mountains of Seir to those of Lebanon. The portion lying to the south of the great plain of Esdraelon was the most completely subjugated; and it seemed proper to determine without further delay to what tribes that portion should belong. The southern part of this territory was given to Judah, and the northern part to Ephraim, and the unprovided half tribe of Manasseh. Thus five tribes were provided for: two-and-a-half on each side of

111. Mounts Ebal and Gerizim.

the river Jordan. This first distribution of territory seemed a suitable occasion for the removal of the tabernacle from Gilgal to the interior of the conquered country. Shiloh, in the territory of Ephraim, and near the centre of the land, was the place chosen; and there it continued above 450 years, until the time of Samuel. It appears to have been on the way to this place that the Israelites, in passing by the mountains of Ebal and Gerizim, went through the august and striking ceremonial which Moses had long before directed to be celebrated in that place, and whereby he had wisely provided that the assembled people should, on taking possession of their inheritance, once more solemnly declare their acceptance of the institutions which had been given to them (Deut. xxvii.) The fundamental laws were inscribed on plastered pillars, and sacrifices were offered on a large altar of unhewn stone. Then, six of the tribes stood on Mount Ebal, and the other six tribes on Mount Gerizim; while the ark with the priests and Levites was stationed in the valley between. In that vast audience, the loud voices of the Levites proclaimed blessings on the obedient, and curses on the disobedient to the law; and each clause of blessing and of curse was met by a grand responsive "AMEN!" from the thousands of Israel— for the blessings from Gerizim, and for the curses from Ebal.

6. The five or six following years were consumed in a desultory warfare with the unconquered states. It would appear that the existing population did not yet need all the country, and found enough to occupy them in what they had already acquired. At all events, the first ardour of action had so much subsided, that at length Joshua rebuked the tribes for their backwardness in taking full possession of their heritage. Anxious, however, that the territorial distribution should be settled before his death, he determined that all that remained to be done with regard to such a distribution should be at once effected, leaving the tribes to assist one another in getting complete possession of the domains which fell to them. As it appeared probable that the portions already given were too large in proportion to the whole, it was deemed necessary that properly qualified persons should be sent through the land to survey it, and to enter the particulars in a book. It is not improbable that some kind of map was constructed on this occasion; and, altogether, the circumstance is interesting as indicating the earliest territorial survey on record.

7. The result of this operation manifested that too much

land had been given at the previous distribution, and that the seven remaining tribes could not be adequately provided for out of what remained; and room was therefore made for two other tribes in the portion which had been assigned to Judah, and for one in that which had been given to Ephraim. To prevent disputes, the seven portions were distributed by lot to the seven tribes; and that the determination of the lot were divinely directed was evinced by the fact, that the position and territory given to each of the tribes corresponded exactly to the prophetic descriptions given by Jacob and by Moses. The lot gave to Simeon and Dan the two portions which had been formed out of the territory of Judah, and to Benjamin that which had been taken from Ephraim. The four portions in the north, forming what was afterwards called Galilee, were assigned by the lot to Zebulun, Issachar, Asher, and Naphtali. The tribe of Levi had no territory assigned to it; but each of the tribes gave four towns with their suburbs for the residence of the Levites, whereby the members of that tribe were equally and judiciously dispersed through the country; and, although there was but one tabernacle and one altar, a determinate localization, in every tribe, was made of the institutions and officers of the Divine King. Of the forty-eight cities given to the tribe of Levi, thirteen were allotted to the priesthood, all in the tribes of Judah and Benjamin. Six of the forty-eight, at proper distances from each other, were made cities of refuge for the man-slayer. These were, on the west of the Jordan, Hebron in Judah, Shechem in Ephraim, and Kedesh in Naphtali; and on the east, Bezer in the wilderness, Ramoth in Gilead, and Golan in Bashan.

8. This important operation having been completed under the direction of Joshua and Eleazer, the high-priest, it seemed proper to dismiss to their homes the warriors of the tribes beyond the Jordan, who, according to agreement, had hitherto accompanied the other tribes, and assisted them in their warfare. Joshua, therefore, called them together, and, after acknowledging their services, and exhorting them to maintain their allegiance to the Divine King, and their union with the other tribes, sent them away with his blessing. The returning tribes having crossed the Jordan, erected, at the passage

of Bethabara, a great altar, which threatened to produce a serious misunderstanding between them and the tribes on this side the river. The law allowed but one altar for sacrifices; and it was hastily concluded that the trans-Jordanic tribes designed to destroy the unity of the nation, by setting up a separate altar and a separate establishment on their side the river. This apprehension so awakened the indignation and zeal of the other tribes, that they assembled in large numbers at Shiloh, bent on making war with their brethren, unless a satisfactory explanation were afforded. Delegates were sent to remonstrate with them, and to invite them to come and share the country west of the Jordan, if they deemed that river so great a barrier as to disconnect them from the central altar and establishment at Shiloh. The charge was, however, repelled with horror by the suspected tribes, who explained that the altar was not intended by them for sacrifices, but for an abiding monument of their common origin, interest, polity, and worship—of that very unity which they were charged with an intention to dissever. This statement was received with great satisfaction, and the name of *Ed*, " a Witness," was given to the altar of memorial.

9. Joshua appears to have lived about fourteen years after the second division of the lands. During this period, the people ceased to prosecute the war against the Canaanites. It would seem that the several tribes having as much land and as many towns as they at present wanted, applied themselves to agriculture and the pursuits of settled life, and each tribe became too much engrossed in its own concerns to assist the others in getting full possession of their territory. It was well that they took so early and decided a turn towards their intended vocation as an agricultural people, and that the old inhabitants were not too rapidly expelled before the Hebrews were able to take their place and to occupy their cities; but it was dangerous to them as the peculiar people, that they were in a position to form connections with the idolaters, and to be contaminated by their abominations. There was also reason to fear that the Canaanites, by being left alone, would in time gather strength again to make head against the chosen race. All this happened accordingly, but not in the time of Joshua.

10. Although the old patriarchal idolatries **and those** of Egypt were secretly practised by some individuals, yet the people were, upon the whole, obedient to the Divine King, and therefore prosperous, during the life of Joshua.   To confirm them in their obedience, Joshua, in his latter days, convened two general assemblies, in which he earnestly exhorted them to be faithful to God; and on the last occasion he caused the covenant, by which the Lord had become their sovereign, to be solemnly acknowledged and renewed.   As a standing memorial of this transaction, a stone was set up under a tree that grew near the sanctuary, and a record of it was made in the Book of the Law.   Soon after this, **the** illustrious warrior and devoted upholder **of the theocratical institutions, died at the age of 110 years.**

CHAPTER III. B.C. 1426 to 1285.

PALESTINE.		EGYPT.		EVENTS AND PERSONS.	
	B. C.		B. C.		B. C
Othniel delivers Israel	1405	Amun-men . . .	1408	Musæus the Poet, Mi-	
Ehud	1323	Remeses I.	1395	nos, King of Crete	1405
Shamgar	1305	Osirei I. (Armais) .	1385	Eleusinian Mysteries	
Deborah and Barak .	1285	Remeses II. (Miamun)		introduced at Athens	1356
		or the Great . .	1355	The Isthmian Games	
		Pthahmen Thmeioftep?		instituted . . .	1326
		(Amenophis) . .	1289	Orpheus the Poet.	

1. WE now enter upon the time of the Judges, a period of 331 years (1426 to 1095 B. C.), during which we shall find the Hebrew nation afflicted or prosperous, in proportion to their neglect or observance of the conditions of their covenant with their Divine King. When they turned from God, and worshipped idols, He humbled them before their enemies, by whom they were subjected to the yoke of bondage; and when at length, in their misery, they repented and turned to God, he sent them deliverers, named " Judges," under whom they continued prosperous, until they sinned again, when they were again punished.

2. During the generation which had taken the covenant under Joshua, idolatry, although it had never been wholly eradicated, was never allowed to predominate in the nation. Soon, however, the idols of Canaan began to receive that homage which had formerly been given to those of Mesopotamia and Egypt. This increasing tendency to idolatry arose from the continued remissness of the Israelites in their conduct towards the Canaanites. Only a few tribes made war upon them, and these soon grew weary of the contest. In most cases where they had the ascendency, they were content to hold the Canaanites under tribute, although this had been forbidden by an express law; and their intercourse becoming gradually more intimate, they engaged in affairs of commerce, and intermarried with the native inhabitants.

3. Joshua has been blamed by some for not asking permission to appoint a successor in the government; but his

office was one in which no successor was needed. He was a military commander, not a civil governor. The Lord himself, enthroned in the Tabernacle, was the political and civil, as well as the religious, head of the nation; and there were established means of obtaining the commands of the Divine King on all questions that could arise, through the instrumentality of his chief minister, the high-priest. In those days the functions of general government were so simple that this theocratical institution contained every element of stability and safety, had its principles and advantages been properly understood by the people. The administration of justice among them had been well provided for; the business of public instruction was in the hands of the Levites, in their several cities; and the internal concerns of the several tribes were sufficiently cared for by their own patriarchal or family chiefs and elders.

4. The only military operations of any note shortly after the death of Joshua, consisted in the endeavours of the tribe of Judah, assisted by Simeon, to get full possession of its territory. In this it seems to have succeeded generally; but it was unable to expel the Jebusites from the strong fortress which formed the upper town of Jerusalem. In one action against Adoni-bezek, in Bezek, ten thousand Canaanites were slain, and the king was taken prisoner. His thumbs and great toes were cut off, in retribution for the manner in which he had been wont to treat his own captives; for he himself declared that seventy kings, whose thumbs and great toes he had cut off, gathered their bread under his table.

5. The high-priest Eleazer did not long outlive Joshua, and he was succeeded by his son Phinehas. Early in his administration, "the angel of the Lord," who had appeared to Joshua at Gilgal, again appeared to the people when assembled before the tabernacle at Shiloh, and, having solemnly reprehended their conduct with regard to the Canaanites, threatened no longer to vouchsafe Almighty power for their expulsion, but to leave the remainder of the Canaanites for a test and trial of their faithfulness. This authoritative rebuke produced some effect, and moved them to such cries and tears as caused the place to be called Bochim (*weepers*).

6. But the impression produced was of short duration. The last five chapters of the book of Judges relate events which belong to the time of Phinehas, and give a melancholy view of the moral condition of the nation at this period. The tribe of Dan being pressed for room in its southern allotment, and being unable to get possession of the portions of territory which were successfully defended by the Canaanites, sent out a portion of its members to seek for a situation where they might more easily form a settlement. This they found near the source of the Jordan, where they took the town of Leshem or Laish from the inhabitants, who were living in security, and changed its name to Dan,—under which name it is often celebrated as the most northerly town of Palestine in the popular phrase, "from Dan (in the north) to Beersheba (in the south)," which described the whole length of the land. On this occasion a modified system of idolatry was introduced into this tribe. The depravity of the inhabitants of the Benjamite city of Gibeah, and the grievous maltreatment of a Levite and his wife, roused the other tribes to warlike operations, on the refusal of the Benjamites to give up the offenders. This infatuated tribe had some success in the first and second actions; but in a third, their reverse was so complete, and the ensuing carnage so dreadful, that the tribe was nearly exterminated, and never wholly recovered the blow, but ever after remained the smallest tribe in Israel.

7. To punish the disorders, which these circumstances illustrate rather than describe, the Lord in his anger brought the nation into subjection to a distant and unexpected enemy, Chushan Rishathaim, a king from beyond the Euphrates, who kept the Israelites under severe tributary bondage for eight years. At the end of that time they turned to the Divine King against whom they had so grievously revolted; and he moved Othniel, the nephew of Caleb, to act for their deliverance After some desultory warfare, a general action was fought, in which the complete victory of the Israelites effected their deliverance from the Mesopotamian yoke. After this, Othniel, as "judge" or regent for the Divine King, directed the foreign and military policy of southern Israel for forty years, during which time the people continued true to their allegiance, and dwelt in peace.

8. On his death, the Israelites again returned to their idolatrous practices, and were punished by their jealous neighbours and relatives, the Moabites, who, finding the chosen people not invincible, ventured a battle, and, being victorious, reduced to subjection the tribes beyond Jordan, and, at length, also the southern tribes on this side the river. Eglon, the king, then fixed his residence at Jericho, as the best means of establishing his power, by controlling the communications of the tribes which the river separated. The Hebrews were kept under tribute for eighteen years; at the expiration of which, one of the tribute-bearers, Ehud of Benjamin, secretly slew the king, whose death struck the Moabites with such consternation, that the Israelites were enabled, under the conduct of Ehud, to shake off their yoke. This man's deed was murder; but in the East, such acts are considered as sanctioned by public objects and successful results.

9. The victory over the Moabites was followed by a repose of eighty years, at the end of which the Philistines first invaded the land of Judah. But their force was encountered by a body of husbandmen, under the conduct of Shamgar, who, although armed only with the instruments which they employed in goading their oxen,* repelled them with great slaughter. If Shamgar, in consequence of this victory, became judge in southern Israel, it does not appear that he lived long to enjoy that honour.

10. In the 200 years which had elapsed since their discomfiture by Joshua, the northern Canaanites had gradually recovered such power as enabled them to form another confederacy against the Israelites, headed by Jabin, king of Hazor. He had at his disposal a large army, comprehending 900 iron-armed chariots of war, which the Israelites regarded with peculiar dread. With such a force, commanded by Sisera, one of the ablest generals of that age, he grievously oppressed the northern tribes for twenty years; and his yoke appears to have been more intolerable than any which they had previously sustained. At the end of that time, Deborah, a prophetess of Mount Ephraim, was moved by a Divine im-

---

* These ox-goads, which are still used in the East, were good substitutes for spears. They are often eight feet long, armed at one end with a sharp point, for goading the oxen and at the other with a kind of spade or paddle for clearing the plough of clay, &c.

pulse to exhort Barak, of the tribe of Naphtali, to undertake
the deliverance of the afflicted tribes. With some reluctance
ne accepted the call, on condition that she went with him.
He assembled 10,000 men, near Mount Tabor, with whom,
confiding in God, he gave battle to the numerous hosts of
Jabin in the plain of Esdraelon. The Canaanites were completely routed; and a sudden inundation of the river Kishon
swept away great numbers of the fugitives. Sisera found re-
.uge in the tent of a pastoral chief, a Kenite, named Heber,
whose wife Jael offered him hospitality and protection; but
while he slept, she treacherously slew him, by driving a tent-
pin through his temples, and nailing his head to the ground.
This great victory was celebrated by Deborah in a song of
thanksgiving, abounding in the richest ornaments of sacre
oriental poetry. Judges iv. 5.

CHAPTER IV.   B. C. 1285 TO 1157.

PALESTINE.		B.C.	EGYPT.	B. C.	EVENTS AND PERSONS.	B. C
ᵉon	. . . .	1242	Pthah-men-Septhah		The Argonautic Expe-	
Abimelech	. . . .	1236	(Sethos)	1269	dition	1263
Tola	. . . . . .	1232	Osirei II. (Rampses) .	1255	The Pythian Games in-	
Jair	. . . . .	1210	Amenophthis . . .	1245	stituted	1263
Jephthah	. . . .	1198	Remeses III. . . .	1235	The rape of Helen by	
Ibzan	. . . . . .	1182	Remeses IV. (Amme-		Paris	1198
Elon	. . . . .	1176	nemes)	1205	Troy taken by the	
Abdon	. . . . .	1165	Remeses V. (Thuoris)	1195	Greeks	1184
Eli	. . . . . .	1157	Remeses VI. . . .	1180		
			Remeses VII. . . .	1170		

1. THE defeat of Sisera was followed by a repose of forty
years. At the end of that time the Midianites, Amalekites,
and other nomad tribes, began to invade Palestine in great
numbers, treading down the cultivated lands under the feet
of their numerous herds, seizing the fruits of the ground,
taking away the cattle, plundering men and houses, and,
in short, ravaging the country as the Bedouin Arabs are wont
to do at the present time, when there is no power sufficient
to restrain them. Like them also, the Midianites withdrew
on the approach of winter, and returned in the early summer
to gather that which the Israelites had sown, and for which
they had laboured. This oppression continued for seven
years, and became so grievous, that many of the people sought
refuge in the dens and caves of the wilderness; and it is perhaps to this period that we should refer the migration to the
land of Moab of that Elimelech, the touching history of whose
widow and daughter-in-law forms the beautiful episode contained in the book of Ruth.

2. In their deep trouble, the Israelites at length cried to
the God who had so often delivered them in time past. A
prophet was then sent to rebuke their ingratitude; but also
to promise deliverance. Accordingly, as Gideon, a man of
the tribe of Manasseh, was secretly threshing wheat in a
winepress, to hide it from the Midianites, an angel of God
appeared to him, and commissioned him to undertake the
deliverance of his country. Gideon first sought to decline so

high a trust, and then requested a token that the commission was indeed from heaven. His request was granted; for, at the touch of the angel's staff, fire broke forth and consumed, as a sacrifice, the kid and the bread which Gideon had set before his visitant, who disappeared, and left him "filled with the Spirit of God,"—a spirit of faith and fortitude, equal to the great enterprise which lay before him. In answer to his prayer, another sign was given to Gideon;—a fleece which he spread out upon the open threshing-floor became wet with dew, while the ground was dry; and again, the fleece alone was dry, while the soil was wet all around.

3. Now strong in faith, Gideon overthrew the altar which his father had erected to Baal, and cut down the trees of the "sacred" grove which he had planted around it. Then proceeding into the country, he blew the trumpet of war, when 32,000 men gathered to his standard. But the Lord knowing the unbelief and distrust that prevailed among them, directed Gideon to proclaim that all who were fearful and faint-hearted might withdraw. Availing themselves of this permission, 22,000 took their departure, so that only 10,000 were left. Even these were too many for the Lord's purpose, which required that the means employed should be so evidently inadequate, that the glory of the deliverance might be entirely his own. Gideon was therefore directed to lead his thirsty troops to the river, and permit them to drink. The greater part bent down to the surface of the water, to imbibe large draughts at ease and leisure; but a few lapped up the water in the hollow of their hands, as men in haste. Those who stooped down to drink were ordered by Gideon to retire to their homes; and by the remainder, who were only 300 in number, the deliverance of Israel was promised. The host which this handful of men had to encounter, lay encamped in the plain of Esdraelon. Encouraged by ascertaining, in a night-visit to their camp, that the Midianites were already dispirited, and might easily be struck with a panic, the Hebrew commander instructed his men to provide themselves with earthen pitchers, and to place in each pitcher a lighted lamp. The pitcher containing the lamp in one hand, and a trumpet in the other, formed the weapons of their warfare. The 300 men, in three bands of 100 each, approached the

sleeping host of Midian, in silence and by night, on different
sides.   At a given signal, they simultaneously broke their
earthen vessels, displayed their lamps, and blew a loud blast
with their trumpets.   The tremendous noise by which the
Midianites were awakened, and the numerous lights all
around, conveyed to their confused senses the notion that they
were surrounded by a mighty host; and, in the darkness,
every one taking his neighbour for an enemy, they slew each
other by thousands.   One hundred and twenty thousand men
were left dead upon the field of battle, and only 15,000 saved
themselves by flight.   The Israelites who shrunk from the
war joined in the pursuit, and hasted to share the spoil.
Gideon displayed the talents of one fit to govern men, by the
tact with which he soothed the jealous pride of the Ephraim
ites, who complained that they had not been called into
action, and by the spirit with which he punished the men of
Succoth and Penuel, who had refused refreshment to his
men, and had derided his enterprise.

4. In the height of their admiration and gratitude, the
people offered to make Gideon king, and to entail the crown
upon his race.   But he was too well acquainted with the pecu-
iar nature of the go-
vernment under which
they had been placed
by God, to listen to a
proposal like this.   He
thereiore replied, "Not
I, nor my son, but Je-
hovah shall reign over
you."   But this great
man was not equally
alive to the religious
obligations of the cove-
nant; for with the pro-
duce of the golden ear-
rings taken from the
Midianites, which were
willingly given to him

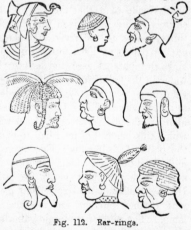

Fig. 112.   Ear-rings.

by the army, he made an ephod, or priest's dress, and ap
pears to have formed a sacerdotal establishment in his own

town, where sacrifices might be regularly offered. However well intended, this was a gross interference with the Tabernacle establishment at Shiloh, and in the end proved a snare to Gideon's own family, and an occasion for idolatry to the nation. Judges viii.

5. Gideon lived forty years after this great victory; and in his time the peace of Israel does not seem to have been again seriously disturbed. The parable of Jotham seems to intimate, that after, or perhaps even before, his death, the offer of the crown had been repeated to his sons, of whom he had, by his several wives, seventy that were legitimate. But they having nobly refused the tempting offer, his spurious son Abimelech succeeded in persuading the people of Shechem to proclaim him king, and to put to death all the other sons of Gideon. Only Jotham, the youngest, escaped; who afterwards from Mount Gerizim administered a cutting rebuke to the Shechemites, in the oldest and most beautiful apologue of antiquity, which represents the bramble as accepting that sovereignty over the trees which had successively been declined by the olive-tree, the fig-tree, and the vine. Three years sufficed to disgust the Shechemites with the king they had set up. They revolted, in consequence of which their city was utterly destroyed by Abimelech, who then proceeded to reduce another revolted town, Thebez, where he was killed by a stone thrown down upon him by a woman. Judges ix.

6. The enemies from whom Tola, of the tribe of Issachar, defended Israel are not named; and of Jair, the Gileadite, we only know that his thirty sons rode on white asses, as chiefs of thirty small towns or villages in Gilead, which belonged to their opulent family. The administration of Tola lasted twenty-three years, and that of Jair twenty-two.

7. After this, the Israelites fell into gross idolatry, in punishment for which their enemies were allowed to oppress them greatly. The Ammonites laid claim to a part of the land beyond Jordan which had been wrested from them by the Amorites, from whom it was conquered by Moses. For eighteen years they greatly distressed the two and half tribes beyond Jordan, and likewise made incursions into Benjamin, Judah, and Ephraim, who had at the same time to defend

themselves against the Philistines.   In these troubles they cried to God, whom they had so grievously insulted; and as they gave signs of true repentance, he delayed not to send them deliverance.

8. Jephthah, the deliverer raised up on this occasion, was an illegitimate son, by "a strange woman," of one Gilead, a person of some note in Manasseh, beyond Jordan. He had no claim to share with his brethren in their patrimony; and, on the death of their father, was excluded with some harshness from the paternal home, and became a wanderer and exile.   A number of men of like broken fortune and unsettled dispositions, joined themselves to him, and they lived upon the prey which they acquired by harassing the Ammonites and other enemies of Israel.   In this kind of predatory warfare, they became skilful, hardy, and bold; and the name of Jephthah was celebrated beyond Jordan as that of a valiant and successful leader. When, therefore, the tribes were encouraged to hope for deliverance, their eyes turned to him, and a deputation was sent to invite him to take the command in the war against the Ammonites.   After some demur, he accepted the invitation, and repaired to Mizpeh of Gilead, where his appointment was solemnly ratified.   His first act was to send an embassy to demand of the Ammonites why they invaded the territories of Israel.   In reply, they advanced the claim of prior occupation, which has been mentioned; to which Jephthah answered, that whoever were the prior occupants, the country belonged to Israel by right of conquest from the Amorites.   Jephthah then went forth to the war, but in departing, rashly vowed to devote in sacrifice to God whatever came forth to meet him on his return triumphant.   In the issue the Ammonites were defeated with great slaughter, and completely subdued.

9. Jephthah had only one child, a virgin daughter, beautiful and young; and she it was who, on his return to Mizpeh, came forth, at the head of the maidens, to greet him with timbrels and dances.   The warrior remembered then the irreversible vow which he had taken, and rent his clothes in the anguish of his soul.   When apprised of her doom, the heroic daughter encouraged her father to fulfil his vow; but whether he did this by shedding her blood in sacrifice, or by devoting

her to a secluded and solitary life, is a point not well deter
mined, and on which different opinions are entertained.

10. The Ephraimites, envying the splendid success of
their brethren in this campaign, and the valuable booty which
they had gained, stirred up a civil war, which terminated very
disastrously for them, for they were defeated with the loss of
42,000 men. Jephthah died, after an administration of six
years.

11. The Judges—Ibzan of Bethlehem, who governed
seven years; Elon of Zebulon, ten years; and Abdon of
Ephraim, eight years; in all, twenty-five years—appear to
have maintained peace. But during this time the Israelites
again relapsed into gross idolatry, and drew on themselves a
rigorous bondage to their western foes the Philistines, who
had by this time become a powerful people. This servitude
lasted forty years; during which, whatever general government existed, appears to have been exercised by Eli the high-
priest (B. ' '57).

CHAPTER V.   B. C. 1155 to 1117.

PALESTINE.		EGYPT.	
	B. C.		B. C.
Samson born	1155	Remeses VIII.	1154
Samson's exploits from . .	1137 to 1117	Remeses IX.	1146
Samson's death	1117	Remeses X.	1122

1. SAMSON was the next deliverer, or rather avenger—for, as his countrymen were become too weak and too spiritless to second his efforts, he was only able to "*begin* to deliver Israel," and to molest the Philistines in transient and desultory attacks.   Samson was a very extraordinary man in bodily endowments, indomitable courage, and tremendous strength ; but he was very feeble in his moral and intellectual character.   His parents were of the tribe of Dan.   An angel announced his birth and declared his vocation to his mother ; and directed that the abstinence and unshorn hair of a Nazarite should distinguish him from his birth.   These were to be the signs of the covenant by which he held his gigantic powers, and on which their continuance was to depend.

2. In early manhood, Samson became enamoured of a damsel of the Philistine town of Timnath, and persuaded his parents to go and ask her in marriage for him.   On the way, he encountered a lion, and without weapons, tore it asunder as if it had been a kid ; but he did not deem the exploit worth relating, even to his parents.   The offer of marriage was accepted ; and after a while, Samson again went to Timnath, to celebrate the nuptials and bring home the bride.   On the way, he turned aside to see what had become of the lion ; and he found a swarm of bees in the dried frame-work of skin and bones which was left, after jackals (probably) had devoured the flesh.   This furnished the subject of the riddle which, according to the custom of these times, he proposed to the guests at the marriage-feast—" Out of the eater came forth meat, and out of the fierce came forth sweetness."   Not being able to solve the riddle, the guests secretly induced Samson's wife, by threats, to extract the secret from him and

reveal it to them. Indignant at his wife for betraying his secret, and at the guests for tampering with her, Samson left her and went home, after he had slain thirty Philistines of Askelon, and given their garments, as his forfeit, to the guests.

3. After his anger had subsided, he went to visit his wife, with a present of a kid; but he found her married to his friend, who had been his bridesman at the wedding. On this and other occasions, he allowed his private wrongs to stimulate him to the exercise of his vindictive mission, which otherwise he appears to have been much disposed to neglect. Fired by the present insult, he vowed and took severe revenge. Collecting three hundred foxes, he tied them together by the tails, in pairs; and then putting a firebrand between every pair, he turned them into the standing corn of the Philistines, which was burnt with fire, along with the shocks of corn, and the vineyards and olive-grounds. The Phili-

113. Syrian Fox.

stines laid the blame upon Samson's wife and her father, and came and burnt them both with fire; but this cruel action was soon after punished by Samson with so great a slaughter, that he deemed it prudent to withdraw to the top of the almost inaccessible rock Etam in the tribe of Judah. Determined to secure so implacable an enemy, the Philistines went in great force against him; but being unable to reach him in this position, they required the Judahites to yield him up. More disposed to dread the consequences of Samson's feats than to glory in them, three thousand men of Judah went to seize their hero, and deliver him up in bonds to the Philistines. He did not resist; and when the enemies and masters of Israel beheld their redoubted foe brought to them as a captive, they raised an exulting shout: but at that moment Samson burst asunder the new ropes with which he was bound, as if they had been burnt tow, and seizing the jaw-bone of an ass that lay near, he fell upon the Philistines, and routed them with the slaughter of a thousand. After this feat, which he very properly felt to be "a great deliverance which God had given to him,"

H

Samson, ready to perish with intense thirst, called upon God
for relief; and immediately water rose from a hollow place
close by, which ever after remained a perennial spring.

4. We next find this very strong yet erring man in the
house of a harlot, in the Philistine city of Gaza. When his
arrival was known, the gates of the city were shut, and a
guard set, to prevent his escape. But he arose in the night,
and not only burst open, but rent away the gates, carried
them off, posts and all, upon his shoulders, and left them
upon a hill on the road to Hebron.

5. Another harlot, named Delilah, dwelling in the vale
of Sorek, proved his ruin. Tempted by the rich bribes of the
Philistine lords, Delilah endeavoured to extract from Samson
the secret of his strength, for it was known that it was in
something more than bones and sinews that he differed from
other men. After some attempts to amuse her, Samson, tired
by her importunities, at length told her that his strength lay
in his hair, as the sign of his devotement, and of the covenant
by which he held his powers. While he slept upon her lap,
she made the seven locks of his hair be cut off; and instantly
the covenant with God being broken, the strength of Samson
departed from him, and he became weak as other men. The
Philistines took him without difficulty, put out his eyes, and
carried him to Gaza, where he was bound with fetters of brass,
and put to a slave's labour in the prison-house. Blind and
in prison, Samson had leisure to repent that he had trifled so
lightly with the gift of God; and with his repentance and
the growth of his hair, it pleased God to renew his strength.
At this time the Philistines held a high day of festival and
thanksgiving, to praise their God Dagon for having delivered
their greatest enemy into their hands; and Samson himself
was brought from the prison, that the assembled people might
behold their wretched victim, triumph in his misery, and
make sport of his blindness. Wearied at length, the fallen
champion applied to the lad who led him by the hand, to let
him lean for rest upon the two pillars which chiefly supported
the roof of the building, upon which three thousand people
were at that time assembled to see the spectacle and celebrate
the feast. Their impious rejoicing in their idol was so displeasing to God, that he granted the prayer of Samson, and

endued him with such strength, that when, embracing the pillars, he bowed himself with all his might, they yielded to the vast force, and broke; whereon the roof, with the mass of people upon it, fell in, and buried in the ruins Samson and the multitude below. At his death, Samson slew a greater number of the Philistines than he had done during his life. Judges, xvi. 4-31.

6. The precise effect of this event upon the relative position of the Israelites and the Philistines does not appear. But a blow which struck down the flower of the Philistine nation was not likely to be inoperative; and it may be inferred from subsequent circumstances, that the Philistines were too much discouraged to maintain their hold upon the Hebrew nation.

CHAPTER VI.

PALESTINE.	EGYPT.	EVENTS—PERSONS.
B.C.	B.C.	B.C.
Samuel born . . . 1149	Remeses XI. . . 1110	Return of the Heraclidæ
Samuel called to be a		into Peloponessus . 1104
Prophet 1137		Which they divide
Commencement of 20		among themselves . 1103
years' servitude to the		Kingdom of Lacedæmon
Philistines . . . 1127		commences . . . 1102
Convention at Mizpeh,		
and Samuel Judge 1107		
Defeat of the Philistines 1107		
End of Samuel's (12		
years) separate admi-		
nistration 1095		

1. As Samson does not appear to have exercised any authority, civil or military, even in the southern portion of Palestine adjoining the Philistine territory to which his operations were confined, he might be described as a scourge of the Philistines rather than a Judge of Israel. Without doubt, the civil government, as far as any existed in such disorderly times, was directed by the high priest—which office, during a portion of Samson's time, appears to have been held by Eli, although, for chronological purposes, his administration is said to begin where the history of Samson ends. Eli judged Israel for forty years after the death of Samson. In the course of his administration, Hannah, the wife of Elkanah, a Levite, who had been barren, and on that account much insulted by another wife of Elkanah, who was fruitful, in her distress prayed to the Lord to give her a son, and vowed that if her suit were granted, she would dedicate that son as a Nazarite to the Lord all the days of his life. The petition was heard, and she called her son Samuel, signifying "heard of God," or "given of God." In accordance with the vow of special dedication, the child had no sooner reached a proper age than he was taken to the tabernacle at Shiloh, and left there under the care of Eli, who soon became much attached to him, and, as he grew up, employed him in personal attendance on himself, and in various services about the tabernacle.

2. Eli himself was descended from Ithamar, the second son of Aaron, and appears to have been the first high priest of the younger branch of the family. We know not on what occasion the elder branch, descended from Eleazer, had been set aside. Eli was a pious man, but of too easy and mild a disposition for his high situation. His gentle rebukes had therefore very little effect upon his two sons, Hophni and Phineas, who proved so degenerate, that they were guilty of the grossest excesses and most criminal abuses of their priestly office; and hence the presentation of offerings and sacrifices became disagreeable and hateful to all the people. Although sensible of their bad conduct, Eli did not interpose his authority to put a stop to it.

3. Thus matters proceeded until the boy Samuel had attained the age of twelve years, when he was called by night, in a very remarkable way, to the prophetic office. On that occasion the destruction and deposition of Eli's house were denounced, on account of the iniquities of his sons and his own criminal neglect,—" because his sons made themselves vile, and he restrained them not." Samuel could not conceal this revelation from Eli. The aged pontiff, in conformity with the usual passive piety of his character, answered meekly, " It is the Lord : let him do what seemeth to him good!" From that time forward Samuel was favoured with frequent communications from God. The youth also conducted himself with so much propriety and discretion, that the people generally looked to him with affection and confidence, as appointed of God to an office which appears to have been for a long time intermitted.

4. Ten years after the call of Samuel, the Israelites, without the consent or authority of their Divine King, whom they ought to have consulted, embarked in an ill-considered war with the Philistines. Being defeated in the first engagement with the loss of 4000 men, they had the presumption to send for the ark of God, out of the tabernacle, that they might fight under its protection. It was borne to the wars by Hophni and Phineas with other priests; and its arrival filled the Philistines with dread, as they identified it with the presence of " the mighty God, that smote the Egyptians with all the plagues." Yet they encouraged one another to fight

manfully to save themselves from such bondage as that in
which they had held the Israelites. Again they were victorious: 30,000 men of Israel fell in the battle; Hophni and
Phineas were slain; and the ark of the covenant was taken.
Eli, now blind with age, and his heart trembling for the ark
of God, sat watching by the way side for the first news from
the battle. He soon heard the disastrous tidings, and when
the messenger announced that "the ark of God was taken,"
he fell off his seat, and, being heavy and old, his neck was
broken by the fall.

5. The Philistines conveyed the ark to Ashdod, and
placed it in the temple of Dagon their god, whose idol bore
a figure half fish and half man. By this they perhaps intended to shew that their god had triumphed over the God
whom the Hebrews worshipped. But He, always jealous of
His glory, delayed not to vindicate it on this occasion. On
successive nights, the image of Dagon was found thrice to
have fallen prostrate before the ark, and the third time it
was broken in pieces. He also smote the Philistines with a
grievous disease, and with swarms of field-mice which marred

the land; and they
were at length com-
pelled to appease the
wrath of the God of
Israel, by trespass-
offerings expressive of
the plagues with
which they had been

114.

visited. These were
five golden mice, and five golden emerods, which they put in
a coffer beside the ark. They then set the ark on a new car,
drawn by milch cows taken from their calves, which, without
guidance, took the right
road to the land of Israel,
and stopped at Beth-
shemesh, a city of the
priests in the tribe of
Judah. The restored
ark, which had been

115.

seven months among the Philistines, was received with great

joy by the people; but this was soon turned into mourning, for not fewer than 50,070 men were struck with sudden death for presuming to look into the ark. This made the men of Bethshemesh as much afraid as the Philistines had been, to have the ark any longer among them, and they invited the inhabitants of the neighbouring town of Kirjath-jearim to send and take it to themselves. They did so, and deposited it in the house of Abinadab, "upon the hill," who set apart his son Eleazer to take care of it. There it remained for eighty-two years, or until the tenth year of the reign of king David.

6. Notwithstanding these signal events, the Israelites, who remained in subjection to the Philistines, continued careless of the obligations of the covenant, and negligent of the worship of God. The exertions of Samuel, however, in the course of time, brought them round to a better state of feeling; and after twenty years, they were disposed to return to their allegiance to their Divine King. Having, therefore, put aside all their strange gods, they held a solemn feast of humiliation for their sins at Mizpeh in Benjamin, and there poured out water before the Lord in token of their grief. Samuel, who was then formally recognised as judge over Israel, earnestly interceded for them, and implored deliverance from the Philistines, who had taken alarm at this large assemblage, and were then advancing to disperse them. This prayer was answered by a thunder-storm so tremendous, and so entirely unexpected at that season of the year, as struck such terror and amazement into the Philistines, that they were easily put to flight, and were pursued and smitten by the Israelites. The consequences of this victory relieved them from the yoke of the Philistines, who were obliged to restore the places taken from Israel, and were not in a condition to give any further disturbance during Samuel's administration.

7. The prophet-judge administered the government with great ability and care; and perhaps made the office of the judge in time of peace, more efficient than it had ever been before. For the regular administration of justice, he took an annual circuit through the land to Bethel, Gilgal, Mizpeh, and Ramah, which last was the place of his usual residence. At that place he erected an altar for sacrifices; and this was

doubtless by special order or permission, as otherwise it would have been contrary to the letter and spirit of the law. Besides, the ark, that most sacred symbol of the Divine Presence, was not then in the tabernacle, and the spot destined for its final resting-place was not yet known.

8. At length Samuel, growing "old and greyheaded," appointed his sons Joel and Abiah to act as his deputies in the southern district of Palestine. They accordingly settled their residence at Beer-sheba; but, in their management of affairs, they proved as unlike their father as Eli's sons had been unlike him. Greedy of gain, and careful only how to turn their public employment to their own private advantage "they took bribes, and perverted judgment."

BOOK IV.

CHAPTER I. B. C. 1095 to 1091.

PALESTINE.		EGYPT.	
	B. C.		B. C.
The Israelites desire a king: Saul		Amun-mai-Pouee . . .	1095
appointed	1095		
Saul defeats the Ammonites . . .	1095		
War with the Philistines	1093		
Saul's first offence	1093		
Jonathan's exploit at Michmash .	1091		

1. THE misconduct of Samuel's sons, his own advanced age, and the seemingly unsettled state in which the government would be left at his death, were the ostensible grounds on which the elders of Israel proceeded in resolving to demand such a change in the government as would give them a human king, "to rule them like the nations." Every nation must have some great central principle on which it can unite as one community. This was particularly necessary in a nation, which, like that of Israel, had a strongly marked sectional division into tribes, whose interests were not always in agreement. Now, this principle had been very efficiently and very beautifully supplied by the theocracy, with its invisible but ever-present Divine King, and the sacred symbols and services. But the right working of this constitution depended on a continued obedience in the people, which they had not manifested, and an appreciation of the system, of which they seem to have been scarcely capable. In short, the principle of this form of government was too refined for them; and, notwithstanding its very numerous concessions to their weakness, they too often failed to comprehend it as *their* principle, and to act up to its requirements. Hence arose internal disorders and confusions, which, although really owing to the shortcomings of the people, yet seemed in some degree imputable to the

practical inefficiency of the central principle, and created the desire for something less sublime and remote,—something visible, tangible, common,—suited to the apprehensions of an unintellectual people. Hence the demand for a king, and for the forms and institutions of a human monarchy, which might form a more sensible state-principle than the theocracy offered.

2. When the elders made their application for this great change in the government to Samuel at Ramah, they found him strongly opposed to their wish. With becoming dignity, he vindicated the purity of his own administration, and chal·lenged any one to charge him with corruption or wrong-doing; he reminded them that they had already a KING, whose power and resources were illimitable, and under whom obedience only was necessary to render their welfare secure; he placed before them, in the most vivid manner, the exactions and services to which they would be subject under human kings, and from which they were now so happily exempt; and, in short, it was his desire that they should rather strive to bring the national character up to the requirements of their present state-principle, than bring down the principle to a lower standard of character. But the elders had made up their minds on the subject, and persisted in their demand. As, therefore, the demand was made in a becoming manner, which referred the whole matter to the Lord through his prophet; as Moses had foreseen and provided for such a contingency; and as it was more than probable, that, in their present temper, the people would set up a king for themselves, unless indulged in their wish, Samuel was at length authorised to yield to their desire, although under a protest.

3. We have now, therefore, to contemplate a new phase of the Jewish history, in which the government was not a pure theocracy, nor a simple monarchy, but a combination of the two. The Lord was still the Supreme King; and the human monarch was to be appointed by him, and the line of succession determined or changed at his pleasure. The king was to wield the ordinary administrative powers of royalty, and its signs and symbols of dignity and honour; but his real position was that of a vice-king,—the minister, regent, or re-

presentative of the Divine King, whose counsel was to be sought, through the sacred oracles, on all occasions of importance, and whose directions, when given, were to be implicitly followed by the sovereign. It must, therefore, be understood that the responsibility of the Hebrew kings to the Lord, was not merely the responsibility under which every one is placed to God for the exercise of the powers entrusted to him; but also the more immediate and particular responsibility of a delegated or representative ruler to the Supreme King of the state which he governs. This was the theory of the Hebrew monarchy, as, by anticipation, it had been settled long before by Moses (Deut. xvii. 14-20); and we shall find in the sequel that the character of the kings, whether good or bad, was determined by their observance or neglect of this fundamental principle. The kings themselves were but too much disposed to forget the fact of their dependence upon the Invisible King.

4. Saul, the son of Kish, of the tribe of Benjamin, had wandered about for three days seeking the strayed asses of his father. Fatigued with the unsuccessful search, he was disposed to abandon it and return home, when, finding himself near Ramah, where Samuel lived, he resolved to consult one who was renowned in all Israel as a man from whom nothing was hidden. Instructed in the Divine designs regarding Saul, the prophet received him with honour. He assured him that the asses which he had sought were already found, and invited him to stay with him until the next morning. Saul was in fact the man on whom the Divine appointment to be the first king of Israel had fallen. A hint of this high destiny, produced from the astonished stranger a modest declaration of his insufficiency. But the prophet gave him the place of honour before all the persons whom—foreknowing the time of his arrival—he had invited to his table. As is still usual in summer, Saul slept on the flat roof of the house; and was called early in the morning by Samuel, who walked forth some way with him on his return home. When they had got beyond the town, they stopped, and Samuel then anointed Saul as the person whom God had chosen to be "captain over his inheritance;" and gave him the first kiss of civil homage.

In token of the reality of these things, and to assure the mind of the bewildered young man, the prophet foretold the inci-

dents of his home-ward journey, and, in parting, desired his attendance on the seventh day following at Gilgal.

116. Kiss of Civil Homage.

5. On the day and at the place appointed, Samuel assembled a general convocation of the tribes for the election of a king. As usual, under the theocracy, the choice of God was manifested by the sacred lot. The tribe of Benjamin was chosen; and of the families of Benjamin, that of Matri was taken; and, finally, the lot fell upon the person of Saul, the son of Kish. Anticipating this result, he had modestly concealed himself, to avoid an honour which he so little desired. But he was found, and brought before the people, who beheld with admiration his comely and dignified person,—for he stood taller, by the head and shoulders than any of the people. A physical superiority over the great body of the people, so manifest, and so highly appreciated in ancient times, procured a willing recognition of the king offered to them. Many persons in the great tribes, however, were dissatisfied that this election had vested the royalty over Israel in the smallest of the tribes, and in a person of so little consequence, even in that tribe, as Saul. They therefore held proudly aloof, and the new king was allowed to return, with a very humble attendance, to his home in Gibeah. Saul, although sensible of the neglect, wisely "held his peace" for the time; and it ultimately appeared that the different tribes could more readily unite around a monarch in his neutral position, than would have been possible to them had a member of one of the more powerful tribes been chosen. Judah would have been reluctant to submit to a king of Ephraim, and the proud and fiery

Ephraimites would not willingly have received a king from Judah. Perhaps, therefore, the choice which appears so strange at the first view, was the only one by which a civil war could have been averted.

6. Soon after these things, the Ammonites, under their king Nahash, took the field on the other side of the Jordan, and laid siege to the important town of Jabesh-Gilead. Being forced to capitulate, the inhabitants could obtain no better terms than that every man should have his right eye put out. To this hard condition they agreed, unless relief should come within seven days. Messengers were immediately despatched to Saul, who had contentedly resumed his usual avocations in Gibeah, and, when the tidings were brought to him, was returning quietly from the fields with his herd. Instantly the spirit of a king was roused within him; and he felt the duties, and claimed the powers of the Lord's anointed. He imperatively summoned the warriors to his standard; and speedily found himself at the head of a very large force, with which he crossed the Jordan, and by a forced march arrived before Jabesh, in time to save the inhabitants from their enemies, who were defeated with great slaughter. This splendid achievement manifested in Saul the qualities which, in these times, were most sought for in a king, and raised him so high in the estimation of the people, that Samuel deemed it proper to call another assembly at Gilgal, to confirm him in the kingdom. Here those who had hitherto manifested discontent, were obliged, by the force of popular opinion, to join in a general and more formal recognition of the new king. It was then that Saul began really to reign.

7. Of the large force which had been collected, Saul retained only three thousand men, with whom he proposed to make war upon the Philistines, who held in possession many strong places in the south, and kept the neighbouring inhabitants in such subjection that they had been deprived of their weapons, and could not even get their implements of husbandry sharpened without going to the Philistine garrisons. Hence, in all the force, Saul and his eldest son, Jonathan, were the only persons who possessed a sword or a spear. The operations against the Philistines were commenced by Jonathan, who, with the thousand men whom his father had placed

under his command, cut off the Philistine garrison at Geba
Interpreting this as a declaration of war, the Philistines delayed not to bring into the field a vast force, which comprehended six thousand horsemen and three thousand chariots of
war. Saul, on his part, had summoned all the tribes to send
their levies to Gilgal. This they did in sufficient numbers;
but while they remained there waiting for Samuel, who had
appointed to come and offer sacrifices, great numbers of the
men slunk away, being appalled at the formidable aspect of
the Philistine army. Saul was confessedly in a difficult position, and his obedience to the principle of the theocracy was
severely tested. It failed; for, becoming impatient at the
delay of Samuel, he called for the victims, and himself offered
the sacrifices. By this act he not only seemed to make a claim
to exercise the priestly office, as kings did in other countries,
but gave indications of the dispositions which in the end proved
his ruin. He was a brave and able commander; but he too
often forgot that, in his political capacity, he was but the vassal
of the Divine King; and he did not always execute the orders
he received, but made exceptions according to his own views.
Just as the sacrifices had been offered, Samuel arrived, and
strongly testified the Divine displeasure at this disobedience,
which he declared had manifested the unfitness of Saul to be
the founder of a race of kings. He then quitted the camp;
and Saul, hiding his concern, numbered his force, which he
found dwindled away to six hundred men. Not daring to
encounter the Philistine host with this handful of men, he
marched with them to his own town of Gibeah.

8. The main body of the Philistines remained at Mich-
mash; but they frequently sallied out in parties, and ravaged
the country without opposition. At length a bold plan was
formed by Jonathan, who communicated it only to his armour-
bearer, and the two secretly withdrew themselves from the
camp. They found means to ascend a steep cliff, where the
enemy least of all expected an attack; and early in the morning they fell upon the advanced guards of the Philistines.
Some were slain by the sword, and the others thrown into
such consternation, that they slew one another, mistaking
friends for foes. As soon as Saul got intelligence of what had
happened, he took advantage of the confusion into which they

were already thrown, and fell upon the Philistines with such fury, that they were soon utterly routed. That the pursuit of the enemy might not be retarded, Saul, in the heat of the chase, proclaimed death to any one who should taste food before the night. Ignorant of this, Jonathan, happening to taste some wild honey, had well nigh fallen a sacrifice to the rash vow of his father, but was saved by the interposition of the people.

CHAPTER II. B. C. 1095 to 1050.

PALESTINE.	B. C.	EGYPT	EVENTS AND PERSONS	B. C.
War with the Amalekites . . .	1095	Amun-rueses? from 1080 to about 1760, after which the succession is doubtful for ninety years.	Latinus, fifth king of the Latins . . .	1095
Saul's second offence and rejection . .	1079		Kingdom of Athens ends with Codrus	1070
David born	1079		Medon, the first Archon of Athens .	1070
David anointed . .	1070			
David slays Goliath .	1065			
David marries Michal	1060			
David's first flight to Gath, &c. . . .	1059			

1. SEVERAL following years were distinguished by successful warfare with the enemies of Israel,—with Moab and Ammon in the east, with Edom in the south, with the Philistines in the west, and with the Syrian kings of Zobah in the north. At length, in the tenth or eleventh year of his reign, Saul received orders, through Samuel, to execute the Lord's "fierce wrath" upon the Amalekites, who had formerly been doomed to utter extermination for opposing the Israelites when they came out of Egypt. The result of the war put it fully in the king's power to fulfil his commission; but he thought proper to retain the best of the cattle as booty, and to bring back the Amalekite king Agag as a prisoner. Here again Saul ventured to use his own discretion where his commission left him none. For this the Divine decree, excluding his descendants from the throne, was again and irrevocably pronounced by Samuel, who met him at Gilgal on his return. The stern prophet then directed the Amalekite king to be brought forth and slain by the sword, after which he departed to his own home, and went no more to see Saul to the day of his death, though he ceased not to bemoan his misconduct and the forfeiture it had incurred. But, during the years in which Samuel mourned for Saul, the king himself seemed increasing in strength and power; he became respected at home and feared abroad; while the many virtues of his excellent son Jonathan, who was greatly beloved by the people, seemed to render his dynasty secure. Saul himself, however, appears to

THE BATTLE OF AZOTUS *Palestine.*

have had sad misgivings on this subject, and we may perhaps impute to the constant brooding of his mind upon the doom pronounced by the prophet, those fits of morbid melancholy into which he frequently fell. His general temper, at the same time, became sour, irritable, and sanguinary.

2. At length, about the twenty-fifth year of Saul's reign, Samuel received the Divine mandate, to take measures for anointing the person whom the Lord had chosen to displace the race of Saul in the throne of Israel. For this purpose he was to proceed to Bethlehem, and there anoint one of the sons of a man named Jesse. This was a delicate commission, which, if known, might, as the prophet apprehended, induce Saul to slay him; and he therefore veiled it under the form of a public sacrifice. The prophet appears to have made known his real purpose only to Jesse, who caused all his sons to pass before him, when they were rejected, one after another, until the youngest, David, was sent for from the fields, where he was with the sheep. This youth was the destined king; and Samuel anointed him as such in the midst of his elder brethren, who, as well as himself, were probably kept in ignorance of the purport of this act. Samuel returned to his own home, and David continued to tend his father's flock. David was not more distinguished by the comeliness of his person than by his accomplishments and valour; he was skilled in music and poetical composition, and he had, without weapons, slain a lion and a bear which attacked his flock.

3. Meanwhile, the king's fits of melancholy madness went on increasing in frequency and duration, and no cure was found for his disordered mind. At length, some persons who had observed that Saul was much affected by music, suggested that the soothing powers of the harp should be tried; and another then recommended

117. Grand Egyptian Harps.

"the son of Jesse" as an accomplished master of that instru-

ment, and withal, a man of valour. Saul therefore delayed
not to send to Jesse, commanding him to send his son to
court. Little thinking that in him he beheld his successor
on the throne, Saul received the youthful minstrel with favour
When the fits came upon him, David played on the harp, and
under its soothing strains his mind soon recovered its usual
tone. This service, together with his other engaging qualities, and his discreet behaviour, won the heart of the king,
who conferred upon him the distinguished and confidential
post of his armour-bearer.

4. Since their last great discomfiture, the Philistines had
recruited their strength, and in the thirtieth year of Saul's
reign, and the twentieth of David's life, they again took the
field against the Israelites. It curiously illustrates the nature
of warfare in those times, to find that the presence, in the
army of the Philistines, of one enormous giant about nine or
ten feet high, filled them with confidence, and struck the

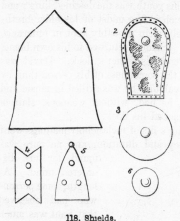

118. Shields.

I The Tsenna, or Great Shield. 2. Common Egyptian
Shield. 3. Target. 4. 5. Ancient Shields of unknown tribes. 6. Roundel.

Israelites with dread.
The giant, whose name
was Goliath, had a hel-
met of brass upon his
head, and he was armed
with a brazen coat of
mail, the weight of
which was no less than
six hundred shekels.
He had also greaves of
brass upon his legs, and
a target of brass be-
tween his shoulders;
and a man bearing his
shield went before him.
His weapons were of
course proportioned to
his enormous bulk; as
an instance of which,
we are informed, that the staff of his spear was like a weaver's
beam, and that its head contained six hundred shekels of
iron. He presented himself daily between the two armies,
and, with insulting language, defied the Israelites to produce

a champion who might, in single combat with him, decide the quarrel between the nations. This was repeated many days; but no Israelite was found bold enough to accept the challenge. At this juncture David, who, when his services were no longer needed at court, had returned to his father, arrived

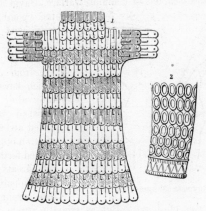

119. Coats of Mail.

1. Egyptian tigulated. 2. Sleeve of ring-mail, Ionian.

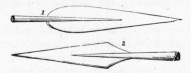

120. Spear Heads.

at the camp to visit his elder brethren who were with the army. Hearing the insolent vaunts of the proud Pagan, witnessing the dismay of the people, and learning that high rewards had been offered to the man who should overcome the giant, David offered himself for the combat. He was accordingly brought before the king, who failed to recognise him under the altered appearance which a year or two on the verge of manhood produces, but, contrasting the bulk and known prowess of the giant with the inexperience and light frame of the young man, earnestly disuaded him

from the enterprize.   But as David expressed his strong con·
fidence that the God of Israel, who had delivered him from
the lion and the bear when he tended his father's flock,
would also deliver him from the Philistine, Saul at length
allowed him to go forth against Goliath.   Refusing all armour
of proof and weapons of common warfare, David advanced to

the combat, armed
only with his shep·
herd's sling and a few
smooth pebbles picked
up from the brook
which flowed through
the valley.   The as·
tonished giant felt in·
sulted at being offered
such an opponent, and
poured forth such hor·
rid threats as might
have appalled any one
less strong in faith

121. Egyptian Slingers and Sling.

than the son of Jesse.   But as Goliath strode forward to
meet David, the latter slung one of his smooth stones with
so sure an aim and so strong an arm, that it smote his
opponent in the middle of the forehead and brought him to
the ground.

5. The king lost no time in following up this blow, and
attacked the astonished Philistines with such vigour that they
immediately gave way and were defeated with tremendous
slaughter.   Triumphant was the return of Saul; but it mor·
tified his pride to perceive that David was on all hands re·
garded as the hero of the day: and when the damsels made
this the burden of their triumphal song—" Saul has slain his
thousands, and David his ten thousands!" he could not con·
ceal his resentment that the honours of victory should be
thus proportioned.   From a fretful expression which he let
fall, it seems more than likely that he then first suspected
that David was " the man after God's own heart," to whom
his throne was to be given.   His inquiries probably confirmed
this impression, and thenceforth he lost no opportunity of ex·
posing David to disgrace and danger.   But all the schemes

laid for his ruin served only to make more prominent David's valour in the field, and the wisdom and generosity of his general conduct. Finding that the honours which were designed as snares for him—including that of giving him his daughter Michal in marriage—really exalted David, Saul could no longer confine his dark passions to his own bosom, but charged his son Jonathan and others to take some opportunity of destroying the son of Jesse for him. He little suspected that a most tender friendship, " passing the love of women," had grown up between Jonathan and David. To Jonathan, in particular, was this celebrated friendship highly honourable; for it was not unknown to him that the son of Jesse was destined to exclude himself and his children from the throne of Israel. But with a generosity of feeling, of which there is scarcely another example, he cheerfully acquiesced in the superior claims of David, and was the most ardent admirer of his person and character. He could even find pleasure in picturing the time when David should sit upon the throne, and when he should himself be next to him in place, as nearest to him in love, and find in him the protector and guardian of the very children whom narrow minds might have suspected to be in the utmost danger from his claims.

6. On the present occasion Jonathan gave his friend timely notice of danger, and spoke so forcibly to his father, that his better feelings overcame his insane horror of David, and he promised to make no further attempt upon his life. But soon after this, David, having commanded an expedition against the Philistines, so distinguished himself as to increase the admiration of the people, and to revive the hatred of Saul. When he resumed his place at court, and was one day playing on his harp to soothe the perturbed spirit of the king, he narrowly escaped death from a javelin which Saul threw with the intention of pinning him to the wall. He then withdrew to his own house, where he was followed by men whom the king sent to despatch him. But they were amused and deceived by David's wife Michal, Saul's own daughter, while her husband was let down from the window in a basket and made his escape to Samuel at Ramah. Repeated attempts to take him thence or slay him there, the last of which was

made by the king in person, were defeated by the special interposition of Providence. But Saul, brooding gloomily over his doom, still cherished his cruel purpose against him; and on one occasion he even threw his javelin at Jonathan for speaking in favour of his absent friend. This being made known to David, he resolved, after a private interview and tender parting with Jonathan, to withdraw himself effectually from the designs upon his life by retiring to a foreign land. For this purpose he made choice of Gath, one of the five Philistine states. In this choice he was probably guided by the consideration that the Philistines, from their enmity to Saul, were less likely than any other neighbouring nation to give him up at the demand of the king.

7. The tabernacle had by this time been removed from Shiloh to Nob, in the tribe of Benjamin; and David, with his few followers, called there on his way, and procured from the high priest, Ahimelech, a supply of provisions and the only weapon in his possession—the very sword which David himself had taken from Goliath, and which had been laid up in the tabernacle as a trophy of that victory. This assistance David obtained under the unjustifiable pretence of being on a private mission from the king. He then proceeded to Gath; but finding that the Philistines cherished revengeful recollections of his former exploits against them, he feigned himself mad, and by that means escaped their resentment.

8. David then left the country of the Philistines and repaired to the wild district of Adullam, in the tribe of Judah. Here there was a large and not easily accessible cave, which formed an excellent shelter for himself, and the men of broken fortunes and reckless character, about four hundred in number, who resorted to him, and of whom he became the captain.

9. From Adullam David went to the land of Moab for the purpose of placing his parents in safety there, lest they should become exposed to the blind fury with which Saul was now animated. He was perhaps inclined to remain there himself; but it was of importance that his dangers and conduct should keep him in the view of his admiring countrymen, and a prophet was therefore sent to command his return to the land of Judah. He obeyed, and found refuge in the forest of Hareth.

CHAPTER III.   B.C. 1059 to 1055.

PALESTINE.

	B. C.		B. C.
David's wanderings	1059 to 1054	Saul's third offence	1055
Death of Samuel	1057	Saul defeated and slain by the Phi-	
David's second flight to Gath	1055	listines	1055

1. The mind of Saul was of too coarse a mould to understand that it was possible for David to know his high destinies, and yet abide God's own time, without taking any questionable measures to advance them. He persuaded himself that David had organized an extensive conspiracy against his life and government; he suspected every one about him of being engaged in this conspiracy, and believed that his son Jonathan had been drawn into it. He was in a most sanguinary mood, and craved for some objects on which to wreak his fury. Unhappily such objects were found in the high-priest and others of the sacerdotal order. One Doeg, an Edomite in the employment of Saul, had been present at Nob when David was there; and he gave an exaggerated report of the assistance which Ahimelech had given to the fugitive. On hearing this, Saul sent for the pontiff, and the rest of the priests then at Nob, and, accusing them of traitorous practices, ordered them to be slain. His guards refused this barbarous office; but Doeg and other strangers executed the king's order without compunction. Eighty-five of the priestly race perished: nor did this satisfy the sanguinary king, for he sent to Nob, ordering man, woman, child, and every living creature, to be put to the sword. None escaped but Abiathar; and he fled to David, who was greatly shocked at the tidings which he brought. Thus another and almost final step was taken in the completion of that doom which had many years before been pronounced upon the house of Eli. This, however, was no excuse for Saul, whose tenderness towards the Amalekites, whom he was commanded to destroy, is strikingly contrasted with his shocking immolation of the priests of God, whom it was his duty to protect.

2. Meanwhile, David found an opportunity of employing his troop for the benefit of his country, by relieving the town of Keilah from the incursions of the Philistines. He then entered that town; which Saul no sooner heard, than he marched to lay siege to it. But David, being informed by the sacred oracle, which Abiathar, who acted as his priest, consulted for him, that the inhabitants would deliver him up, withdrew into the wild country in the eastern part of Judah, towards the Dead Sea, and found refuge in the wilderness of Ziph. While he was there, Jonathan came to him privately, to encourage him to trust in God, and to renew their covenant of friendship and peace. This was the last time these devoted friends saw each other.

3. Soon after this, some ill-disposed persons of the neighbourhood went to Gibeah, and acquainted Saul with the place of David's retreat. The king immediately marched thither with a sufficient force; but David, being warned of his approach, retreated southward into the wilderness of Maon, before his arrival. Saul followed him thither; and was close upon him, when he was providentially called off to repel an unexpected incursion of the Philistines. This gave David an opportunity of withdrawing to Engedi, among the rocky fastnesses which border the Dead Sea; and to that quarter Saul pursued him with three thousand men, after he had repulsed the Philistines. Here, being one day weary, the king withdrew into a cave to take some rest. In the providence of God, it happened that this was the very cave in whose interior recesses David and his men lay concealed; and whilst Saul slept, David advanced softly, and cut off the skirt of his robe. When the king went out of the cave, David followed him at some distance, and at length called to him, and displayed the skirt in evidence of his innocence. Saul could not but feel that the man who had taken the skirt could quite as easily have taken his life; and struck by this magnanimity, his stern heart was for the time subdued. " Is that thy voice, my son David!" he cried, and then he wept. He acknowledged that he had been foolish and criminal; he admitted that the son of Jesse was worthy of the destinies which awaited him; and he exacted from him a promise, that when ne became king he would not root out the family of his pre-

decessor, as eastern kings were wont to do   Saul then withdrew : but David had too little confidence in his good resolu-
tions to make any alteration in his own position.

4. The death of Samuel took place shortly after this, in
the ninety-second year of his age. He appears to have retained his judicial authority, even after Saul became king ;
and he was much and deservedly lamented by the people before whom he had acted a public part from his very cradle,
with equal credit to himself and benefit to his country. Soon
afterwards, David retreated southward into the desert of
Paran. The shepherds of southern Israel led their flocks into those distant pastures in the proper season ; and the presence of David and his men, at this time, effectually protected
them from the Bedouin tribes, by which they were in general
much molested. Afterwards returning to the wilderness of
Maon, David heard that a rich sheep-master, called Nabal,
with whose shepherds his men had been very friendly in the
desert, was making great preparations for the entertainment
of his people during the shearing of his numerous flocks of
sheep. David being in great want of provisions sent a
respectful message to solicit a supply from him. Nabal, who
was of a churlish disposition, refused the application with insult ; at which ungracious return for the protection which had
been given to his flocks in the desert, David was so much
enraged, that he hastily determined to inflict a severer punishment than the occasion warranted, by bearing fire and sword
to the homestead of the brutish sheep-master.

5. Some such resolution on his part was foreseen by such
of the shepherds then present as had been out into the desert ;
but the execution of it was prevented by the prudent conduct
of Abigail, the wife of Nabal, a very excellent and beautiful
woman, whom David married after Nabal's death. Here it
is right to mention that after David fled from court, Saul, to
wound him in the tenderest point, obliged his daughter,
Michal, the first wife of David, to marry another husband.

6. David again retreated into the wilderness of Ziph,
which coming to the knowledge of Saul, he, notwithstanding
his recent convictions, again went in search of him with 3000
men. While the King of Israel lay encamped and surrounded
by his troops, during the darkness and stillness of the night, and

M

when all were fast asleep, David, accompanied by his nephew Abishai, penetrated, undiscovered, to the place where the monarch lay, and took away the spear which was stuck in the ground near his head, and the cruse of water which stood by his side. In the morning, he called to the king from the hill-side, and displayed these manifest tokens that the king's life had been completely in his power. His remonstrance was attended with the same result as on the former occasion. Saul was deeply affected, and, having acknowledged that he had acted "foolishly," returned to Gibeah.

7. The strong faith by which David had been hitherto sustained, now began in some degree to give way under these continued persecutions; and apprehending that, if he remained any longer in the country, he should one day perish by the hand of Saul, he resolved again to seek refuge with the Philistines of Gath. This very questionable step brought him into dangers quite as imminent as those from which he fled, and involved him in much insincere conduct which cannot be contemplated without pain. Achish, the king of Gath, received him and his men with pleasure, probably because he calculated that persons so persecuted by Saul, would render effectual service in the war against him, for which the Philistine states were then making preparations. After being for some time hospitably entertained at Gath, the king gave to David the border town of Ziklag, that he and his men might dwell there with their families and possessions. While at this place, David employed his men from time to time in expeditions against the Amalekites and other nations of the south; and by the spoil thus acquired his men were greatly enriched. But, as these nations were friends and allies of the Philistines, Achish was led to believe that his operations were directed against his own countrymen the Israelites, which gave the king of Gath great satisfaction—in the belief that by thus making himself abhorred in Israel, he had rooted himself in the service of the Philistines. This duplicity, however, soon brought its own punishment; for, when the Philistines were ready for the war against Saul, David found that no ground was left him on which he could decline the invitation of Achish, to go with him against Israel. He was only saved from his difficulty by the jealousy of the princes of the other

Philistine states, who, justly suspecting the sincerity of his alleged enmity against his own people, compelled Achish to send him back to Ziklag. On his return, David found that the Amalekites had taken advantage of his absence to burn and pillage the place, and had carried away as captives all the people, chiefly women and children, who had been left there. He immediately pursued after them, and having at length overtaken them, when they deemed themselves in safety, cut them in pieces, and not only recovered all that they had taken, but obtained abundant spoil, which they had collected in other places, and out of which he sent valuable gifts to his friends in Judah.

8. Meanwhile the Philistine army continued its march into the land of Israel, and penetrated to the eastern part of the great battle-field of Esdraelon; by which time Saul had formed an opposing camp on the mountains of Gilboa. When he beheld the vast force which the Philistine states had, by a mighty effort, brought into the field, dire misgiving as to the result arose in his mind; and now, at last, in this extremity, he sought counsel of God. But the Lord answered him not by any of the usual means,—by dreams, by *Urim*, nor by prophets. Finding himself thus forsaken, he had recourse to a witch at Endor, not far from Gilboa, to whom he repaired by night in disguise, and conjured her to evoke the spirit of Samuel that he might ask counsel of him in this fearful emergency. Accordingly, an aged and mantled figure arose, which Saul took to be the ghost of Samuel, though whether it were really so or not has been much questioned. The king bowed himself reverently, and told the reason for which he had called him from the dead. The figure, in reply, told him that God had taken the crown from his house, and given it to a worthier man; that, on the next day, the Philistines would triumph over Israel; and that he and his sons should be slain in the battle. The king swooned at these heavy tidings, but soon recovered; and having taken some refreshment, returned the same night to the camp.

9. The next morning the two armies engaged, when the Israelites gave way before the Philistines, and maintained a running fight until they had fallen back upon Mount Gilboa, from which they had advanced to meet the enemy. Here

they attempted to rally, but in vain : Jonathan and two other
of Saul's sons were killed, and the army was thrown into
complete disorder.   At length Saul himself was desperately
wounded ; and fearing that he would fall into the hands of
the enemy, and be ignominiously treated by them, he prayed
his armour-bearer to thrust him through ; and when that
faithful follower refused, he took his own sword, fell upon it,
and died.   This example was followed by the armour-bearer.

10. The next morning, when the Philistines went over
the field of battle, they found the bodies of Saul and his sons.
They cut off their heads, and sent them, with their armour,
into Philistia as trophies of their victory ; and the bodies
were shamefully gibbetted upon the walls of the neighbouring town of Bethshan, near the Jordan.   But the people of
Jabesh Gilead, on the other side of the river, mindful of their
ancient obligations to their king, went over by night and
stole away the bodies, which they burned, and then buried
the remains under a tree.

11. Three days after his return to Ziklag, the news of
this action and its results were first brought to David by an
Amalekite.   This man, in roaming over the field of battle,
had found the body of Saul, which he divested of the royal
diadem and armlets, and, in expectation of great rewards,
hastened with them to David, whose appointment to the
throne appears to have been by this time well known not
only to the Israelites but to their neighbours.   To enhance
his claims of reward, he pretended that the wounded king
had fallen by his hand.   But he grievously misunderstood
the character of David, who rent his clothes in bitter afflic-
tion, and ordered the Amalekite to be slain for laying his
hands upon " the Lord's anointed."   David then poured forth
his grief for Israel, for Saul, and for Jonathan, his friend, in
one of the most beautiful elegiac odes to be found in any
language.

CHAPTER IV.   B.C. 1055 TO 1034.

B.C.

David begins to reign over Judah in
Hebron 1055
Abner sets up Ishbosheth, son of Saul,
as king, ... 1055
Abner comes over to David, and is as-
sassinated by Joab 1048
Ishbosheth assassinated 1047
David becomes king of all Israel . 1047
Takes the fortress of Jebus in Jeru-
salem 1046

B.C.

Removes the Ark of the Covenant to
Jerusalem 1044
Designs to build a temple, but is told
to leave that work for his son . . 1040
Sin in the matter of Bathsheba and
Uriah 1035
Is reproved by Nathan, and re-
pents 1034

1. SAUL being dead, David inquired of God what course
he should take, and was directed to repair to Hebron, the
principal town in the tribe of Judah.   At that place the men
of Judah publicly anointed him as their king.   But through
the able management of Abner, a near relative of the late
king, and the chief commander of his forces, the other tribes
acknowledged Ishbosheth, the only surviving son of Saul,
whose residence was fixed at Mahanaim, eastward of the
Jordan.   For two years no hostile acts took place between
the two kingdoms; but, at the end of that time, war was
commenced by Abner, with the view of bringing Judah
under obedience to the house of Saul.   To oppose him David
sent Joab, his sister's son, who, with his brothers Abishai
and the swift-footed Asahel, had been amongst his most active and devoted followers in all his wanderings.   The most
remarkable action in this war took place at Gibeon, where
the forces of Abner were defeated and put to flight.   Abner
being closely pursued by Asahel, and having in vain entreated
him to desist, smote him dead with his spear.   At length a
number of Benjamites rallied under Abner, and faced the
pursuers, when the opposing tribes came to a parley; and
Joab, being persuaded by Abner to prevent the further effu-
sion of kindred blood, drew off his forces, and went home.
In most of the other actions of this war David had the advantage, and his interest in the nation daily increased. while
that of Ishbosheth declined.

2. One so able and experienced as Abner could not but apprehend the final result; and being stimulated by a personal dispute with Ishbosheth, he resolved to withdraw from him, and give to David that support by which alone the house of Saul was upheld. Having obtained authority from the other tribes to treat with David, he repaired to Hebron, and was there received and entertained with all honour and respect; and after having conferred with the king, withdrew with the intention of completing the transaction. Joab just then returned from a military expedition, and being informed of what had taken place, he became jealously apprehensive that such a man as Abner would soon supplant him with David; and professing to believe that the whole was a snare laid by Abner, he reproached the king, in no very measured terms, for the reception he had given to him. He also burned to avenge the death of his brother, which, indeed, the popular ideas connected with "blood-revenge," seemed to impose upon him as a duty. He therefore despatched a messenger to recall Abner, in the king's name, to Hebron. He met him at the gate of the town, and drawing him aside, as if to speak with him privately, treacherously stabbed him. This was likely to have the very worst effect upon the pending negotiations. David, by the abhorrence he expressed at this cruel and treacherous deed, by his lamentations, and by a magnificent funeral, in which he appeared himself as a mourner, evidenced that he had no part in the murder; and of this the people were satisfied. But the influence of Joab with the soldiers was too great to allow the king, at that time, to inflict on him the punishment he deserved. The loss of Abner rendered the condition of Ishbosheth utterly hopeless; and not long after, two of his own officers, expecting great rewards from David, murdered him in his bed, and hastened with his head to Hebron. But no sooner had David heard their boastful confession, and seen the head of his rival, than, with great indignation, he condemned the assassins to an ignominious death, for the crime by which they had hoped to win his favour.

3. The tribes, now looking upon David as the man who had been specially nominated by the Divine Head of their theocracy, and as one whose military services in the time of Saul entitled him more than any living man to the distinction,

unanimously offered him the crown. Having accepted the offer, with conditions annexed to it, David was, in the presence of the elders of all the tribes, anointed a second time at Hebron, and proclaimed king over all Israel. He had then reigned seven and a half years as king of Judah only.

4. The resources of united Israel being now at his disposal, David turned his attention to such military enterprises as might consolidate and extend his empire. His first act was to gain possession of the fortress which was still held by the Jebusites in Mount Zion. This fortress being deemed impregnable, the attempt to take it was derided by the Jebusites. It was, however, carried by storm, under the conduct of Joab, who was in consequence appointed captain-general of the forces of the whole kingdom, as he had been before of those of Judah. David then made Jerusalem the metropolis of his realm, and fixed his residence upon Mount Zion. His success in accomplishing what for many ages had resisted all the efforts of the Israelites, seemed a most auspicious commencement of David's reign, and even attracted the attention of foreigners. Hiram, king of Tyre, sent ambassadors to congratulate him on his accession to the throne, and to enter into a league with him. As the Phœnicians were well skilled in the fine and useful arts, David was glad to avail himself of their assistance in building a palace in the captured city.

5. The Philistines regarded with apprehension the increasing prosperity of the Israelites; and to keep it in check, invaded the south with a large army. They had some successes at first, David not being prepared to meet them in the field; but when he had collected his forces, he gave them battle, and discomfited them so completely in two different engagements, that they were never again able to give any serious disturbance to Israel.

6. Having now a respite from war, David formed the design of removing to his new capital the ark of the covenant, which had so long remained in obscurity at Kirjath-jearim. A vast company of priests and Levites, chiefs and elders, from all parts of the land, attended at this important solemnity; and numerous instruments of music sounded in harmony with the glad feelings of the people. But, through ignorance or inadvertence, the ark, which should have been borne on the

shoulders of the Levites, was put upon a car drawn by oxen. On the way the animals stumbled, and Uzzah, the son of Abinadab, put forth his hand to support the tottering ark, for

which he was struck dead upon the spot, none but priests being allowed to touch it on pain of death (Numb. iv. 15). This judgment threw a damp

122.

over the whole proceeding; and David, being afraid to take the ark farther, left it in the care of Obed-edom, a Levite, whose house was near at hand. This person experienced the Divine favour and blessing in a very remarkable manner, during the three months the ark remained under his roof. The news of this encouraged David to resume his original design, which he did with the more confidence, as he had meanwhile taken care to acquaint himself with the prescribed observances for the orderly removal of the ark. It was accordingly removed with great pomp and ceremony, and deposited in a tabernacle which David had provided for it.

7. About five years after, when the king was inhabiting his house of cedar, and God had given him rest from all his enemies, he meditated the design of building a temple in which the ark of the Lord might be placed, instead of being deposited " within curtains," or in a tent, as hitherto. This design was at first encouraged by the prophet Nathan; but he was afterwards instructed to tell David that this work was less appropriate for him, who had been a warrior from his youth, and had shed much blood, than for his son, who should enjoy in prosperity and peace the rewards of his father's victories. Nevertheless, the design itself was highly commended, as betokening proper sentiments; and for this, and for his faithful allegiance to the Supreme King of Israel, it was promised that the sceptre should be perpetuated in his family. To this was added an intimation—sufficiently intelligible to him, and which filled him with joy—that the long-promised Messiah, the Anointed of God, should be numbered among his descendants. To David this was an honour greater than his crown; and in very beautiful and elegant language he

expressed his adoration and gratitude. Since he was himself precluded from building the temple, it became an object of interest to him, during the rest of his life, to provide the materials for it, and to form arrangements and lay down rules for the more imposing and orderly celebration of the ritual worship which the law had prescribed. He divided the priests and Levites, who had become very numerous, into bands, and fixed a regular rotation of service. Music, instrumental and vocal, was also introduced by him into the sacred services. A great number of the sacred songs to be used in these services were composed by himself. These are to this day preserved to us in the Book of Psalms.

8. The next measures of David were calculated, if not designed, to give a peaceable and prosperous reign to his successor, by subduing or weakening all the neighbouring powers likely to disturb his repose. In successive campaigns he completed the reduction of the Philistines, and took possession of Gath and its towns, using them as barrier towns for Judah; he utterly subdued the Moabites, and dismantled all their strongholds; he cleared his eastern frontier to the Euphrates, and made the Syrians of Zobah and Damascus tributary, and brought the Edomites under the like subjection, after he had defeated them with great slaughter in the valley of Salt. From all these wars, which appear to have occupied about three years, he returned to Jerusalem with rich spoils, which he laid up for the use of the future temple. To the same use he applied the presents which he received from foreign kings whose attention was drawn to his victories, and who deemed it expedient to propitiate so great a conqueror.

9. The Scriptures describe David as "a man after God's own heart." By this we are not to understand that David always acted rightly, or that God approved of all he did. Its meaning is, that, in his public capacity, as king of Israel, he acted in accordance with the true theory of the theocratical government; was always alive to his dependence on the Supreme King; took his own true place in the system, and aspired to no other; and conducted all his undertakings with reference to the Supreme will. He constantly calls himself "the servant (or vassal) of Jehovah:" and that, and no other, was the true place for the human king of Israel to fill. By

I

thus limiting the description of David as "a man after God's own heart," we are left free from any necessity of vindicating all his acts, or of upholding him as an immaculate character, which he was very far from being. The basis of his character, and the general tone of his conduct, were good,—were better than we usually find among men. But the same ardent temperament which sometimes betrayed his judgment in his public acts, led him into great errors and crimes; it also made him the first to discover his lapse, and the last to forgive himself. Who can depict the sins of David in stronger language than he does himself? Who was ever more submissive to punishment, or more convinced of his unworthiness to receive forgiveness and consolation?

10. We find him engaged in a war with the Ammonites, in the eighteenth year of his reign, to avenge the insulting treatment which his ambassadors had received from their king. The conduct of this war David intrusted to Joab, and remained himself at Jerusalem. There, while sauntering upon the roof of his palace, after the noon-day sleep which is usual in the East, he perceived a woman whose great beauty attracted his great regard. She proved to be Bathsheba, the wife of Uriah, an officer of Canaanitish origin, then absent with the army, besieging Rabbah, the capital of Ammon. David sent for her, and, under the influence of criminal passion, became an adulterer. This first crime was followed by a greater; for, to cover his own sin, and to save the woman from the doom of an adulteress, he sent for Uriah to Jerusalem. Having heard from him the particulars of the war which he pretended to require, the king dismissed him to his own home. But Uriah, considering that it ill became a soldier to seek his bed while his companions lay on the hard ground, under the canopy of heaven, exposed to all the attacks of the enemy, remained all night in the hall of the palace with the guards, and returned to the wars without having seen Bathsheba. This cost him his life; for David, seeing no other way to prevent the consequences he apprehended, made him the bearer of an order to Joab to expose him to certain death in some perilous enterprise against the enemy. He was obeyed by that unscrupulous general; and when David heard that Uriah was dead, he sent for Bath-

sheba and made her his wife. He had already several wives, as was customary in those times; and among them was Michal, whom he had long ago reclaimed from the man to whom she had been given by Saul.

11. David thought all was now safe; but he was much mistaken. The prophet Nathan was sent to him, and by a fictitious tale of oppression applicable to the case (2 Sam. xii. 1–4), so kindled the anger of David that he not only sentenced the supposed offender to restore fourfold, according to the law, but condemned the criminal to death. Instantly the prophet exclaimed—"Thou art the man!" and proceeded, in the name of the Lord, to rebuke him for his heinous transgression, and to announce the punishments which it became his justice to inflict.

12. No sooner were the eyes of David thus opened than he instantly confessed his crimes with great humility and contrition, and submitted himself to the chastisements of God. This becoming repentance averted the sentence of death from himself, but it was transferred to the offspring of his crime, then newly born. To mark the divine displeasure against sin, the rest of David's life was full of troubles from his children, three more of whom died untimely deaths; thus, in some sense, completing a fourfold retaliation for the murder of Uriah.

13. The war with the Ammonites was successful. Rabbah, the metropolis, which was the last to yield, was taken; and the people generally were so completely subjected, that David put them to hard labour and servile employments in the fields, woods, and brick-kilns. Among the spoils was the very costly crown of the king, which David appropriated to his own use, and wore on state occasions.

CHAPTER V. B.C. 1034 to 1015.

PALESTINE.	B.C.
Solomon born	1033
Absalom's vengeance on Amnon .	1030
Absalom recalled	1027
His rebellion and death	1023
David numbers the people . . .	1017
Rehoboam born	1015
Adonijah's rebellion	1015
Solomon proclaimed king . . .	1015
David dies	1015

EVENTS AND PERSONS.	B C
Medon, king of Argos	1038
Alba, sixth king of the Latins . .	1028
Archippus, third archon of Athens .	1014
Hiram, king of Tyre	

1. The threatened troubles in the house of David were not long in breaking out. Amnon, his eldest son, dishonoured his half-sister, Tamar, who was the full sister of Absalom. This injury excited in the mind of Absalom a resentment which only blood could satisfy. He said nothing for a time. But after two years, when all seemed to be forgotten, he invited all the royal family to a feast with which he celebrated the shearing of his sheep. Amnon was among the guests; and, at a given signal from their master, he was set upon and murdered by the servants of Absalom. On this, all the others mounted their mules, and fled in haste to Jerusalem; while Absalom himself lost no time in seeking refuge at the court of his maternal grandfather, Talmai, king of Geshur. He remained there three years; for although David, after the first burst of indignation and grief, would have been willing to recal him, he was prevented by the dread of public opinion and the demands of justice. At the end of the three years, however, the king, through the contrivance and intercession of Joab, was induced "to call home his banished;" but a regard for appearances excluded Absalom from the presence of his father until two years after his return to Jerusalem.

2. Absalom was now the eldest living son of David, and, in ordinary circumstances, might have been considered the heir-apparent to the throne. But it was already known to David that Solomon, his eldest surviving son by Bathsheba was destined by God to be his successor. The Lord, as we

have already seen, reserved the right of appointing whom
he pleased to the crown, although, in the absence of any
special appointment, it was supposed to descend in the ordinary course of succession.   It is more than probable that
this destination of the crown of David was known to
Absalom, and that the attempt to secure it in his father's
lifetime was made with the design of averting his own exclusion.   Had he been sure of succeeding when his father died,
he would probably have waited till then, for David was
already old.   At all events, he soon began to affect great
state, made much display of his chariots and guards, and
appeared in public with a splendid retinue of fifty men.   All
this pomp the more enhanced the condescension with which
he behaved to the people, and the interest he took in the
affairs of the suitors at the royal court.   These arts of popularity, with his handsome person and engaging manners,
quite won the hearts of the undiscerning multitude; and
when at length he ventured to raise the standard of open
rebellion, and to proclaim himself king, at Hebron, the people
flocked to him in crowds, and David was nearly deserted,
except by his guards and some faithful followers.   Confounded
at this intelligence, David abandoned Jerusalem in haste, to
proceed to the country beyond the Jordan, where the distance
would allow him more time for collecting his resources and
considering his course of action.   Deeply humbled at what
he considered as the punishment of God for his sins, David
ascended the Mount of Olives, on the upper road to Jericho,
as a mourner, weeping, barefoot, and with shrouded head.

3. On his way David was deeply wounded by false intelligence of the ungrateful desertion of Mephibosheth, the son of
Jonathan, whom, for his father's sake, he had treated with
much kindness and distinction, and to whom he had restored
the lands of Saul.   These lands he now too hastily bestowed
on the treacherous informant, Ziba, who had managed them
for Mephibosheth.   When he afterwards discovered his error,
and found that it was only his lameness which prevented the
son of his friend from following him, Ziba's connections were
too powerful to allow him to revoke the grant entirely, and
he directed that the land should be divided between them.
Among the remarkable incidents of this mournful journey

was the abusive and insulting conduct of a man named
Shimei, of the family of Saul, who manifested the most unseemly exultation at the forlorn condition of the king. Yet
the chastened David would not allow his people to avenge
this wrong.

4. The fugitives rested themselves in " the plains of the
wilderness;" but soon crossed the Jordan, in consequence of
information that Absalom had been advised to pursue them
with 12,000 men, and smite them before an army could be
collected. This, in fact, was the best course which Absalom
could have taken to complete his enterprise at one stroke.
It was the advice of David's chief councillor, Ahithophel,
who was renowned in all Israel for his sagacity, and whose
desertion to Absalom seemed one of the most serious of the
king's disasters. Nevertheless, Hushai, the friend of David,
who also had found a place in the council of Absalom, contrived to get this advice rejected in favour of the very different course recommended by himself. Finding his counsel
thus neglected, and foreseeing the consequences, the traitorous
Ahithophel went home and hanged himself.

5. Meanwhile David fixed his residence at Mahanaim,
beyond Jordan, where Ishbosheth had formerly held his
court. When Absalom heard where he was, he followed
him across the river with a powerful army, under the direction of his cousin Amasa. David and his general had not
been idle, but had collected a force, which, although small
in comparison, seemed to men who trusted in the righteousness of their cause, sufficient for the contest. David divided
his force into three battalions, and entrusted the command to
Joab, Abishai, and Ittai; for the troops refused to allow him
to risk his own valuable life in the battle. Still feeling all
a father's unreasoning love for his guilty son, the last words
of David to his commanders charged them to respect the life
of Absalom. This charge was but little regarded. The
army of Absalom was defeated by the better disciplined troops
of David, and the prince himself fled upon a swift mule; but
as he passed under an oak, the long hair which he so carefully cherished became entangled in the projecting boughs,
from which he was left suspended. In this situation he was
found by Joab, who slew him on the spot. His death ended

the war: the rebels dispersed, and went every man to his
home.   The king's joy at the victory was greatly damped

by the news of his son's
death.   He shut him-
self up in the chamber
over the city gate; and
the returning warriors,
who expected the re-
ward of his presence
and praise, heard only,
as they entered, his
loud and bitter lamen-
tations for his lost Ab-
salom.   At length Joab
went to him, and by
representing the pro-
bably serious conse-
quences of disgusting
the troops by making
them feel that their
victory was a crime, he
induced him to appear

123. Absalom's Tomb.

in public, and give his faithful soldiers the satisfaction they
had earned.

6. As the mass of the people had hailed Absalom as king,
David, with commendable delicacy, abstained from resuming
the crown as a matter of right; but resolved to tarry at
Mahanaim until formally invited back by the tribes.   The
Israelites generally were, by this time, thoroughly ashamed
of the rebellion, and quite ready to return to their allegiance.
But the want of unanimity among the tribes, and other circumstances, occasioned such delay, that Judah was the first
to invite the king to resume his throne at Jerusalem.   He
accordingly returned.   This seems to have been a wrong
step; for the other tribes were offended that he had returned
on the sole invitation of Judah, without their concurrence;
and at length the dissension became so great, that the Israel
ites, as distinguished from the Judahites, refused to recognise
the act, or to acknowledge David as king; and, appointing
one Sheba of Benjamin, perhaps of Saul's family, for their

leader, they raised the standard of revolt, with the usual cry of civil war—" To your tents, O Israel !"

7. David, partly with the view of conciliating those who had followed Absalom, appointed Amasa his commander-in-chief, in the place of Joab. Him he now ordered out in pursuit of Sheba; but as he failed to assemble the forces of Judah within the limited time, David, who dreaded delay, sent out Abishai with the royal guards. With this force Joab went as a volunteer.* While they rested at Gibeon, Amasa came up with the force which he had at length got together. As he came on, Joab advanced to meet him; and. under the cover of a friendly salute, gave him a mortal stab, as he had formerly given Abner. Having thus treacherously removed his rival, and confiding in the attachment of the troops he had so often led to victory, he assumed the chief command, and the soldiers readily, perhaps gladly, followed their former general. The fact that they had to deal with so experienced a commander as Joab, appears to have helped to discourage the partisans of Sheba, who, finding himself abandoned by the greater part of his followers, as Joab approached, deemed it expedient to withdraw with his few remaining adherents into the fortified town of Abel-beth-maachah in Naphtali. But when Joab appeared under the walls, the inhabitants, to save themselves, threw over to him the rebel's head; and the war being thus ended, Joab returned to Jerusalem. David detested his conduct, and was mortified at his presumption; but he dared not call him to account for the murder of Amasa, or remove him from the place which he had assumed.

8. After these things a famine of three years afflicted the people : and as the principles of the theocracy, guaranteed to the Israelites prosperity and plenty as long as they continued in obedience, every public calamity was justly regarded as a punishment for sin. David, therefore, somewhat tardily, sought to know the cause of this famine. He was told that, although so long after the event, it was a punishment for innocent blood

---

* As these persons were all related to the king, it may be well to define the relationship. David had two sisters, Zeruiah and Abigail. Zeruiah was the mother of Joab, Abishai, and Asahel (whom Abner slew); and Abigail was the mother of Amasa. They were all therefore David's nephews, and cousins of his sons. 1 Chron. ii. 13, 17

which had been left unatoned, namely, the blood of the Gibeonites, whose safety Israel had guaranteed by a covenant of peace ; but who had been massacred by Saul, on some pretext or other, in considerable numbers. On learning this, David required the remnant of the Gibeonites to name the expiation they required ; and they vindictively asked the death of seven of Saul's descendants. The king could not gainsay them ; and accordingly two sons of Saul by his concubine Rizpah, and the five sons of Merab, his eldest daughter, were yielded up to them. Thus were all the descendants of Saul destroyed, except Mephibosheth, the son of Jonathan, whom David had cherished, and now exempted for his father's sake. The exposure of the bodies, beyond the day of execution, which the Gibeonites demanded, was contrary to the habits of the Israelites, and justly repugnant to their feelings. Rizpah, the mother of Saul's sons, remained disconsolately, night and day, watching the bodies of her children, to protect them from the birds and beasts of prey. When this came to David's knowledge, he ordered the bodies to be taken down and deposited, with the bones of Saul and Jonathan, in the family sepulchre.

9. Now that the Israelites had been weakened by two rebellions and by three years of famine, the Philistines deemed the opportunity favourable for trying to shake off the yoke which they had borne with much impatience. They therefore renewed the war, but were defeated in four engagements, and finally subdued. Among the Philistines were some families of gigantic stature, and in this campaign they brought several of Goliath's family into the field. One of them had nearly overpowered David ; but he was rescued, and the giant killed by Abishai. After this the people would never allow David to go to the wars in person, " lest he should quench the light of Israel."

10. The next year David, that he might know the real extent of his power, and that all competent Israelites should be enrolled for military service, ordered Joab to take a census of the adult male population. The schemes of enlarged dominion, with a view to which this census was probably ordered to be taken, were contrary to that divine policy which required Israel to remain a compact and isolated people ; and

the enrolment for such purposes seriously infringed the liberties of the nation. It also manifested great distrust of the Supreme King, who was known to be willing and able to give victory in every lawful enterprise, whether by many or by few. On these grounds the act was displeasing to God; and it was distasteful even to Joab, who, after a vain remonstrance, proceeded to execute the order with great reluctance. The return which he made of men twenty years old and upwards, was 900,000 in the tribes of Israel, and 400,000 in Judah alone,—amounting in all to 1,300,000. By this we see that the population had more than doubled since the nation left Egypt and entered Palestine. The total numbers may be reckoned at considerably more than 5,000,000. When David received this account of the numbers of his people, "his heart smote him," and he became alive to the heinousness of his offence. At that moment the prophet Gad came commissioned to offer him the choice of three punishments :—seven years of famine—three months of defeat and loss in war—or three days of pestilence. He chose the last; and immediately the country was visited with a pestilence which in two days destroyed 70,000 men. David then vehemently interceded for his people, pleading that he alone had sinned, and praying that he and his might alone bear the punishment. His intercession prevailed, and the plague was stayed.

11. The eldest surviving son of David was Adonijah, who resembled Absalom in comeliness and in ambition. Provoked at the prospect of his younger brother Solomon being considered heir to the throne, he plotted to secure the crown before the king's death, which his age and feebleness shewed to be near at hand. He gained over Joab and Abiathar the high-priest to his cause; but the other high-priest,* Zadok, with the valiant Benaiah, the commander of the guards, and the great body of the "worthies," remained faithful to the cause of Solomon, and thereby evinced their adherence to the great principle of the government,—the supremacy of the Divine King, and his right to bestow the crown according to

* Abiathar will be remembered as the son of Ahimelech, who fled to David after the massacre at Nob. He naturally succeeded as high priest; but Saul gave that dignity to Zadok, thereby restoring the pontificate to the older line of Eleazer. When David succeeded to both kingdoms, he was unwilling to remove either and therefore gave them co-ordinate powers.

his pleasure. Having taken all the preliminary measures which seemed necessary, Adonijah invited his supporters to a splendid feast in one of the suburbs of Jerusalem, near the fountain of the king's garden. Here he was proclaimed king, with great acclamation, by his adherents. The news speedily reached the city, and was communicated to the king by Bathsheba and the prophet Nathan. Now Adonijah was very dear to the heart of David; and it is more than likely that, if left to his own feelings, he would have been willing that his eldest son should reign. But he was too much alive to the principle of the government to consider that he had any will in the matter, after the will of the Lord had been declared. He therefore immediately issued orders to Zadok the priest, and to the officers of the court and army, to take Solomon, and anoint and proclaim him king. The prince was immediately mounted upon the king's own mule, and escorted by all the court and the royal guards to the fountain of Gihon, where he was anointed by Zadok with the sacred oil; when the trumpets sounded, and the assembled concourse rent the air with shouts of "Long live King Solomon!"

12. When Adonijah and his party heard of this prompt and decided procedure, they were struck with fear, and dispersed to their own homes. Adonijah himself fled to the altar, which was a sanctuary, whence none but murderers could be taken. Hearing of this, Solomon sent to tell him that his safety depended upon his future conduct, and directed him to retire to his own house. Soon after, in a general assembly of the nation, the election of Solomon was ratified by the assent of the people; and he was again solemnly anointed by the high-priest. On this occasion, David gathered up the remnant of his declining strength, and addressed the convention in a very forcible and touching harangue. He took pains to impress upon his audience the true character of the government, and its peculiar subservience to the Divine King. He then adverted to the temple, which had been so long before his view; mentioned his own extensive preparations for it; urged them to assist Solomon with heart and hand in the great work which lay before him; and recommended an adherence to the plans and models which he had provided. He concluded with a devout thanksgiving to the Lord for all

his mercies to him and to the nation. Solomon then ascended the throne of his father; and his accession was celebrated with feastings and sacrifices.

13. On a subsequent occasion, David, feeling his end rapidly approaching, sent for Solomon, and earnestly impressed upon him the duty of obedience in all things to the Divine King. He had now done with life; and gave it up, at the age of seventy years, of which he had reigned forty—seven as king of Judah only, and thirty-three as king of all Israel. Amid the lamentations of all his people, the remains of David were deposited in a splendid tomb, which he had prepared for himself on Mount Zion.

CHAPTER VI.   B. C. 1015 TO 975.

PALESTINE.	B. C.
Solomon king	1015
Adonijah and Joab slain	1015
Solomon weds an Egyptian princess	1013
The foundation of the Temple laid .	1012
The Temple finished	1005
Solomon seduced to idolatry . . .	978
Solomon dies: Rehoboam succeeds	975
Revolt of the ten tribes . . .	975

GENERAL HISTORY.

	B. C.
Capetus, 7th king of the Latins . .	9??
Thersippus, 4th Archon of Athens	995
Tadmor built	991
City of Samos built . . . . . .,	986
Shishak (Sheshonk I., Sesonchis), king of Egypt	981

1. SOLOMON was nearly twenty years old when he began
to reign. His natural talents were of the highest order, and
had been improved by careful education; he was endowed
with profound sagacity, quick penetration, and great decision
of character; and no man ever possessed in a more eminent
degree those collective talents and attainments to which the
ancients gave the name of wisdom. He had not long ascended
the throne when his sagacity detected the secret traitorous
designs which Adonijah still entertained. This prince had
the adroitness to interest Bathsheba, the king's mother, in a
scheme which he had formed of espousing Abishag, one of the
wives of the late king, whom he had taken in his latter days.
No sooner was this named by Bathsheba to Solomon, than he
recognised in the insidious demand a plan formed by Adonijah
to accredit his old pretensions; and as this was a breach of
the conditions on which his life had been spared, he ordered
him to be slain. Abiathar appears to have had some part in
this intrigue; on which account, as well as for his first defection, he was deposed from the joint high-priesthood to the
rank of a common priest, and ordered to withdraw to his town
of Anathoth. With some other persons, Solomon dealt according to the last instructions which his father had given
him. Joab, when he heard what had been done to Adonijah
and Abiathar, doubted not that his own death was determined,
and therefore fled for refuge to the altar. But the altar was
allowed to be no refuge to so old a murderer: he was torn
thence, and put to the sword by order of the king. This was
an act of astonishing vigour for so young a ruler, when we

consider the influence of Joab with the army, which had secured him complete impunity in the time of David. The valiant Benaiah was appointed captain-general in his stead; and Zadok remained the sole high-priest.

2. Solomon was not unmindful of Shimei, the Benjamite, who had cursed David and pelted him with stones when he fled from Absalom. David had not found it prudent to punish him; but Solomon was not under the same restraint. He ordered him to fix his residence in Jerusalem, and not to leave it on any occasion on pain of death. For a time he was attentive to this injunction; but after two years he left the city, and went to Gath in pursuit of two runaway slaves, and was, on his return, put to death.

3. Through the conquests of his father and the wise measures which he had taken to consolidate his power, Solomon was a great king, especially when the extent of his dominion is compared with the small dimensions of kingdoms in those times. His dominions reached from the Mediterranean to the Euphrates, and from the Red Sea and Arabia to the utmost Lebanon. The tributary states were held in complete subjection, and being still governed by their native princes, made Solomon a "king of kings." The Canaanites who still remained in the land, had become peaceable and obedient subjects, or useful and laborious servants. His treasures also were immense, composed chiefly of the spoils won from many nations by his victorious father, and treasured up by him for the very purpose of sustaining the magnificence and aggrandizing the kingdom of his son. Solomon sought for an alliance becoming his high estate, and found it in a marriage with the king of Egypt's daughter. It was a proud thing for Israel that their king could in such a matter treat on terms of equality with the power which had in old times so long held them under the yoke. The Egyptian princess was received with great magnificence; and Solomon lodged her in "the city of David," on Mount Zion, until he should build for her a superb palace.

4. During the time of David, in which the tabernacle and the ark had been separate from each other, an irregular practice had crept in of sacrificing to God and burning incense at other places than the tabernacle. The altars for these ser-

vices were chiefly upon hills covered with trees, and were called " high places." As this was also the practice of the surrounding heathens, it was very dangerous, and, in fact, paved the way for the idolatries into which the Israelites in after times fell. It had been strictly prohibited by the law of Moses (Lev. xvii. 3-5 ; Deut. xii. 2-5). The principal high place was at Gibeon ; and at one of the religious festivals Solomon proceeded thither, in solemn pomp, with all his court, the officers of the state and army, and the chiefs and elders of the people, to render his homage to Jehovah, and to offer sacrifices to him. With this homage and with these sacrifices God was well pleased ; and the night following he manifested himself to Solomon in a dream, and offered to bestow upon him whatever blessing he might choose. The young king evinced the wisdom he already possessed, by asking an understanding heart to enable him to discharge the awful responsibilities that rested on him, in governing the numerous people and the various interests under his sway. Because he had made so excellent a choice from among all the gifts which the Lord of the Universe had to bestow, not only was surpassing wisdom given to him, but—what he had *not* asked—glory, and riches, and length of days, were added to the gift. His extraordinary sagacity was early shown in his judicial decisions, one example of which is given in the celebrated case of the two women living together, each of whom had a child. One of the children died in the night, and the living child was claimed by both the mothers, with equal apparent truth and zeal. When the case came before the king, he saw there was no way of discovering the real mother of the living child, but by an appeal to the truthfulness of maternal affection, and he therefore ordered the living child to be cut in two and one half given to each. The earnestness with which one of the women entreated that the life of the child might be spared, at once discovered the real mother.

5. Solomon had a great taste for magnificence, which he displayed in many ways. In the state, he introduced a most skilful organization of all its departments, which were severally entrusted to men whose abilities had been tried in the time of David ; and the splendour and beautiful order of every de-

partment in the court claimed admiration. But the inordinate magnificence and extent of all the regal establishments may be justly blamed, when we learn that the expenses were too great for even his large resources; so that at length the royal profusion could only be supported by such oppressive exactions upon the people, as in the next reign led to the division of his dominion into two kingdoms. Some idea of this extravagant magnificence may be formed from the fact, that he had 4000 stalls or stables for the horses of his various carriages. The provisions required by the court for one day, amounted to thirty bushels of fine flour, sixty bushels of common flour, ten fat oxen, twenty oxen from the pastures, and a hundred sheep, besides venison and poultry of all description. A household requiring such quantities of food must have consisted of several thousand persons; but it is likely that the royal guards were also supplied from this store.

6. It is said that Solomon's wisdom greatly exceeded that of the wisest men, Jewish or foreign, of his own day; there were none equal to him among the people of the east or the Egyptians, who were justly famous for their knowledge of every useful science. Three thousand proverbs, many of which remain to us, embodied his moral sayings and sage remarks on human character. A thousand and five songs, of which only the Canticles and 127th Psalm remain, ranked him among the first of Hebrew poets; and his perfect knowledge of all kinds of plants, beasts, birds, and fishes, was shown by writings which are supposed to have been lost in the Babylonian captivity.

7. An embassy of condolence and congratulation from Hiram, king of Tyre, kept open the friendly relations with that king, which David had cultivated. It also led to an arrangement under which the king of Tyre engaged to bring from Lebanon, and to land at the port of Joppa, the timber which Solomon required for the building of the temple. For this he was to pay in corn and oil; for the Tyrians having only a small tract of territory, and being chiefly employed in commerce and manufactures, obtained their provisions chiefly from the fertile lands of Canaan. In return for this, in the ordinary course of traffic, the Israelites received the manufactures of the Phœnicians and the products of foreign lands.

The timber, when landed at Joppa, was conveyed by the Tyrians to Jerusalem; and they also assisted in preparing the stones for the building. Three years were spent in these preparations: and in the fourth year, the foundation of the temple was laid, and in seven years the fabric was completed (B. C. 1005). The temple appears to have been a truly splendid structure, and great wealth was consumed in its various utensils of precious metal, the whole of which were executed by Phœnician artists supplied by Hiram. From the connection of Solomon with Egypt, it is also probable that he availed himself of the talent which, in every branch of art, that country abundantly supplied. To foreigners certainly much of the beauty and perfection of the celebrated temple was owing; for the Israelites being chiefly an agricultural people, had but little skill in those arts of design and ornament which the undertakings of Solomon required. The general plan of the temple seems to have much resembled that of the tabernacle; being composed of extensive courts for worship and sacrifice in the open air, in front of an oblong building, comparatively of small dimensions, but in all its parts rich and elaborate beyond description. This was not, like our churches, for the use of the worshippers. It was never entered by them; but was the abode of the Divine symbols, which were the same as in the tabernacle; the ark with its hovering cherubim, and the Shechinah, or radiant symbol of the Divine presence, being within the interior or most sacred of the two apartments into which the building was divided.

8. A high feast was held on the day when the temple was dedicated to its destined purpose, and when the sacred services commenced. On that day Solomon appeared upon a scaffold before the temple, and poured forth a long and most sublime prayer, at the conclusion of which the Divine complacency was evinced by "the glory of the Lord," filling the whole house, as it had aforetime filled the tabernacle; after which the radiance concentrated over the ark, and there rested as the symbol of the Divine presence and occupancy. The first victims were also consumed by supernatural fire, which was afterwards constantly kept up as the sacred fire of the temple.

9. The remainder of king Solomon's reign is a history

N

rather of peaceful undertakings than of warlike exploits. He built a number of splendid palaces, with pleasure-grounds, and basins of water. Of these the most celebrated was "the house of the forest of Lebanon," all the plate and furniture of which seems to have been of pure gold, while in the hall hung two hundred golden bucklers, each of which must have been worth fifteen hundred pounds, and three hundred smaller ones, each worth half the former. There also was the royal hall of audience and of judgment, where the king sat publicly upon a lofty throne of ivory and gold. Many cities were built, others rebuilt, and others fortified by Solomon. Of the former the most celebrated was Tadmor in the eastern wilderness (B. C. 991), better known by its later name of Palmyra, whose splendid ruins excite to this day the admiration and wonder of travellers. These, however, are not the ruins of Solomon's buildings, but of others erected in after ages on the same site.

10. The king also engaged in maritime and inland commerce. Being possessed of Eziongeber, a port on the Red Sea, which opens into the Indian Ocean, he united with king

124. Baboon.

Hiram in sending ships into the eastern seas, which, after an absence of three years, returned laden with the valuable products of distant climes — gold, silver, ivory, beautiful and costly woods, and precious stones; gums, spices, and perfumes; and collections of curious plants, animals, and birds (among which apes and peacocks are particularly named), which must have ministered much delight to the enquiring mind of Solomon. He also carried on a great trade in the fine linens, the yarn, the horses, and the chariots of the Egyptians; which he bought by his factors of the Egyptians, and sold at an enhanced price to the Syrian nations. From these sources, and from the tribute of the subject nations.

vast treasure came into the royal coffers. We are told that
the commercial voyages alone brought, in one year, no less
than 666 talents of gold, which some compute at £3,646,350
sterling. As for silver, it was of no account in his days; and
the previously costly wood of the cedar became as common
as that of the sycamore had been. But most of this prosperity
was rather the result of a temporary excitement, than of a
regular development of the national resources. Even the
commercial enterprises were monopolies of the crown; and the
greater part of the wealth arising from all sources went into
the royal treasury, and was there absorbed in empty splendour, spent on foreigners, or consumed in extravagance. We
are not therefore surprised that, in his later years, when some
of the sources of supply had declined, while the cost of the
royal establishment was undiminished, Solomon was obliged
to resort to oppressive exactions from his own people, which
had well nigh ruined the house of David in popular esteem.
It is true, however, that, taking his reign in the whole, the
nation was prosperous, as the long continued peace enabled
the population to increase without check, while every man
could attend to his lands without distraction. Hence we are
told that in his days "Judah and Israel dwelt safely, every
man under his vine and under his fig-tree, from Dan even
to Beersheba."

11. The vast knowledge of Solomon, his profound sagacity, and the order and splendour of his court, attracted many
foreign princes to Jerusalem. The most celebrated of these
visitors was the queen of Sheba, supposed, on sufficient
grounds, to have come from southern Arabia; but who is
thought by some to have been the queen of Abyssinia, which
is the firm belief of the Abyssinians themselves to this day.
The distance from which she came, the costly gifts which
she brought, and her splendid train, excited much admiration.
The king satisfactorily solved the "hard questions" by which
she tried his wisdom; and all that she heard and saw led
her to confess that the reality greatly exceeded the scarcely
credible rumours which had reached her distant land.

12. Unfortunately, that vain and costly appendage of
royal state in the east, a large seraglio of women, was
deemed by Solomon necessary to his magnificence. He had

no fewer than 700 wives of high family, and 300 secondary
or concubine wives. Many of these wives were foreigners
and idolators from the neighbouring nations; and they, in
his latter days, drew him astray, not only to participate in
their acts of homage to their native idols, but to build
temples to their honour and for their worship, on the hills
facing Jerusalem, and in front of the Lord's own temple.
Here he joined in sacrifices to Chemosh or Peor, the obscene

125. Ashtaroth.

idol of the Moabites, to Moloch the
god of the Ammonites, and to Ashtaroth the goddess of the Sidonians.
These doings greatly provoked the
Divine indignation. The splendid
endowments of Solomon served the
more to aggravate his offence; and
at length it was solemnly announced
to him, that since he had broken
the covenant by which he held his
crown from the Divine King, the
kingdom should be rent from him, and given to his servant.
Nevertheless it was added, that, for David's sake, this should
not be done in his time, but in the time of his son; and
that, also for the sake of David, one tribe, that of Judah
(with which Benjamin had now coalesced), should remain
under the dominion of his house.

13. This prophecy was soon after made known by the
prophet Ahijah to Jeroboam, an Ephraimite, who, as a man
of activity and talent, had attracted the notice of Solomon,
and had been by him made overseer of the workmen from
the tribes of Joseph, employed in the public service. The
prophet accompanied the message by the significant act of
rending his own new garment into twelve pieces, ten of which
he gave to Jeroboam, and reserved only two for the house of
David. It was then announced that the dominion over the
ten tribes was given to him; and that it should be confirmed
to his descendants, if he and they maintained their allegiance
to the Divine King. This soon came to the knowledge of
Solomon, whose attempts to destroy the destined rival of his
son, taught Jeroboam the prudence of leaving the country.
He retired into Egypt, where he was well received by the

king, Shishak, and protected by him till the death of Solomon. The repose of the king's latter days was also disturbed by the revolt of the Edomites and the Syrians of Damascus There is reason to hope, that these just punishments opened the eyes of Solomon to the enormity of his offences, and that his last days were repentant. He died about the sixtieth year of his age, after a reign of forty years. B.C. 975.

14. Solomon may have left many sons, but the only one known to history is his successor, Rehoboam, who was born the year before his father's accession, and was therefore forty-one years of age when he ascended the throne.

15. The tribes were now determined to relieve themselves from the burdens, which, in the later years of his reign, had been imposed upon them by Solomon. They therefore recalled Jeroboam from Egypt; and, with him at their head, applied to Rehoboam for redress of the grievances under which they had laboured. It is evident that the ten tribes were predisposed to separate themselves from Judah, and establish an independent government. Their sentiments were influenced chiefly by those of Ephraim, which proud and powerful tribe could not brook that the sovereignty should be in the great rival tribe of Judah. They were, therefore, in all probability, rather glad than sorry when a rough refusal of redress from Rehoboam gave them a reasonable pretext for revolt, and for abandoning their allegiance to the house of David. Accordingly, they openly revolted, and made Jeroboam their king.

16. As this separation was in accordance with the intentions of the Divine King, to punish the house of David for the guilt of Solomon, the Sacred Oracle forbade Rehoboam to pursue the design which he had formed of reducing the revolted tribes to obedience by force of arms.

BOOK V

CHAPTER I. Israel from B.C. 975 to 918.

JUDAH.	B.C.	ISRAEL.	B.C.	GENERAL HISTORY.	B.C
Rehoboam	975	Jeroboam I.	975	Phorbas, 5th Archon of	
Ahijah	958	Nadab	954	Athens	954
Asa	955	Baasha	953	Osorkon I., King of	
Azariah, High-Priest	958	Elah	930	Egypt	945
		Zimri and Omri	929	Benhadad, King of Syria	940
		Omri dies	918	Lycurgus born	926
				Takelothe, King of Egypt	925

1. Jeroboam made the ancient city of Shechem, in his own tribe of Ephraim, the seat of his government ; and he had also a summer residence at Tirzah in Manasseh. Although released from its dependence on Judah, the new kingdom, which was called, by way of distinction, the kingdom of Israel, was still under allegiance to the Divine King, and bound, as much as Judah, by all the obligations of the ancient covenants. In both, therefore, we are to view the continued operation of the theocratical system, for the purpose of preserving the knowledge of the true God upon the earth. Both the kingdoms prospered or were humbled in proportion as their conduct advanced or hindered that great object.

2. Jeroboam, whatever may have been his original intentions, soon renounced the peculiar institutions of Judaism. Although the kingdoms were separated, there remained, according to the law, but one temple and one altar, one ecclesiastical establishment, for both. To the place of that temple and that altar all the descendants of Jacob were still absolutely required to repair three times every year, and that place was Jerusalem, the metropolis of the rival kingdom. Fearing that this might ultimately lead to the re-union of the tribes, and to the extinction of his separate kingdom, Jeroboam most presumptuously and wickedly dared to abrogate

the unity of the *nation* (which might still have been maintained under two *kingdoms*), by forbidding his subjects to repair to Jerusalem, to render their homage to the Divine King. He alleged that the distance made the journey burdensome to them : and, therefore, he established two places, towards the opposite extremities of his own kingdom, to which they might resort. These were Bethel in the south, and Dan in the north. Having himself resided in Egypt, and recollecting the readiness with which the Israelites had, in the wilderness, set up a figure of the Egyptian ox-god (Mnevis) as the symbol of the true God, he now reverted to that superstition, and set up " golden calves" at Dan and Bethel, as objects of religious service and homage. He did not deny the God of Israel, and turn to other gods ; but for political objects, he prevented the access of his subjects to the true symbols of the Divine Presence, and caused them to worship Him under forbidden and degrading symbols.

3. To their very great honour, no priests or Levites could be found who would connect themselves with this abomination. After a vain attempt to stem the evil, the Levites abandoned their cities and possessions, and removed into the kingdom of Judah. The priests were already there, for their towns were all within the territories of Judah. Jeroboam could not induce any respectable persons to arrogate the priestly office, and, therefore, the lowest and most unprincipled of the people became the fitting priests of the golden calves. As to the high-priesthood he took that office to himself, according to the practice in Egypt and other countries, where the sovereign was also supreme pontiff. As such, he officiated at high festivals, one of which, the Feast of Tabernacles, he presumed to change from the seventh to the eighth month. These innovations were so shocking to every mind well imbued with the principles of the theocracy and the true religion, that, by degrees, a large proportion of the most valuable men in Israel removed into the sister kingdom. By this and other accessions, the kingdom of Judah soon became, in real strength and power, less unequal to that of Israel, than the proportion between two and ten tribes would seem to indicate. Indeed, Judah was already a *formed* kingdom, with well-organized resources and establishments, and with much

treasure ; so that the balance of power may even be deemed to have inclined in its favour.

4. Jeroboam was not allowed to remain long unwarned. He was officiating as high-priest at Bethel, at *his* feast of tabernacles, when a prophet appeared and foretold that a future king of Judah, Josiah by name, should profane and destroy the very altar at which he was then burning incense. The power by which the prophet spoke was evinced by the instant withering of the hand which the king stretched forth to lay hold on the prophet ; and not less by its being instantly restored at that prophet's prayer. This, however, had no abiding effect upon Jeroboam ; he persisted in his evil ways, which at length brought ruin upon his house. This doom was announced to his wife by the prophet who had anointed him for the kingdom. Ahijah was now blind with age ; but when the queen, disguised, went to consult him about a beloved son who was dangerously ill, he knew her, and not only told her that the child should die, but that the dynasty of Jeroboam should soon be extinguished ; and that the Israelites, for their iniquities, should, in the end, be carried away as captives beyond the Euphrates. After a reign of twenty-two years Jeroboam died, and was succeeded by his son Nadab, in the second year of Asa, king of Judah.

5. Nadab reigned only two years, during which he adhered to the system of his father. He was then murdered by a person called Baasha, of the tribe of Issachar, who usurped the crown and put to death the whole family of Jeroboam.

6. Baasha's government was as offensive to God as it was oppressive to the people, great numbers of whom sought quiet in Judah. Displeased at this, Baasha engaged in a sort of skirmishing warfare with Asa, and took Ramah of Benjamin, which he began to fortify with the view of controlling the intercourse between the two kingdoms. But he was called off to defend his own country from the Syrians, whose assistance had been bought by the king of Judah with gold from the temple. Persisting in evil, Baasha incurred for his house the doom which had been inflicted on that of Jeroboam. He died after a reign of twenty-three years.

7. Elah, his son. reigned little more than one year, when he was murdered at a feast by Zimri, a military commander,

who then mounted the throne. The army, which was in the field against the Philistines, no sooner heard of this than they declared in favour of their own commander Omri, who immediately led them against his rival. He was at Tirzah; and when Omri arrived, Zimri, despairing of the result, withdrew to his haram, which he set on fire, and perished, with all that belonged to him, in the flames.

8. The people, like the army, had refused to recognize the murderous Zimri as king, and had chosen one for themselves named Tibni, in whom Omri now found another competitor. It was not until after six years of civil war that Omri mastered this opposition and remained undoubted king (B. C. 923.) The most memorable act of his reign was the foundation of a new metropolis in a very advantageous situation (B. C. 918.) He called it Shemron or (as afterwards softened in the Greek into Samaria), after the name of the person (Shemer) to whom the ground had originally belonged. Omri reigned eleven years, and died in the thirty-ninth year of Asa, king of Judah.

CHAPTER II   JUDAH FROM 975 TO 889.

JUDAH.	B.C.	ISRAEL.	B.C.	EGYPT.	B.C.
Rehoboam	975	Jeroboam I.	975	Orsokon II., king	906
Abijah	958	Nadab	954	Shishak (Shes ork) II.	8.\
Asa	955	Baasha	953	to about 86` : after	
Jehoshaphat	914	Elah	930	which a blank t`l the	
———— Dies	889	Zimri and Omri	929	reign of Boc v v's,	
Johanan, high-priest of		Ahab	918	who ascendee b	
the Jews	896	Ahaziah	897	throne in . .	ˤ
		Jehoram	896		

GENERAL HISTORY.

	B.C.
Megacles, 6th Archon of Athens	923
Hesiod, the poet	915
Homer flourished about	907
Diogenetes, 7th Archon of Athens	893

1. In Judah, the conduct of Rehoboam was without re
proach during the three first years of his reign. After that
he, and his subjects with him, fell into the same gross idolatry and abominable practices, which had proved the ruin of
the Canaanites. To punish them for this apostasy, God allowed an invasion of the land by Shishak, king of Egypt,
(B.C. 970), who took some of the fortified towns, entered
Jerusalem, and carried off the treasures of the temple and the
palace. As this produced repentance, the remainder of the
reign was prosperous. Rehoboam reigned seventeen years.

2. Abijah, the son of Rehoboam by a grand-daughter of
Absalom, succeeded his father. He was an active and martial prince, and he resolved to endeavour, by force of arms, to
bring back the ten tribes to obedience. He raised a large
army for that service ; and was met by Jeroboam with an
rmy twice as large. Before the battle, Abijah harangued
ue opposing force from Mount Zemaraim. He asserted the
indefeasible right of the house of David to reign over all the
tribes ; he alleged that, in the revolt, undue advantage had
been taken of Rehoboam's inexperience ; and he gathered
confidence of success from the adherence of Judah to the
theocratical institutions, which Israel had so heinously forsaken. This reliance gained him the victory. Jeroboam

lost two-thirds of his immense army, and never recovered the strength he then lost. Abijah was thus enabled to advance his frontier, by taking from Israel several border towns, among which we find the name of Bethel, where was one of the golden calves. We are not, however, told that he destroyed that idol; and it would appear that the town itself was ultimately recovered by Israel; perhaps on the death of Abijah, which soon followed, after a short reign of three years.

3. Asa, who then ascended the throne, was a prince of great piety and virtue. He ruled quietly for ten years, which he employed in the reformation of the abuses of former reigns. He destroyed all idols and their altars, and employed all the means in his power to restore the pure worship of God, and re-establish the principles of the theocratical government. His own adhesion to these principles, which required implicit confidence in the Divine King, was severely tried by an invasion of the country by a vast host of the Cushites (called Ethiopians), under Zerah their king (B.C. 941). Strong in the confidence that it was equally in the Lord's power to give the victory with few as with many, the pious Asa advanced with a comparatively small force, to his southern frontier, to meet this immense host. In that confidence, the Cushites were totally overthrown before him, and the victory gave him the abundant spoil and numerous cattle of this pastoral horde. This repulsion of a torrent which had threatened to overwhelm all the neighbouring states, and which must have been regarded with general apprehension, could not but enhance his credit in the adjoining countries.

4. Five following years of profound peace he employed, under the advice of the prophet Azariah, in pursuing his reformations with a still more vigorous and less sparing hand. Even his own grandmother, the guardian of his youth, was banished from court on account of her idolatries. These reforms put the kingdom in such advantageous contrast with that of Israel, that the well disposed subjects of that kingdom removed in great numbers into Judah. Alarmed at this, Baasha of Israel, took the measures which have been already mentioned to check the communication between the two kingdoms. The conduct of Asa, in hiring the Syrians with the gold of the temple, to make a diversion in his favour, did not

become his character, nor evince that confidence in the Great King which he had on more trying occasions exemplified. He also imprisoned the prophet Jehu, the son of Hanani, who reproved him for his conduct on this occasion. His latter years were also stained by several acts of oppression; and when afflicted with a grievous disease in the feet, he manifested more confidence in his physicians, and less in God, than was considered becoming. He died after a reign of forty-one years, and was honoured by his subjects with a magnificent funeral; for the Jews, like other Orientals, were in the habit of making known, by funeral testimonials, the estimation in which they held their deceased kings.

5. The excellent father was succeeded by the still more excellent son, Jehoshaphat. The first act of his reign was to remove the high places and the groves, which Asa had left untouched. Then, becoming convinced that the most effectual means of preventing the return of the corruptions which had with so much difficulty been rooted out, was to provide for the suitable instruction of the people, in the third year of his reign, he sent out, through all the cities of Judah, a number of chiefs or "princes," whose rank and influence secured respect and attention to the priests and Levites who, with them, were to instruct the people in the law of Moses. The king himself made a tour through his kingdom to see that due effect was in this matter given to his intentions.

6. Having made this the first object of his care, Jehoshaphat found leisure to examine and reform the abuses which had crept into various departments of the state, and to develope the civil and military resources of the country. His cares were rewarded by the increasing numbers and prosperity of his people, by their happiness, and by the exemption from war which his manifest preparedness for it secured. All the men fit to bear arms were regularly enrolled, and were found to be no less than 1,160,000—being not materially fewer than the number returned for all the tribes (except Levi and Benjamin) in the time of David. Of these a certain proportion was kept in service, to act as royal guards at Jerusalem, to garrison the fortresses, and to protect the northern frontier from the kings of Israel. The effective order which the king thus established throughout his king

dom procured for him the respect of foreign states, while
Edom was retained in its subjection, and the Philistines dared
not withhold their tribute.

7. The grand error of Jehoshaphat's reign was the
alliance which he contracted with the idolatrous Ahab, king
of Israel, who thought it safer to have the king of Judah for
a friend than an enemy, and therefore paid court to him.
The alliance was soon cemented by a marriage between
Ahab's daughter Athaliah, and Jehoram the son of Jehoshaphat. In consequence of this connection a friendly intercourse was established between the two kings; and on a
visit paid by Jehoshaphat to the court of Ahab he allowed
himself to be persuaded to accompany him in an expedition
to recover Ramoth-Gilead from the Syrians. In that action
Ahab was killed, and Jehoshaphat narrowly escaped with his
life to Jerusalem. On his arrival he was severely reproved
by the prophet Jehu for so injurious and improper a connection. The king testified his repentance in the best possible
way by prosecuting his reformations with renewed vigour.
A personal tour through the kingdom evinced the sincerity
of his endeavour to bring his subjects into a right state of
feeling towards the God of their fathers. In this tour the
king discovered many abuses and irregularities in the administration of justice; and he therefore established local courts
in every important town, with a right of appeal to the superior courts at Jerusalem. To all these courts competent
judges were appointed; and they were dismissed to their
duties with a plain and forcible charge from the king.

8. The next undertaking of Jehoshaphat was an attempt
to reopen the maritime traffic which Solomon had carried on
by way of the Red Sea. But he unfortunately allowed Ahaziah, the king of Israel, to become a partner in the enterprise,
in consequence of which the Lord refused to prosper the
design, and the ships were destroyed by a storm almost as
soon as they had left the port of Ezion-Geber. Ahaziah
wished to renew the attempt; but Jehoshaphat refused, and
appears to have abandoned the project altogether.

9. Very soon after this, Jehoshaphat obtained a very
signal deliverance from a formidable and quite unexpected
invasion from the south, by a large force composed of Moab-

ites and Ammonites, together with some Arabian tribes whom they had engaged in the enterprise. They came by the way of Edom, and had arrived as far as En-gedi before Jehoshaphat was well aware of their presence. He had no resource but to throw himself unreservedly upon the covenanted protection of the Great King; and this confidence was rewarded by the promise of deliverance. In fact, the Judahites had no occasion to draw a sword; for there arose such a spirit of discord among the invaders, that after the Ammonites and Moabites had quarrelled with and destroyed their Arabian auxiliaries, they repeated the same process between themselves; so that the people under Jehoshaphat had nothing to do but collect the spoil which they left. This was so large that it took three days to gather it together; after which they returned with great joy to Jerusalem, and before they entered the city held a solemn thanksgiving in the valley of Shaveh.

10. The king of Judah was probably induced, by his resentment at the invasion of the Moabites, to give his aid to the king of Israel, Jehoram, in the attempt to re-establish over that people the dominion of Israel, from which they had revolted on the death of Ahab. The allies got into a position of imminent danger, and their deliverance was declared to be solely owing to the divine favour towards Jehoshaphat. B. C. 895.

11. Not long after this Jehoshaphat died, having lived sixty years, and reigned twenty-five. He was undoubtedly the greatest of the Hebrew kings since Solomon, and the most faithful since David. B. C. 889.

CHAPTER III. Israel from B.C. 918 to 897.

ISRAEL.	B. C.	JUDAH.
Ahab, king	918	Jehoshaphat, king 91
The great drought begins	910	
Return of rain—plenty	906	
Benhadad's invasion	901	
Naboth slain: and Ahab doomed	899	
Ahab slain in battle at Ramoth-Gilead	897	

1. OMRI was succeeded by his son Ahab, the events of whose reign are related at greater length than those of any other king of Israel. His reign was for the most part contemporary with that of Jehoshaphat in Judah. In both their public and private character there never was a greater contrast than between these two kings. We have seen how zealously Jehoshaphat laboured to restore and establish the knowledge and the worship of the true God among his people. But Ahab exceeded all former kings in his abominations. His predecessors had been content to make religion an implement of human policy, by the unwarrantable worship of God, under the profane symbol of the golden calves; but Ahab betook himself to the worship of foreign gods instead of the God of Israel. The preference appears to have been given to Baal, the great sun-god of the Phœnicians; which is to be ascribed to the influence of Ahab's wife Jezebel, who was a daughter of Ethbaal, king of Tyre,—an unscrupulous and wicked woman, who was very zealous for her national idol. She soon procured his worship to be established in the land of Israel; and as the religious sentiments of the people had been corrupted by the worship of the golden calves, it is not wonderful that they very readily transferred their homage to an idolatry pleasant to the natural depravity of man. Jehovah was not formally rejected or abandoned; but Baal received at least equal worship from the multitude, and greater from the court.

2. To stem the tide of corruption, and to prevent the total apostacy of Israel, God raised up a man endued with

extraordinary gifts and powers, ardent zeal, and stern virtues, such as the time required.   This was Elijah, the Tishbite,* by far the greatest prophet, both in word and deed, which had appeared since Moses.   He is introduced abruptly, as boldly announcing to Ahab in person the national punishment of a long drought, and consequent scarcity, not to be removed but by his own intercession.   This last condition made it necessary for the prophet to withdraw himself from the presence and solicitations of the king.   When, therefore, the drought began to be felt, in the eighth year of Ahab's reign, Elijah retired beyond the Jordan, and concealed himself in a cavern beside the brook Cherith, where Providence directed ravens to furnish him with regular supplies of bread and meat, morning and evening.   When the brook was dried up for want of rain, the prophet crossed the country to Sarepta, a town in the kingdom of Jezebel's father, to which also the drought and famine had extended.   He remained at this place two years, lodging with a poor widow and her son; and during all that time of famine, they were supported through the miraculous inexhaustion of a handful of flour and a little oil, the only remaining food of the poor woman when the prophet met with her.

3. Three years had Elijah remained in obscurity—one year by the brook Cherith, and two in Sarepta.   During this time Israel suffered greatly; and Ahab had sought for the prophet in every quarter, convinced that the remedy was in his hands.   God, intending now to give rain, and to remove the famine, ordered the prophet to return to the land of Israel.   On the way, he met Obadiah, comptroller of the king's household, who had been sent out to seek forage for the cattle.   This person, at the risk of his own life, had sheltered many holy persons in a cave, and supplied them with victuals, during a recent persecution by Jezebel.   Elijah sent Obadiah back to announce his reappearance to Ahab, who then came out to meet him.   When the king saw him, he said, "Art thou he who troubleth Israel?"   But the prophet sternly retorted the charge, alleging that the apostacy of himself and his people was the cause of the national suffer-

* So called, from his native place. which was probably Thebez, a town of Manasseh beyond Jordan

ing. He further required the king to convene a general assembly of his priests and people at Carmel.

4. In that great assembly there were no fewer than 450 priests of Baal. Elijah proposed that these priests should call upon Baal, and that he should call upon the name of Jehovah, and that the Deity who should make it appear that he had heard their prayers, by consuming with fire from heaven the sacrifices to be offered, should be acknowledged as the true God. It was impossible for the priests of Baal to decline so fair a trial, especially as fire was the congenial element of the god they worshipped. Accordingly, they prepared their altar, and laid out upon it their sacrifices, and continued, with frantic invocations and lacerations of their flesh, to ask the required sign, until above half the day was spent; but no sign in heaven or earth answered to their cry. Then Elijah rose, and, after some biting ridicule of the im-

126. Persian Devotee.

potent god and his votaries, proceeded to repair an old altar, which had formerly been erected there. Upon this he placed his sacrifices, and called solemnly upon the God of Israel to manifest his power. He was instantly answered by fire from heaven,—so intense, that it consumed not only the victims and the wood, but the very stones and dust of the place, and absorbed the water which had been poured profusely on the whole. At this astounding display of miraculous power, the people fell on their faces, crying, "The Lord, he is the God; the Lord, he is the God." At the instance of the prophet, they evinced the sincerity of their conviction, by seizing the priests of Baal and destroying them all. The prophet then went to the top of Carmel, and prayed for rain. A small cloud arising from the sea was the first answer to his prayer, and that welcome sign was soon followed by abundant and heavy rain.

5. Learning that Jezebel had vowed his death, on account of the slaughter of Baal's priests, the prophet withdrew to Beersheba, where he left his servant, and proceeded alone across the desert to Horeb, "the Mount of God." Here,

J

where the law had been originally delivered, the Lord manl-
fested himself to his servant—not in the whirlwind, the
earthquake, or the fire—but in "a still small voice," which
spoke comfort to his now desolate soul, and encouraged him
by the assurance, that whereas he deemed that he was himself the only worshipper of God left in Israel, there were
indeed seven thousand who had not bowed the knee to Baal.
He was then directed to return home; and on the way he
met with Elisha, ploughing in the field. Knowing that this
person was his destined successor, he intimated the fact by
casting over him his mantle. Elisha then went with him,
and remained in attendance upon him.

6. Now Israel was invaded by Benhadad, king of Syria*
of Damascus, at the head of a numerous army, with which he
invested Samaria. The kingdom was too much exhausted
by the recent famine to allow Ahab to make any effectual
resistance. But although he was unworthy of any help, yet
God, for the glory of his own great name, sent a prophet to
promise him victory, and to instruct him how to act. Benhadad
was in consequence defeated, and with difficulty saved his
life by flight. Yet the next year he made another invasion
with a more powerful force, hoping to bring the Israelites to
action in the plain; for he had arrived at the foolish conclusion, that the God of Israel (to whom he ascribed his previous
defeat) was indeed a God of the mountains, but not a God of
the valleys. To correct so dishonouring a notion of his power,
the Lord again gave the victory to Ahab. But instead of
following up this success, Ahab concluded a league of amity
with Benhadad, which was so displeasing to God, that a prophet was sent to announce the evils which would befal his
house, through the neglect of this opportunity of breaking
the Syrian power.

7. It was not until nine years after the transactions at
Mount Carmel, that Elijah and Ahab had another interview,
which was the last. The prophet came to denounce the
Divine vengeance against him and his family, for killing
Naboth under the forms of law, in order to obtain possession
of a vineyard which that person had refused to part with.

---

* The "kings of Syria," in the Scriptural history, were the kings of that portion of
Syria of which Damascus was the capital.

For his great wickedness the prophet declared that his posterity should be cut off; and that, for this iniquity in particular, dogs should lap his own blood in the place where they lapped the blood of Naboth; and that dogs should eat the flesh of Jezebel under the wall of Jezreel. On hearing this dreadful denunciation, the king manifested some signs of humiliation and contrition, in consequence of which the heaviest part of this doom was postponed from his own time to that of his successor.

127. Dog.

8. The last act of Ahab's reign was the expedition against the Syrians, in which Jehoshaphat took part, as noticed in the preceding chapter.   When that excellent prince was invited to go with the army, he was not satisfied with the assurances of success which the "false prophets" of Ahab gave in great abundance; but wished to see "a prophet of the Lord beside."   Ahab therefore sent for a prophet named Micaiah, whom he nevertheless declared that he hated, because he did not prophesy good concerning him, but evil. Micaiah verified this when he arrived, by telling him that if he went, he would never return alive.   On this the indignant king commanded him to be kept in prison until his return "in peace;" which the unflinching prophet persisted would never happen.   The kings went against the Syrians; but before the battle began, Ahab, secretly alarmed at the prediction of Micaiah, invidiously proposed to Jehoshaphat that he should take the chief command, and appear in his royal robes, while he himself would wear an ordinary dress.   He hoped to favour his own escape, by exposing the king of Judah.   In fact, Jehoshaphat being taken for the king of Israel, was in great danger of his life; but Ahab escaped not. An arrow shot at random by a Syrian soldier penetrated the joints of his coat of mail, and inflicted a mortal wound.   He immediately retired from the field to have the wound dressed; but fearing to discourage his men, quickly returned, and re-

mained in the field till he died in his chariot. When this
was known, the army was commanded to disperse. The
washing of Ahab's chariot in the pool of Samaria, to which
city his body was taken, caused a modified fulfilment of the
prediction that dogs should lick his blood as they had licked
the blood of Naboth; but this doom was again, and more
literally (as to the place), accomplished in the person of his
son.

CHAPTER IV. Judah from B. C. 389 to 809

JUDAH.		ISRAEL.		GENERAL HISTORY.	
	B. C.		B. C.		B C
Jehoram or Joram, king	889	Jehoram or Joram, king	896	Phidon, king of Argos	867
Ahaziah, king	885	Jehu, king	884	Carthage founded	869
Athaliah, queen	884	Jehoahaz, king	856	Pherecles, 8th Archon of Athens	863
Joash or Jehoash, king	878	Jehoash or Joash, king	839	Ariphron, 9th Archon of Athens	846
Zechariah, high priest	850	Jeroboam II., king	823	Thespieus, 10th Archon of Athens	826
Amariah, high priest	846			Bocchoris (Pehor, Bakhor), king of Egypt	812
Amaziah, king	838				
Amaziah dies	809				

1. In the kingdom of Judah, Jehoshaphat was succeeded by his son Jehoram or Joram, who has before been mentioned as having married Ahab's daughter, Athaliah. He was thirty-eight years of age when he began to reign, and proved a very degenerate son of an excellent father. The first act of his reign was the murder of his six brothers, and some of the chief persons of the nation. He was also persuaded by Athaliah to subvert the worship of the Lord, and to introduce the corruptions which prevailed in the sister kingdom. For this, the prophet Elisha, by letter, denounced the Divine vengeance upon him and upon his house. This was speedily executed. The Edomites threw off the yoke, as had long before been foretold (Gen. xxvii. 40), and Libnah, on his southern frontier, revolted. The Philistines harassed him on the west; and he was invaded from the south by the Arabians, who plundered his country and palaces, carrying into captivity all his wives except Athaliah, and all his sons except Ahaziah, the youngest. Lastly, to fill up the measure of his punishments, he was afflicted with a horrible disease in his bowels, of which he died after a torturing illness of two years and a reign of eight.

2. Ahaziah, called also Jehoahaz, who then ascended the throne, was twenty-two years old. He was as bad as his father, and associated as much by character as by birth with the house of Ahab. He joined his uncle Jehoram, the

reigning king of Israel, in another effort to recover Ramoth-Gilead from the Syrians.   After they had returned to Jezreel in consequence of a wound which Jehoram received, both the kings were slain in the conspiracy of Jehu, who was commissioned to exterminate the house of Ahab.   The servants of Ahaziah were allowed to convey his body to Jerusalem, for burial in the royal sepulchre.   He reigned only one year.

3. When Athaliah saw that her son was dead, she resolved to take the sovereign power into her own hands.   She therefore destroyed all of the royal family whose present or prospective claims stood in the way of her ambition.   No one escaped, except her grandson Joash, the son of Ahaziah, an infant of a year old.   He was hidden from her rage, with his nurse, in the chambers of the temple, by his aunt Jehosheba, the wife of the high-priest.   Athaliah now ruled Judah with a high hand.   She established the worship of Baal through the land, and persecuted the faithful few who still adhered to the worship of Jehovah.   Thus six years passed ; when Jehoiada, the high-priest, resolved to endure her usurpation and profligacy no longer, but to produce Joash, then seven years old, to the people as their king.   Having engaged the Levites to support the design, a time was fixed for its execution.   On that day the avenues and gates of the temple being strictly guarded by well-armed Levites, the young prince was carried into the inner court of the temple, under a strong escort of priests, and was there anointed and proclaimed king of Judah.

128. Ancient Egyptian Trumpets.

4. The blast of the trumpets, and the shouts and acclamations of the people, attracted the attention of Athaliah, who repaired in haste to the temple.   A glance revealed to her the hateful truth, and she turned away with a cry of "Treason!"   But no one moved in her

favour, not even when, by order of Jehoiada, the guards seized her and led her forth to inevitable death. The high-priest now solemnly charged the king and people to renew the national covenant with God, and to serve and worship him only. He then led the willing people to destroy the temple and idols of Baal, whose priests and prophets were also slain. In reading the account of these transactions, we must bear in mind that, under the theocracy, idolatry was not merely a religious error, but high treason against the Supreme Head of the commonwealth.

5. While the young king acted under the direction of Jehoiada, he reigned well, and order was restored to the kingdom. But after the death of that eminent person, he fell under the influence of bad advisers—idolaters at heart—by whom he was seduced from the worship of the true God to those abominations through which the nation had already suffered so deeply. This provoked the Divine anger, of which he was repeatedly warned by the prophets. At length, when the king and people were celebrating a festival in the temple, Zechariah, the son and successor of Jehoiada, remonstrated so strongly against his conduct, that the indignant king commanded Zechariah, his cousin, and the son of his benefactor, to be stoned, even in that sacred place ; and his cruel and unjust command was but too readily obeyed by the apostate multitude. Many evils fell upon Judah for these iniquities. The land was invaded by the Syrians, who ravaged the country and plundered Jerusalem. Many of the inhabitants, as well as of the king's court and household, were put to the sword, and the invaders withdrew with immense booty to Damascus. Shortly after this, Joash, being afflicted with grievous diseases, was assassinated by two of his attendants, after a reign of forty and a life of forty-seven years.

6. Amaziah, the son of Joash, was twenty-five years old when he succeeded his father. He began his reign well, and re-established the worship of Jehovah ; but he, like all his predecessors, continued the unsanctioned practice of offering sacrifices in the high places. When he was settled in the throne, he brought the murderers of his father to condign punishment ; but he shewed his respect for the law (Deut. xxiv, 16) by sparing their children, contrary to the general prac-

tice of the East. Afterwards, about the twelfth year of his reign (B. C. 827), he undertook to reduce to obedience the Edomites, who had revolted in the reign of his father. He

129. Ruined Temple, Petra.

got together 300,000 men for this expedition; and not deeming this a sufficient number, hired 100,000 warriors from the king of Israel, for 100 talents of silver. This was displeasing to God, who ordered him, by a prophet, to send them back again; and he manifested a just sense of his position, as the viceroy of the Divine King, by his compliance, which involved the loss of the money he had advanced. The Israelites were very far from being pleased at their dismissal, and testified their resentment by the ravages and barbarities which they committed on their way home. Amaziah was rewarded for his obedience by a complete victory over the Edomites, of whom he slew ten thousand in battle; and ten thousand more whom he had taken prisoners, he unjustifiably destroyed, by casting them down from the cliffs of their native mountains. He took the metro-

130. Petra, from above the Amphitheatre.

polis, Selah, and changed its name to Joktheel. This is, in

all probability, the lately discovered Petra, whose marvellous excavations have been regarded with much admiration.

7. The savage cruelty of Amaziah to the captive Edomites was not the only evil connected with this expedition ; for, having brought away with him the idols of Edom, he, with wonderful infatuation, set them up as objects of religious homage at Jerusalem ; and the services of God's temple were once more forsaken or eclipsed. After repeated warnings, his doom went forth from God, and its execution speedily followed. Puffed up with his victory, over Edom, he formed the wild project of bringing the ten tribes under obedience to the house of David, and provoked Joash, the king of Israel, to hostilities, notwithstanding his endeavour to avoid them. In the first action the army of Amaziah was completely routed; he was himself taken prisoner and carried in triumph to his own capital, which was taken, and the fortifications demolished. The rapacious conqueror stript even the temple of its treasures ; but at his departure he left Amaziah in possession of his dishonoured crown. The disgrace which Amaziah had brought upon the nation was so intolerable to his own subjects, that a powerful conspiracy was formed against him. and he was killed at Lachish, to which place he had fled for safety (B. C. 809). He reigned twenty-nine years.

CHAPTER V. Israel from B.C. 897 to 771

ISRAEL.		JUDAH.		GENERAL HISTORY	
	B.C.		B.C.		B.C.
Ahaziah, king . .	897	Jehoram, king . .	889	Hazael, king of Syria	884
Translation of Elijah	896	Ahaziah king .	886	Benhadad II., king of	
Jehoram or Joram, king	896	Athaliah, king . . .	885	Syria	886
Jehu, king	884	Joash or Jehoash, king	878	Kingdom of Macedon	
Jehoahaz, king . . .	856	Amaziah, king . . .	838	begins	814
Jehoash, king . . .	839	Uzziah or Azariah, king	809	Jonah's prophesy against	
Jeroboam II., king .	823	Menahem, king . .	770	Nineveh	800
Interregnum	783			Kingdom of Lydia be-	
Zechariah and Shallum,				gins	797
kings	771			Monarchy ends in Co-	
The prophets Jonah,				rinth	778
Amos, Hoshea, flourish				So, Sabaco or Sabakoph,	
in the time of Jero-				king of Egypt . .	778
boam II.—Isaiah be-					
gins in the last year					
of Uzziah.					

1. AHAB was succeeded, in Israel, by his son Ahaziah, who adhered to the abominations which his father had added to those of Jeroboam. The chief events of his reign were the revolt of the Moabites, and his unfortunate alliance with Jehoshaphat in the attempt to recover the maritime traffic by the Red Sea. Being greatly injured by a fall from the lattice of an upper chamber, Ahaziah sent messengers to consult the oracle of Baal-Zebub, the fly-god of Ekron, respecting his recovery. The messengers were intercepted by Elijah the prophet, who sent them back, and afterwards went himself, to denounce, as a punishment of his impious abandonment of the God of Israel, and his resorting to foreign idols, that he should rise no more from the bed on which he had lain down. Accordingly he died, after a reign of two years.

2. Having no sons, Ahaziah was succeeded by his brother Jehoram or Joram. He removed the foreign and recent idolatries; but would not interfere with the golden calves of Jeroboam, probably on account of the political considerations connected with their worship. The first year of this reign was distinguished by one of the most extraordinary events in Biblical history,—the translation to heaven of the prophet Elijah, who was taken away by a whirlwind in a chariot and horses of fire. Elisha was present; and on him the mantle

and the power of his master devolved. This was soon proved; for the Jordan, when smitten by the prophetic mantle, opened to give him passage, as it had before done to Elijah; at his word the bitter waters of Jericho were made sweet; and, soon after, his curse brought bears from the wood to destroy some young men who mocked at the translation of Elijah and insulted his successor. By these signs Elisha, although a man of different temperament and habits, became known to all Israel as one invested with the spirit and power Elijah.

3. The beginning of Jehoram's reign was prosperous; for, as Elisha declared, on account of Jehoshaphat having joined him in the enterprise, his army was, by a special inter-position of Providence, delivered from circumstances of great danger, and enabled to subdue the Moabites, who had revolted in the preceding reign. In this campaign, the king of Moab, when besieged by the allies in his capital, and pressed to ex-tremities, offered up in sacrifice his eldest son, upon the wall of the city, hoping thus to render his idols propitious. Hor-ror-struck at such a sight, the allies raised the siege and re-turned home. Elisha also returned to Samaria, where, in his prophetic capacity, he wrought several signal miracles, which gave him a great and useful influence with the people.

4. The partial reformations with which Jehoram com-menced his reign, were not the result of decided principles. They were, therefore, soon abandoned, or not carried out; and both king and people speedily relapsed into the former idolatries. This was punished by a new invasion by the Syrians under their king Benhadad. He subdued the whole country to the metropolis, Samaria, which he could only hope to reduce by famine, and to which, therefore, he laid siege. The famine and attendant miseries which were experienced in Samaria during this siege defy description. The extremity of hunger at length became so great, that every kind of edible substance, however unusual or unwholesome, was devoured; and some women were known to have eaten the flesh of their own children. When the king heard of this he rent his robes with horror and anguish of soul, and disclosed the penitential sackcloth which he wore next his skin. But he was still as far as ever from a right mind. His indignat

turned against Elisha, whom he supposed to have the power to avert these evils; and he swore that he should be put to death that day. Aware of this intention, the prophet refused to admit the king's messenger into the house he occupied. Jehoram himself followed, perhaps to countermand the order he had given; and to him the prophet announced an immediate deliverance, and a superabundance of provisions in Samaria on the following day. This seemed incredible to some of those who heard the announcement. But the night following it was found that the Syrians had raised the siege and fled away in great alarm, leaving every thing behind them. They had miraculously been made to hear a noise of a vast host of chariots and horses, which led them to conclude that the Israelites had purchased relief from the neighbouring states; hence their panic and its consequences. The delivered and famished citizens rushed upon the forsaken camp, in which they found rich spoils and great abundance of food.

5. Towards the end of this reign, the king of Syria, Benhadad, was secretly murdered in his sick-bed by Hazael, one of his chief officers, who then usurped the throne. Soon after this, Jehoram determined to make another effort to recover Ramoth-Gilead from the Syrians; and, as we have seen in the previous chapter, persuaded Ahaziah, the king of Judah, to go with him. The king of Israel was severely wounded and obliged to leave the army and retire to Jezreel, and was soon followed by Ahaziah. Long before this, when in Horeb, Elijah had been commissioned to anoint, as king of Israel, Jehu, the son of Nimshi, who was to execute the doom of extermination upon the house of Ahab. This charge he had delayed to execute, and it now therefore devolved upon Elisha. Now, Jehu was one of the generals left in charge of the military operations before Ramoth-Gilead after the king had departed. One of the "sons of the prophets" was sent to anoint him there, and to charge him at once to execute his commission as the Lord's avenger upon the house of Ahab. Jehu was popular with the army; and when the officers heard of this appointment they hailed it with acclamations and immediately proclaimed him publicly as king of Israel. They then followed Jehu to Jezreel, whither.

with his usual promptitude, he determined to proceed at once before any others could convey the tidings. When his approach was discovered from the walls of that city, Jehoram, quite ignorant of these transactions, and being impatient to know whether he returned from the war in triumph or defeat, went forth to meet him, accompanied by the king of Judah. But when they met in the fatal field of Naboth, after a few bitter words Jehu slew him, and his body was left unburied in the open field. Ahaziah of Judah, being of the house of Ahab by his mother Athaliah, was also slain; but his body was conveyed for interment to Jerusalem.

6. As Jehu entered Jezreel, the queen-mother Jezebel presented herself, royally arrayed, at a window of the palace; but at the command of Jehu, she was cast down by her own servants, and dashed to pieces, and trodden under foot by the horses. It was found, not long after, that her body had been devoured by dogs, according to the prediction of Elijah. The rest of Ahab's family, seventy in number, who were at Samaria, were killed, and their heads sent to Jehu by the men in authority there, in evidence of their obedience to the new king. After he had rooted out all of the doomed race that were in Jezreel, he proceeded himself to Samaria, and extirpated all who bore affinity to the family. The establishment at Samaria for the service of Baal,—temple, idol, and priests,—were totally destroyed by Jehu; and he denounced a similar fate against whoever should attempt to revive what he had overthrown. The consequence of this severe proceeding was, that the idolatry of Baal never again gained head in Israel; although idolatry itself was far from being destroyed. Indeed, Jehu made no attempt to interfere with the golden calves; and, altogether, his zeal, although effective and vehement in operation, only led him to do what coincided with his own interest or humour. For the completeness with which he had accomplished his avenging mission, it was promised to Jehu that his dynasty should endure for four generations. The defects of his obedience probably prevented a more extended duration; but still his family sat on the throne above a hundred years, which is longer than the rule of any other dynasty in Israel. The result of the war east of the Jordan was, that Hazael proved victorious.

and deprived Israel of all its possessions on that side the river. Jehu reigned twenty-eight years.

7. He was succeeded by his son Jehoahaz, who also adhered to the schismatical worship and institutions of the golden calves. For this the Syrians were allowed to extend their power to the west of the Jordan, and so to prevail, that at length the whole force left to the king of Israel consisted of no more than fifty horsemen, ten chariots, and 10,000 infantry. Jehoahaz reigned seventeen years.

8. Joash, his son, then ascended the throne. Soon after he visited the prophet Elisha when on his deathbed, and was encouraged by the dying prophet, who assured him of three successive victories over the Syrians. He accordingly ventured to rise against them, and succeeded in expelling them from his dominions. He also repulsed the Moabites, who invaded his territories. These successes procured for troubled Israel a few years of tranquillity and peace. Joash reigned sixteen years.

9. Jeroboam II. then succeeded his father. He was as bad as most of his predecessors; and the condition of the Israelites was daily becoming more depressed. The country was successively invaded by the Syrians, Moabites, Ammonites, and Edomites; who, however, were severally defeated and driven off by Jeroboam, encouraged by the prophet Jonah (B. C. 823). Jeroboam reigned forty-one years. During this reign the Lord began by his prophets to warn the Israelites of the doom of captivity and dispersion, which their crimes would speedily bring down upon them. The prophets were Hosea, Amos, and Jonah.

10. The reign of Jeroboam was followed by an interregnum of eleven years, occasioned probably by the infancy of his son Zechariah. It was at this period that the prophet Jonah was sent on his reluctant mission to Nineveh, of which an interesting account is given in the book that bears his name. During the interregnum, the country fell into such a state of anarchy and confusion, that at length the remedy was adopted of calling Zechariah to the throne of his fathers.

11. Zechariah, the last king of the race of Jehu, wielded the sceptre of Israel only six months. He was not equal

to the emergencies of the times, and was put to death by one Shallum, who usurped the government. Thus endured as promised, and ended as foretold, the dynasty of Jehu.

12. During the period embraced by this chapter, the prophets Jonah, Amos, and Hosea, flourished and prophesied. Jonah appears to have lived in the time of Jeroboam II.; he was a native of Gath-hepher, in Zebulon. The book which bears his name is occupied by a narrative of his mission to Nineveh, to warn that great city of an impending destruction, which was averted by the repentance and humiliation of the inhabitants. Amos belonged to the same time: he was a dresser of sycamore fruit, and began to prophesy at Bethel; but being driven thence by Amaziah, the high-priest of the golden calf, he retired to Tekoah in Judah, and found employment as a herdsman. It is from this place that his written prophesies are dated. They are replete with images drawn from the objects in rural life, with which his avocations made him conversant: and their object is to denounce the destruction of the surrounding nations; to alarm the negligent by the declaration of national punishments; and to hold forth comforting promises of the future Messiah. Hosea lived at the same time with Amos, but appears to have survived him. Little is known of his history; but he is supposed to have been of the kingdom of Israel, as his denunciations of vengeance, mixed with promises of mercy, are chiefly directed against the iniquities into which the ten tribes had fallen.

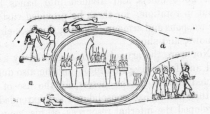

CHAPTER VI. JUDAH FROM 809 TO 696.

JUDAH.		ISRAEL.		GENERAL HISTOR.	
	B. C.		B. C.		B. C.
Uzziah or Azariah, king	809	First Interregnum	783	Agamestor, 11th Archon of Athens	800
Jotham, king	757	Zechariah and Shallum,			
Ahaz, king	741	kings	771	Æschylus, 12th Archon of Athens	778
Hezekiah, king	725	Menahem, king	770		
Hezekiah dies	696	Pekahiah, king	760	Æra of the 1st Olympiad	776
Ahitub II., high-priest	800	Pekah, king	758		
Zadok II., high-priest	771	Second Interregnum	738	Ephori commence in Lacedemon	760
The prophets Isaiah,		Hoshea, king	729		
Naham, Micah, and		Samaria taken	721	Decennial Archons begin at Athens	754
Habakkuk, flourish				Rome founded	753
after Uzziah.					

1. In the kingdom of Judah, Uzziah, otherwise called Azariah, was but five years old when his father was slain. He was sixteen before he was formally called to the throne : and it is disputed by chronologers, whether we should count the fifty-two years of his reign from the beginning or from the end of the eleven intervening years. In the first half of his reign, this king behaved well, and was mindful of his true place as viceroy of the Divine King. He accordingly prospered in all his undertakings. His arms were successful against the Philistines, the Arabians, and the Ammonites. He restored and fortified the walls of Jerusalem, and planted on them engines of defence, for discharging arrows and great stones; he organised the military force of the nation into a kind of militia, composed of 307,500 men, under the command of 2600 chiefs, and divided into bands liable to be called out in rotation ; for these he provided vast stores of all kinds of weapons and armour,—spears, shields, helmets, breast-plates, bows, and slings.

2. Nor were the arts of peace neglected by king Uzziah: he loved and fostered agriculture; and he also dug wells, and constructed towers in the desert, for the use of the flocks. At length, when he had consolidated and extended his power, and developed the internal resources of his country, Uzziah fell. His prosperity engendered the pride which became his ruin. In the twenty-fourth year of his reign, incited pro-

bably by the example of the neighbouring kings, who united
the regal and pontifical functions, Uzziah, unmindful of the
fate of Dathan and Abiram, dared to attempt the exercise of
one of the principal functions of the priests, by entering the
holy place to burn incense at the golden altar. But, in the
very act, he was smitten with leprosy, and was thrust forth
by the priests. He continued a leper all the rest of his life,
and lived apart as such,—the public functions of the government being administered by his son Jotham, as soon as he
became of sufficient age. His whole reign was fifty-two
years, being, with the sole exception of Manasseh's, the longest
in the Hebrew annals. In this reign Isaiah began to prophesy in Judah.

3. Jotham was a meritorious prince, and prospered accordingly. He re-
pelled an invasion of
the Ammonites, and
laid them under a
yearly tribute; and
he built various
cities, castles, and
towers, in different
parts of his domi-
nions. Besides the
time that he acted

131. Castle.

as regent during the leprosy of his father, Jotham reigned
sixteen years in Jerusalem.

4. Ahaz, then twenty years old, ascended the throne.
He proved an unworthy son of a good father, being equally
forgetful of his allegiance to the Lord as his King, and of his
reverence to him as his God. He apostatised not only to
the idolatries of the surrounding heathen, but to that of the
golden calves. He erected images and altars to various idols
in different parts of Jerusalem, and adopted all the horrid
rites by which their worship was celebrated. So intense was
the passion of this prince for idolatry, that it rather resembled
the insatiate craving of a drunkard than the reverence of a
worshipper. The Syrian idolatry appears to have been that
which he most admired; for he introduced the idols and
altars of that country, and altered the temple and its ser-

vises after the model of those of Damascus. At length he shut up the sacred building altogether. To punish him for these crimes, his kingly state was brought very low. In the early part of his reign, a formidable confederacy was formed against him by Pekah, king of Israel, and Rezin, king of Syria, with the fixed intention of dethroning the house of David and of bestowing the crown on some person whom we only know as " Tabeal's son." In this war, Rezin stripped Judah of its external territories, and carried away great numbers of Jews as captives to Damascus. Pekah was equally success-ful : he slew in one day 120,000 men of Judah, and carried away 200,000 as captives to Samaria. But he was induced to treat them well, and to send them back again, at the in-stance of the prophet Obed and other persons of influence, who refused to hold their brethren in bondage, and were in this supported by public feeling in Israel. This shews that, after all, the separation had not produced an exasperated state of feeling between the nations. After this, the allies besieged Jerusalem, but were unable to take it; while the general distress was aggravated by the incursions of the Edomites on the south and the Philistines on the west, who took several cities and villages in the low country, and settled in them.

5. In this extremity, Ahaz sought the assistance of Tig-lath-pileser, the king of Assyria, to whom he sent an embassy, declaring himself his vassal, and bearing a subsidy of all the sacred and the royal treasures. Glad of a pretext for inter-ference, Tiglath-pileser readily promised the assistance thus required. Accordingly, he defeated and slew the king of Syria, and took possession of his dominions; he also made himself master of all the Hebrew possessions beyond Jordan, and sent away captive, into Assyria and Media, the three tribes—Reuben, Gad, and Manasseh.* Ahaz visited the Assyrian king at Damascus, to congratulate him, and to render him homage. He found, however, that although temporarily relieved from an imminent danger, he had little cause to rejoice in the result. He had become the tributary

---

* There was only half of Manasseh beyond Jordan; but the king of Assyria com-pleted the tribe for captivity, by adding the other half which was west of the Jordan.

of a foreign power; and instead of a rival, he had now a powerful and overbearing master for his neighbour. Little is known of his future reign, except that he persisted in his old courses, and lived, it would seem, under the odium of the whole nation for having been the apparent cause of the captivity into which three tribes of Israel had fallen. When, therefore, he died, after an inglorious and disastrous reign of sixteen years, he was refused a place in the royal sepulchres, although a grave in Jerusalem was allowed him. In this reign Micah delivered the prophesy contained in the book which bears his name.

6. Hezekiah, the son of Ahaz, was twenty-five years old when he ascended the throne. In all respects his character was the very reverse of that of his father, entitling him to rank as one of the very best kings of David's line; indeed, the Scriptures seems to give him the preference to them all (2 Kings, xviii. 5). The characteristics of a good king under the Hebrew system of government have been so often mentioned, that it is scarcely needful to repeat that they consisted in a faithful obedience to the revealed will of God— first, in his general character, as Creator and sole Lord of the Universe; secondly, in his more particular character, as the God who had made Israel his chosen people, and to whom, therefore, he was a national God, as distinguished from the national gods of the heathen around; and, thirdly, in the still more intimate character of the actual KING and political Head of the nation, and who, as being incapable of error, exacted, and was entitled to, the most unlimited and confiding obedience. In all these characters Hezekiah understood him; and hence he also understood his own true position in the state. The first act of his reign was to open and purify the temple, and to extirpate all the idolatries which his father had sanctioned or introduced. He even went so far as to destroy the brazen serpent of Moses, which had been preserved as a memorial, the people having manifested a disposition to burn incense to it as a holy relic.

7. This conduct of Hezekiah was rewarded by prosperity in all his undertakings. He subdued the Philistines; and at length ventured to withhold the yearly tribute which his father had agreed to pay to the Assyrians. Shalmaneser, the

son and successor of Tiglath-pileser, was too much occupied in other quarters to pay much attention to Hezekiah; but in the sixth year of his reign, he carried away into captivity the flower of the seven tribes of Israel on the west side of Jordan, thus completing the ruin of the ten tribes. This event appears to have made a salutary impression on Judah, and probably afforded much aid to Hezekiah in his reformations. These were more radical than any former kings, however well-disposed, had thought necessary; for Hezekiah not only abolished idolatry and restored the worship of God, but he revived the national observances, which had been altogether neglected in former reigns,—such as the passover, which he celebrated at Jerusalem with greater solemnity than had been observed since the time of Solomon. Not only his own subjects, but the desolate remnants of the ten tribes were invited to this great feast; many of them came, but others mocked and refused.

8. At length the Assyrians, having subdued the small nations between the Mediterranean and the Euphrates, found leisure to call Hezekiah to account for his arrears of tribute. Shalmaneser was dead, and had been succeeded by his son Sennacherib, who invaded Judah with a mighty host. Hezekiah, disappointed of assistance which he had expected from Egypt, did not consider it safe to attempt to oppose him; but made his intercessions, and offered to furnish any tribute which the Assyrian might think proper to impose. He accordingly paid the heavy ransom of three hundred talents of silver and thirty talents of gold, although this obliged him not only to exhaust the sacred and the royal treasures, but to strip off the gold which covered the doors and pillars of the temple. Sennacherib took the money, and went towards Egypt, which he intended next to invade; but on the way he changed his mind, and resolved not to leave unbroken in his rear a power so well inclined to ally itself with the Egyptians. He, therefore, took the strong towns of the south; and, while he laid siege to Libnah and Lachish, sent his general Rabshakeh against Jerusalem. The language which this man used in summoning Hezekiah to surrender, was in the highest degree offensive and blasphemous. Hezekiah, with humble confidence, referred the matter to God, and was answered by

the promise of deliverance.   Accordingly, a rumour reached
Sennacherib that Tirhakah the Ethiopian, king of Upper
Egypt, was marching with an immense army to cut off his
retreat; so that he deemed it prudent to abandon his operations, but not without sending a boastful and threatening
letter to Hezekiah respecting his future intentions.   But the
very night after, the Assyrian host of 180,000 were destroyed
by " a blast," which may be understood to have been the
simoom, or hot pestilential wind which sometimes blows in
those regions.   The baffled tyrant hastened home to Nineveh,
where he behaved with great severity to the captive Israelites.
But his career was short; for, seven weeks after his return,
he was slain by his own sons while worshipping in the temple
of Nisroc, the great idol of the Assyrians.   The parricides
fled, and left the throne open to their younger brother Esarhaddon.

9. The same year Hezekiah was taken ill, apparently
with the plague; and was warned by the prophet Isaiah to
prepare for death. But
he so fervently and de-
voutly prayed for his
recovery, that the pro-
phet was sent back
with a second message,
promising a prolonga-
tion of his life for fifteen
years.   To assure him
that his recovery was
indeed miraculous, and
not " a chance," and

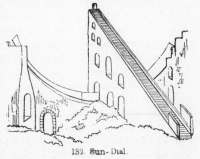

132. Sun-Dial.

to give him confidence in the promise, a token was given in
the going backward of the sun's shadow ten degrees, as
measured by the sun-dial of Ahaz, which was probably something of the same kind as the architectural dial at Delhi,
which is also used as an observatory.

10. The great loss which the Assyrians had sustained in
Palestine, enabled the governor of Babylon, Merodach-bala-
dan, to declare himself independent; and he naturally desired to form amicable relations with the monarch in whose
dominions the Assyrian power had been so greatly disabled.

To congratulate Hezekiah on his recovery, and to inquire concerning the attendant miracle, were, however, the ostensible objects of the embassy which the Babylonians sent to Jerusalem. Highly flattered by such an embassy from so distant a quarter, Hezekiah forgat his usual discretion, and to convince the ambassadors of his importance, and that he was a desirable ally, he made to them a very ostentatious display of his treasures and armouries. Because he had indulged in this vainglory, instead of referring all his power and greatness to that Divine King who had cared for and protected him and his people, the Lord was displeased; and the prophet Isaiah was commissioned to warn him, and to humble him by the intimation that the day was coming when all the treasure which he and his fathers had laid up should be spoil for the Babylonians, and when his descendants should be servants in the palace of the king of Babylon. The remainder of his own reign, however, which lasted for twenty-nine years, was peaceful and prosperous.

11. *Sacred Writers.*—The prophet Joel is generally supposed to have delivered his predictions during the reign of Uzziah; but his whole history is perfectly unknown, and it is even uncertain whether he belonged to the kingdom of Judah or that of Israel. In nervous and animated language, he endeavours to awaken the people to repentance, by announcing the devastation of their fields, and consequent famine, as the punishment of their sins. In the reign of Hezekiah, several eminent prophets flourished, some of whom, however, had begun to prophesy before his reign. At the head of them, and indeed of all the prophets, stands Isaiah. We know little of him, except that he was the son of one Amoz, and that he discharged the prophetic office in the reigns of Uzziah, Jotham, Ahaz, and Hezekiah, before the last of whom he probably died; although there is Jewish tradition which alleges that he survived to the time of Manasseh, by whose order he was sawn asunder. His prophetic ministry, therefore, extends over the whole period which also embraced the prophets Amos, Hoshea, Joel, and Micah. His extensive predictions embrace every matter in which the Jews or their neighbours were interested. They are delivered with marvellous sublimity of thought and language, especially in

those portions in which he foretells the advent of the Messiah, and the circumstances attending his birth, his ministry, his death and the ultimate glory of his kingdom. Micah prophesied in the reigns of Jotham, Ahaz, and Hezekiah. He was a native of Morasthi, a small town in the southern part of Judah ; and this is all we know of him. His prophesies relate to both the kingdoms, which he invites to repentance by threatenings and promises. He also spoke of the Messiah, and named Bethlehem as the place of his birth. Nahum appears to have prophesied in the time of Hezekiah, and not long after the subversion of the kingdom of Israel by Shalmanezer. The principal object of his prophesy is to declare the future downfall of that great Assyrian power by which Israel had lately been desolated, and to which Judah was then tributary.

Tower of Babel.

CHAPTER VII. B.C. 771 to 721.

ISRAEL.	B.C.	ASSYRIA.	B.C.	EGYPT.	B.C.
Shallum	771	New Dynasty	821	Sebechon, or Sheebet	722
Menahem	770	Pul or Belus II.	790	Tirhakah (Ethiopian)	710
Pekaiah	760	Invades Israel	770		
Pekah	759	Tiglath-pileser	747	GENERAL HISTORY	
Second Interregnum	739	Invades Israel	740	Tatius, king of Rome	746
Hoshea	730	Shalmaneser	729	First recorded eclipse of	
Samaria taken	721			the moon, March 19th	720
Nahum the prophet	713	BABYLON.			
Micah	750	Nabonassar	747		
		Nadius	733		
		Chinzirus	731		
JUDAH.		Jugæus	726		
Jotham	757	Merodach-baladan	721		
Ahaz	741	These are viceroys under			
Hezekiah	725	Assyria, up to and be-			
Dies	696	yond this time.			

1. In Israel, Shallum did not long retain the power he had acquired by the death of Zechariah, the last of Jehu's house. He was in his turn assassinated by Menahem, about a month after he ascended the throne.

2. But the act of Menahem was not sanctioned by public opinion, and the nation generally refused to acknowledge his authority. The land was thus distracted by internal commotions, when the Assyrians first made their appearance in these parts, under Pul their king, the father of Tiglath-pileser. This conqueror was advancing to invade Israel, when Menahem made submission to him, and, by the payment of one thousand talents of silver, procured his assistance against his refractory subjects. Menahem exercised with great barbarity the power he had thus acquired by foreign help; and the heavy annual tribute which he had engaged to pay the Assyrians in some degree compelled him to extort large sums of money from the people. The kings of Israel had no sacred treasury to draw from, like those of Judah ; and in eastern countries, where there is no regular system of finance, extraordinary demands are met by the exaction of large contributions in money from those who are supposed to be in possession of wealth. Israel was thus in a most miserable con-

dition. The land became impoverished; the people were in a state of exasperation; and the Assyrians, having so largely profited by the invasion of Israel, were ready to avail themselves of any pretext for repeating the experiment. The state of religion and morals corresponded with this external condition. With the rapid growth of idolatry, and the neglect of that religious system which was the true glory of the nation, the people lost all love for the good and the beautiful, and gave themselves up to the grossest abominations that the heart of man can conceive. It was evident that the nation was ripening fast for that destruction which the prophets had foretold. After a troubled reign of ten years, Menahem died.

3. Pekahiah, his son, reigned two years, and was then put to death by Pekah, the commander of the forces.

4. Pekah then ascended the throne. The principal events of this reign were those which arose from the alliance of Pekah with Rezin, king of Syria, against Ahaz, king of Judah, as related in the preceding chapter. Pekah was victorious in this war, which induced Ahaz to apply to Tiglathpileser, the son of Pul, king of Assyria, who came and chastised the belligerents into quietness, after which he removed the tribes beyond Jordan to Media and Assyria. After a reign of twenty years, Pekah was slain by Hoshea.

5. Ten years of the most cruel anarchy elapsed before Hoshea was able to establish himself on the throne. About this time the Egyptians became seriously alarmed at the progress of the Assyrians in their neighbourhood; and So or Sabaco, the king of Egypt, adopted the policy of procuring employment for them elsewhere, to avert their attention from his own country. To this end he induced Hoshea in Israel, and Hezekiah in Judah, by insincere promises of support, to hold back the tribute they had paid to the Assyrians. This soon brought Shalmaneser, the son of Tiglath-pileser, with a mighty host into Palestine. Having easily subdued the country, he advanced to lay siege to the metropolis, in which Hoshea had shut himself with the remnant of his forces. It was not taken until the third year, and in the interval the inhabitants endured great privation and distress. At length it fell; and Shalmaneser extinguished the kingdom of Israel, and sent Hoshea in chains to Nineveh. Thus perished the

kingdom of Israel, which was annexed to the Assyrian crown under an Assyrian governor, after it had endured, as a separate state, 271 years, under seventeen kings.

6. The king of Assyria adopted the policy which appears to have been usually followed in those times with regard to such countries or provinces as the conqueror designed to incorporate with his own dominions. The flower of the nation, composed of all who were distinguished for their rank or wealth, for their abilities or personal qualifications, and for their knowledge of arms and useful arts, were taken away to the region beyond the Euphrates, in which the three tribes carried off by Tiglath-pileser were already settled. Their place was partly supplied by the inhabitants of other conquered countries in distant parts. In the present case, the new settlers in Israel were brought from the region of the Lower Tigris and Euphrates; and being intended merely to keep the land occupied, were a far less numerous and valuable population than that which they had displaced. This design was more fully worked out by Esarhaddon, the son of Sennacherib, who gleaned the remnant left in the land, and substituted more foreigners. The new comers gradually combined with the dregs of the Israelites who remained in the country, and the population thus formed took the name of Samaritans from the city of Samaria. They were all idolaters; but, according to the notions of local and national deities which then prevailed, they deemed themselves bound to know something of " the god of the country" in which they had settled. To this they were further impelled by the increase and boldness of lions and

133. Lion.

other beasts of prey in the depopulated country, which they ascribed to His anger against them. The desired knowledge they obtained from a priest who fixed his residence at Bethel, and the result was, that they combined the worship of the true God with that of their own idols. Very gradually, however, their system purified itself from the idolatrous dross, and the Samaritans at length rested in a system of belief as pure as that of the Jews, although less regular in some of its observances. In some respects their creed may have been the purer of the two, seeing that it was based entirely upon the Books of Moses, whereas that of the Jews became encumbered with a great mass of oral traditions.

7. As henceforth the Jews only, that is, the inhabitants of the kingdom of Judah, have historical existence, it may be well to offer a few concluding remarks regarding the ten tribes, who were earlier brought under the yoke of bondage by the Assyrians. They were settled in Assyria and Media, and nothing of their further history is known. Much, however, has been conjectured; and their destiny has often been made a subject of inquiry and dispute. Many believe that they are destined to take part in those purposes of divine mercy for which their brethren of Judah have been kept for so many ages separate and apart among the nations, a wonder and a byword in them all. In this belief they have sought for them, and have found in various countries, and under a variety of disguising circumstances, races or tribes of men whom, from analogous customs, rites, and features, they have supposed to be descendants of the ten tribes. Such have been found in Asia, Europe, and America, among heathens, Moslems, Jews, and Christians. All these identifications cannot be true; and there are none of them which quite satisfy the mind, for many of the analogies rest on circumstances which belonged to the Israelites, not as the sons of Abraham, but only as Orientals.

8. It is to be borne in mind that the land of Israel was not altogether divested of its inhabitants, as many of the poorer people were allowed to remain. Then, also, the proclamation of Cyrus, under which the Jews eventually returned to build again their city and temple, was addressed not to the tribes of Judah and Benjamin alone but to *all* the people of Jehovah (Ezra i. 1, 3); and being proclaimed throughout the Persian empire, which included the former dominions of Assyria, it is probable that not a few of the ten tribes were

induced to return to Palestine. Those who were inclined to remove, would naturally attach themselves here and there to a caravan of merchants, and return to the land of their fathers. But as they arrived one after another, in small parties, no mention of their return could be expected in a history so concise. There might have been Israelites in the great caravan of Zerubbabel; and, at all events, it is more than probable that most of them returned when they heard of the prosperity of their brethren in Palestine. At whatever time it may have been, it is certain that many did return; for the history mentions Israelites as settled in Galilee and Peræa before the time of Christ. (1 Macc. v. 9, 24.) But connecting themselves with the tribe of Judah, they finally lost the distinctive name of Israelites, and all the Hebrews were indiscriminately designated as Jews.

9. Something similar may very safely be supposed to have occurred beyond the Euphrates, where a very large proportion of the Judahites thought proper to remain. It is likely that still greater numbers of the Israelites who had lived in these countries two centuries longer, would feel little inclination to exchange the comforts they had accumulated for the prospects which Palestine offered. But as the old jealousy between Judah and Israel had by this time ceased, those Israelites who remained east of the Euphrates joined themselves to the tribe of Judah, which was in possession of the Temple, and consequently they too received the name of Jews. If this view as to the amalgamation of the ten with the two tribes rests upon better grounds than that which reserves for the former a separate existence, all inquiry after the "lost tribes" must needs be superfluous.

CHAPTER VIII.   B. C. 698 TO 588.

JUDAH.	B. C.
Manasseh	698
Judah invaded by the Assyrians . . .	674
Amon	643
Josiah	641
Jehoahaz . . .	610
Jehoiakim . . .	610
Jehoiachin . . .	598
Zedekiah	598
Jerusalem taken . .	588

PROPHETS.

Zephaniah	630
Jeremiah	628
Habakkuk	607
Daniel	603
Ezekiel	594
Obadiah	587

EGYPT.

Tirhakah	689
The twelve kings.	
Psammitichus (Psamatik) I. . . .	664
Necho	610
Psammitichus (Psamatik) II.	600
Psamatik III., Apries, (Pharaoh Hophra) .	596

ASSYRIA.	B. C.
Esarhaddon	710
Medes and Babylonians revolt . . .	710
Babylon regained . .	680
Ninus III.	667
Nebuchadonozor . .	658
Sarac or Sardanapalus II.	606
Nineveh taken by the Medes and Babylonians	606

BABYLON.

Apronadius	699
Regibelus	693
Misoessimordak . .	692
Interregnum . . .	688
Asaradin or Esarhaddon (of Assyria) .	680
Saosduchin	667
Chyniladen	647
Nabopolassar . .	617
Labynetus I. . . .	625

BABYLONIAN EMPIRE.

Nebuchadnezzar . .	606
Evil-merodach . .	561

MEDES.

Revolt from Assyria	710
Dejoces or Artæus .	703
Phraortes	663
Cyaxares I.	608
Astyages	601

GENERAL HISTORY	B. C
Creon, 1st annual Archon of Athens . .	684
Tyrtæus, the poet .	684
Terpander, the poet .	675
Tullus Hostilius, king of Rome	672
Byzantium built . .	658
Ancus Martius, king of Rome	640
Thrasybulus, tyrant of Miletus	634
Kingdom and city of Cyrene founded . .	630
Periander, tyrant of Corinth	629
Draco, lawgiver of Athens	624
Tarquinius Priscus, king of Rome . . .	610
Alcæus, the poet . .	607
Sappho, the poetess .	600
Solon, lawgiver of Athens	594
Thales of Miletus . .	594
The Pythian games instituted	591
Anacharsis, the Scythian	590

1. MANASSEH, the son of Hezekiah, was but twelve years old when his father died. Wicked counsellors corrupted his youth. They imbued his mind with the worst principles of religion and government, and brought him up in a settled dislike to the wholesome reformations of his father, which he seemed to have made it the business of his life to subvert. Whatever God declared to be most repugnant to him—whatever good men the most abhor—were the very objects of his depraved choice and appetite. He not only built altars for all the heavenly bodies, but set up an idol in the very sanctuary of God, which no one had hitherto dared to pro-

fane; he devoted his children to Moloch, by making them
pass through the fire in the valley of Hinnom; and the
people, depraved by his example, became in all respects far
worse than the Canaanites, who had been rooted out to make
room for them. The righteous few, who still remained
faithful to the truth, were grievously persecuted; and injustice
and crime were at this time so rampant, that innocent blood
flowed abundantly in Jerusalem. Even the prophets, whom
God sent t warn the apostate king, were not spared; and
it is believed that the great prophet Isaiah was by his order
sawn asunder.

2. The threatened doom was at length inflicted. By the
twenty-second year of his reign, Esarhaddon, king of Assyria,
had repaired the losses which the death of Sennacherib had
occasioned. Having invaded Palestine, he removed the
remnant which lingered upon the mountains of Israel, and
dispatched his generals against Jerusalem. The city was
taken and Manasseh was sent in chains to Babylon, which
the Assyrians had recovered, where he was thrown into a
dungeon. There he had leisure for thought; and the remembrance of what he had been, of what he had lost, and
how he had lost it, filled him with poignant sorrow. At
length his heart was softened; he wept, and turned repen-
tingly to the Lord, from whom he had revolted. God heard
the moaning of the prisoner, and had pity upon him, and
forgave him, and inclined the heart of the successor of
Esarhaddon to restore him to his kingdom. The remainder
of his reign was good, and he found ample employment in
undoing all that he had before done. His reign of fifty-five
years was the longest which occurred in either Judah or
Israel.

3. Amon, his son, succeeded at the age of twenty-two
years. But although brought up in the best days of his
father, he followed the example of the worst. He was slain
in a conspiracy by his own servants, after a short reign of
two years.

4. Josiah was only eight years old when the people, after
having punished the murderers of his father, made him king.
His guardianship devolved upon the high-priest, who bestowed upon him an education worthy of a king. Josiah

began very early to manifest the good dispositions and excellent character which distinguished his reign. As early as the age of twelve he interested himself in seeing Jerusalem purged of the idolatries which his father had in his short reign introduced. Afterwards he conducted this expurgation in person, not only in his own dominions, but throughout the territories which had belonged to Ephraim, Manasseh, Zebulun, and Naphtali. On this occasion he executed the sentence against the altar at Bethel, denounced to the first Jeroboam 350 years before, when Josiah had been appointed to this work *by name*.

5. In the eighteenth year of his reign, the Temple was put in complete order and repair. In the course of these labours, the original book of the law, as written by the hand of Moses, and deposited beside the ark, was discovered by Hilkiah the high-priest. From this venerable copy the prophesies of Moses, foretelling the desolation of the land and the ruin of the Temple, were read to the king. With intense concern Josiah rent his clothes, and sent to the prophetess Huldah to ask how these things were to be understood. She confirmed the denunciation, and said that the threatened evils were near at hand; but she added that the good king himself should be removed from this world before they came. The same year the king celebrated a great passover, such as had not been in any former reign. In short, no king surpassed, or perhaps equalled, Josiah in well-directed zeal for the Lord, and in efforts to extirpate idolatry and restore the true religion.

6. In the year 606 B. C., Nineveh was besieged by the Medes and Babylonians, who had revolted from Assyria. Taking advantage of these affairs, the king of Egypt marched an army to possess himself of Carchemish, an important pass of the Euphrates. He marched through Palestine. But Josiah, as a tributary to the Assyrians, felt himself bound to oppose his passage. He was defeated, and mortally wounded in a battle at Megiddo, and soon after died at Jerusalem, sincerely lamented by all his people, and bewailed by the prophet Jeremiah. He left three sons, Eliakim, Jehoahaz or Shallum, and Zedekiah.

7. Jehoahaz or Shallum, the second of these sons, was

elected king by the people. We know not the cause of this preference, which was very little justified by his conduct during the three months of his reign, in which he manifested a disposition to imitate the worst of his predecessors. At the end of the three months, Necho returned triumphant from the Euphrates, and came to Jerusalem to reap the fruits of his victory at Megiddo. He laid on the city a heavy tribute, and deposed Jehoahaz, and carried him away captive into Egypt, where he died. Necho bestowed the crown on Josiah's eldest son, Eliakim, whose name he changed to Jehoiakim, in token of subjection.

8. Jehoiakim was twenty-five years old when he ascended the throne as the vassal of Egypt. He trod in the steps of his idolatrous predecessors, and the people imitated his example. The Babylonians wished to succeed to the western empire of the Assyrians, and not to destroy it. Nabopolassar, the king of Babylon, while besieging Nineveh, beheld, therefore, with displeasure the disturbances west of the Euphrates, and sent his son Nebuchadnezzar to reduce the provinces to obedience. In this he succeeded, and Jehoiakim, among the rest, became his vassal, and continued such for three years. During this time Nineveh was taken, and Nabopolassar, dying soon after, was succeeded by his son Nebuchadnezzar. While the attention of the new monarch was otherwise engaged, Jehoiakim had the temerity to revolt from him. To this he was probably incited by the king of Egypt, who undertook a second expedition against Carchemish, which Nebuchadnezzar had recovered. He was defeated by the Babylonian, and stripped of all his possessions between the Euphrates and the Nile. Nebuchadnezzar then besieged and took Jerusalem; and among other spoil, carried away a portion of the sacred vessels of the Temple, which he lodged in the temple of Belus at Babylon. Certain of the royal family and of the nobles were also taken away as hostages for the fidelity of the king and people. Among these were the prophet Daniel and his companions. Upon the whole, Nebuchadnezzar behaved more leniently than might have been expected, owing, probably, to a desire of maintaining Judah, if possible, as a frontier state between himself and Egypt. He did not even depose Jehoiakim.

who, uncorrected by adversity, proved the same remorseless tyrant, regardless of God and man. It does not appear that he again revolted, but after some years his conduct appeared so displeasing to the king of Babylon, who was then in the north of Syria, that he sent a number of local auxiliaries against him. They took him prisoner and carried him to Nebuchadnezzar, who put him in fetters, and designed to take him to Babylon. But he first proceeded with him to Jerusalem, where he died.

9. On Nebuchadnezzar's arrival at Jerusalem, he was little pleased to find that, without consulting him, the people had in the meantime raised to the throne Jehoiachin (or Jeconiah or Coniah), the son of Jehoiakim. This prince, in the brief interval of three months, had found time to evince the most depraved dispositions. He surrendered to Nebuchadnezzar, and was taken to Babylon, where he spent the rest of his days. Nebuchadnezzar made Zedekiah, the third son of Josiah, king; but left him a much impoverished kingdom. All the portable wealth that could be found in the palace or the Temple, was seized and sent off to Babylon: and, along with the deposed king, were taken away all the persons of note, and all the skilful craftsmen of the kingdom.

10. In appointing Zedekiah to the throne, Nebuchadnezzar exacted from him a very solemn oath of allegiance. Accordingly, when in the fourth year of his reign, the kings of Edom, Moab, Ammon, and Tyre, invited him to join them in a confederacy to shake off the Babylonian yoke, he would not listen to their proposals. But Zedekiah set an example of iniquity to his people, which they willingly followed. They were rapidly ripening for the destruction which had been so long foretold; and which was brought about by means of the revolt of Zedekiah from the king of Babylon, in the ninth year of his reign. This step was taken in reliance upon Pharaoh Hophra, king of Egypt, in spite of the earnest remonstrances of Jeremiah, who repeatedly and in the face of cruel treatment, warned both the king and people, that their only hope of safety and quiet lay in their adhesion to Nebuchadnezzar.

11. In consequence of this revolt, the Babylonian king invaded Judæa with a great army, and, after taking most of

K

the principal towns, sat down before Jerusalem. Early in
the next year the Egyptians marched an army to the relief
of their ally; but being intimidated by the alacrity with
which the Babylonians raised the siege and advanced to give
them battle, they returned home without risking an engagement. The return of the Chaldeans to the siege, destroyed
all the hopes which the approach of the Egyptian succours
had excited. The siege was now prosecuted with redoubled
vigour; and at length Jerusalem was taken by storm at midnight, in the eleventh year of Zedekiah, and in the eighteenth
month from the commencement of the siege. Dreadful was
the carnage. The people, young and old, were slaughtered
wherever they appeared; and even the temple was no refuge
for them: the sacred courts streamed with blood. Zedekiah
himself, with his family and some friends, contrived to escape
from the city; but he was overtaken and captured in the
plains of Jericho. He was sent in chains to Nebuchadnezzar,
who had left the conclusion of the war to his generals, and
was then at Riblah in Syria. After sternly reproving him
for his ungrateful conduct, the conqueror ordered all the sons
of Zedekiah to be slain before his eyes, and then his own eyes
to be put out, thus making the slaughter of his children the
last sight on which his tortured memory could dwell. He
was afterwards sent in fetters of brass to Babylon, where he
remained until his death.

12. Nebuchadnezzar appears to have felt that his purposes had not been fully executed by the army, or else he was
urged by the Edomites and others to exceed his first intentions. He therefore sent Nebuzaradan, the captain of the
guard, with a sufficient force, to complete the desolation of
Judah and Jerusalem. He burned the city and the temple
to the ground; he collected and sent to Babylon all the gold
and silver which former spoilers had left; and he transported
all the people who had been left behind in Jehoiachin's captivity, save only the poor of the land, who were left to be
vine-dressers and husbandmen. Four years after, Nebuzaradan again entered Judæa, and gleaned a few more of the
miserable inhabitants, whom he sent off to Babylon.

13. Thus was the land left desolate; and thus ended the
kingdom of Judah and the reign of David's house, after it had

endured 404 years, under twenty kings. It is remarkable that the king of Babylon made no attempt to colonize the country he had depopulated, as was done by the Assyrians in Israel; and thus, in the providence of God, the land was left vacant, to be re-occupied by the Jews after seventy years of captivity and punishment.

14. *Sacred Writers.*—Zephaniah prophesied in the early part of Josiah's reign; and his reprehension of the existing abuses would appear to have roused that excellent prince to undertake those reformations which honoured his reign.— About the middle of that reign Jeremiah began to prophesy, and he lived through the succeeding reigns to see the fulfilment of his own predictions of the captivity of Judah. He was a priest of Anathoth, a place about three miles north o Jerusalem. After the death of Josiah, he met with great opposition from the kings and courtiers, by which his spirit was much afflicted. After the destruction of Jerusalem, he went, reluctantly, to Egypt, with a remnant of the Jews. What afterwards happened to him is not known with certainty; but it is said that his countrymen in Egypt were so offended by his faithful remonstrances, that they stoned him to death. The prophesies and "lamentations" of Jeremiah, indicate a man deeply conscious of the evil days on which he had fallen, and over which he mourned intensely.—Habakkuk, who delivered his short prophesy in the reign of Jehoiakim, declared, with much sublimity of style and grandeur of imagery, the approaching calamities of the nation, and pointed out the consolations which the faithful might still claim.—Ezekiel was of the sacerdotal race, and was one of the captives whom Nebuchadnezzar carried into Babylonia, along with king Jehoiachin. There, by the river Chebar, which falls into the Euphrates, he had visions of God, and delivered prophesies confirmatory of those which Jeremiah at the same time delivered in Judæa.—The short prophesy of Obadiah is almost wholly directed against the Edomites, and is supposed to have been delivered in the very few years which elapsed between the destruction of Jerusalem and the desolation of Edom by Nebuchadnezzar.

BOOK VI.

CHAPTER I. 588 to 535.

BABYLON.	B. C.	MEDIA.	B. C.	GENERAL HISTORY	B C.
Nebuchadnezzar con-		Cyaxares II. (Darius)	641	Servius Tullius, King	
quers Egypt . . .	570	—— succeeds Belshaz-		of Rome	578
His insanity	568	zar at Babylon . .	553	Anaximander. . . .	568
His recovery and death	561	Cyrus succeeds his		Phalaris, tyrant of	
Evil-Merodach . . .	561	uncle Darius . .	551	Agrigentum . . .	567
Jehoiachin released .	561	—— completes the for-		Cleobulus	564
Belshazzar, or Neriglis-		mation of the Persian		Croesus, King of Lydia	562
sar	558	Empire, by recover-		Pisistratus, tyrant of	
Nabonadius—viceroy	553	ing Babylon from Na-		Athens	560
Cyrus, the Persian, takes		bonadius	536	Anaximenes . . .	556
Babylon	536			Pythagoras	539
End of captivity . .	535			Simonides the poet .	537

IN order to preserve the continuity of the history of Palestine, it is necessary to follow into their exile that favoured race, on whose account the Holy Land has acquired that celebrity which must ever attach to its name.

1. Again, the children of Abraham, the chosen people, were in exile, and the land of their inheritance lay desolate. But we are not on that account to imagine that the purposes for which they had been set apart as a peculiar people among the nations, had been rendered nugatory. This was by no means the case. They were still destined to fulfil their vocation of keeping alive in the world the knowledge of the true God, the Creator of all things, and of being the depositaries of his designs towards the race of man.

2. The later exiles found themselves not altogether strangers at Babylon. Their countrymen of the earlier captivities were settled in various stations and employments, and some of them held posts of trust under the government. By that government they were regarded not as prisoners, but as useful emigrants; and after a while they appear to have experienced no other inconveniences than those which naturally

flowed from their regrets for their own pleasant land, from
their position as foreigners in a strange country; from the
derision of the natives at the peculiarities of their religion;
and, probably, from a distinctive poll-tax from which the
Babylonians were exempt.   This much may be gathered from
dispersed intimations; but the principal known facts of the
captivity are connected with the history of Daniel, one of the
earlier exiles, who rose to the highest distinction under the
Babylonian kings.

3. Daniel was one of the young men of high family who
were carried away as hostages for the fidelity of king Jehoiachin.   He and some others were put under the chief eunuch,
to be properly trained in the language and learning of the
Chaldeans, to fit them for employments at the court.   This
training lasted three years, when they were examined in the
presence of the king; and Daniel and three of his friends
were found to have made far greater progress than any of
those who had been educated with them.   They were therefore enrolled among the magians or learned men.

4. A few years after Nebuchadnezzar was greatly troubled
with a dream, which made a profound impression upon his
mind; but the particulars of which quite passed from his memory when he awoke.   Great importance was attached to
dreams in those days, and men skilled in the sciences were
supposed to be able to discover their meaning.   Therefore,
the king sent for his court magians, and required them not
only to interpret the dream, but to discover the dream itself,
which he had forgotten.   This they declared to be impossible;
on which the exasperated tyrant ordered all the magians to
be massacred.   Daniel and his friends, although not present,
were included in such a sentence.   On learning this, he
begged a respite for the whole body, undertaking to find,
through his God, the solution of the difficulty.   The respite
was granted; and at the earnest prayer of Daniel, the Lord
made the secret known to him.   A colossal image which the
king saw, with a head of gold, arms and breast of silver,
belly and thighs of brass, legs of iron, and toes partly iron
and partly clay, was struck down by a stone, which itself grew
and filled the whole earth.   This, in the interpretation of
Daniel, figured forth " the things to come;" describing by

characteristic symbols the succession of empires to the end of time; and it is wonderful to observe how precisely the greater part of what was then future has since been accomplished. The king was not only satisfied but astonished; he was almost ready to pay divine honours to Daniel; and raised him at once to the eminent station of Archimagus, or chief of the magians, and governor of the metropolitan province of Babylon. His three friends, also, were, at his request, promoted to places of trust and honour.

5. Not long after, Nebuchadnezzar set up a colossal image in the plains of Dura, and commanded that, when music sounded, every one should worship it, on pain of death. He soon learned that this command was utterly neglected by Daniel's three friends, Shadrach, Meshach, and Abednego; and his rage grew so high, at the example of disobedience given by persons in their high station, that he ordered them to be at once cast into "the burning furnace." The heat of the furnace was so great as to destroy the men who cast them in; but they themselves remained unhurt, and not even a hair of their heads was singed. They came forth when the king called them; and he was so much astonished and convinced by this prodigy, that he publicly acknowledged the greatness of the God whom they served.

6. There appeared to have been some good and generous

134. Ancient Babylonians.

qualities in the character of Nebuchadnezzar; but the pride with which he contemplated the grandeur of his empire, and the magnificence of his undertakings, was most inordinate, and he required to be taught that "the Most High ruleth over all the kingdoms of the earth, and giveth them to whomsoever he will." He was warned of this in a dream, which was interpreted to him by Daniel; but, neglecting the warning, "his heart was changed from man's, and a beast's heart was given to him." He was afflicted with a madness which made him think himself a beast, and, acting as such, he remained constantly abroad in the fields, living upon wild herbs. In this debased and forlorn condition the mighty conqueror remained seven years, when he was restored to his reason and his throne; and one of his first acts was to issue a proclamation, humbly acknowledging the signs and wonders which the Most High God had wrought towards him, and declaring his conviction, that "those who walk in pride he is able to abase." He died soon after. He was succeeded by Evil-Merodach, who had administered the government during the insanity of

185. Ancient Babylonians.

his father. On his accession, he released Jehoiachin from his long confinement, and gave him the first place among the fallen kings who sat at his table in Babylon. After three years, Evil-Merodach was defeated, and killed in a battle with the combined Medes and Persians under Cyrus.

7. His son Belshazzar succeeded. Of him nothing is recorded but the circumstances in which his reign concluded. There was a great festival, which Belshazzar celebrated by a magnificent feast to all his nobles. They talked of their gods, whose power had proved so much greater than that of the gods of other nations; and this suggested to the king to send for the sacred vessels of the temple of Jerusalem, to be used as wine-cups in their riotings. While thus profanely engaged, their attention was arrested by a mysterious hand, tracing on the wall words which no one understood. The magians tried in vain to interpret them. Daniel was then sent for, and he, after solemnly rebuking the king for his profanation of that Great Name which his proud grandfather had been compelled to honour, explained the terrible purport of the inscription to be, that the end both of his

life and dynasty was close at hand. He lost his life that very night by the conspiracy of two nobles, whom he had grievously wronged; and a year after, the death of his son, a boy, named Laborosoarchad, left the heritage to Darius (or Cyaxares) the Mede, who accordingly took possession of the kingdom. Thus the Babylonian empire was merged in that of the Medes and Persians.

8. A very high place in the favour of Darius was occupied by Daniel; and in re-distributing the government of the provinces, the prophet was set at the head of all. This excited the jealousy and discontent of many, and the destruction of Daniel was determined. His hands were too clean, and his conduct too upright, to allow them to hope that they could fasten any charge upon him, except on the score of his religion. They therefore persuaded the weak old king to issue a decree, that no one should, for thirty days, make prayer to any god but himself, under pain of being cast alive into the den of lions. Daniel, however, made no change in his usual habits of prayer to the God of Israel, with his face turned towards Jerusalem. He was, therefore, accused to Darius, who saw too late the folly into which he had been drawn, and would fain have spared his friend. But being reminded, that among the Medes and Persians a royal decree could not be revoked or altered, he reluctantly consented that his own should take effect. Daniel was then thrown into the den of lions. The unhappy king spent the night in sorrow; and early in the morning he hastened to the den, hoping that perhaps the Mighty God whom Daniel served had not allowed him to perish. The cheerful voice of the prophet from within the den answered to the call, for the lions had not been allowed to hurt him. Daniel was taken from the den, and his accusers cast in; and on them the lions had no mercy. This produced from Darius a remarkable proclamation of the greatness and supremacy of " the Most High God," whom Daniel served.

9. Darius occupied the throne of Babylon only two years; and on his death it was usurped by a Babylonian noble, named Nabonadius. Cyrus, the illustrious nephew of Darius, was for several years too much engaged in other wars to attend to him. But, at length, he led his troops against

Babylon. The city held out for two years against him; and was then only taken by the remarkable stratagem of diverting the course of the river Euphrates, which flowed through the city, and entering by night through the dry channel This taking of Babylon, with all its circumstances, was minutely described by the prophet Isaiah, and Cyrus mentioned by name, above a century before that conqueror was born.

10. The prophet Daniel was still alive when Babylon was taken by Cyrus; and there is reason to conclude, that this venerable personage was high in the esteem of that conqueror. In some decrees, Cyrus intimates his knowledge of those prophesies in Isaiah which speak of himself, and there is little question that Daniel had called his attention to them. We know that the prophet had at this time looked much into the writings of former prophets (Dan. ix. 1, 2), and had ascertained that the duration of the captivity was to be seventy years (Jer. xxv. 11, 12 ; xxix. 10); and now he found that the expiration of the seventy years left the sovereign power in the hands of Cyrus, of whom Isaiah had so particularly prophesied as the person destined " to restore the captivities of Judah." The communication of these facts must have made a strong impression on the conqueror, accompanied as it was by the claim, that the Jehovah whom the Hebrews worshipped was He who had raised him up, and had given to him all that greatness and glory by which he was now surrounded.

11. *Sacred Writers.*—The most eminent writer of this period was Daniel, whose history has been given above. He lived throughout the captivity in great esteem and honour. He did not return with his countrymen to Judæa, but remained at Babylon, and probably died soon after, either there or at Susa, from which metropolitan city the last of his visions is dated, when he was about ninety-four years old. His writings are in the form of visions, which describe, almost with the distinctness of history, the events of future times. The Messiah is also mentioned by him ; and the time of his coming is set down with such precision, as produced among the Jews a general expectation of his advent at the time when Jesus Christ appeared.

CHAPTER II. B. C. 535 to 516.

THE JEWS.	B.C	PERSIAN EMPIRE.	B. C.	GENERAL B. C.	B C
Return to Jerusalem under Zerubbabel	535	Cyrus		Tarquinius Superbus, King of Rome	534
Jeshua, high-priest	535	Cambyses	529	Anacreon	532
Rebuilding of the city and second Temple begun	535	Smerdis, the Magian	521	Polycrates, tyrant of Samos	531
Temple finished	516	Darius Hystaspes	521	Hippias and Hipparchus at Athens	527
				Confucius, in China	520

1. ANIMATED by the impressions thus made upon his mind, Cyrus, in the very year that Babylon was taken, issued a decree, in which, after acknowledging the supremacy of the Lord, and that to Him he owed all his kingdoms, he gave full permission to the Jews, in any part of his dominions, to return to their own land, and to rebuild the city and Temple of Jerusalem. No sooner were the favourable dispositions of the king thus made known, than the members of the later captivity—those of the tribes of Judah, Benjamin, and Levi—repaired in large numbers to Babylon from their different places of residence; some to make preparations for their journey; and others, who had no intention to return themselves, to assist those who had. Most of the existing race had been born in Babylonia, and in the course of years families had established themselves in the country, and formed connections, and gathered around them comforts which were not easily abandoned. Hence, only a zealous minority were disposed to avail themselves of the decree in their favour: the great bulk of the people choosing to remain in the land of their exile; and it has always been the opinion of the Jews, that the more illustrious portion of their nation remained in Chaldea.

2. The first return caravan was organised and directed by Zerubbabel, the grandson of king Jehoiachin, and by Jeshua, a grandson of the last high-priest Jozadak. The number of persons who joined them was about 50,000, including above 7000 male and female servants. Before they

departed, Cyrus caused to be restored to them the more valuable of the sacred utensils, which had been removed by Nebuchadnezzar, and preserved by his successors, and which were now destined to be again employed in the service of the sanctuary. Zerubbabel was also entrusted with large contributions towards the expense of rebuilding the Temple, from the Jews who chose to remain behind. The beasts of burden in this caravan exceeded eight thousand. In the book of Ezra, the names of the families which returned in this first colony, and in those which followed are carefully given.

3. The incidents of the journey are not related. On reaching Palestine, the caravan repaired at once to Jerusalem, which they found utterly ruined and desolate. Before they separated to seek habitations for themselves, they raised a large sum by voluntary contributions towards the rebuilding of the Temple. They then employed themselves in securing dwellings and necessaries for their families ; and at the ensuing Feast of Tabernacles again repaired to Jerusalem, where sacrifices were offered on an altar erected upon the ruins of the Temple. After this the people applied themselves zealously to the necessary preparations for the restoration of that edifice. In a year from the departure from Babylon the preparations were sufficiently advanced to allow the work to be commenced ; and, accordingly, the foundations of the second Temple were then laid with great rejoicings and songs of thanksgiving. While the work proceeded, the Samaritans manifested a desire to assist in the work, and to claim a community of worship in the new Temple. This was declined by the Jews, on the ground that the decree of the Persian king extended only to the race of Israel.

4. Being thus frustrated in their design, the Samaritans employed every means they could devise to thwart the undertaking. Their origin appears to have given them considerable influence at the Persian court , and although they could not act openly against the plain decree of Cyrus, an unscrupulous use of their money and influence among the officers of the government enabled them to raise such obstructions that the people were much discouraged, and the work proceeded but languidly, and at length was suspended altogether. This was one cause of the enmity which always afterwards sub-

sisted between the Jews and the Samaritans. The suspension
of the work commenced in the time of Cyrus, and continued
through the reigns of Cambyses and Smerdis, to the second
year of Darius Hystaspes. In this long interval the people
gradually lost all heart for the work, and were disposed to
conclude that the set time for it had not yet arrived. From
this lethargy they were roused by the exhortations and reproaches of the prophet Haggai; and the building was resumed with fresh zeal. This zeal was indeed somewhat
damped by the discouraging regrets of the old men, who had
seen in their youth the Temple of Solomon, and who clearly
perceived that this would be a far inferior building. But to
obviate this discouragement the prophet Haggai was commissioned to declare that the ultimate glory of this second
Temple should greatly exceed that of the first,—not by
greater splendour of fabric, but by the presence within its
walls of the Messiah, so long expected and foretold—" the
desire of all nations." Haggai ii. 1-9.

5. The renewal of the work roused afresh the opposition
of the Samaritans, whose representations induced Tatnai, the
Persian governor of Syria, to write home for instructions,
stating that the Jews alleged the authority of a decree of
Cyrus for their proceedings. The result was happy; for,
after some search, the decree was found. It not only authorised the erection of the Temple, but directed the local
government to afford assistance and supplies, which the Jews
had not ventured to require, but which the rescript of Darius
now commanded to be given. Under the impulse thus imparted the work proceeded with spirit; and, four years after,
it was completed. The dedication was celebrated with great
solemnity and joy ; and soon after, it was made fit for the
old ritual worship, which was resumed at the ensuing passover.

6. The Jews being now in some sense restored to their
own land, it is proper to mention the footing on which they
stood as a people. Like all the surrounding nations, they
were under tribute to the Persians, and subject to the general
policy of that government. They appear to have been
favourably considered by it, at first on account of Daniel, and
afterwards on account of the hatred of idolatry which was

common to the Jews and to the Persians.* They were allowed the free exercise of their religion and laws, and the internal government was directed by a governor of their own nation, or by the high-priest when there was no other governor. There was, in fact, a distinct commonwealth, with its own peculiar institutions; and although responsible to the Persian king, and to his deputy the governor-general of Syria, it was more secure under the protection of the Persian monarchy than, considering its feeble condition, it would have been in complete independence. With regard to religion, the dreadful lesson taught by the desolation of the land, the destruction of the Temple, and the captivity of the people, had effectually cured the Jews of that tendency to idolatry which had been their ruin. But, as time went on, the distortion of character which had been restrained in one direction broke forth in another; and although they no longer went formally astray from a religion which did not suit their carnal minds, they, by many vain and mischievous fancies, fabricated a religion suited to their own dispositions out of the ritual to which they formally adhered.

7. *Sacred Writers.*—The prophet Haggai was the first of the three prophets who were commissioned to make known the will of God to the Jews after their return from captivity. He is supposed to have been born at Babylon, and to have returned with Zerubbabel, under the edict of Cyrus. The object of his prophesy was to stimulate the building of the Temple.—Zechariah was also one of the returned exiles; and his prophesies were delivered at the same time, and with the same object. He also speaks of more remote times,—the coming of Christ, and the Roman war.

* The Persians worshipped the sun as a symbol of the Deity, and the fire as a symbol of the sun. They could not endure idolatrous *images*.

CHAPTER III.   B. C. 516 to 444.

THE JEWS.

	B. C.
Jehoiakim, high-priest	483
Esther succeeds queen Vashti	464
Ezra sent to Jerusalem	457
Mordecai exalted	451
Eliashib, high-priest	453

PERSIAN EMPIRE.

	B. C
Xerxes or Ahasuerus	485
Artaxerxes Longimanus	464

GENERAL HISTORY.

Harmodius and Aristogiton at Athens	513
Consular government established at Rome	509
First dictator (Lartius) at Rome	498
Coriolanus banished	491
The Persians defeated at Marathon	490
Xerxes makes his expedition into Greece	480
The stand at Thermopylæ	479
Xerxes, defeated at Platæa and Mycale, retires from Greece	479
First Decimvirs at Rome	451

REMARKABLE PERSONS.

L. Junius Brutus	509
Porsenna	507
Coriolanus	490
Leonidas	491
Aristides	486
Æschylus	486
Pindar	480
Themistocles	480
Pausanius	479
Cimon (banished)	470
Anaxagoras	470
Pericles	468
Sophocles	463
Herodotus	445

1. It does not appear that the restored Jews experienced any further molestation in the lifetime of Darius Hystaspes, who reigned thirty-six years, and died B. C. 485. He was succeeded by his son Xerxes; and as he is the Ahasuerus of Ezra (iv. 6), it would appear that he was friendly to the Jews, notwithstanding the attempts made by the Samaritans to prejudice his mind against them. He was succeeded in B. C. 564, by his son Artaxerxes Longimanus, whose long reign embraces several circumstances of great interest to the Jewish people.

2. Early in this reign they proceeded to rebuild Jerusalem on a regular plan, and to surround it with a wall. This last procedure excited a ferment of opposition from the Samaritans and others, who succeeded in alarming the Persian government lest its dominion in these parts should be endangered by the fortification of a city, noted of old for its turbulent character, as well as for the power of its former kings. Hence, an order was obtained that the building of the walls should not be allowed. It was not long, however,

before Artaxerxes ascertained the present position and character of the Jewish people, and the favourable sentiments of Cyrus and Darius Hystaspes towards them, as manifested in the conduct and edicts of these princes. He learned also the veneration with which the God of the Hebrews had been regarded by the most eminent of his predecessors. All this is manifested in the terms of the commission by which, in the seventh year of this reign, Ezra, the priest and scribe, was authorised to proceed to Jerusalem to set in order whatever related to the service and worship of Jehovah. He was not, however, authorised to rebuild the walls.

3. Such a commission as that with which Ezra was invested had become highly necessary; for after the death of the first leaders of the restoration, the high-priest Jeshua, the governor Zerubbabel, and the prophets Haggai and Zechariah, both the civil and ecclesiastical state became very unsettled, and had remained so for many years. The commission granted to Ezra was very extensive, and its terms were so precisely applicable to the circumstances of the Jewish people, as to suggest that it was procured from the king by some of the powerful Jews who remained beyond the Euphrates. As governor, Ezra was authorized to appoint superior and inferior judges, to rectify abuses, to enforce the observance of the law, and to punish the refractory with fines, imprisonment, or even death, according to the degree of their offences. Such of the Jews as thought proper, were invited to go back with Ezra, and from those who chose to remain, he was authorized to collect contributions for the use of the Temple. To this fund the king himself and his council liberally contributed; and the ministers of the royal revenues west of the Euphrates were enjoined to furnish Ezra with what he might require, within certain limits, of silver, wheat, wine, oil, and salt, in order that the sacrifices and offerings of the Temple should be constantly kept up; all of which is said to have been done in order to avert from the king and his sons, the wrath of the God of the Hebrews, who, it is very evident, was held in much honour at the Persian court.

4. An exemption from all taxes was also promised to persons engaged in the service of the Temple; but this boon did not induce any of the Levitical tribe to join the caravan

which assembled on the banks of the river Ahava, in Baby·
lonia; and it was with some difficulty that Ezra at last
induced some of the priestly families to go with him.   The
whole caravan was composed of 1754 adult males,—making,
with wives and children, about 6000 persons.   As a party
thus composed had little military strength, and as the journey
across the desert was then, as it always has been, dangerous,
from the predatory Arab tribes by which it is infested,
they felt considerable anxiety on this account.   But Ezra,
from having said much to the king of the Lord's power to
protect and deliver those that trusted in him, felt disinclined
to apply for a guard of soldiers; and thought it better that
the party should, in a solemn act of fasting and prayer, cast
themselves upon the care of their God.   Their confidence
was rewarded by the perfect safety with which their journey
was accomplished.   In four months they arrived at Jerusalem.

5. Having deposited in the Temple the donations with
which he was charged, and imparted his commission to the
royal officers in that quarter, Ezra applied himself earnestly
to the work he had undertaken.   He does not himself record
any of his acts particularly, excepting the removal of the
foreign and idolatrous women, whom many of the people, and
even of the priests and Levites, had married, contrary to the
law.   But we are informed by Nehemiah, that Ezra caused
the law to be publicly read to the assembled people, and to
be explained by interpreters to those who understood only
the Chaldean dialect, in which they had been brought up.
This doubtless gave occasion for the increase of the copies of
the law; and it is generally understood that Ezra collected
and revised the sacred books which compose the Old Testament, and arranged them in the form which they now bear.

6. While Ezra was engaged in these labours, a great
danger threatened the Jews who remained beyond the
Euphrates.   In the third year of his reign, the Persian king
had put away his queen Vashti, and had taken in her place
a beautiful Jewish damsel named Esther, the niece of Mordecai, a Benjamite, and one of the officers of the palace.
Years passed away, in the course of which the chief place in
the king's favour was acquired by Haman, an Amalekite.

INTERIOR OF THE CHURCH OF THE HOLY SEPULCHRE
Palestine.

To him the king commanded that all his servants and officers should bow in that peculiar manner, by which the Persians testified the highest respect. This act of homage was refused by Mordecai,* who constantly allowed the great man to pass by without shewing that respect which all others paid. This attracted the attention and excited the inquiries of Haman; and learning, probably, that all other rigid Jews would act in the same manner, he vowed the extinction of the whole race.

136.

Having fixed, by lot, what he considered a propitious day for the execution of his design, he proceeded to the king, and without naming the people, but describing them, in general terms, as of peculiar customs and unpleasant manners, and of a refractory and rebellious disposition, he obtained an order for their extermination. Couriers were accordingly sent to all the provinces, commanding that the Jews everywhere, without regard to age or sex, should be utterly extirpated on the thirteenth day of the month Adar, and their property taken as a prey. When this became known in Shushan (Susa) the metropolis, all the Jews there declared their concern in loud lamentations, and by garments of mourning. On learning these things from Mordecai, Esther, at his desire, undertook to intercede with the king in behalf of her people.

7. This was an undertaking of great peril; for it was death for any one to appear before the king uncalled, and she had not for some time been invited to his presence. She

* The precise ground of this refusal is not well known. Some think that it was because the form of homage was deemed idolatrous by Mordecai; others, that he would not bow to one of the race which had been doomed to extermination as the implacable enemies of Israel.

went, however, attended by her maidens and the king, happening to be in good humour, extended to her the golden sceptre, by which act her intrusion was forgiven. She invited the king and Haman to a banquet, at which she improved the favourable opening with such consummate tact, that the design of Haman appeared in the king's view as a plot for the destruction of the queen and her people; and in his rage he commanded him to be hanged upon a high gallows which he had himself prepared for Mordecai. It was less easy to revoke the murderous order which had at Haman's instance been issued, by reason of that peculiar practice of the Persians which made the word of the king a law that could not be altered. All that could be done was to allow the Jews to stand upon their defence against those who might attempt to put the first order into execution. These conflicting orders occasioned much bloodshed in different parts; but the Jewish nation was preserved, and the deliverance is to this day commemorated by an annual feast, called Purim.

8. There is yet another incident in this remarkable history. In the interval, after the first order had been issued, the king's attention was providentially drawn to the fact, that a domestic plot against his life had been formerly detected and made known by Mordecai. He then asked what reward had been conferred on the man to whom he owed his life; and hearing that he had received no mark of favour, he sent for Haman, and asked him what ought to be done for the man "whom the king delighted to honour." Supposing that the king referred to himself, Haman enumerated distinctions of the very highest class, bordering on those which belonged to royalty itself; he was, therefore, utterly confounded when the king told him to see that all these honours were bestowed upon Mordecai the Jew,—the very Mordecai for whom he had just prepared a gallows fifty cubits high. Haman obeyed in silence; and on his downfall, which immediately followed, Mordecai was promoted to his place, which gave him power to be very useful to his nation.

9. *Sacred Writers.*—The history of Ezra has been mentioned, and some allusion has been made to his labour in arranging and revising the sacred books. Of these labours

he says nothing himself; but the constant tradition of the Jews has been, that he collected as many copies of the sacred books as he could obtain; and by correcting the errors of former copyists, and by adding in various places what appeared necessary to illustrate, connect, or explain the context, he produced one perfect copy, which became the exemplar for all subsequent transcribers. Ezra was probably the author of the book which bears his name; and to him also the authorship of the books of Chronicles has been usually ascribed.

Tomb of Ezra

CHAPTER IV. B. C. 444 to 312.

THE JEWS.	B. C.	PERSIAN EMPIRE.	B. C
Nehemiah	444	Artaxerxes Longimanus	423
Builds the walls of Jerusalem	444	Darius Nothus	423
Returns to Persia	432	Artaxerxes Mnemon	404
Comes again to Jerusalem	424	Ochus	381
End of Old Testament canon	420	Darius Codomanus	335
Joiada, high-priest	413	Conquered by Alexander	331
Jonathan or Jehu, high-priest	373		
Jaddua or Jaddus, high-priest	341		
Onias	321		

EVENTS.	B. C.	PERSONS.	B. C
First Censors at Rome	443	Euripides	442
Peloponnesian War begins	431	Phidias	440
Egypt revolts from the Persians	414	Aristophanes	434
Death of Cyrus the younger	401	Socrates	429
Retreat of the Ten Thousand	401	Democritus	428
Peace of Antalcidas	387	Thucydides	426
Battle of Mantinea, and death of		Hippocrates	425
Epaminondas	363	Alcibiades	420
Birth of Alexander the Great	356	Appius Claudius	419
Egypt recovered by the Persians	350	Euclid	404
Carthaginians defeated by Timoleon	340	Zeuxis	397
Battle of Chæronea	340	Camillus (Roman dictator)	390
Philip, king of Macedon, killed	336	Plato	389
Alexander defeats the Persians on the		Epaminondas	375
Granicus	334	Diogenes	372
——— at Issus	333	T. Manlius Torquatus	361
Takes Tyre, visits Jerusalem, acquires		Timoleon	346
Egypt, founds Alexandria	332	Aristotle	345
Defeats Darius at Arbela	331	Phocion	343
Persian Empire ends	331	Demosthenes	338
Alexander dies, and his conquests		Apelles	334
shared by his generals	324		

1. It was not until the twentieth year of Artaxerxes that the Jews received the long-desired permission to build the walls of Jerusalem. This permission was obtained by a Jew called Nehemiah, who held the high office of the royal cup-bearer, and whose concern that "the city of his fathers' sepulchres lay waste" having been noticed by the king, led to the inquiries which induced this result. Nehemiah himself was granted leave of absence, and invested with full powers, as governor of the province, to enable him to execute his own designs, which circumstances had rendered coincident with the existing policy of the Persian government. He carried orders to the royal officers west of the Euphrates, to

render him ll possible assistance, and to furnish from the king's forests in Lebanon such timber as he might require. Thus commissioned, Nehemiah proceeded to Judæa, escorted by a body of Persian officers and cavalry. In this person we have another instance of the liberality with which the great eastern monarchies treated persons of a different religion, and of foreign and captive origin. The rank and authority of Nehemiah at the Persian court are evinced by the commission itself, and by the great retinue which was allowed him; and his wealth is shown by the numerous servants he maintained, and the open table he kept at Jerusalem, which, with the other expenses of the governor, he defrayed from his own purse, declining to receive from the Jews the allowances belonging to his office.

2. A large town without walls offered so little inducement to the people, and so much temptation to enemies, that Nehemiah found Jerusalem unbuilt, and with a most scanty population. On making known his commission to the principal persons of the nation, he found them all disposed to engage zealously in the undertaking. The building of the new wall was accordingly commenced upon the old foundations. The Samaritans, and other enemies of the Jews, took alarm at this movement, and endeavoured in every possible way to thwart the design. The Jews were, however, too much in earnest to be discouraged; they armed the workmen, and still further protected them by a guard of armed citizens, as they worked in bands upon different parts of the wall. Thus, by the most arduous and patriotic exertions, the whole wall, with its gates and towers, was finished in the short space of fifty-two days. This great work being accomplished, the governor took measures to induce a sufficient number of the people to come and settle in the city. The neglected service of the Temple was re-established, and care was taken that the people should be properly instructed in the law of Moses. The public reading of the law, and its interpretation, under the direction of Ezra, as mentioned in the former chapter, took place at this time, with every encouragement from Nehemiah. This ended in a joyful celebration of the Feast of Tabernacles, which had, since the days of Joshua, been neglected and almost forgotten; and after

this the people were found to be in so devout a frame of mind, that Ezra and Nehemiah seized the occasion to engage them to enter into a solemn covenant to serve God with singleness of heart, and to obey in all things the law of Moses. Of such covenants we have had more than one previous example. This one was sealed by the principal heads of families, as representing the whole of the people.

3. After twelve years Nehemiah returned to Persia, his leave of absence having apparently expired. His absence was not supplied by the presence of any person uniting the same degree of power and influence in the nation. The consequence was that the people soon began to neglect the divine law, and to contract mischievous connections with the heathen nations by whom they were surrounded. This misconduct was by no means confined to the inferior classes of the people; but the evil example was set by the leading men, by the priests, and even by the high-priest himself. The intelligence of such proceedings at length brought Nehemiah back again from the Persian court. He applied a vigorous and unsparing hand to the reformation of these abuses. The Jews who had married heathen females were compelled to part from them; the observance of the Sabbath was enforced; and the condition of the people was much improved by the abolition of illegal usury, which had operated in bringing great numbers of the poor under personal servitude to the rich.

Here, properly speaking, the history of the Old Testament closes; and our further information is obtained from Josephus, and from the books of the Maccabees.

4. After Nehemiah, Judæa ceased to form a distinct government, and was annexed to the satrapy of Syria. The internal government was, however, administered by the high-priests, under the appointment of the satraps of Syria. This annexation of the civil government to the pontificate, soon made that office one of high ambition to the different members of the sacerdotal family, and gave occasion to most disgraceful contests among them. At the time which we have now reached, there had been three high-priests since the return from Babylon, namely, Jeshua, Joachim, and Eliashib.

This last died in B. C. 413, and was succeeded by his son Joiada or Judas, whose pontificate extended to B. C. 373. Until the death of Joiada nothing particularly worthy of notice occurs in the history of the Jews. They remained quiet under the Persian government, to which they were as much attached as they could be to any foreign rule, and to which they were always faithful.

5. The death of Joiada occurred in the thirty-first year of Artaxerxes Mnemon, when the satrapy of Syria was vested in Bagoses. Joiada was succeeded by his son Johanan or Jehu. But soon after Joshua, another son of the late high-priest, arrived at Jerusalem, and claimed that high office on the ground of having been appointed by Bagoses. This occasioned a violent dispute between the two brothers in the interior court of the Temple, and Joshua was slain in that sacred place. On hearing of this, Bagoses repaired to Jerusalem, and after sternly rebuking the Jews for thus defiling the Temple of their God, he imposed as a punishment a heavy tax upon the lambs offered in sacrifice, which was not remitted until after the death of Artaxerxes, when Bagoses was recalled to Persia, and the tax was not enforced by his successor.

6. In the next reign, that of Ochus, the Phœnicians revolted from the Persian yoke; and in this affair the Jews appear to have been partially involved; for after the fall of Sidon, the king went and took Jericho, and sent the inhabitants into exile. It was in the eighteenth year of this reign that the high-priest Johanan died, and was succeeded by his son Jaddua. It would seem that Jaddua was a just pontiff, who endeavoured to uphold the reforms of Nehemiah. Of this he gave a remarkable proof by expelling his own brother Manasses for marrying the daughter of Sanballat, the Cuthite governor of Samaria. Manasses then repaired to that personage; and the Samaritans, not being allowed access to the Temple at Jerusalem, were induced, by the presence of a member of the pontifical family among them, to think of having a Temple for themselves. Sanballat accordingly obtained from Darius Codomanus permission to build a Temple for them on Mount Gerizim, and when it was finished, Manasses became their high-priest. This measure greatly widened the

breach between the Jews and the Samaritans. Each party contended for the exclusive claims of its own Temple. The Jews alleged that sacrifices ought to be offered only at Jerusalem; but the Samaritans affirmed that the true place of sacrifice was Mount Gerizim, where they alleged Joshua had built the first altar. The continuance and growth of this controversy produced that mortal antipathy between the two nations to which there is more than one allusion in the New Testament. Luke ix. 51-56; John iv. 9-29; viii. 48.

7. It was in the time of Jaddua that the great event arrived which had long been foreshewn in the prophetic visions of Daniel (ii. 39; xi. 4). The great victory over the Persian king, at Issus, opened up the south to Alexander the Great, who commenced operations in Syria, and, while engaged in the siege of Tyre, summoned the neighbouring nations to render their submission. The Samaritans obeyed the summons very early, and were treated with indulgence; but it does not seem that any attention was paid to it by the Jews. Therefore, after he had destroyed Tyre, he turned aside on his way to Gaza, to march against Jerusalem. As he approached, his hostile purposes are said to have been averted by an imposing and submissive procession of the priests and citizens, headed by the high-priest in his pontifical robes. In him the conqueror is said to have recognised the person who in a dream had foretold to him the conquest of the Persian empire. If so, it was quite in the power of Jaddua to fulfil this dream by showing him these prophesies of Daniel, in which his existence and victories had been clearly foretold. That the high-priest brought these prophesies to his knowledge, might account for the favour with which the Jews, notwithstanding the tardiness of their submission, were treated by Alexander. But the Greek historians who have written the history of Alexander, have no record

137. Alexander the Great.

of his visiting Jerusalem; and the whole story of the interview between him and the high-priest wants confirmation.
However, when the Jews submitted, the conqueror, at their
special request, secured to them the indisturbed enjoyment of
their national laws, with exemption from tribute every seventh
year; but he demurred when the latter privilege was also
sought by the Samaritans. While he was absent, conquering Egypt, the Samaritans gave him so much displeasure
that, so far from rendering them any favour, he expelled them
from Samaria and re-peopled it by a colony of Macedonians.
The dispossessed Samaritans then repaired to the city of
Shechem, between Mounts Ebal and Gerizim, which became
their metropolis.

8. After the death of Alexander, the vast empire which
he had won was divided among his generals, and Judæa,
from its situation between Egypt and Syria, suffered dread-
fully, and was deeply involved in the bitter contests in which
his successors were soon engaged against each other. It is
our purpose not to relate the particulars of these contests, but
to glean from them the facts which directly affected the condition of the Jewish people.

9. In the first division of Alexander's empire, Syria, with
Palestine, devolved to Laomedon, and Egypt to Ptolemy Lagus.
Between them a war arose, and the former was defeated by
Nicanor, one of the generals of Ptolemy. All the provinces
of Laomedon then submitted to Ptolemy; but the Jews manifested so much reluctance to violate their engagements, that
Ptolemy advanced against Jerusalem with a large army and
laid close siege to the city. Knowing that the religious
veneration of the Jews for the seventh day prevented them
from fighting thereon, he assaulted and took the city on the
Sabbath. But he did not treat them with severity; for
although he sent a large number of Jews into Egypt, it was
rather as colonists than as prisoners. Indeed, before this,
many Jews had been removed to Egypt by Alexander, to
help to people his new city of Alexandria, where they were
allowed civic privileges of the first class, the same as the
Greek inhabitants enjoyed. These privileges were confirmed
by Ptolemy, who also advanced many of those he took away
to places of authority and trust, in consequence of which

Q

many more went to Egypt of their own accord. Eight years after, Ptolemy transported another large body of them, whom he settled in the provinces of Lybia and Cyrene. By successive deportations of this description, and by the voluntary removals of Jews who sought under the shadow of the Egyptian throne the peace which they could not find in their own country, Egypt became, and long continued, an important seat of the Jewish population.

10. *Sacred Writers.*—The book of Nehemiah has the singularity of being written in the first person, and was, therefore, without doubt, the production of the eminent man whose name it bears. It gives a clear and plain account of his administration, and has more than any other portion of Scripture, the effect of an autobiographical narrative. Malachi, the last of the prophets, belonged to the time of Nehemiah. Nothing whatever is known of him. He reproved the abuses which Nehemiah laboured to correct. It is remarkable that his prophesy closes the Old Testament with an announcement of John the Baptist, with whose birth and ministry the history of the New Testament opens.

CHAPTER V. B.C. 314 to 187.

THE JEWS.	B.C.	EGYPT.	B.C.	SYRIA.	B C
Simon I. High-priest	302	Ptolemy Lagus	324	Seleucus I. Nicator	312
Eleazer	283	P. Philadelphus	284	Antiochus I. Soter	280
Manasses	251	P. Euergetes I.	246	Antiochus II. Theos	261
Onias II.	225	P. Philopator	220	Seleucus II. Callinicus	246
Simon II.	211	E. Epiphanes	204	Seleucus III. Keraunus	226
Onias III.	191			Antiochus III. the Great	223
				Seleucus IV. Philopator	187

GENERAL HISTORY.	B.C.	REMARKABLE PERSONS.	B.C
Æra of the Seleucidæ begins	312	Antipater, *ob.*	319
Alexander's generals take the title of		Eumenes, *ob.*	315
kings	306	Antigonus	311
Antigonus defeated and killed	301	Demetrius Poliorcetes	307
Seleucia on the Tigris built	291	Epicurus	295
The Septuagint translation of the Old		Theocritus	281
Testament	184	Berosus	268
Pyrrhus, King of Epirus, enters Italy	280	Manetho	261
First Punic war begins	264	Callimachus	260
Regulus taken prisoner	256	Hanno	257
The Temple of Janus shut'	235	Regulus	258
The Colossus of Rhodes overthrown	224	Hamilcar	248
Second Punic war begins	218	Archimedes	236
The battle of Cannæ	216	Apollonius	230
Hannibal defeated in Africa by Scipio	202	Plautus	220
Second Punic war ends	201	Hannibal	220
Hannibal goes to Antiochus III.	195	Q. Fabius Maximus	216
First Roman army in Asia, under		Zeno	210
Scipio Asiaticus : defeats Antiochus	190	Asdrubal	211
		Scipio Africanus	204
		Scipio Asiaticus	190

1. Ptolemy Lagus did not long remain in undisturbed possession of Palestine, which, with Phœnicia and Cœle-Syria, was wrested from him by Antigonus, one of the most ambitious and turbulent of the generals who shared the empire of Alexander. But after he had been overthrown and slain by Seleucus and Lysimachus, in the decisive battle of Ipsus, Ptolemy quietly recovered and retained this important province ; and by the wisdom and justice of his government promoted the prosperity and gained the affections of the Jewish people. During his reign, Simon the Just, a most excellent high-priest, repaired and improved the city and temple of Jerusalem, and provided both with strong and lofty walls. He is also understood to have completed the canon of the Old Testament Scriptures by adding the books of Ezra, Nehemiah,

Chronicles, Esther, and the prophesies of Malachi. In B.C. 300, he succeeded Onias, the successor of Jaddua, and died in B.C. 291.

2. Meanwhile a power arose in Asia, which was by far

the greatest of those which were formed out of the spoils of Alexander's empire. It was founded by Seleucus, who took the title of King of Syria. His dominion extended from the Euxine to the borders of Arabia, and from the Mediterranean to the Indus. His eastern capital was Seleucia, on the Tigris, and his western Antioch. Both

138. Antioch.

these cities, and many others, were founded by him. Being, like Ptolemy, convinced of the value of the Jews as good and faithful citizens, he endeavoured to attract them to his new cities in Asia Minor by the offer of the same privileges as Ptolemy had allowed them in Egypt. Many Jews accepted the invitation ; and hence, in later periods, we find them established in considerable numbers in the principal cities of Asia Minor as well as of Egypt.

3. Ptolemy Philadelphus succeeded his father Ptolemy Lagus in B.C. 285. He confirmed to the Jews all their former privileges. He induced large numbers of them to settle in Egypt, and to promote that object ransomed many who had been sold for slaves. This king was a great patron of literature, and spared no cost in procuring curious books for the famous library which he established at Alexandria. He caused the Hebrew Scriptures to be translated into Greek, and deposited in that library. This important translation still exists under the name of the Septuagint, from the tradition that *seventy* persons were employed in the translation. The prophesies of the Hebrew books had lately attracted some at-

tention, and the authentic history of a people so closely connected with Egypt as the Jews, must have been deemed interesting.   These were probably the reasons which led Philadelphus to desire this translation.   By its means the religion of the Jews became better known to the heathen, and we afterwards hear of magnificent presents being sent by them to the Temple of Jerusalem.   The translation may be referred to the year B.C. 278 ; a correct copy of the original also was provided by the care of Eleazer the high-priest, son of Simon the Just.

4. Ptolemy Euergetes, the next king of Egypt, considerably enlarged the privileges of the Jews, and testified his respect for their God, by offering a vast number of victims in sacrifice at Jerusalem.

5. In the next reign, that of Ptolemy Philopator, the peace which the Jews had enjoyed under the Egyptian kings began to be seriously disturbed.   Antiochus III. surnamed the Great, king of Syria, greatly desired to annex to his own dominions the provinces of Palestine which had been held by the kings of Egypt, whom he made some vigorous efforts to dispossess.   But, after being for a time successful, he was at length defeated with great loss by Philopater, who soon after repaired to Jerusalem, and offered many sacrifices to Jehovah in acknowledgment of his recent victory   Unfortunately the beauty and

139.   Antiochus the Great

richness of the building attracted his attention, and he desired to view the interior.   This was resisted by the high-priest Simon II. who informed him that it was unlawful even for priests to enter the inner sanctuary.   The king persisted ; but as he was walking across the inner court to enter the sacred place, a sudden dread and horror came over him, and he fell speechless to the ground.   He was carried out, half dead, by his attendants.   This circumstance, acting upon an ill constituted mind, filled the king with great resentment against the Jewish people, and, on his return to Egypt, he raised a bitter persecution against those who had settled in that land. He took away their high privileges, and caused them to be enrolled with the lowest class of the native Egyptians; and many were, on various alleged grounds, consigned to slavery and to death. It is even said that he contemplated the extirpation of the Jewish race, and that, beginning with those of Egypt, he caused a large number of them to be brought together at Alexandria, with the view of having them publicly destroyed by elephants in the hippodrome. A vast multitude of people assembled to view the horrid spectacle, and the king himself was present with his court. The elephants, to render them furious, had been previously inebriated with wine and frankincense; but instead of slaying the victims exposed to their rage, they turned their fury upon the spectators, of whom great numbers were destroyed, while the Jews remained altogether unhurt. Public opinion recognised in this an interposition of Heaven in their behalf; and we are told that Philopator desisted from his designs, and restored to the Jews their former privileges. The whole of this account, however, rests on authority in which implicit confidence cannot be placed.

6. Philopator died in B.C. 205, leaving the crown to Ptolemy Epiphanes, then a child of five years old. Antiochus the Great had meanwhile, by a series of successes in the east, greatly extended his authority and power; and having now returned to the west, he deemed the conjuncture favourable for a fresh attempt to wrest the Syrian provinces from the Egyptian crown. He succeeded; and the Jews manifested great readiness in placing themselves under his rule. Considering their general attachment to Egypt, this must be accounted for by their resentment at the treatment of Philopator, and by their satisfaction at the kindness and liberality of Antiochus to the numerous Jews who were settled in his dominions on both sides of the Euphrates. Antiochus was much gratified by the proofs of attachment which he received; and when he visited Jerusalem in B.C. 198, he conferred on it such favours as he knew were best calculated to win the hearts of the inhabitants. He promised to restore the city to its ancient splendour, and to repair the Temple at his own cost; he made provision for the regular performance of the sacred services, and he guaranteed the Temple from the intrusion of strangers. By bestowing these favours, with the

confirmation of their political privileges, Antiochus shewed
that he well understood the remarkable people with whom he
had to deal.

7. The troubles in which Antiochus became involved with
the Romans, who now began to take part in the affairs of
Western Asia, little concerned the Jews. They might have
continued to enjoy tranquillity under his successor ; for Seleucus Philopator was as well disposed towards the Jews as
his father had been, and gave orders that the charges for the
public worship should continue to be defrayed out of his own
treasury. An unhappy altercation, however, between Onias
III. and Simon the governor of the Temple, changed the
aspect of affairs. The latter, in consequence of this quarrel,
sent to the king a very exaggerated account of the wealth
contained in the Temple ; and Seleucus, being in great want
of money, determined to appropriate all this treasure to himself. He therefore sent his treasurer Heliodorus to seize it
and bring it to Antioch. When this functionary arrived at
Jerusalem, Onias endeavoured to dissuade him from his purpose, assuring him that the fund was not considerable, and
that it was devoted to charitable uses. But Heliodorus per
sisted in executing his commission, and was about to enter
the Temple, when he was terror-struck by an awful vision,
and quickly withdrew not only from the Temple but from the
city, which he declared to be under the protection of a power
which no man could withstand.

8. The high-priest soon followed him to Antioch, to com
plain to Seleucus of the misconduct of Simon, which he placed
in so strong a light as to procure his banishment from Jeru
salem, whereby peace was once more restored to the city

CHAPTER VI. B. C. 175 to 169.

THE JEWS		EGYPT.		SYRIA	
	B. C.		B. C.		B ?
Jason, High-priest	174	Ptolemy Philometor		Antiochus IV. Epi-	
Menelaus, High-priest	172	and Ptolemy Phys-		phanes	17
		con	175		

1. The Jews had now been so long under the Greek monarchs of Egypt and Syria, that they had become well acquainted with the customs, the literature, and the philo-

sophy of the Greeks. A large party regarded the manners of that people with preference, and their religion without displeasure, and were willing to sink the distinctive peculiarities of their own practices and faith. Of this number was Jesus, the brother of the high-priest Onias, whose predilections were manifested by the Greek name of Jason which he assumed. He offered

140. Antiochus Epiphanes.

a large sum of money for the high-priesthood to Antiochus Epiphanes, who succeeded Seleucus Philopator in B. C. 175.

His offer was accepted. Onias was called to An-tioch, and kept there a prisoner at large; and Jason took his place. The party which gathered around this man was con-siderable; for not only was there among the edu-cated classes a strong lean-ing towards the Greek customs, to which he was known to be favourable,

141. Athletic Exercises.

but the citizenship of Antioch, which he had been empowered to bestow, was to them an object of great desire. Jason delayed not to establish at Jerusalem a gymnasium for athletic exercises, which soon became so popular, that even the priests neglected the Temple services to be present at the games. Jason also established an academy for bringing up the Hebrew youth after the manner of the Greeks; and by every kind of influence he encouraged the adoption of Greek customs and habits, not only of external life, but of action and thought. It appears, however, that the Jews generally, and even his own adherents, were not prepared to go so far as himself; and when he sent some young men to Tyre, to assist at the games celebrated there in honour of the Tyrian Hercules, and entrusted them with large sums of money to expend in sacrifices to that idol, they chose rather to give the money for the building of ships. Jason did not long enjoy his ill-gotten dignity; for after three years he was supplanted in turn by his younger brother Onias IV. or Menelaus, who offered the king 300 talents more for that dignity than Jason had given. Jason fled to the country of the Ammonites.

142. Ancient Light Vessel Pompeii.

Menelaus proved even more wicked than his brother. One of his first acts was to abstract some of the golden vessels of the Temple, and to send them secretly to Tyre for sale. The fact, however, transpired, and excited considerable ferment, especially among the numerous Jews at Antioch, where the exiled high-priest, the venerable Onias, took such notice of it, as gave deep offence to his brother, who prevailed on Andronicus, the king's deputy at Antioch, to put him to death; for which deed Andronicus was himself slain on the same spot by order of the king, when he returned to the capital.

2. Soon after Antiochus engaged in a war with Egypt. He invaded that country twice with success; but a rumour

L

of his death was believed in Palestine. This, together with the absence of the Syrian forces, encouraged the exiled Jason to attempt the recovery of his lost power. With a body of 1000 men, assisted by friends within the city, he surprised Jerusalem, and inflicted great severities upon the adherents of Menelaus, who himself sought refuge in the castle. The return of Antiochus, however, compelled him to abandon the city and relinquish the power which he thought he had recovered; and after wandering from place to place, he died miserably in Lacedæmonia. Antiochus, provoked at the satisfaction which the news of his death was reported to have given the Jews, chose to consider the transaction as a revolt, and to punish it accordingly. The city was abandoned to the fury and license of the soldiers for three days, during which 4000 of the inhabitants were slain, and nearly an equal number carried away and sold for slaves. The king, conducted by the impious Menelaus, then entered the Temple, which he plundered of all its treasures, vessels, and golden ornaments, and carried away 1800 talents of gold and silver to Antioch. But he did not quit the place until he had offered to the people and their God, the outrage, of sacrificing a large hog upon the altar of burnt-offerings. Menelaus was left in the high-priesthood; for although he was hated by the people, no one dared to move against one who stood so high in the favour of the king.

3. In another invasion of Egypt, Antiochus was met by the Roman ambassadors, who, in the name of the Senate, commanded him to desist from the enterprise, and, drawing a circle around him on the sand, forbade him to quit it until he decided between the friendship and the enmity of Rome. He bent his proud heart to the hard task of obedience, and turned homeward with the formidable army he had assembled for this enterprise. Burning with the sense of this disgrace, he failed not to wreak a portion of his wrath on the Jews as he returned. The baffled tyrant detached Apollonius to Jerusalem with an army of 22,000 men, commanding him to destroy the city, to massacre the male inhabitants, and to sell the women and children for slaves. Apollonius entered the city peaceably, and gave no sign of his intentions until the first Sabbath-day after his arrival. Then, while the people

were engaged in the solemn worship of the Most High, he executed his dreadful commission with unrelenting ferocity. After having slain great multitudes of the people, and sent away 10,000 captives, he plundered the town, after which it was set on fire, and the wall demolished. The Temple was allowed to stand, but its service was altogether abandoned; for it was commanded by a fortress which the Syrians erected, and from which the soldiers assaulted all who went there to worship. Thus, in the month of June, B. C. 168, the daily sacrifices of the Temple ceased, and the city of Jerusalem was deserted.

4. Antiochus next issued a decree, enjoining the establishment of the Grecian form of idolatry throughout his wide dominions, that the various nations under his sway might, by the relinquishment of their distinctive observances, "become one people." When we consider the variety of the forms of worship among the different nations in the empire of Antiochus, it is scarcely credible that so wild a project was seriously entertained; nor is it likely that the decree was exclusively levelled against the Jewish people; but it is more probable, that his object was to find a pretext for plundering the temples of the recusants; and as the temples were, from their sanctity, the great banks of deposit in those times, their spoils offered great temptations to so needy a king as Antiochus. Although the Temple of the Jews had been already plundered, his hatred to that people was gratified by the sufferings in which this law involved them; and so rigidly was it enforced, that death was the penalty of disobedience. What reception this decree met with among the heathen, is scarcely known; but, except the Jews and the Persians, there were few nations likely to offer any serious opposition. Officers were especially appointed to enforce the decree in every province. In the different towns, many of the Jews submitted to sacrifice to idols, and to profane the Sabbath. The Samaritans consented to receive the statue of Jupiter Xenius into their temple on Mount Gerizim: and the Lord's Temple at Jerusalem was dedicated to Jupiter Olympius, his statue placed therein, and sacrifices regularly offered to him. Such of the Jews as refused to share in this worship, or to evince their conformity by eating swine's flesh, were cruelly

massacred, or subjected to the most exquisite tortures. The same proceedings were repeated in other towns; for the idol altars, groves, and statues were everywhere set up, and everywhere the tests of obedience were exacted. It was not long, however, before Antiochus perceived that, in as far as the Jews were concerned, his decree was less effectual than he had expected. He therefore issued another decree, forbidding, under pain of death, the worship of Jehovah, and the observance of the distinctive requirements of the Mosaical law, such as circumcision and the Sabbath. He went further, and endeavoured to extinguish the law itself, forbidding it to be read, and commanding every copy to be given up under pain of death. It was in this emergency that the Jews commenced reading lessons from the prophets, instead of the law, in their synagogues; and when afterwards they resumed the reading of the law, they did not cease to read the prophets; whence arose the subsequent use of *both* the books of the law and of the prophets in their synagogues. Many, as we have said, apostatized under these trying circumstances; but many also were found faithful unto death, and many others went forth to wander in deserts and in mountains, in dens and caves of the earth, subsisting on such herbs and roots as they could find in those solitary places.

5. Astonished at the obstinacy which the Jews manifested, Antiochus, mistrusting the zeal of his officers, repaired himself to Jerusalem to see that his decreee was rigidly enforced. It were charity to suppose that Antiochus Epiphanes had by this time become mad; for it is difficult otherwise to imagine how any human creature would endure to witness, much less to take delight in, the horrid tortures and cruel deaths to which the unhappy recusants were subjected. As examples of these dreadful transactions, the historian relates at length the case of the venerable Eleazer, who, in his ninetieth year, chose rather to die than to eat the forbidden flesh of swine; and of the heroic mother and her seven sons, who nobly set the tyrant at defiance, and professed their faith and hope that "the king of the world would raise up those that died for his laws to everlasting life."

BOOK VII.

CHAPTER I. B. C. 167 to 163.

THE JEWS.	B. C.	EGYPT.	B. C.	SYRIA.	B. C.
Menelaus, High-priest	172	P. Philometor and P.		Antiochus (IV.) Epi-	
Judas Maccabæus . .	163	Physcon	175	phanes	175
Alcimus	161			Antiochus (V.) Eu-	
				pator	164

1. THE persecution by Antiochus had raged about half a year, when God raised up deliverance for his people in the noble family of the Asamoneans, Mattathias and his sons, better known as the Maccabees. Asamoneus, from whom the family took its name, was the great-grandfather of Mattathias, a priest descended from Phinehas, the son of Eleazer, the elder branch of the family of Aaron. This Mattathias was a person of consequence and influence in his native city of Modin, for which reason the king's commissioner at that place was anxious that he should there set the example of compliance with the royal mandate. But Mattathias, on his own behalf and that of his sons, repelled with indignation the inducements which were offered; and in a transport of holy zeal, he ran and smote down a Jew who at that moment advanced to offer sacrifice at the idol altar. By this act the sword was drawn, which was to be sheathed no more till Israel was free. Animated by the same impulse, his sons and a few others gathered around Mattathias, and fell upon and slew the commissioner himself and his attendants; after which they passed through the city, calling upon all who were zealous for the law of God to follow them. Many were roused by their call; but as the number was as yet small to meet the enemy, they withdrew for a time into the wilderness. They were speedily followed thither by the king's troops, and being attacked on the Sabbath day, many suffered themselves

to be slain without offering the least resistance.   Mattathias saw the fatal consequences of this scruple, as it had for a long time been usual for the enemies of the Jews to attack them on a day when it was known they would not fight.   He therefore directed that henceforth they should stand on their defence even on the Sabbath day; and this order, being properly confirmed, guided the future practice of the Jewish people, who still, however, refused to act, except on the defensive, on the sacred day.

2. The standard of revolt being now erected, all who were zealous for liberty and truth repaired to it, so that Mattathias soon found himself sufficiently strong to act on the offensive.   They then left their retreat, and went, chiefly by night, throughout the country, pulling down the idolatrous altars, and destroying their persecutors wherever they met with them.   They also re-opened the synagogues, enforced the rites enjoined by the law, and recovered many of the sacred books which had fallen into the hands of the heathen. A year of such exertions greatly improved the aspect of affairs, when death arrested the career of the heroic priest. He left five sons, John, Simon, Judas, Eleazer, and Jonathan. The dying advice of the father was, that the judicious Simon should be their counsellor, and the valiant Judas their captain.   Judas is said to have derived his surname of Maccabeus from a cabalistic word formed out of M. C. B. J., the initial letters of the words contained in the sacred text which he bore upon his standard.*   He proved himself a bold and able commander, and, in many respects, may be considered one of the greatest heroes which the Jewish nation ever produced.   With a force not exceeding 6000 men he took the field against the large and well-disciplined armies of Antiochus, commanded by warriors of reputation, and defeated them all.   In the first instance, the defeat of Apollonius the governor of Samaria, enabled him to make himself master of some of the principal towns and fortresses of Judæa, from which he expelled the Jews who had turned to idolatry.   Then a powerful army under a great general

* The text was Exod. xv. 11.   *Mi Chamoka Baalim Jehovah,* "Who is like unto thee among the gods, O Lord!"

called Seron, took the field against Judas. After encouraging his men, who were somewhat alarmed at the immense disparity of numbers, the hero fell upon the enemy with great fury, so that their force was broken and they fled before him. This victory made the name of Judas renowned in all the neighbouring states. Antiochus himself saw that this revolt required more attention than he had given to it, and resolving to crush it, he repeatedly sent formidable armies into Judæa, commanded by his most able officers. But the valiant Maccabeus maintained his ground, and in one year defeated the Syrians five times, in as many pitched battles. The last of these engagements was with Lysias the regent of Syria, during the absence of Antiochus in Persia, whose army amounted to 60,000 choice infantry and 5000 horse. This formidable army was met by Judas with only 10,000 men to Bethzur; and after calling on God,— "Cast them down with the sword of them that love thee,"— he assailed them with such vigour that thousands of them were slain and the rest put to flight. Lysias was astonished at the desperate valour of the Jews, and conducted the remnant of his army back to Antioch.

3. This great success encouraged Judas to march at once to Jerusalem. He gained possession of the city and the Temple, and after purifying both from every trace of the Syrian idolatries, the Temple was consecrated anew to the service of God, and the daily sacrifices and worship were resumed after a calamitous interruption of three years. This new dedication of the Temple and revival of their worship, was ever after celebrated by a feast which occurred about the winter solstice. John x. 22.

4. The Jews were not, however, able to expel the Syrian garrison from the fortress which had been built by Apollonius to overlook the Temple. They therefore protected the Temple itself by surrounding it with high walls and towers, within which they kept a valiant and watchful garrison.

5. In the east, Antiochus appears to have been little more successful than were his generals in the west. He was repulsed in an attempt to plunder the rich temple at Elymais in Persia, and withdrew in anger and shame to Ecbatana. There news reached him of the repeated losses which his arms

had sustained in Judæa, and that the country was in possession of the Jews. On receiving this intelligence, his rage passed all bounds, and he denounced the most horrible vengeance upon that land and people. But while the words were in his mouth, he was smitten with a loathsome and incurable disease, in which he lingered under the most excruciating torments. In his last days, he confessed to those around him that he was smitten by the hand of God, in punishment for his desecration of the Temple and his persecution of the Jews. "I perceive, therefore," he said, "that for this cause these troubles come upon me; and behold, I perish through grief in a strange land." He died in the beginning of B. C. 164.

6. Although the Jews were thus delivered from the most inveterate enemy they had ever known, the war was still carried on by the regent Lysias, in the name of Antiochus Eupator, a child, the son of the late king. But although this army was much stronger than the last, it was completely routed; and then the regent, confessing the wickedness of contending with the mighty God who defended the Jewish people, offered peace on reasonable terms, which the Jewish leaders thought it right to accept, and in obtaining which the Roman ambassadors used their commanding influence. The high-priest Menelaus took this occasion to return home and resume his pontificate. 2 Macc. xi.

7. The Jews at Jerusalem were, however, still much annoyed by the presence of the Syrian garrison in the castle. Judas, therefore, laid siege to this fortress, determined, if possible, to rid the capital of so serious an inconvenience. There were many apostate Jews in the castle; and they, dreading the treatment they might expect from the orthodox Jews, if it fell into their hands, withdrew secretly and hastened to Antioch, where their representations invited the regent and the young king to undertake a new war against Judæa. The army which was raised for this purpose, was evidently intended to extinguish the nation. It consisted of 100,000 foot, 20,000 horse, 32 war elephants, and 300 chariots armed with scythes. With this mighty host, Lysias proceeded southward and besieged Bethsura, a strong fortress which had been built to protect the frontier towards Idumæa.

Judas could not induce his men to risk a pitched battle with such a host; but they fell upon the invaders by night, and before they knew who had entered their camp, four thousand of them were dead men. The Jews drew off in safety by break of day. The next morning they came to battle; and Judas, to avoid being surrounded by the Syrians, was forced to withdraw to Jerusalem, which had by this time been put in a good state of defence. In this battle Judas lost his brother Eleazer, who was crushed to death by the fall of an elephant, which he himself slew under the erroneous impression that the king rode upon it. 1 Macc. vi. 18-47; 2 Macc. xiii. 15-22.

8. The Jews were now in great peril; for the Syrian army, after taking Bethsura, and placing a strong garrison there, advanced to Jerusalem, which they closely besieged, and, in all human probability, would have soon taken. But at this juncture the regent received intelligence that Philip, a rival regent, whom the late king had appointed on his death-bed, had entered Syria with a large army, and had taken possession of Antioch. He therefore concluded a hasty treaty with the Jews, granting all their demands. He then threw down the strong walls around the Temple mount, in violation of the treaty, and hastened to encounter Philip, whom he utterly overthrew (1 Macc. vi. 48-65; 2 Macc. xiii. 3-23). Menelaus, the apostate high-priest, who had again deserted to the Syrians, and had encouraged the expedition in the hope of obtaining the government of Judæa, being viewed by them as the real author of their disasters, was, by the royal order, smothered, by being thrown into an ash-pit at Berea. Judas himself was now recognised as governor of Judæa; and it is from this year (B. C. 163) that his accession to the principality is usually dated.

CHAPTER II. B. C. 163 to 143.

ASMONEAN PRINCES.	B. C.	EGYPT.	B. C.	SYRIA.	B. C.
Judas Maccabeus	163	Ptolemy Philometor	160	Demetrius Soter	162
Alcimus, High-priest	163	Ptolemy Physcon	145	Alexander Balas	150
Jonathan	160			Demetrius Nicator	145
High-priest	153			Antiochus (VI.) Theos.	144
				Tryphon	143

GENERAL HISTORY.

	B. C.
Demetrius Soter defeated and killed by Alexander Balas	150
Third Punic War begins, and lasts three years	149
Carthage destroyed by Scipio Nasica	148
Corinth destroyed by L. Mummius	148

1. THE vacant high-priesthood was given to Alcimus or Jacimus, to the exclusion of the rightful successor, Onias, the son of that Onias who had been murdered at Antioch at the instigation of Mene-

laus. This disappointment induced Onias to retire into Egypt. He was there received with favour by Ptolemy Philometor, and used his influence to obtain leave to found a temple for the numerous Jews in that country. It was built at On or Heliopolis, " the city of the sun," after the model of the Temple at Jerusalem, but not so large or magnificent. Onias was appointed high-priest : there

143. On or Heliopolis.

were also inferior priests and Levites, and the services were conducted as at Jerusalem, until the time of Vespasian, in whose reign both temples were destroyed.

2. Alcimus, the new high-priest, was a man of loose principles, which, with his known attachment to the Grecian idolatries, rendered him so obnoxious to the Jews, that they very soon expelled him from the land.

3. Shortly after, Antiochus Eupator, and the regent Lysias, were defeated and slain by Demetrius Soter, the rightful heir to the throne,* who had hitherto been detained as a hostage at Rome. This prince was no sooner established on the Syrian throne than all the Jewish traitors and apostates, with Alcimus at their head, came around him with many grievous complaints against Judas and his party; and Alcimus made it appear that his own expulsion was an act of strong contempt towards that power by which he had been invested with the pontificate. Listening to these complaints, Demetrius re-appointed Alcimus to the high-priesthood, and sent Bacchides, the governor of Mesopotamia, to re-instate him in his office, and take vengeance on his enemies. This commander entered the country without any hostile manifestations; and many Jews, who, relying on his fair professions, had put themselves into his power, were treacherously slain. Bacchides then, having met with no opposition, left the country in charge of Alcimus, with a force considered sufficient to secure him in his place. But he had no sooner withdrawn, than Judas, who had retired before him, appeared again, and easily recovered the position which he had seemed for the moment to abandon. Alcimus, being unable to offer any effectual resistance, again repaired to Antioch, with renewed and more earnest complaints to the king. Another and more powerful army was accordingly sent into Judæa, under Nicanor. He was twice defeated by Judas—the last time so completely, that of 35,000 men, not one escaped alive to bear the tidings to Antioch. This great victory procured the nation an interval of rest, and was deemed of so much importance by the Jews, that they established an annual festival of commemoration. 1 Macc. vii. 4-50; 2 Macc. xiv. 2-16; xv. 1-37.

4. A step was then taken by Judas, which some have praised, and others blamed; but which will probably be con-

---

* Demetrius was the son of Seleucus Philopator, who was succeeded by his brother Antiochus Epiphanes, who left the crown to his son Antiochus Eupator.

sidered, by those who are the most intimately acquainted with the history of the time, to be the best which could have been taken under all the circumstances. He sent an embassy to Rome, to solicit the friendship of that powerful nation, whose influence had for some time been paramount in Syria and in Egypt. It quite consisted with the policy of the Roman senate to weaken the great states, by forming alliances with the lesser nations which depended on them. The Jewish ambassadors were therefore received with favour, and the Romans readily concluded a treaty, which could not possibly be injurious to themselves, and might yet be of some advantage to the Jews. The immediate result of this alliance was, that the senate sent a missive to Demetrius, commanding him, on pain of their displeasure, to abstain from persecuting the Jews in time to come. But before the ambassadors returned, the valiant Judas had met his death, in a desperate conflict with Bacchides and Alcimus, who had been sent to avenge the destruction of Nicanor and his host. The brothers of Judas, Simon, and Jonathan, having made a truce, deposited the body of the hero in the family sepulchre at Modin, which was not far off, and all Israel mourned for him many days, crying, " How is the valiant fallen, that delivered Israel !"

5. The death of their great leader threw the Jews into such consternation, that the Syrians easily reaped the fruits of their victory. They reduced Jerusalem, and slew many of the adherents of the Maccabees; and Alcimus was once more restored to the high-priesthood. Incapable of profiting by experience, this man persisted in his former courses. He made many innovations in the religion of his country, in order to produce a greater conformity to the practices of the heathen. At length, with the view of admitting the Gentiles equally with the Jews to the inner courts of the temple, he proceeded to break down the separating wall, when he was suddenly cut off in the full career of his guilt, and died in the most dreadful agonies. On the occurrence of this event, Bacchides, who had remained in the country, returned to Syria, and the Jews were left for two years unmolested. Jonathan, the youngest brother of Judas, who had been elected by the orthodox Jews as their prince and leader in his place, employed

this interval in establishing a regular government, in strength-
ening the walls and fortifications of Jerusalem, and in effecting various important reforms in the civil and ecclesiastical
affairs of his country.

6. After two years, the adverse faction, growing uneasy
at the prospect of continued peace, recommenced their operations. They conspired to seize Jonathan, and all his adherents
throughout the land, in one night; and invited Bacchides to
aid their project by a military force. This became known to
Jonathan, who, after putting fifty of the leading conspirators
to death, withdrew with Simon and his friends to Bethbasi in
the wilderness, not feeling strong enough to meet Bacchides
in the field. This was a strong post; and the dilapidated
fortifications having been put into complete repair, the besieged were enabled to hold out so long, and so to harass the
enemy by daring sallies and excursions, that Bacchides at
length grew weary of an expedition from which so little
honour was to be won, and put those to death who had engaged him in it. In this mood he listened to the overtures of
peace made by Jonathan, and, after an exchange of prisoners,
withdrew his forces, engaging to trouble the land no more.

7. Three years after this, a conjuncture of affairs arose in
Syria highly favourable to the Jewish cause. A claim was
set up by Alexander Balas to the
crown of Syria, which not only
gave the reigning king, Demetrius,
sufficient employment for all his
disposable forces, but made it the
interest of the competitors to outbid each other for the support and
favour of so warlike a people as
the Jews had now become. Jonathan had, meanwhile, been pro-

144. Alexander Balas.

ceeding quietly with his improvements and repairs, which,
while they enhanced his reputation, gave the promise of stability to his government. When the competitors began to
court his friendship, the remembrance of the wrongs which
Demetrius had inflicted upon the nation, no less than good
policy, induced him to espouse the cause of Alexander, who,
in return, offered him the high-priesthood. That office had

been vacant seven years, and, with the unanimous consent
and approbation of the people, it was accepted by Jonathan.
It will be remembered that the Maccabees were descended
from the eldest branch of the family of Aaron. Together
with the offer of the priesthood, Balas sent to Jonathan a
purple robe and a crown, as ethnarch or prince of Judæa.
The chief ecclesiastical, as well as civil power, was then, with
the full sanction of public opinion, assumed by Jonathan, in
the seventh month of the same year, at the Feast of Tabernacles (B. C. 153), and remained in the family until the
usurpation of Herod.

8. Hearing of this, king Demetrius, resolving to outbid
Alexander, sent a long list of privileges and immunities
which he would grant to the Jews, and of honours which
he would bestow upon Jonathan. But, distrusting his sincerity, the people, when the letter was read to them, agreed
with their leaders in adhering to the cause of Alexander
Balas. That cause was successful; and when Alexander
was at Ptolemais, to espouse the king of Egypt's daughter,
he gratefully acknowledged the efficient assistance he had received from Jonathan during the struggle, and treated him
with distinguished honours.

9. Prosperity ruined Alexander Balas. The misconduct
of the ministers to whom he abandoned all the affairs of government, alienated his friends and encouraged his enemies,
and in the fifth year his head was laid at the feet of the
younger Demetrius, the son of Demetrius Soter, by Zabdiel,
with whom, after all had been lost, the royal fugitive had
sought a refuge in Arabia.

10. As Jonathan had remained true to Balas in this
struggle, his enemies hailed the success of Demetrius Nicator
as the signal for his overthrow; and, through their representations, he was summoned to Antioch. He went, carrying
with him valuable presents, and conducted himself so dis-
creetly, that, so far from disturbing him, Demetrius not only
confirmed him in the dignities he had received from Balas,
but added all the valuable privileges which had been offered
by his father, when he had endeavoured to outbid Balas for
the friendship of Jonathan.

11. Among his other public acts, Jonathan renewed the

treaty with the Romans, and formed another with the Lacedæmonians. His government of seventeen years was in the highest degree beneficial to his country, and tended much to give to the peculiar institutions of the people, which he laboured to renovate, that determinate character which was essential to their continuance. His end was afflicting. Disgusted by the perfidy of Demetrius, who cancelled the privileges he had granted, as soon as he was relieved from the danger by which he was threatened, the Jews eagerly espoused the cause of a young son of Alexander Balas, who was brought forward by Tryphon, formerly governor of Antioch. Eventually this youth was raised to the throne, under the name of Antiochus Epiphanes. But Tryphon had used him only for his own objects, and contemplated his removal to make room for himself. To this he saw an obstacle in the known attachment of Jonathan to the house of Balas; and this obstacle he resolved to remove by his death, which he treacherously and barbarously accomplished at Ptolemais, where Jonathan was slain, with a thousand men who attended him as guards. This was speedily followed by the murder of the young king; and Tryphon placed on his own head the blood-stained crown.

CHAPTER III. B. C. 143 TO 78.

ASMONEAN PRINCES.		SYRIA.		GENERAL HISTORY.	
	B.C.		B.C.		B.C.
Simon	143	Tryphon	143	Scipio Nasica . . .	136
John Hyrcanus . . .	135	Antiochus (VII.), Si-		Tiberius Gracchus, tri-	
Aristobulus	107	detes	139	bune	133
Alexander Jannæus .	106	Demetrius Nicator II.	130	Mithridates the Great	123
Queen Alexandra . .	79	Alexander Zebina . .	127	Caius Gracchus, tribune	121
		Antiochus (VIII.),		Caius Marius, tribune	119
		Grypus	123	Jugurthine war begins	
EGYPT.		Antiochus (IX.), Cy-		(5 years)	111
	B.C.	zicenus	111	Julius Cæsar born . .	100
Ptolemy Physcon . .	144	Antiochus VIII. and		The civil war between	
Ptolemy Lathyrus . .	116	IX. contemporane-		Marius and Sylla (6	
Ptolemy Alexander .	88	ously	100	years)	88
		Philip and Antiochus		Sylla, dictator (3	
		(X.), Pius	93	years . . . 82 to 79	
		Demetrius Eucærus .	92	Cicero's first Oration .	81
		Tigranes, King of Ar-			
		menia	83		

1. WHEN the Jews heard of the massacre at Ptolemais, and the death of their honoured high-priest, they were filled with consternation and sorrow. To avert the dangers which this state of discouragement threatened, Simon, the only surviving brother of Judas and Jonathan, called the people together in the Temple, and offered himself as their leader. The people were encouraged and animated by the terms in which the offer was made, and they accepted it with joy. The first act of Simon was to put the country in a state of complete defence, by repairing all the fortresses, and storing them with provisions and munitions of war. Then considering that, bad as the conduct of Demetrius Nicator had been, that of Tryphon was much worse, Simon sent an embassy to the former, offering to acknowledge his sovereignty, and to assist him against Tryphon. Demetrius, who led an indolent and dissipated life at Laodicea, and left the war to his generals, saw the value of this offer, which he gladly accepted, and, in return, agreed to acknowledge Simon as the high-priest and prince of the Jews, to relinquish all claim upon them for tribute, customs, and taxes, and to grant an amnesty for all past offences against himself. This being committed to writing in the form of a royal edict, and properly ratified, amounted

to a charter of freedom and independence; and was so considered by both parties. Accordingly, with this year (B. C. 143), the Jews commenced a new epoch, dating from it as from the first year of " the freedom of Jerusalem." This era is used on the coins of Simon, as well as by Josephus, and by the author of the first book of Maccabees.

2. The next care of Simon was to reduce the fortresses which still held out; and he had the inexpressible satisfaction of compelling the Syrian garrison in the citadel of Jerusalem, which had so long been a standing grievance to the Maccabees, to surrender. He made his son John commander of the forces, and ultimately sent him with king Demetrius to the wars in the East, where, from his exploits in Hyrcania, he acquired the surname of Hyrcanus. In the third year of his reign, he renewed the alliance with the Romans and Lacedæmonians, and sent, as a present to the former, a great shield of gold, worth fifty thousand pounds. The senate was pleased, and wrote to all the kings in these parts, commanding them to consider the Jews as friends and allies of the Romans. The next year Antiochus Sidetes ascended the Syrian throne, his brother Demetrius being held in bondage by the Parthians. He confirmed to Simon all the grants of his pre-

145. Parthians.

decessor, and added the regal prerogative of coining money When, however, he had subdued and slain the usurper Tryphon, he altered his tone, and demanded back the strongholds which Simon had taken, and the tribute which had been relinquished. He sent a powerful army to enforce his demand; which was met and defeated by the Jews under the conduct of Simon's two eldest sons, John and Judas. This victory procured an interval of repose, during which Simon and two of his sons were treacherously murdered, while on a visit at Jericho to his son-in-law, Ptolemy, who aspired to his office

R

and power (B.C. 136).   He sent also to destroy John Hyrcanus, who, however, had timely warning, and fled to Jerusalem,
where the people elected him in his father's room, and shut
their gates against the murderer.   Baffled in this, Ptolemy
applied to Antiochus for an army to assist him in bringing
the country again under the Syrian yoke.   Without waiting for his movements, Hyrcanus marched against him, and
besieged him in a fortress near Jericho, to which he had fled.
The siege was, however, broken up when the sabbatical year
opened, and Ptolemy sought refuge beyond the Jordan until
Antiochus should arrive (B.C. 135).   What afterwards became of him is not known.

3. Antiochus arrived soon after, with a large army, and
besieged Hyrcanus in Jerusalem, which was reduced to great
extremities for want of provisions.   When the Feast of Tabernacles approached, Hyrcanus begged a week's respite for the
celebration of the festival.   This was not only granted, but
the king supplied victims for the sacrifices, and was in the
end so much mollified that he concluded a peace, although he
knew that the city lay at his mercy.   But he again reduced
the country under the Syrian dominion, dismantled Jerusalem, and exacted tribute for the fortresses which were held
out of Judæa.   Antiochus was, not long after, killed in a
battle with the Parthians, from whom Demetrius contrived to
escape.   Of the confusion occasioned by these events, Hyrcanus availed himself to enlarge his territories, as well as to recover the independence of Judæa; and no sort of service, tribute, or homage, was ever after paid by him or his descendants to the kings of Syria.

4. The next exploit of their prince must have been very
acceptable to the antipathies of the Jews; for he invaded
Samaria, took Shechem, the chief seat of the Samaritans, and
destroyed their temple on Mount Gerizim.

5. The next year (B.C. 129), Hyrcanus attacked the Idu-
means (Edomites), who, during the Captivity, had established
themselves in the southern part of Judæa, having Hebron for
their capital, and had since maintained themselves there.
Having subdued them, Hyrcanus gave them the choice of
adopting the Jewish religion, or of quitting the country and
seeking a settlement elsewhere.   They accepted the former

alternative, and afterwards gradually incorporated with the Jews, so as not ultimately to be distinguishable from them.

6. In the course of the two following years, two several embassies were sent to Rome, and obtained decrees highly favourable to Hyrcanus and to the Jewish nation, chiefly as securing them against the aggressions of their neighbours. By his alliances, his consolidation of the government, his conquests, and the wealth which they afforded, Hyrcanus succeeded in raising the nation to a position of much greater dignity and power than it had occupied since the return from Babylon. After enjoying several years of peace and honour, he died B.C. 106.

7. The principality was left by Hyrcanus to his wife; but the government was seized by his eldest son Aristobulus; and as his mother refused to relinquish her claim, he sent her to prison, where he left her to die of hunger. He also imprisoned the three youngest of his brothers; but shewed some affection for Antigonus, the next in age to himself, and employed him in public business. Aristobulus was the first who assumed the royal title and diadem. He extended his dominion by subduing the Itureans, who, like the Edomites before, chose rather to accept the Jewish religion than to abandon their country. The short reign of Aristobulus was brought to its close through his remorse and horror at discovering that it was an unjust suspicion which had caused him to put to death Antigonus, the brother whom he had trusted and loved.

8. Immediately after his death, his three imprisoned brothers were liberated, and the eldest of them, Alexander Jannæus, was advanced to the throne. He had talents for war, which enabled him to enlarge his dominions, although, in other respects, his reign was far from happy. He subdued the Philistines, who accepted the alternative of adopting the Jewish religion. Moab, Ammon, Gilead, and part of Arabia Petræa, also yielded to his arms. This reign was, however, much troubled by the Pharisees, a sect whose name occurs first in the time of Hyrcanus, but who must have arisen earlier, as they had then attained to much power and importance. Their turbulent character and lofty pretensions induced Alexander to follow the example of Hyrcanus in attaching himself to the rival sect of the Sadducees. This,

as well as the general disfavour with which he regarded the principles of the more powerful body, led them to detest his person and government; and they lost no opportunity of exasperating the mind of the people against him by vilifying his administration, and by all sorts of charges and insinuations against his conduct and character. His return with loss and disgrace from the siege of Amathus beyond the Jordan, damaged his reputation with the people, and gave increased boldness to the Pharisees. At length they openly assaulted him while engaged in the most sacred act of the ritual service. At the feast of tabernacles, as he stood at the altar, performing the functions of his office, the Pharisees, and the multitude incited by them, cast at him the citrons which the Jews usually carried in their hands on that occasion. This was the commencement of a civil war, which lasted nine years, in which all parties suffered, and in which above 50,000 persons perished. During this war, both parties committed the most shocking barbarities on each other. The concluding act of it was the taking of Bethone by Alexander. He then brought 800 of the prisoners to Jerusalem, and caused them all to be crucified in one day, and their wives and children put to death before their eyes; while he sat feasting with his women in view of the horrid spectacle.

9. Alexander spent three years more in reducing the fortresses which had fallen into hostile hands during these troubles, and in extending his power beyond the Jordan; where, it should be observed, the country was chiefly occupied by, or under the control of, tribes of Arabian origin, which had settled in these parts; and hence the whole country beyond Jordan, excepting the northernmost part, came ultimately to be considered as part of Arabia, and is so named by ancient geographers.

10. Returning victorious to Jerusalem, Alexander abandoned himself to luxury, drunkenness, and sloth, which brought on a quartan ague, under which he languished for three years and then died. B.C. 82.

11. Before his death, Alexander delivered the government to his wife Alexandra, and appointed her the guardian of the young princes. Following the dying counsels of her late husband, she convened the leaders of the Pharisees, and

committed to them the management of affairs. With this they were so wonderfully mollified, that they not only secured her own peaceful succession, but bestowed a most magnificent funeral on their old enemy. Being now the dominant party, and, in fact, greatly exceeding the other party in popularity and numbers, the queen soon became a mere tool in their hands. She was obliged to yield to their most unreasonable demands; and they used their power with no sparing or gentle hand. They raised a grievous persecution against the Sadducees, and, in general, used their authority in a most oppressive and arbitrary manner,—especially against the former friends and adherents of Alexander Jannæus. Many of the most valuable persons, finding that the queen was unable to protect them, abandoned Jerusalem, and withdrew to obscure towns.

CHAPTER IV. B.C. 78 to 54.

ASAMONEAN PRINCES.	EGYPT.	GENERAL HISTORY.
B.C.	B.C.	B.C.
? Alexandra, with Hyrcanus II. as priest . 78	Ptolemy Auletes . 64	Spartacus 71
Hyrcanus II. king . . 69		Lucullus defeats Mithridates and Tigranes 69
Aristobulus 69	ROMAN GOVERNORS.	The Cataline conspiracy 63
Hyrcanus II. restored . 63	B.C.	Cicero 63
	Gabinius 58	Catullus 60
	Crassus 55	1st Triumvirate: Pompey, J. Cæsar, and
	SYRIA.	Crassus 60
	B.C.	Cicero banished . . . 58
	Antiochus (XI.) Asiaticus 69	Sallust 57
	Dethroned by Pompey, and Syria made a Roman province . . . 65	

1. ALEXANDRA had two sons. The elder, Hyrcanus, who was a man of quiet habits and indolent temper, was raised to the high priesthood. The other son, Aristobulus, was of a more ardent and impetuous temperament, and took no pains to conceal his dislike of his mother's proceedings, and of the conduct of the Pharisees. He, with the principal men of the party, which had been paramount in the time of his father, appeared before the throne, and asked permission to quit the country, or to reside in the frontier towns, out of the way of the Pharisees. The request was granted, excepting that they were not permitted to withdraw to those towns in which the queen kept her treasures. Aristobulus was afterwards entrusted with some forces to relieve Damascus; but he only used the occasion as an opportunity of making himself agreeable to the soldiers, and returned without having done any thing of importance. After a peaceful reign of nine years, Queen Alexandra fell sick, and died, after having, in her last days, as one who had nothing more to do with government, refused to nominate her successor.

2. The Pharisees, however, placed Hyrcanus II. on the throne. But he reigned only three months; for his brother Aristobulus, having got possession of most of the fortresses of the kingdom, during the illness of his mother, advanced his own claims to the sovereignty. The people, who had grown

weary of the Pharisees, and knew that the imbecile Hyrcanus was entirely in their hands, supported this movement;
the soldiers also de-
serted to the popular
Aristobulus. Hyrca-
nus, with little reluc-
tance, then resigned
the mitre and the
crown, and withdrew
into private life, which
better suited his cha-
racter and habits.

3. In his retire-
ment, Hyrcanus fell
under the designing
counsels of Antipater
(originally Antipas),
an Idumean, who had
been much in the
confidence of Alexan-
der Jannæus and his
wife Alexandra : by
them he had been
appointed governor of
Idumea, in which office
he had amassed con-

146 Modern Asiatic Crowns.

siderable wealth. By repeated solicitations, and by persuading
him that his brother sought his life, this person at length induced Hyrcanus to escape by night to Petra, the seat of the
Arabian king Aretas, and claim his protection and assistance. Aretas espoused his cause, and brought him back to
Judæa with an army of 50,000 men; and being joined by
many Jews of the same party, he gave battle to Aristobulus,
who was defeated, and obliged to retreat to the temple-mount,
which had by this time become a strong fortress. The siege
of this fortress was carried on with the animosity which has
always been usual in civil wars. Heathen kings had almost
invariably, during a siege, allowed the lambs for sacrifice at
the great festivals to be introduced into the temple; but this
was refused by the party of Hyrcanus, at the passover, al-

though Aristobulus gave, over the walls, money to pay for them.

4. At this time, the Romans, in accordance with the national policy for establishing a universal empire, had a large army in Asia, under the command of the great Pompey, who was warring in Armenia against Tigranes and Mithridates, while some of his officers were employed in Syria. In this emergency, Aristobulus sent to Severus the Roman general, who had taken possession of Damascus, imploring his assist ance against his brother, not forgetting to send a present of 400 talents with the application. Although Hyrcanus offered to buy his aid at the same price, the Roman preferred the cause of Aristobulus, as one whom it might be the most easy to assist, and the most difficult to subdue; and, therefore, he commanded Aretas instantly to withdraw his forces from Judæa, under pain of a war with the Romans. The Arabian

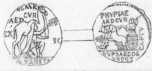

147.

king obeyed at once; but, on his retreat, he was overtaken by Aristobulus, and was defeated in a bloody conflict, in which many of the friends of Hyrcanus perished. Being thus master of the country, Aristobulus anxiously endeavoured to procure from the Romans a recognition of his title. Accordingly, when Pompey soon after came to Damascus, and twelve kings and many ambassadors appeared before him, the ambassadors of Aristobulus were among the number, bearing, as a present, an exquisitely wrought vine of pure gold, valued at 500 talents. His suit was waived for the time, and although his present was accepted, not his own name but that of his father was inscribed upon it, as the donor.

5. The next year, when both Hyrcanus and Aristobulus sent ambassadors to Pompey, inviting him to consider and decide their differences, he put them off to the year ensuing, when they again appeared before him, each furnished with a multitude of witnesses to prove his claim; while another body of Jews came and accused both of them of having changed the government, which had formerly been administered by high-priests, and not by kings. Hyrcanus urged his right as the elder born; which right, Aristobulus contended, was neu

tralised by his incompetency. Pompey, however, still left
the matter undecided, until he should be at leisure to come
himself and settle it at Jerusalem. But the impetuous Aristobulus, perceiving that imbecility in a dependent prince
was far from being objectionable to the Romans, and that the
ultimate decision was likely to be against him, abruptly withdrew to make preparations for war. Enraged at this, Pompey, on his return from an expedition against the Nabathæan
Arabs, marched into Judæa, and summoned Aristobulus, who
was in the strong fortress of Alexandrium, to appear before
him. He obeyed; and Pompey no sooner had him in his
power, than he compelled him to sign an order for all the fortresses to be given up to the Romans. He was then liberated; when, resenting this treatment, he fled to Jerusalem,
determined to stand a siege. But when Pompey advanced,
the gates were opened to his troops by the party of Hyrcanus; and Aristobulus and his party withdrew once more into
the Temple, determined to hold out to the last. Here they
were closely besieged by Pompey, who found his proceedings
greatly facilitated by the strictness with which the Jewish
people observed their Sabbath. It was true, that since the
Maccabæan wars, they would on that day stand on their own
defence; yet they still considered it unlawful to take any
steps to hinder the works or operations of the enemy. The
Romans were, therefore, allowed, without the slightest molestation, to carry on during the Sabbath-days their preparations
for the assaults of the ensuing weeks; by which means they
at length carried the Temple by assault, after a siege of three
months, on the very day which the Jews observed as a fast
for the taking of the city and Temple by Nebuchadnezzar.
A dreadful carnage now ensued, during which the officiating
priests continued, with the utmost composure, their solemn
services at the altar, until they were themselves smitten down
before it without resistance.

6. Pompey had the temerity to enter the Temple itself,
even to the most holy place, with some of his officers; no
one venturing to oppose the act. But curious observers have
remarked, that he was ever after an unprosperous man; and
this is no doubt true in itself, whether it was a consequence
which resulted from this sacrilege or not. In the sanctuary,

the Roman noted with a curious eye the objects presented to his view; but he left untouched all the sacred utensils, and even the treasures of the Temple, which amounted to ten thousand talents of gold. The walls and fortifications of Jerusalem were then demolished by order of Pompey ; who also made no ceremony in reducing the recent "*allies*" of Rome to the condition of a tributary people. He indeed appointed Hyrcanus to be high-priest and prince of the country ; but he required him to pay tribute to the Romans, and forbade him to assume the crown, or extend his territories beyond their ancient limits. The external conquests of the principality were added to Syria, which was erected into a Roman province, and left under the dominion of Scaurus as prefect, with two legions to preserve order. To this date all agree in referring the subjection of Judæa to the Romans. When Pompey left Palestine, he took with him Aristobulus, with his two sons, Alexander and Antigonus, and two of his daughters, to grace his triumph at Rome.

7. Alexander, the eldest son of Aristobulus, escaped from Pompey during the journey to Rome, and got back to his own country. He must, however, have kept quiet for a time, as we do not hear of him till the year B.C. 57, when he had found means to collect a considerable force, with which he seized and garrisoned several strong fortresses, and from them ravaged the whole country. Hyrcanus had no means to oppose him, and as Jerusalem would probably be the next point of attack, he wished to rebuild the walls of the city, but was forbidden by the jealousy of the Romans. On his calling upon them for succour, however, the pro-consul, Gabinius, marched an army into Judæa, and was accompanied by the celebrated Mark Antony, the commander of his cavalry. The Roman troops were joined by those of Hyrcanus, under Antipater; and in the battle which followed, Alexander was completely routed. He sought refuge in the strong fortress of Alexandrium, whence, through the mediation of his mother, he concluded a peace with Gabinius, on condition of surrendering the fortresses held by him, which were then demolished.

8. The general then employed himself in settling the country, after the manner of the Romans. He was probably, in many respects, guided by the advice of Antipater, who

made it his policy to ingratiate himself with the Romans. The most important measure was the change of the government to an aristocracy. Before this, the administration of affairs had been conducted by two sanhedrim, or councils, or courts of justice :—the lesser consisting of twenty-three members, existed in every city, and all these local sanhedrims were subject to the jurisdiction of the Grand Sanhedrim of seventy-two members, which sat at Jerusalem. These were put down by Gabinius, who, in their place, established five separate and independent tribunals—at Jerusalem, Jericho, Gadara, Amathus, and Sepphoris,—giving to each the power of administering summary justice upon the inhabitants of the several districts. This threw the whole power into the hands of the nobles, who presided in these courts; whereas by the former practice the power had ultimately centred in the prince. This, or anything that tended to lower the regal principle of government, was no doubt acceptable to the Jews in general; for they were unwilling to have any king not of the house of David to reign over them, especially as they were at this time anxiously expecting the appearance of the promised Messiah.

9. The next event of importance is the re-appearance of Aristobulus, who, with his younger son Antigonus, escaped from Rome, and returned to his own land, where he soon got together a considerable number of adherents, and excited a revolt, which might have been dangerous, but for the interference of the Romans, who soon defeated his forces, and again made him and his son prisoners. But in sending them back to Rome, Gabinius made such a representation of the services of the mother in suppressing Alexander's insurrection, that the senate liberated the family, and only detained Aristobulus.

10. Not long after this, Gabinius was succeeded in the government of Syria by the celebrated triumvir Crassus, whose insatiable avarice is well known to the students of Roman history. He soon visited Jerusalem with a body of soldiers, and plundered the temple of all the treasures which Pompey had spared, to the value of two millions sterling. His terrible overthrow and death, in the ensuing year, was deemed by the Jews a judgment upon him for this sacrilege.

CHAPTER V. B.C. 54 TO 37.

THE JEWS.		SYRIA.		EGYPT.	
	B.C.	Roman Governors.	B.C.	Ptolemy Auletes.	B.C.
Hyrcanus II.				Cleopatra	51
Antigonus	40	Bibulus	51		
Antigonus beheaded;		Q. Metellus Scipio	50	ROME.	
End of Asamonean		Sextus Cæsar	47	Julius Cæsar	38
Dynasty	37	Cassius	43	II. Triumvirate — Octa-	
		Ventidius	38	vius—Mark Antony	
				—Lepidus	38

GENERAL HISTORY.		PERSONS.	
	B.C.		B.C.
Syria invaded by the Parthians	50	Cornelius Nepos	50
Battle of Pharsalia	49	Varro	49
Cato kills himself at Utica	47	Diodorus Siculus	44
Cæsar reforms the Roman Calendar	46	Trogus Pompeius	41
Cæsar slain in the Senate-house	44	Caius Cassius, ob.	42
Battle of Philippi	42	Marcus Brutus, ob.	42
The Parthians make themselves mas-			
ters of Syria and Asia Minor	40		
The Parthians defeated and expelled			
by Ventidius	39		

1. IN the Roman civil war which broke out between Pompey and Julius Cæsar, the latter, thinking to promote his own interests and to disturb those of his rival in Syria, liberated Aristobulus, and sent him home with two legions of soldiers to reclaim the crown. But he was poisoned in the way by the adherents of Pompey; by whom also his son, Alexander, who had begun to raise forces to assist his father, was seized, brought to Antioch, and after a mock trial, beheaded. Two years after, the surviving son, Antigonus, presented himself before Cæsar when he returned, through Judæa, from his campaign in Egypt, and solicited to be restored to the principality of his father. He mentioned the claims of his family, its wrongs, and how much it had suffered in his cause. But Cæsar was now under a new influence, and he therefore not only rejected the petition, but treated it as an impertinence. The new influence was that of Antipater, who swayed the real power of the province in the name of Hyrcanus. He had employed that power and the near resources of a neighbour, so much to the advantage of

the Romans in this campaign, he had devoted himself so sedulously to Cæsar, and, withal, he had found occasion to display so much valour and conduct, that Cæsar felt grateful to him, and held him in high estimation.

2. Antipater failed not to employ, for the advancement of his own fortunes, the influence he had thus acquired. Cæsar was induced to confirm to Hyrcanus the full and ancient powers of the high-priesthood and the ethnarchy. This had the effect of indirectly restoring the regal character of the government, which had been impaired by the measures of Gabinius, and of destroying the independent jurisdictions which he had established. To do this, and to do it without a direct decree against a popular measure, appears to have been the real object of this restoration. Hyrcanus personally derived no increase of power from it; for at the same time Antipater himself, who had before been admitted to the dignity of Roman citizenship, was appointed Roman procurator of Judæa, which vested in him all the substantial powers of the state. Cæsar also granted permission for rebuilding the walls of Jerusalem which Pompey had destroyed ; and at this and other times, such other signal favours were, through Antipater, bestowed by Cæsar upon the Jewish nation, that in his time the weight of the Roman yoke was scarcely felt. One of the first acts of the new procurator was to raise his two sons, Phasael and Herod, to stations of trust and distinction. Herod was made governor of Galilee, and Phasael governor of Jerusalem. The former exercised himself in clearing his province of the bands of daring robbers by which it was infested. But his mode of action was so sovereign and arbitrary as to attract the notice of the Sanhedrim, which summoned him to Jerusalem to give an account of his conduct. He came indeed, but he came clothed in purple, with a numerous retinue, and bearing a letter from the president of Syria, with express orders for his acquittal. This, with his haughty and imperious carriage, quite intimidated the assembly, until an address from one of their number kindled their resentment as well at his past as present conduct. Perceiving this, Hyrcanus, who was attached to him, adjourned the assembly, and, as advised by that prince, Herod fled from the city in the following night, and went to

Sextus Cæsar at Damascus, who bestowed upon him the government of Cœle-Syria. Burning with resentment, Herod would have marched to Jerusalem to punish the Sanhedrim and depose Hyrcanus, had not his father and brother persuaded him to abandon the design.

3. The greater struggles and confusions in the state of Rome were accompanied by smaller conflicts and troubles in Syria and Palestine; but in all these, it was the lot of the family of Antipater to be always uppermost. After the assassination of Julius Cæsar at Rome by Brutus, Cassius, and their confederates, and of his relative Sextus Cæsar in Syria by Bassus, the flames of war broke forth anew. Cassius being, like others, obliged to withdraw before the paramount influence of Antony and Octavius in Italy, passed over into Syria, and, seizing that province, made head there against the proconsul Dolabella. Cassius was obliged to raise heavy contributions to maintain the large army he had collected. Judæa was assessed in 700 talents; and Antipater commissioned Herod to raise one-half, and Malichus, one of the principal supporters of Hyrcanus, to collect the other. Herod won high favour with Cassius by the speedy payment of his portion; but Malichus, being more dilatory, would have been put to death, had not Hyrcanus redeemed him by paying 100 talents out of his own coffers. This affair seems to have quickened the bad feeling with which Malichus and other leading Jews regarded the power and authority which Antipater had acquired and was acquiring over the nation. They therefore plotted to destroy him and his whole family; and soon after Antipater was poisoned with a glass of wine, which the high-priest's brother was induced to give him at an entertainment in the palace. Herod avenged his father, by inducing Cassius to order Malichus to be slain at Tyre by the Roman soldiers. The party of which Malichus had been the head, countenanced by Hyrcanus himself, then made a vehement struggle to relieve themselves from the grasp of Antipater's sons. They failed, and the failure gave the more strength to Herod and Phasael. Herod upbraided Hyrcanus for the part he had taken in this affair; but he did not come to an open rupture with him, as he wished to bring into his own family the claims of the

Asamonean house by a marriage with Mariamne, the high-priest's accomplished and beautiful grand-daughter.

4. The party adverse to Herod and Phasael, was, however, far from being extinct. It soon found another and more dangerous head in the person of Antigonus, that younger son of Aristobulus, whom there has been more than one occasion to mention. He came to claim his father's throne; and his claim was well supported. But when Antigonus arrived in Judæa with his army, he received from Herod a complete overthrow, and was obliged, for the time, to abandon his enterprise. The next year, after the victory over Brutus at Philippi, Mark Antony passed over into Asia, to secure that important region for the conquerors. It will be remembered that this celebrated man had formerly served in Palestine with Gabinius, and must have been acquainted with the affairs of the Jewish people, and with the persons of their leaders. A deputation, composed of a hundred influential Jews, came to him at Daphne, near Antioch, with complaints against the usurping sons of Antipater. Antony gave them a hearing, and then turning to Hyrcanus, who was present, asked whom *he* thought the most competent to govern the state under himself. To the surprise of many, he named the two brothers, influenced possibly by the projected marriage between Herod and his grand-daughter. On this, Antony, who had received gifts from Herod, and who well remembered the services of Antipater, raised Herod and Phasael to the rank of tetrarchs, and committed the affairs of Judæa to their administration. Not long after, however, when Antony was at Tyre, another more numerous deputation came to him with the same complaints; but Antony ordered the soldiers to disperse them, which was not done without loss of life.

5. Antigonus was not yet disheartened. The Parthians, for a brief period, became masters of Syria, and held possession of Sidon and Ptolemais. Antigonus engaged their assistance by the promise of a thousand talents and five hundred Jewish women, and advanced at the head of a powerful army against Jerusalem; and after many strong efforts, succeeded in recovering the kingdom. Herod escaped by flight; but Hyrcanus and Phasael were thrown into dungeons. Knowing that his death was determined, Phasael dashed out his brains

against the prison walls.   Antigonus dared not incur the odium of destroying his aged uncle; but he barbarously cropped off his ears, and sent him far away to Seleucia in Babylonia, in the safe keeping of the Parthians.

6. Herod made the best of his way to Rome, where he found his friend Antony in the very zenith of his power; and was by him introduced to the favourable notice of Octavius, his coadjutor, by an account of the services which Antipater had rendered to Julius Cæsar in the Egyptian campaign, and of the esteem in which he had been held by that conqueror. All that Herod came prepared to solicit was, that Aristobulus, the brother of his espoused Mariamne, should have the throne of Judæa, purposing himself to govern under him, as he had governed under Hyrcanus. But Antony would hear of nothing less than that he should be king himself, and, with the concurrence of Octavius and of the Senate, he was solemnly inaugurated king of Judæa, in the Capitol of Rome. He had still, however, to gain possession of his kingdom, and this he found an arduous undertaking. The Romans were again masters of Syria; but such assistance as Herod could obtain from them did him more harm than good; and the war lingered on with various success for between two and three years, when, finding that he had tolerably well secured Galilee and Samaria, he led his forces against Jerusalem. He was induced to do this, probably, by the promise of efficient aid from Antony, who had now returned to the East.   While engaged in the siege, Herod completed his marriage with Mariamne, whom he had espoused four years before, hoping by this step to reconcile the people to his government. He was joined before Jerusalem by Sosius, the president of Syria, whom Antony had sent to his assistance with a powerful army, which raised the whole investing force to above 60,000 men. The city withstood a vigorous siege of above half a year, and was then taken by storm.   Exasperated at the obstinate resistance they had encountered, the Roman soldiers pillaged the city, and massacred the inhabitants without mercy. Jerusalem would probably have been destroyed, had not Herod ransomed it with gold.   Antigonus surrendered himself to Sosius, and showing less of the hero than had been expected from him, was treated with contempt.   He was

sent in chains to Antioch, where he was ultimately, at the
solicitation of Herod, put to death, with such contumely as
had never before been shewn by the Romans to a crowned
head.

7. Thus ended the Asamonean dynasty, after it had subsisted 126 years. In its later struggles for existence, the
most devoted and even obstinate attachment to it was evinced
by the great mass of the Jewish people ; and it was because
nothing would induce them to acknowledge one of another
family as king while Antigonus lived, that Herod determined
on procuring his death. After that, the Jews sullenly and
gradually submitted to what they could not avoid, Herod
being upheld by Roman swords.

M

BOOK VIII.

CHAPTER I.   B.C. 37 TO B.C. 4.

THE JEWS.

	B. C.
Herod the Great	37
Birth of John the Baptist announced	6
Birth of Christ announced	5
John the Baptist born	5

EGYPT.

	B. C.
Cleopatra.	
Egypt reduced to a Roman Province by Octavius	31

GENERAL HISTORY.

	B. C.
Lepidus expelled from the Triumvirate	36
War between Octavius and Antony	33
Battle of Actium	31
Octavius invades Egypt, and reduces it to a Roman Province	30
Octavius, Emperor, with the title of Augustus	27

SYRIA.

	B. C.
Roman Governors.	
Plancus	34
Messala Corvinus	27
Agrippa	22
—— again	15
Sentius Saturninus and Titus Volumnius	13

PERSONS.

	B. C.
Mæcenas	31
Agrippa	29
Horace	29
Propertius	27
Titus Livius	25
Tibullus	21
Ovid	20
Vitruvius	15
Dionysius of Halicarnassus	5

1. We now find upon the throne of Judæa the man who comes down to us as Herod " the Great," and who certainly manifested in no common degree the qualities to which greatness has been usually ascribed.   Understanding the epithet, in its conventional use, as not applied to moral goodness, but to certain regal qualities which men have been trained to admire, it must be admitted that Herod had as good claim to be called " the Great" as many of those to whom that distinction has been given.   There is no person who, singly, fills so large a place in the history of the Jews, or whose character has been brought so completely into view.   His resolution and indomitable valour are evinced by his whole history; he was liberal even to extravagance in his expenditure; his views were large and penetrating, and his plans comprehensive; he was magnificent in his buildings and public works; and, at the first view, he appears to us as one of those men who might stand forth as the benefactors of mankind.

2. But a closer inspection shews that all this fair appearance was false and hollow. Ambition, glory, and the praise of men, were the motives of all his great acts—to attain these he aimed at objects far beyond the grasp of the dependent sovereign of so small a state. He was obliged, by his lavish expenditure, to lay the most heavy and oppressive burdens upon his people, and to invent any pretext for cutting down the wealthy and the noble, and confiscating their estates. He was a slave to the most furious passions : his natural disposition was severe and unrelenting, and no regard for human suffering formed an obstacle to the least of his designs. His inexorable cruelties against those whom he suspected or feared, excited against him the hatred of all his subjects,—and then, his only care was how to make that hatred a source of gain, by new exactions and confiscations. Although a Jew by profession, he was in heart a heathen, and it displeased him that the severe principles of that religion which made more account of righteousness than of glory, precluded his subjects from honouring him as the great ones of the heathen were honoured,—by statues, temples, games, and offerings. In a word, the good qualities of Herod, real or seeming, were kept bright for holiday show to the Romans; but the bad ones were displayed without reserve to his own people, to his own kindred, and, above all, to those who stood in his way, or whom he accounted his enemies.

3. The leading acts of his reign class themselves so naturally under the heads of *jealousy* and *pride*, that it may be well thus to arrange them. Of his jealousy, the prime objects were the members and the adherents of the Asamonean house. He began his reign by a most dreadful persecution of the adherents of the fallen Antigonus; and here policy went along with his hatred, for with his exhausted treasury and lavish expenses, he found it exceedingly convenient to put the more affluent of them to death, and confiscate their estates. The blood which he shed, and the inexorable cruelty which he manifested, in the beginning of his reign, made his person and government hateful to the Jews; and hatred rose to abhorrence when the objects of the public love, the last remains of a noble race, became the victims of his murderous jealousy.

4. The old Hyrcanus, it will be remembered, had been

exiled to Babylonia, where he was treated with much consideration, not only by the large body of influential Jews in that quarter, but by the Parthian government. Jealous of the place which the harmless old man occupied in the affection and respect of the Jewish people, Herod decoyed him to Jerusalem, and, after treating him for a time with apparent attention and deference, caused him, at a convenient season, to be slain (B. C. 31). The enormity of this deed is unutterable, when we consider what Hyrcanus had been to Herod and to his father Antipater.

5. The next object of Herod's jealousy was a boy, the grandson of Hyrcanus, and brother of Mariamne. This child was now the lineal representative of the Asamonean house, and, as such, was hateful to Herod; but his life and welfare seemed sufficiently guarded by his relationship to Mariamne. The boy grew up into a youth of wonderful beauty; and the hearts of the Jews were fixed upon him, as the last of the glorious race of the Maccabees. His of right was the high-priesthood, which Herod had bestowed upon an obscure priest of the name of Ananel; but perceiving, at length, that it was no longer safe to withhold the pontificate from him, the king removed Ananel, and gave his place to Aristobulus, then but seventeen years of age. When he first appeared in the gorgeous robes of his office, at the Feast of Tabernacles, the assembled people could not restrain a burst of admiration and delight: and that testimony of affection sealed the doom of Aristobulus. Very soon after, he was drowned, by alleged "accident," while bathing at Jericho; but the whole nation knew that the act was Herod's, and saw through the show of mourning and parade of grief displayed on the occasion.

6. Of his wife, Mariamne, who has been so often named, Herod was doatingly fond ; and this he shewed in his own peculiar manner, by more than once leaving private orders, when he had occasion to leave Judæa, that she should be put to death if he failed to return. This happened to transpire, and gave occasion to jealousy and suspicion on the part of Herod, and to anger and indignation on the part of the high-spirited and virtuous princess. The result was, as usual, death. In the rage of his jealousy and anger, he poured out that life which was the dearest of all to him, and which his groans and

tears could not afterwards restore. The death of her mother Alexandra followed soon after. The two sons of Mariamne by Herod himself, also exciting his jealousy and dislike by resting upon their Asamonean descent through her, and making that their ground of claim to the favour of the people, were at length consigned to the same doom, and were, by their father's order, strangled in the prison-house (B. C. 6). In short, such was his jealous temper, that he spared neither his own family, his friends, nor the noblest, wealthiest, or most powerful of his subjects. It is not wonderful that such conduct procured him the intense hatred of the Jews, and that various plots were laid for his destruction. In such plots a very active part was taken by the Pharisees; but they were all abortive, and only served to increase the distance between the tyrant and his people, and to render the former so suspicious, that the innocent were often cruelly tortured, lest the guilty should escape.

7. The knowledge of how deeply he was disliked by the people, also made him more and more careless of public opinion; and when he supposed that all his enemies were put down, and his power well established, he evinced a marked neglect of the Jewish religion and laws, and as marked a preference of Roman customs and practices. There was, perhaps, policy in this; for he owed everything to the Romans, and had no trust but in their favour. Not being a Levite, or even, by birth a Jew, he did not venture to seize the priesthood. His own policy and that of his successors, was, therefore, to degrade that sacred office, and to render it entirely dependent on his will. From the beginning of his reign to the destruction of the Temple, the hereditary principle of succession to the priesthood was utterly neglected; and the high-priests were set up and removed at pleasure. He destroyed the authority of the Grand Sanhedrim, before which he had formerly been summoned; and he is said to have burned the public genealogies, that no evidence might exist against his claim to be considered an Israelite. In all parts of his kingdom, except Judæa, Herod built temples in the Grecian style of art, set up statues for idolatrous worship, and even dedicated a magnificent theatre and amphitheatre to the celebration of games in honour of Augustus, which, it is known, implied the deification of the

person in whose honour the games were celebrated. His ordinary habits were framed after the manners and customs of
the Romans; and along with the usages, his influence and example failed not to impart the luxuries and vices of that
licentious people.

8. To Herod's *pride* may be ascribed his buildings and
public works. His design to rebuild the Temple in a style and
scale of superior grandeur, may certainly be attributed to his
wish for the glory of being thought another Solomon, rather
than to his piety or zeal. He was likewise sensible of the
fact, that there was scarcely any step he could take by which
he could so well please and soothe the people he had done so
much to exasperate. Accordingly, having obtained their consent, he spent two years in bringing together all the materials
for the work, after which the old fabric was pulled down, and
the new one begun, in the twentieth year of his reign. For
nine or ten years, no less than 18,000 workmen were employed
upon it. The sanctuary, or the actual Temple itself, was completed in a year and a-half; and the rest of the pile, with its
courts, porticoes, offices, and outer buildings, in eight years
more, so as to be fit for the usual services of religion; but the
whole was not completed till long after the death of Herod.
This Temple is that which Christ and his apostles so often
visited, and which is minutely described by Josephus. It
seems in many respects to have been a much more magnificent
pile than the first Temple, built by Solomon, although it may
not have equalled that celebrated structure in its wealth of
gold. It was built with hard white stones of vast size; and,
rising in all its grandeur from the summit of an eminence, it
formed the most conspicuous object in a general view of the
city, and excited the admiration of all beholders. The exterior was covered profusely with solid plates and pinnacles
of gold; and when the rays of the sun were reflected from it,
it shone like a meteor, which the eye could not rest upon.
The noble porticoes which surrounded the Temple courts, also
claimed no small share of admiring wonder. Incalculable
wealth was expended on them; and the refined taste was
gratified, by grace of form and proportion, by vast extent, by
costliness of materials, and by every variety of beauty and
embellishment which art or imagination could devise.

9. Herod also built a magnificent palace for himself, which subsequently became the residence of the Roman procurators at Jerusalem. This, next to the Temple, was considered the finest building in Jerusalem. Many other great works were undertaken by him, not only in his own dominions, but in foreign cities, with the view of spreading the fame of his magnificence in the Roman empire. In many other cities, the traveller might hear in those days, as he went from place to place, that the city walls, the porticoes, the gymnasiums, the theatre, the temple, the bath, the bazaar, the aqueduct, were built by a munificent foreigner, Herod, king of Judæa; or else that he had planted the grove, had founded the public games, or had made rich gifts to the city. Although this lavish expenditure upon foreigners was a grievance to the people over whom he ruled, it must be admitted that his own dominion was by no means overlooked. Many new cities were built by him, and old ones restored; bridges, roads, baths, aqueducts, were formed wherever needed, which gave a new aspect to the country under his reign. At Cæsarea, which was built by him, he framed by art the safest and most convenient port on all the coast. Among the cities rebuilt by him on an enlarged and beautiful plan, was Samaria, to which he gave the name of Sebaste, in honour of Augustus. All these were great, and in themselves useful works; yet we may gather from the Jewish writings, that the people were but little grateful for them, while they groaned under the exactions by which their cost was defrayed.

10. We have seen that Mark Antony was the original patron of Herod, and that to him chiefly he owed his kingdom. In the conflict that eventually arose between Antony and Octavius, Herod adhered to the cause of the former; but at length, not feeling it his interest to connect his fortunes with those of a man whose infatuations were leading to his inevitable ruin, he made a timely and by no means ungraceful transfer of his allegiance to Octavius. To that person the attentions and services of Herod were very acceptable; and when he became the sole master of the Roman world, under the name of Augustus, he continued to manifest towards him the highest degree of favour and personal esteem. By

successive additions, his kingdom was made more extensive
than that of any king since Solomon, and embraced not only
the whole country from Dan to Beersheba, but as extensive
domains beyond the Jordan as had at almost any time belonged to the crown of Israel.   Besides this, he was the
emperor's procurator in Syria, and the governor of that important country undertook nothing without his concurrence.
We may form some notion of the regard which the emperor
had for Herod by the pains which he took from time to time
to settle the troubles that were constantly arising in his
family, and which were as constantly referred to his judgment
and decision.   The most important incidents, as arising
chiefly from the jealousy of Herod's character, have been
mentioned.   The last of them which was named, being the
execution of his two high-spirited and accomplished sons by
Mariamne, took place towards the latter end of his long reign.
B. C. 6.

11. The year after was signalised by the birth of John
the Baptist,—the harbinger of the promised Messiah.

CHAPTER II.   B. C. 5 TO A. D. 23.

PALESTINE.

	B. C.
Herod the Great	37

	A. D.
Archelaus, ethnarch of Judæa, &c.	1
Herod Antipas, tetrarch of Galilee and Perea	1
Herod Philip, tetrarch of Trachonitis, &c.	1

ROMAN PROCURATORS OF JUDÆA.

	A. D.
Coponius	6
Marcus Ambivius	9
Annius Rufus	13
Valerius Gratus	14
Pontius Pilate	25

ROME.

	B. C.
Augustus	27

	A. D.
Tiberius	14

PERSONS.

	B C
Phædrus	4
Cornelius Celsus	17
Valerius Maximus	23
Germanicus	8
Arminius	10

EVENTS.

	A. D.
Jesus Christ born	1
Massacre of the Innocents at Bethlehem	1
Christ in the Temple	9
Jews expelled from Italy	20
Annas removed from the high-priesthood, which he had held 15 years	23

1. THE good understanding between Herod and Augustus, was at length interrupted, in consequence of Herod marching some troops into Arabia Petræa, against king Obodas, with whom he had quarrelled. This was so misrepresented to the emperor, that he was greatly incensed against Herod, and wrote to him saying he should be no longer treated as a friend but as a subject. Accordingly, a commissioner named Cyrenius, was sent into Judæa to register the taxable population, with a view to the imposition of that capitation or poll-tax, usually paid by the inhabitants of the subject provinces, but from which Herod's dominion had been hitherto exempt. The registration was completed; but the tax itself was not imposed, as proper explanations restored the good understanding between Herod and the emperor.

2. As, under the decree of registration, the people were to be enrolled in their paternal towns, many persons who had settled in other places, had now to journey to the seat of the

families to which they belonged. Those of the house and lineage of David repaired to Bethlehem. Among them was a carpenter named Joseph, with his wife Mary, from Nazareth in Galilee. As the caravanserai was too crowded by previous comers to afford them any accommodation, they lodged in the stable belonging to it. Here Mary gave birth to a son, and cradled him in the manger. That son was JESUS CHRIST, the Messiah, so long foretold, whose day so many kings and prophets had desired to see. Nor was that illustrious birth without such heavenly celebration as became its importance. Hosts of rejoicing angels sang of "peace on earth, and good will to man;" and by them the shepherds, who lay abroad at night in the plain, watching their flocks, were directed to the birth-place of the Redeemer.

3. Not long after, Jerusalem was astonished by the arrival of three sages from the distant east, inquiring for the new-born king, saying, that they had seen "his star," and had come to offer him their gifts and homage. They found him in the manger at Bethlehem; and then repaired to their own country without returning to Jerusalem, as Herod had desired. The jealousy of that tyrant had been awakened by their inquiry for the "King of the Jews;" and as their neglect to return prevented him from distinguishing the object of their homage, he had the inconceivable barbarity to order that all the children in Bethlehem under two years of age should be put to death, trusting that the intended victim would fall in the general slaughter; but Joseph had previously been warned in a dream to take his wife and the infant to the land of Egypt, whence they did not return till after the death of Herod.

4. That event was not long delayed. In the sixty-ninth year of his age, Herod fell ill of the disease which occasioned his death. That disease was in his bowels, and not only put him to the most cruel tortures, but rendered him altogether loathsome to himself and others. The natural ferocity of his temper could not be tamed by such experience. Knowing that the nation would little regret his demise, he ordered the persons of chief note to be confined in a tower, and all of them to be slain when his own death took place, that there might be cause for weeping in Jerusalem. This savage

order was not executed. After a reign of thirty-seven years,
Herod died in the seventieth year of his age.

5. By his will, which was, of course, left subject to the
approval of the emperor, Herod divided his dominions among
his three sons, Archelaus, Herod Antipas, and Herod Philip.
To Archelaus he bequeathed what was regarded as properly
the kingdom, namely, Judæa, Samaria, and Idumæa; to
Antipas was left the tetrarchy of Galilee and Perea; and
Philip was appointed tetrarch of the territory formed by the
districts of Trachonitis, Gaulonitis, Batanea, and Paneas.
The relative value of the territories may be estimated by the
revenue derived from them. Archelaus' territory yielded 600
talents a-year, that of Antipas 200, that of Philip 100. This
distribution was confirmed by Augustus, excepting that he
recognised Archelaus as ethnarch only, reserving the title of
king as the future reward of his good conduct in the government. His subjects, however, regarded him as their king
and entertained favourable anticipations of his reign. But
he soon shewed himself as great a tyrant as his father, without the redeeming qualities that had been sometimes visible
in Herod. At the very beginning of his reign, his refusal of
a popular demand, raised a commotion in the temple, to quell
which he let loose the soldiers upon the people, whereby not
fewer than 3000 persons were destroyed. This and other
acts revived the general unpopularity of the rule of the
Herodian family; and, therefore, when the several members
of that family, interested in the will of Herod, proceeded to
Rome to promote their claims, a deputation of Jews also went
to petition that they might be no longer harassed by a show
of independence, but should be allowed to live according to
their own laws under a Roman governor. Their suit was,
however, refused, and the will of Herod was confirmed.

6. On his return, Archelaus conducted himself with great
harshness towards his refractory subjects. This produced new
disorders; and the ensuing years were disturbed by insurrections against the Romans by pretenders to the crown, and by
powerful bands of brigands, who kept the kingdom in continual alarm, and checked the communications between one
part of the country and another. At length the mal-administration of Archelaus, and his unfitness to govern, became

so evident, that the complaints of his subjects were no longer treated with neglect at Rome. In the tenth year of his reign he was deposed, and banished to Vienne in Gaul.

7. At the same time Judæa was reduced to the form of a Roman province, annexed to Syria, and governed by Roman procurators. This change threw into the rough hands of strangers those powers which the kings had previously exercised. Thus, tribute was paid directly to the Romans; the power of life and death was taken away; and justice was administered in the name and by the laws of Rome. The procurators were appointed directly by the emperors, and the place of their residence was Cæsarea, which hence became the reputed capital of the province. A magnificent palace which Herod had built there for himself, became the residence of the procurators. At the great festivals, the procurators usually visited Jerusalem, attended by some cohorts (or regiments) of soldiers, with the view of repressing any disturbance which might arise in so vast a concourse of discontented people. Six cohorts were constantly kept in Judæa, of which five were generally at Cæsarea, and one always at Jerusalem. A part of the Jerusalem cohort was quartered in the tower of Antonia, so as to command the Temple and the prætorium or palace of the governor.

8. The duty of the procurator was to maintain good order in his province, to collect the imperial revenues, and to administer justice. Some of those who came to Judæa, held independent jurisdiction, while others were dependent on the president or general governor of Syria, whose seat was at Antioch. The tribute paid to the Romans was peculiarly galling to the Jews, many of whom, arguing on abstract tenets, without reference to its being compulsory, held that it was "unlawful" for the chosen people of God to pay tribute to the heathen. The persons holding this doctrine, or making it a cover for their restlessness, were called "zealots;" and under that name they are distinguished in the few sad pages that remain of the Jewish history. Such people were not likely to admit of any middle course, nor indeed was there any such course open to them. They raised numerous insurrections against the Roman government, or united in formidable bodies of brigands; and considering all those Jews who

were willing to rest quiet under the Romans, as unworthy and degenerate sons of Israel, they counted them as enemies, and treated them as such. The effect of this was increasing disorder, insecurity, and rapine.

9. Even the more quietly disposed who, from seeing no hope of deliverance, were disposed to submit to the Roman yoke, detested the tribute in their hearts: and hence those Jews who assisted in the collection, and were called "publicans," were disliked beyond all men, being regarded as betrayers of their country's liberties, and extortioners in behalf of the Romans. This feeling naturally threw the office of collector or publican into the hands of men of low character, whose conduct generally justified the dislike with which they were regarded. The lofty notions entertained by the Jews of their national privileges as the peculiar people of Jehovah, rather than any enlarged and patriotic views of public liberty, fostered those feelings of hatred to the Roman government. Besides, the Romans, being idolaters, were looked upon by the Jews with disgust, as polluted and abominable men, with whom they could not sit at the same table or mix in any social intercourse. This marked and avowed abhorrence of the Jews to the persons of the Romans, was by no means calculated to produce in that overbearing people a kind feeling towards their tributaries.

10. But for their national peculiarities and prejudices the Jews would have had no good ground for complaint. They were allowed the free exercise of their own religious rites; they worshipped in their temple and synagogues without restraint; they followed their own customs, and were still in a great degree governed by their own laws.

CHAPTER III. A. D. 25 TO 36.

PALESTINE.	A. D.	EVENTS.	A. D.
Galilee—Herod Antipas	1	John the Baptist begins his ministry	28
Trachonitis—Herod Philip	1	Jews baptised by John	29
Judæa—Pontius Pilate	25	John imprisoned by Antipas	30
Marcellus	35	Jesus begins his ministry	30
Marullus	36	John the Baptist beheaded	32
		Jesus crucified	33
ROME.		Stephen martyred	34
Tiberius	14	Conversion of Saul	36

1. The important changes in Judæa consequent upon its becoming a Roman province, did not extend to the tetrarchies of Herod Antipas and Philip, who governed their territories without the direct intervention of the Romans. The former of these personages is repeatedly mentioned in the gospels by the name of Herod. He sedulously cultivated the favour of the emperor Tiberius, who succeeded Augustus in A. D. 14, and gave his name to the city which he built on the western border of the lake of Gennesareth, from which also the lake itself soon acquired the name of Tiberias.

2. The Roman procurators of Judæa were often changed; and, with rare exceptions, every succeeding one was worse, in character and conduct, than his predecessor. The first of them of whom there is anything remarkable to record is Pontius Pilate, whose name the gospels have made familiar to every reader. He came into the province in A. D. 25, and continued in it ten years. His conduct from the first excited the dissatisfaction of the people. He was an impetuous, greedy, sanguinary, and obstinate tyrant, who sold justice, plundered the people, and slew the innocent. Although the abhorrence in which idolatrous images were held by the Jews, was perfectly well known to all the Romans, he persisted in bringing into Jerusalem the images which were on the military ensigns; and by this

and oth r acts of insult and oppression, he raised frequent tumults among even those of the Jewish people who were the most inclined to submit to the Roman government.

3. But the government of Pilate is made chiefly memorable by the public appearance, ministry, and death of JESUS CHRIST. His birth has already been mentioned. Of his history, while he remained in private life, that is, until he attained the age of thirty years, little further is known than that he remained with his parents at Nazareth in Galilee, to which town they had returned as soon as the death of Herod rendered it safe for

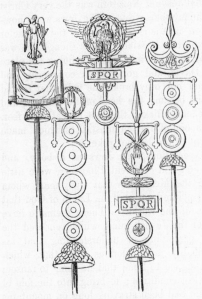

148. Roman Standards.

them to leave Egypt. His actual appearance as the expected Messiah, was harbingered by John the Baptist, who had lived in the solitudes of the wilderness, clad in hairy raiment, and subsisting on locusts and wild honey, and came thence to the river Jordan, where, by his preaching of repentance and remission of sins, with his baptism of those who came to him, he attracted great attention. But the interest of his countrymen was increased when he announced that he came but as a forerunner of One whose sandal-thong he was not himself worthy to unloose. This accorded with the expectations then prevalent among the Jewish people, that the time for the coming of the long-desired Messiah, the Deliverer, was very near. This expectation was founded on a calculation of the time mentioned by Daniel the prophet,[*] which calculation still remains as one of the strongest evidences that Jesus of Nazareth was the very Christ of whom Moses and the prophets wrote. The Jews were, however, utterly mistaken in their conception of the character and offices of the expected Messiah. They thought he was to appear as a great and glorious king, claiming his place upon the throne of David, and going forth conquering and to conquer, until Israel not only broke the yoke that fretted her neck, but until she became the head of the nations, and the proudest of her enemies licked the dust beneath her feet. This expectation was one of the circumstances which made the nation so impatient of the Roman yoke.

4. With such expectations, the Jews as a body, and especially the proud and self-confident Pharisees, were little prepared to recognise the Messiah in that lowly man, whom soon after the Baptist pointed out as "the Lamb of God that taketh away the sins of the world." There seems to have been a thick mist over the Jewish mind, which rendered the nation incapable of perceiving or understanding that his mission was indescribably more glorious than that which their worldly minds assigned to him; that he came to ransom mankind from their lost condition; to bring into the fold of God other sheep, which had been straying long on mountains and in wildernesses of ignorance and ungodliness; to bring into the world a hope full of immortality; and to furnish mankind with higher and purer motives, feelings, and principles of action than had yet been known on the earth. This the Jews would not and could not understand, as they liked far better to see in the Messiah a great king and warrior, clad with the visible glory of his father David. Although, therefore, they confessed that no man ever spake as he spoke, that no man ever did such marvellous things as he did; although he raised the dead, healed all manner of diseases, gave sight to the blind and hearing to the deaf, and fed seven thousand with the bread of ten people, yet they refused to receive him as "the Christ of God." Nay, more, the claims which he

[*] "Seventy weeks," meaning weeks of years, or seventy multiplied by seven being 490 years.

advanced were, as coming from him, so opposed to rooted opinions, by which the national pride was flattered; his announcement of the termination of the Mosaical system was so abhorrent to the same feeling; his reproofs of the reigning evils were so unsparing, that he was not only rejected but hated by the teachers and leaders of the people. They spared no pains to accomplish his death; and at length, three years after the commencement of his ministry, at the Passover of the year A. D. 33, they brought him to the scourge, the thorny crown, the transfixing nails, and the cross of a Roman execution.

5. In that act of blood the doom of the Jewish nation was sealed. The rent veil of the Temple indicated the end of the Mosaic dispensation, and the completion of the purposes for which the descendants of Abraham had hitherto been preserved as a nation. The light of Israel went out in that darkness which overspread the land when the dying Saviour cried " It is finished !"

But the grave could not retain him. On the third day he rose, and after meeting several times with his followers, discoursing with them and partaking of their food, on the fortieth day he ascended, visibly, up into the heavens from which he came. Soon after, at the feast of Pentecost, he sent down upon his chosen followers that enlightenment of the Holy Spirit, which was needful to qualify them for making known his doctrines to all the world.

6. The Roman governor, Pilate, being the person in whom rested the power of life and death, necessarily took part in the death of Christ. To ensure the conviction of Jesus, the Jews charged him with a political crime, that of sedition. Had the power been with them, they would have stoned him. Pilate, however, saw very plainly that there was no real ground of charge against him, and was reluctant to condemn him. But, on the other hand, he was at that time anxious to gratify the Jewish people, and was fearful of the impressions which the jealous and suspicious Tiberius might receive from their accounts of the transaction. He therefore yielded to their clamour; but, in doing so, vainly sought to clear his own hands from the stain

of innocent blood, and to cast it upon their heads. They received it gladly, shouting, "His blood be on us, and on our children!"—and awfully were their words fulfilled. Christ himself, not long before his death, predicted that the existing generation should not pass away before their city and Temple should be destroyed, with fearful sufferings of the people.

7. In the year that Christ was crucified, the tetrarch Philip died; and as he had no sons, his territories were annexed to the Roman province of Syria. As to the surviving tetrarch, Herod Antipas, he put John the Baptist in prison, on account of his public reprobation of a very unseemly act of which he had been guilty. He took Herodias, the wife of his living brother, and married her himself, putting away his former legitimate wife, a daughter of the king of Arabia-Petræa. Herod had no wish or intention to put John to death, but was reluctantly induced to do so in compliance with a foolish vow which the dancing of the daughter of Herodias extracted from him. He afterwards happened to be at Jerusalem when Christ was brought before Pilate, and that person, hearing that the accused belonged to Galilee, sent him to the tetrarch of that district. Herod was glad to see him, having heard much of his preaching and miracles; but, finding that Jesus was not disposed to gratify his curiosity, he treated him with insult, and sent him back to Pilate. This civility between the governor and the tetrarch, at the expense of Jesus, paved the way for making up a misunderstanding which had existed between them.

8. Pilate retained his government some years longer, and continued his oppressions and exactions, among which may be reckoned his attempt to drain the treasury of the Temple, under cover of making it chargeable for the expenses of carrying an aqueduct into Jerusalem. At length, a gross outrage upon the Samaritans, in which a number of innocent people were put to the sword, occasioned such complaints to Vitellius, the governor of Syria, that he ordered Pilate home, to give an account of his conduct to the emperor.

Tiberius was dead before he arrived, and his successor, Caligula, banished him to Vienne in Gaul, where he is said to have perished miserably by his own hand.

9. After having sent Pilate home, Vitellius himself went to Jerusalem (although he had been there lately) to allay the ferment which had arisen among the Jews. He was accompanied by Herod, and acted with temper and discretion. He removed the high-priest, appointed Marcellus procurator for the interim, and received the oaths of allegiance to the new emperor.

10. Marcellus was soon superseded as procurator by Mar... who was sent out by Caligula.

CHAPTER IV.   A. D. 36 TO 64.

PALESTINE.

	A. D.
Herod Antipas in Galilee, &c.	1
King Herod Agrippa in Trachonitis, &c.	38
Herod Agrippa, king of Judæa	41

ROMAN PROCURATORS.

	A. D.
Cuspius Fadius	44
Tiberius Alexander	46
Ventidius Cumanus	47
Felix	52
Porcius Festus	60
Albinus	63

ROME.

	A. D.
Caligula	37
Claudius	41
Nero	54

GENERAL HISTORY.

	A. D.
Jewish embassy to Caligula	40
Claudius's expedition into Britain	43
Martyrdom of James the Elder	44
Council of Apostles at Jerusalem	49
Paul imprisoned at Jerusalem	59
Paul's first visit to Rome	61
Martyrdom of James the Less	62
Paul liberated	63

PERSONS.

	A. D.
Columella	32
Philo Judæus	39
Persius	37
Seneca	52
Petronius Arbiter	61
Lucan	62
Quintus Curtius	64

1. WE must now remind the reader of the two sons of
Herod the Great by the Asamonean Mariamne, whom their
father had put to death. One of them, Aristobulus, left a
son called Herod Agrippa, who was sent to Rome, and brought
up there in the imperial family. While Tiberius lived, he
attached himself to Caligula, and became his intimate friend
and companion. An unguarded expression of the wish that
his friend might soon be emperor, was reported to Tiberius,
who threw him into prison, laden with chains. The first act
of Caligula, when he came to the throne, was to liberate
Herod Agrippa, and to bestow on him a chain of gold, of the
same weight as the one of iron which he had worn for his
sake. Nor was this all: he bestowed on him the tetrarchy
of his late uncle Philip, together with that of Abilene, with
the title of king. This unexpected advancement of his
nephew was highly unpalatable to Herod Antipas, who,
greatly coveting the royal title himself, went to Rome to
endeavour to obtain it; but in seeking it he lost all, and was
sent to join Pilate at Vienne in Gaul. His territory was
given to the fortunate Agrippa; Judæa and Samaria were

added a few years after; so that the kingdom of Herod the Great was once more reconstructed in behalf of his grandson.

2. The government of Agrippa was acceptable to the Jews. He was anxious to satisfy them; and his influence at Rome enabled him to be of real use to them. Caligula grew intoxicated with power, and wished to be worshipped as a god. The Jews were likely to have been in much difficulty through their resistance to the introduction of his image into their Temple. The emperor was greatly enraged; but at length the solicitations of Agrippa gave effect to the remonstrances of a deputation from the Jews, and the Temple was reluctantly exempted from the threatened pollution. Caligula died soon after; and the part taken by Agrippa in promoting the succession of Claudius, procured him the gratitude and favour of that emperor. It was he who added Judæa to his kingdom.

3. It appears to have been less from an intolerant disposition, than from a wish to please the Jews, at all hazards, that Herod Agrippa persecuted the Christians. He put the apostle James, the brother of John, to death, and Peter escaped only through the interposition of an angel.

4. Latterly the mind of Herod was so inflated by the sense of his increasing power and greatness, that he received with complacency the salutations of the people, who, on some public occasion, hailed him as a god in the theatre of Cæsarea. A grievous and loathsome disease with which he was immediately smitten, and of which he soon died, convinced him and them that he was a mortal man.

5. His son Agrippa was only seventeen years of age, and was deemed too young to be put in possession of the dominions of his father. When, however, three years after, his uncle Herod, king of Chalcis, died, the emperor gave him that kingdom, to which was annexed the government of the Temple at Jerusalem, and the power of appointing and removing the high-priests. Afterwards a more important kingdom was given him for that of Chalcis. It was composed of the provinces of Batanea, Gaulonitis, Trachonitis, and Abilene. But on the death of Herod Agrippa, Judæa was again reduced to the condition of a Roman province, in which state it afterwards remained.

6. Under the successive governments of Cuspius Fadius, of Tiberius Alexander, and of Ventidius Cumanus, which together occupied not more than eight years, various acts of tumult, popular frenzy, delusion, and crime, afford indications to the careful observer of the commencement of that troubled condition of society which ended in the destruction of Jerusalem and the ruin of the nation.

7. After these, Claudius gave the government of Judæa to his freedman, Felix. He was the brother of Pallas, the celebrated freedman and favourite of that emperor. The common observation, that the government of a slave is always tyrannous, was confirmed in the case of Felix. He acted with great severity, and with utter disregard of public opinion. He began his government by clearing the country of the numerous banditti, and the clandestine assassins called Sicarii,* by whom it was infested. The great principle of conduct in Felix was the same as that ascribed to Turkish Pashas in our day,—he was bent on making a fortune for himself during the limited period of his government. To this end there was nothing mean, cruel, unjust, or extortionate to which he did not resort; and this conduct went far to extend and strengthen that impatience of the Roman yoke, which had long existed, and which was soon to rise to a kind of madness. Indeed it was such already; for constantly were enthusiasts and impostors starting up, declaring themselves divinely commissioned to deliver the nation from the Roman bondage. The general expectation of such a deliverer, secured followers for the wildest of those impostors ; and so numerous were they, that scarcely a day passed in which several of them were not put to death. The deluded people who listened to them were destroyed like vermin by the Roman troops. The procurator is the same Felix whose name occurs in the Acts of the Apostles (xxiv.)—the same who " trembled" when the apostle reasoned before him " of righteousness, temperance, and judgment to come,"—the same who kept Paul in prison, expecting to obtain money for his ransom. About that time, however, his government became so intolerable to the Jews, that they

---

* They obtained this name from using poniards bent like the Roman *Sicæ*. It was their practice to mingle with the crowds, having these poniards under their garments, and then using them as they saw occasion.

sent a deputation to complain of his conduct to the emperor Nero. He was then recalled; and the influence of his brother Pallas alone preserved him from a severer punishment.

8. Felix was succeeded by Porcius Festus, whose character in history is much fairer than that of his predecessor. He proceeded to act with great vigour against the robbers and Sicarii, who again swarmed in the land, and acted with incredible boldness, spreading terror through the very heart of Jerusalem. He next applied himself to allay the discords which raged between the superior and inferior priests, and which, in a country where the ecclesiastical institutions were still so prominent as in Judæa, could not be carried on without involving all the interests of the state. No one can examine the history of this period without perceiving that the leaders of the people, whether priests or laymen, were, as Josephus, who knew them well, describes, as vile miscreants as ever lived. The immediate cause of quarrel among the priests was connected with the frequent changes of the persons holding the office of the high-priest, and the extravagant claims of the persons who had once enjoyed that dignity. These, in the course of time, formed a considerable body, and as they all claimed the pontifical portion out of the tithes, there was not enough left for the subsistence of the inferior priesthood. The vigour with which the claim was enforced, and the vehemence with which it was resisted, led to the most scandalous outrages. They engaged partisans and employed assassins against each other; and not only was the country kept in a continual ferment, but the very sanctuary was often desecrated by their broils, and stained with their blood. By his resolute conduct and wholesome severities, Festus in some degree subdued this disgraceful strife. He received much trouble from the enthusiasts and false prophets who from time to time appeared, exciting the multitude by their promises of deliverance. In the midst of these labours Festus died, after he had held the government only two years.

9. Albinus, his successor, thought only of enriching himself. His severities were reserved for poor rogues who could produce no money; but the most atrocious criminals who could bribe sufficiently high, were sure of impunity. As crime yielded him a rich harvest of bribes and ransoms, he

was but little anxious to put it down, and his course of action gave it great encouragement; so that he was declared to be the real head of all the robbers in the country.

10. But bad as Albinus was, he was greatly surpassed in oppression and cruelty by Gessius Florus, who was sent out to supersede him. This man seems, indeed, to have been the very worst, as he was the last, of the Roman governors. Other governors had been tyrannical, cruel, avaricious; but the tyranny of Florus knew no bounds, his cruelty was a habit, and his avarice was utterly insatiable. He gave protection to all robbers who would divide the spoil with him, and thus practically gave a license to all kinds of violence and spoliation. His mal-administration was so outrageous as must have insured his disgrace, had it been made a subject of complaint at Rome; and the knowledge of this made him do his utmost to urge on the tendencies of the people to intestine commotion and open revolt, hoping that, in the storm, the voice of complaint against him would not be heard, and that a wider field for spoliation would be opened up. The measures of Florus can, however, only be said to have hastened by a few years that result which the madness of the people had made inevitable

CHAPTER V. A. D. 64 TO 70.

JUDÆA.		ROME.	
	A. D.		A. D.
Gessius Florus, Procurator	64	Nero	54
War with the Romans	65	Galba	68
Vespasian invades Judæa	68	Otho	69
Titus takes and destroys Jerusalem	70	Vitellius	69
		Vespasian	69

1. THE condition of the country became so deplorable, that a great number of the well-disposed inhabitants sought in foreign countries that peace which was denied them in their own. The land was distracted by tumult, and over-run by robbers, who, professing to be actuated by zeal for liberty and religion, plundered, without mercy, the defence-less towns and villages which refused to give in their adhesion to what was called the patriot cause. Meanwhile justice was sold by the Roman governor, and even the sacred office of the high-priesthood was offered to the highest bidder. Hence those who got that dignity were often profligate wretches, who, having obtained the office by bribes, used it for their own purposes, and maintained themselves in it by the darkest iniquities. Being of different sects and parties, of which there was now a great number, they, and the leading men of the nation, acted with all the animosity of sectarianism against each other. With such examples in their superiors, the ordinary priests and the scribes became, in the highest degree, dissolute and unprincipled; while the mass of the people abandoned themselves to all evil; and seditions, ex-tortions, and robberies, were matters of every day occurrence. The bands of society were loosened; and it became clear that the nation was fast ripening for destruction.

2. Some transactions at Cæsarea gave occasion for the actual outbreak. That place, the seat of the Roman gover-nor, was built by Herod, and had a mixed population of Syrians and Jews. It was disputed between these two classes, to which of them the city really belonged. The dis-

pute had been referred to the emperor, and about this time the decree was announced in favour of the Syrians, whose boundless exultation greatly exasperated all the Jews, who had felt a prodigious interest in the question. This, with insults on their religion, of which the governor refused to take cognizance, fanned into a flame the smouldering embers of revolt. Acting upon the impulse thus given, a party of hot-brained young men surprised a Roman garrison at Massada, near the Dead Sea, and put all the soldiers to the sword. The act was recognised at Jerusalem, where the leaders of the nation openly threw off their allegiance, by the refusal of the priests any longer to offer up the usual sacrifices for the prosperity of the Roman empire. There also the popular party rose upon and slew the Roman garrison; and the palace and the public offices were destroyed by fire. Indescribable barbarities were also committed by the " patriot" party upon the quietly-disposed citizens. This example produced a general insurrection, in which the Jews on the. one side, and the Romans and Syrians on the other, attacked each other with the greatest fury; and in every city there was war, massacre, and spoliation.

3. On the first news of this revolt, the president of Syria, Cestius Gallus, marched a powerful army into Judæa, and advanced against Jerusalem. Strange to say, he was defeated by the insurgents with great slaughter; and the military engines which fell into the hands of the victors, were of great use to them in the subsequent defence of the city. The honour of Rome was now engaged to avenge this disgrace, and no thinking man for a moment doubted the result. Nero sent the able and experienced Vespasian into Syria (who was accompanied by his son Titus), with the quality of president, tᴏ take the conduct of the war.

4. Vespasian commenced operations in the spring of A. D. 67, with an army of 60,000 men. Instead of going at once to Jerusalem, he employed himself in reducing Galilee, and in recovering the fortresses which had been taken by the insurgents. In this he met with considerable resistance, and had many occasions of witnessing the desperate valour of the insurgents. At Jotapata he was opposed by Josephus, the historian of the war, to whom the pro-

visional Jewish government had confided the defence of Galilee. The fortress fell, and Josephus was taken alive. He was at first treated rather roughly, but afterwards with consideration and respect. At the commencement of the campaign, the Romans behaved with great severity wherever they came. No mercy was shown to age or sex; but cities, towns, and villages were cruelly ravaged and destroyed. Nor were these desolations confined to Judæa; for in many foreign cities in which Jews were settled, they were slaughtered in multitudes by the Roman soldiers and the other inhabitants. Some idea of these dreadful massacres may be formed from the facts, that above 20,000 Jews were slain in one day at Cæsarea, 13,000 in one night at Scythopolis, 50,000 at Alexandria, 8000 at Joppa, and above 10,000 at Damascus. Nor need we wonder at such extent of destruction among a people who were so infatuated as to rush into a warfare, in which, according to Josephus, the odds were so fearfully against them.

5. Though the war was steadily prosecuted, Vespasian evinced no haste to march against Jerusalem; and when urged by his impatient officers, he told them that it was better to let the Jews destroy one another. In fact, he knew well how destructively the factions were raging against each other in Jerusalem. There were three of these factions, afterwards reduced to two, holding possession of different parts of the city. They wasted their strength in cruel conflicts with each other; in which they even destroyed the storehouses of corn and provisions which formed the only resource against famine in the threatened siege. In one thing, however, they all agreed,—in harassing, plundering, and destroying the citizens and nobles who did not enter into their views. Thus they obtained little real benefit from the respite which arose from the attention of the Roman army being diverted for a while from them by the revolution which at this time happened in imperial Rome, in consequence of the death of Nero. Galba, Otho, Vitellius, were invested with the purple in quick succession; and at length, with general approbation, Vespasian himself was declared emperor by the army in Judæa. He then departed for Rome, leaving the conduct of the war to his son Titus.

6. At the feast of the Passover, in the ensuing year. when the city of Jerusalem was, as usual at tnat time, crowded with people from all quarters, the Roman army appeared before the walls. It was probably his anxiety to save the city and the Temple, that induced Titus to commence the siege at this season; as it might have been expected, that where such multitudes were shut up in an ill-provisioned city, famine alone would soon make a surrender inevitable. The besieged were very earnestly invited to open their gates to the Romans, and were with all sincerity assured of their liberty and safety. Josephus was also commissioned to harangue them, and to point out to them the folly of supposing that they could hold out against, or successfully resist, the might of Rome. But all warning and counsel were treated with insult and scorn; and the factions expressed the resolution of defending the place to the very last, in the confidence that God would not permit his Temple and city to fall before the heathen. Such repeated refusals of mercy and compassion, and the very desperate defence made by the besieged, compelled Titus, much against his own will, to become the unconscious instrument of accomplishing that doom of the city and the Temple, which Christ had nearly forty years before denounced. The folly of resistance was so clear to Titus, that he became exasperated at the unpleasant task which their obstinacy imposed upon him. Resolved that none of them should escape, but such as surrendered to him, he raised around the city a strong wall of circumvallation, strengthened with towers. This great work was accomplished in the short space of three days.

7. The city was very strong, being enclosed by three walls, one within another; and then there was the Temple, which itself was an exceedingly strong fortress. All these defences were successively carried by the Romans, although every step was desperately contested by the besieged.

CHAPTER VI. A. D. 70 to 1076.

1. AFTER the Roman armies were withdrawn from Jerusalem, many of the Jews returned to dwell among its ruins,
though the Roman emperor, indignant at the late rebellion,
had placed a garrison of 800 troops on Mount Zion, in order
to prevent any attempt to rebuild the city. A portion of the
country was yet, indeed, unscathed by the flames of war; the
towns on the coast, submitting to the Romans, escaped the
horrors of a siege and the penalties of rebellion, while the
provinces beyond Jordan enjoyed tranquillity under the rule
of the conquerors. But the Jews were discontented and rebellious under the yoke of Rome; they still fondly believed
that an earthly Messiah was shortly to arise, to free them from
bondage, and to give them the dominion of the whole earth.
They accordingly listened to the tales of every impostor, and
were easily seduced into rebellion by vain hopes of national
glory, that were never realised. Hence their continual insurrections, which exposed them still farther to the vengeance of
the conquerors, and accelerated the crisis of their fate, when
they were to be driven altogether from their own land, and
dispersed over the face of the earth. In the course of these
commotions great cruelties were committed; but in the end
the Jews were everywhere borne down by the discipline of
the Roman legions, and paid the penalty of their rebellion
with their lives. By acts of mutual cruelty, the animosity of
both parties was inflamed; the sword of persecution was let
loose against the Jewish religion by their conquerors; the
rite of circumcision, the reading of the law, and the observance
of the Jewish Sabbath, and all the other memorials of the
national faith, were forbidden. In the city of Jerusalem,
which was to a certain extent repaired, and received the
name of Ælia Capitolina, a colony of Greeks and Latins was
established, in order to preclude the return of the Jews, and
all further hopes of the restoration of their kingdom. But

the policy of the Romans was of no avail against the deep-rooted prejudices of this infatuated people; and no sooner had a new impostor arisen, of the name of Simon Barcochab (*son of a star*), than the deluded Israelites hailed him as the light that was to dawn in the latter days, and usher in the day of their long-expected rest. They accordingly crowded to his standard; and in a short time he had mustered a powerful army of 200,000 devoted followers. Owing to the absence of the Roman legions, engaged at that time in distant service, important advantages were gained, and Jerusalem was again occupied by the insurgent Jews, besides about fifty castles, and numbers of open towns. But this career of success was speedily terminated by the arrival of Severus, afterwards emperor, with a large and well-appointed body of legionary troops; the Jews were overwhelmed by numbers, discipline, and military skill; their cities were taken and destroyed; and Bither, where the leader of the rebellion, Barcochab, had made his last stand, was stormed with great slaughter, and himself slain. Of the Jews, it is estimated that 580,000 died on the field, and the remnant that escaped mostly perished by famine and disease, or amid the flames of their ruined cities. Under these ruthless devastations the country was at last converted into a desert; the inhabitants were either slain or driven into exile; and the divine denunciations were now fully accomplished against this misguided people, that they should be scattered among all the nations of the earth.

2. The victors having thus satiated their vengeance, began in due time to relax their stern and intolerant policy. Under the mild rule of Antoninus Pius, the Jews were restored to their ancient privileges, to the freedom of worship, and to all their other national rites. They were now mingled with the nations, and were found dwelling in all parts of the Roman empire; and their general condition under the Roman emperors was not unfavourable. The numerous remains of that people, though they were excluded from the precincts of Jerusalem, were permitted to form and to maintain considerable establishments both in Italy and in the provinces, to acquire the freedom of Rome, to enjoy municipal honours, and to obtain at the same time an exemption from burdensome and expensive offices. The moderation or indifference of the

Romans gave a legal sanction to the form of ecclesiastical police which was instituted by the vanquished sect. The patriarch, who had fixed his residence at Tiberias, was empowered to appoint his subordinate ministers to exercise a domestic jurisdiction, and to receive from his dispersed brethren an annual contribution. New synagogues were frequently erected in the principal cities of the empire ; and the sabbaths, the fasts, and the festivals, which were either commanded by the Mosaic law, or enjoined by the traditions of the rabbins, were celebrated in the most solemn and public manner. Such gentle treatment insensibly mollified the stern temper of the Jews, and, awakened from their dream of misinterpreted prophecy and conquest, they assumed the behaviour of peaceable and industrious subjects.

3. No great change appears to have taken place in the condition of Palestine, until Constantine ascended the imperial throne. He was, as is well known, the first Christian emperor ; and under his powerful patronage, and that of his mother the Empress Helena, splendid structures were everywhere erected in the Holy Land, in honour of the Christian faith. The land was gradually overspread with memorials of Christianity; and chapels, altars, and houses of prayer marked every spot which was memorable for any of the sayings or doings of the Saviour. The Jews beheld with indignation the rise of these Christian monuments within the precincts of the holy city. They were as much opposed to the Christian worship as to the heathen idolatry, but their influence was now at an end. Scattered in distant parts, they could no longer act with consistency or vigour ; yet, so attached were they to their peculiar rites, that, however faint the chance of success, they were ready in crowds to rally round the standard of their ancient faith, wherever it was displayed, and to follow any daring leader into the field. But the time was past. They were rejected by the divine decree, and were no longer to be assembled as a nation in their own land. Jerusalem was now filled with the emblems of a new faith, and crowds of pilgrims were attracted from the most distant countries, by the eager desire of contemplating the place of the Redeemer's passion, and of all the previous incidents of his holy life. These visits were encouraged from various

T

motives. They evinced, no doubt, the zeal of the new converts; and being at once an apparent proof of piety and a real source of profit, they were encouraged by the clergy at Jerusalem.

4. The reign of Julian was a new era in the history of Palestine, and the Jews anticipated, from his declared enmity to Christianity, his favour for their own faith. The policy of this heathen emperor countenanced them in this belief, when he endeavoured, by rebuilding the Temple of Jerusalem in its former splendour, to discredit the truth of those prophesies which declared the extinction of the ritual service. He chose the commanding eminence of Mount Moriah for the site of a new structure, which was to eclipse the splendour of the Christian church on the adjacent hill of Calvary; and he resolved to establish a Jewish order of priests, who might revive the observance of the Mosaic rites, together with as numerous a colony of Jews as could be collected, in the holy city. Such was still the ardour of the national faith, that the Jews crowded from all parts, and exasperated, by their insolent triumph, the hostility of the Christian inhabitants. All now joined with unwearied zeal in the sacred work of rebuilding the Temple. Liberal contributions poured in from all quarters; men and women joined in the pious labour; and the authority of the monarch was seconded by the enthusiasm of the people. But this last effort of expiring zeal was unsuccessful; no Temple ever arose on the ruins of the heathen edifices; and a Mohammedan mosque still stands on the ground of the Jewish Temple. The work, from whatever cause, was abandoned; and as it was only undertaken during the last six months of Julian's reign, the fact seems sufficiently explained by the absence and death of the emperor, and by the new maxims that were adopted during the Christian reign that succeeded, without the aid of the alleged miracle to which it has been usually ascribed.

5. After the death of Julian, it was the policy of the Christian emperors to depress the Jews in Palestine, though they were not ill-treated throughout the provinces, and were even granted considerable privileges and immunities. But it is astonishing how carefully fathers instilled into the minds

of their children, along with their ancient faith, the fondly cherished delusion, that some new and happier era of freedom and independence was yet to dawn on Israel; and how eagerly the children, imbibing this idea, became the prey of every impostor, and, under the blind impulse of enthusiasm, rashly entered into new conflicts with their enemies in the field, where they perished, the willing victims of a hopeless cause. About the beginning of the seventh century, the peace of Judæa was seriously disturbed by the Persian invasion of Khosroes. The Greeks and the Persians were for a long period rivals for the dominion of the east; and Khosroes, the grandson of Nushirvan, now invading the Roman empire, stormed and sacked the city of Antioch. From Syria the flood of invasion rolled southward on Palestine, and the Persian army was joined by the Jews to the number of 24,000, still burning with the love of independence. The Christians and Jews were inflamed against each other by a long course of deep injuries given and received. Those of the former nation within the walls of Jerusalem were massacred without mercy by their Christian enemies, while the Jews on the outside were burning with the desire of revenge. The advance of the Persians secured the triumph. The city was stormed by the combined armies, and the Jews were satiated with a full measure of revenge. The Christians neither sought nor found mercy; it was estimated that 90,000 of them perished in the storming of the city. Some were sold for slaves, and others were bought for the purpose of being slaughtered. The city was sacked, and the magnificent monuments of the Christian faith were mostly consumed by fire. But this, like all the other triumphs of the Jews, was short-lived. The eastern emperor, Heraclius, was roused from inglorious sloth by the triumphs of the Persian arms, and by the approach of the victorious force to the walls of his own capital. He quickly assembled his veteran armies, by whose aid he defeated the troops of Khosroes; and in the course of a few successful campaigns recovered all the provinces that had been overrun. He visited Jerusalem after his victories in the lowly guise of a pilgrim, and prepared new triumphs for the Christians in the restoration of the magnificent churches which had been destroyed, and

N

in the persecution of the Jews, and their banishment, as before, from the holy city, which they were now forbidden to
approach within a nearer distance than three miles.

6. Palestine continued to own the sway of the Greek
emperor till the rise of the Arabian power in the East.   The
followers of Mohammed, extending their doctrines and their
dominion by fire and sword, rapidly subdued Arabia, Syria,
and Egypt, when, about the year 637, the victorious Omar
turned his arms against Jerusalem.   After a siege of four
months, during which the Arabs suffered extremely from the
inclemency of the winter, a capitulation was proposed and
agreed to, when the conqueror entered the city seated on a
red camel, which carried a bag of corn and dates, and without guards, or any other precaution.   Omar was assassinated
at Medinah, in the year 644, after which, the East was for
two hundred years distracted by the bloody wars that ensued
among the Ommiades, the Abbassides, and the Fatimite
caliphs; and Palestine having become an object of contest between them, was for a like period a scene of devastation and
trouble.   In the year 868, the capital was conquered by
Achmet, a Turk; but was again recovered by the caliphs of
Baghdad in the year 906.   It was reduced by Mohammed
Ikschid, of the Turkish race.   Towards the end of the tenth
century, the holy city was taken possession of by Ortok; and
in 1076, by Meleschah, a Turk.   It was retaken by the
Ortokides, and finally by the Fatimites, who held possession
of it when the Crusaders made their first appearance in the
Holy Land.

CHAPTER VII.   A. D. 1076 to 1203.

1. JERUSALEM, though it was in possession of Moslem chiefs, was still revered as a holy city by both Christian and Jew, and was visited by pilgrims from every quarter; among others by Peter the hermit, a native of Amiens. The pathetic tale which he brought to Europe, of the injuries and insults which the Christian pilgrims suffered from the infidels, who possessed and profaned the holy city, excited the deepest sympathy among the people and princes of Christendom. Councils were summoned, and were attended by bishops, a numerous train of ecclesiastics, and by thousands of the laity. The mixed multitude were harangued by the zealous enthusiasts of this sacred cause; their pity and indignation were alternately roused by the sufferings of their brethren in the Holy Land; the flame of enthusiasm was propagated by sympathy and example; and the eager champions of the cross, the flower of the European chivalry, assembled in martial array, to march against the enemies of their common faith. To defray the necessary expenses of the expedition, princes alienated their provinces, nobles their lands and castles, peasants their cattle and instruments of husbandry; and vast armies were transported to Palestine, in order to accomplish the deliverance of the holy sepulchre. These rude and undisciplined bands died in great numbers on reaching the shores of Asia, from disease, famine, and fatigue; and of the first Crusaders, it is estimated that 300,000 had perished before a single city was rescued from the infidels. Of the leaders in the Christian host, the first rank is due to Godfrey, Duke of Brabant and Bouillon, who was accompanied by his two brothers, Eustace the elder, who had succeeded to the county of Boulogne, and Baldwin the younger. The other chiefs were, Robert of France, the brother of King Philip; Robert, Duke of Normandy, the son of William the Conqueror; Bohemond, the son of Robert Guiscard; Tancred his cousin, and Raymond of Thoulouse. The vast armies that were

collected under the guidance of these leaders arrived by various routes at Constantinople, the Greek capital; after having lost, some say, half their number, in the intermediate march through untried regions, by famine, disease, and the assaults of the inhabitants into whose countries they had made so unexpected an irruption. After some time spent in the capital of the East, they crossed to the opposite shore of Asia. Having taken the towns of Nice and Antioch in the year 1098, they, about a year after, laid siege to Jerusalem, and carried it by assault, with a prodigious slaughter of the garrison and inhabitants, which was continued for three days, without respect either to age or sex.

2. Eight days after the capture of Jerusalem, the Latin chiefs proceeded to the election of a king, who should preside over their conquests in Palestine, and Godfrey of Bouillon was unanimously raised to this high office. But if it was an honourable office, it was also one of danger; he was not chosen to sway a peaceful sceptre; and he was summoned to the field in the first fortnight of his reign, to defend his capital against the sultan of Egypt, who approached with a powerful army. The signal overthrow of the latter in the battle of Ascalon confirmed the stability of the Latin throne, and enabled Godfrey to extend on every side his infant kingdom, which consisted only of Jerusalem and Jaffa, with about twenty villages and towns of the adjacent districts. The fortified castles, in which the Mohammedans had taken refuge, and from which they made incursions into the open country, were reduced; the maritime cities of Læodicea, Tripoli, Tyre, and Ascalon, were besieged and taken; and the Christian kingdom thus included a range of sea-coast from Scanderoon to the borders of Egypt. Although the province of Antioch claimed independence, the courts of Edessa and Tripoli owned themselves the vassals of the king of Jerusalem; and the four cities of Hems, Hamah, Damascus, and Aleppo, were the only relics of the Mohammedan conquests in Syria. The feudal institutions of Europe were introduced into this kingdom in all their purity; and a code of laws, called the Assize of Jerusalem, was drawn up and deposited in the sepulchre of the Saviour, as an unerring guide in all doubtful questions that might be brought before the tribunals of the holy city.

3. Godfrey was succeeded by his brother Baldwin I., who ruled with vigour and success. In 1118 his nephew, Baldwin II., ascended the throne, and still maintained the interests of the kingdom. Melisandra his daughter, married Fulk, Count of Anjou, who, in right of his wife, acquired the kingdom of Jerusalem. He lost his life by a fall from his horse, after having reigned twelve years. His son, Baldwin III., ruled in Jerusalem twenty years; and his reign was remarkable as the era of the second Crusade, and of the rise of the various orders of knighthood,—the hospitallers, templars, and cavaliers.

4. The military force of the first Crusaders, wasted by fatigue, and by losses in the field, was no longer able to oppose the hosts of Turks and Saracens by which it was surrounded. The first victories of the Europeans, and their rapid success, extended far and wide the terror of their arms. But this alarm having subsided, the Mohammedan chiefs collected their armies, and commenced a vigorous attack on the European posts, scattered over a wide extent of country, and gained some important advantages. The accounts of these disasters that were circulated in Europe excited the liveliest sympathy of all Christians for their suffering brethren in the Holy Land, for the defence of which the European princes now entered into a new coalition. A second Crusade was the consequence. It was undertaken by Conrad III., emperor of Germany, and Louis VII. king of France, and was even more unfortunate than the first expedition. In the course of a tedious march through an unhealthy and hostile country, more than half the army of Conrad was wasted by famine and the sword, and not above a tenth part ever reached the Syrian shore. The subsequent battles with the Saracens reduced them to a miserable remnant; and on his return with his shattered forces from this unfortunate campaign, the emperor was met by Louis and the French troops, who arrived in better condition at the scene of action. The French army, rashly advancing into the heart of the country, was assaulted and overwhelmed by an innumerable host of Turks; and the king with great difficulty made his escape, and finally took shipping with his knights and nobles, leaving his plebeian infantry to the sword of the victorious enemy. The two princes proceeding to Jerusalem, united the poor remains of their once mighty armies to the Latin troops in Syria, and laid a fruitless siege to Damascus, which was the termination of the second Crusade.

5. The defeat and dispersion of these armies tended greatly to weaken the Christian cause in the Holy Land, and to shake the foundations of the Latin throne at Jerusalem. Baldwin, the son of Melisandra and the Count of Anjou, together with his brother Amaury or Almeric, long maintained the war with considerable success against the infidels. Baldwin, dying, was succeeded by his brother, who, after a reign of eleven years, transmitted the throne to his son Baldwin IV., disabled both in mind and body by the disease of leprosy. Sybilla, the mother of Baldwin, was the next heiress, who chose for her second husband, and consequently for king of Jerusalem, Guy of Lusignan, base in character, but handsome in his person. This choice was universally blamed, and excited the hatred of Count Raymond, who had been excluded from the succession and regency, and who, entertaining an implacable hatred against the king, was seduced into a traitorous correspondence with the Sultan. Many of the barons were also so dissatisfied, that they refused to take the oath of allegiance to the new king.

6. It was in the midst of these internal dissensions that the kingdom of the Latins was assailed by a new enemy, namely, the Sultan Saladin, who joined much generosity of character to valour, policy, and military skill. He had risen from a private station to the sovereignty of Egypt, and he had been for years extending his influence and dominions. A fortress had been seized by a soldier of fortune, Reginald of Chatillon, from which he issued with his followers to pillage the caravans and insult the Mohammedans, and he even threatened the holy cities of Medina and Mecca. Saladin complained of these injuries, and being refused satisfaction, invaded the Holy Land with an army of 80,000 horse and foot He advanced against Tiberias, to which he laid siege; and a decisive battle was hazarded by the king of Jerusalem, in defence of this important place. The two armies met on the plain of Tiberias, and in a sanguinary conflict, which lasted two days, the Christians were completely overthrown, with the loss of 30,000 men. The king, the Marquis of

Montserrat, and the master of the templars, with many of their followers, were made prisoners; and two hundred and thirty gallant knights of the cross were cruelly led out to execution after the battle. This great victory placed the whole country at the mercy of the conqueror. The Christians were left without a head; the towns and castles, drained of their governors, fell successively before Saladin's victorious force; and scarcely had three months elapsed when he appeared in arms before the gates of Jerusalem.

7. This city was in no condition to sustain a protracted siege. It was crowded with fugitives from every quarter, who here sought an asylum from the destroying sword; a disorderly throng of 100,000 persons was confined within the walls, but there were few soldiers. The queen was alarmed for the fate of her captive husband, and her government was feeble and indecisive. A defence was, however, maintained for fourteen days, during which the besiegers had effected a breach in the wall, and only waited the Sultan's orders for the assault. This last extremity was averted by a capitulation, by which it was agreed that all the Franks and Latins should quit Jerusalem, receiving a safe conduct to the ports of Syria and Egypt, that the inhabitants should be ransomed for a sum of money, and that those who were unable to pay it should remain slaves. These conditions were liberally interpreted and greatly mitigated by the generosity of the Sultan, who allowed the poor to be ransomed by wholesale for a moderate sum, and freely dismissed about 3000 more. In his interview with the Queen, he displayed the kindness and courtesy of his disposition, comforting her with his words, and even with his tears; he distributed liberal alms among the widows and orphans of those who were slain, and allowed the warlike knights of the hospital to continue their care of the sick for another year. He made his triumphant entry into the city, with waving banners and martial music; the Christian Church was converted into a mosque, and the glittering cross was taken down and dragged through the streets, amid the shouts of the Moslems. The whole country now submitted to the Sultan, whose victorious progress was first arrested by the resistance of Tyre, which was gallantly defended by Conrad. The Sultan, being foiled in all his at-

tempts to take this place, was finally compelled to raise the siege, and o retreat to Damascus.

8. The capture of Jerusalem by the infidels, and the decline of the Christian cause in Palestine, excited the deepest sorrow; the slumbering zeal of the European powers was aroused, and new expeditions were fitted out for the recovery of the holy city. Philip, king of France, Frederick Barbarossa, the emperor of Germany, and Richard I. of England, surnamed Cœur-de-Lion, assembled a large force, and, with the aid of Flanders, Frise, and Denmark, filled about 200 vessels with their troops. The first armaments landed at Tyre, the only remaining inlet of the Christians into the Holy Land, and no time was lost in commencing the celebrated siege of Acre, which was maintained with an enthusiasm that mocked at danger, and by feats of valour that were the theme of wonder, even in that romantic age. This memorable siege lasted for nearly two years, and was attended with a prodigious loss of men on both sides. At length, in the spring of the second year, the royal fleets of France and England cast anchor in the bay, with powerful reinforcements, and the brave defenders of Acre were reduced to capitulate. A ransom was demanded for their lives and liberties, of 200,000 pieces of gold, the deliverance of 100 nobles, and 1500 inferior captives, and the restoration of the holy cross, which had been taken at the battle of Tiberias. Thus was an important town and harbour obtained by the Christians, but by an enormous sacrifice of men. The host that surrounded Acre amounted at different periods to 600,000 ; of these, 100,000 were slain during the siege of two years, a greater number perished by shipwreck and disease, and it is computed that only a very small remnant reached their native shores. The place was taken possession of by the Christians on the 12th of July 1191.

9. The capture of Acre was the prelude to farther operations against the enemy. Richard determined to commence the siege of Ascalon, about a hundred miles distant, and his march to this place was a continual battle of eleven days. He was opposed by Saladin with an army of 300,000 combatants ; and on this occasion was fought one of the most memorable battles of this or any other age. Saladin was de-

feated with the loss of 40,000 men, and the victorious Richard
obtained possession of Ascalon, and the other towns of Judæa.
A severe winter interrupted the operations of the field. But
Richard, issuing from his winter quarters with the first gleam
of spring, advanced with his army within sight of Jerusalem,
the great object of his enterprise. Saladin had chosen Jerusalem for his head-quarters, where the sudden appearance of
the Christian conqueror spread universal consternation. The
holy city was, however, relieved by the hasty retreat of the
English king, discouraged by the difficulties of the enterprise
and the murmurs of his troops. In the meantime, the
town of Jaffa was vigorously assaulted by Saladin with a formidable force, and was on the point of surrendering, when
Richard, hastening to its relief, encountered the besieging
army of Saracens and Turks, amounting to 60,000 men, who
yielded to the vigour of his attack. In the meantime, the
miseries of a protracted war began to be severely felt, and the
energetic views of Richard were obstructed by the discontent
of his troops. Negociations were commenced, which were
broken off, and as often resumed. The views of both parties
varied with the fortune of war. At last, however, both Saladin and Richard were equally desirous of terminating an un-
popular and ruinous contest. The first demands of Richard
were, the restitution of Jerusalem, Palestine, and the true
cross. These terms were rejected by the Sultan, who would
not part with the sovereignty of Palestine, or listen to any
proposition for dismembering his dominions. A truce was at
length concluded for three years, by which it was stipulated
that the Latin Christians should have liberty to visit the holy
city without being liable to tribute; that the fort of Ascalon
should be dismantled; and that Jaffa and Tyre, with the intervening territory, should be surrendered to the Europeans.
Soon after the conclusion of this treaty Richard embarked for
Europe; and Saladin, his great rival, did not survive many
months the conclusion of peace.

10. The fourth Crusade was encouraged by the zeal of
Pope Celestine III. It was directed against the Greek empire, which was too feeble to resist so formidable an attack;
and the result was its conquest by the Latins, who ruled over
it for fifty-seven years.

CHAPTER VIII. A.D. 1203 to 1850.

1. In the meantime, though partial successes were gained by the armies of the Crusaders in Palestine, their power was on the decline.   A truce for six years had been concluded with Saphadin, the brother and successor of the Sultan Saladin.   The sovereign of the Latin kingdom at this time was Mary, the daughter of Isabella by Conrad of Tyre, Almeric and his wife being dead.   In order to strengthen the government of Jerusalem, it was resolved to request the king of France, Philip Augustus, to provide a husband for Mary. John de Brienne, one of the most accomplished cavaliers in Europe, of tried valour and experience in war, was chosen; and the Christian chiefs were so elated by this union, that they sought a pretence for breaking the subsisting truce between them and the Sultan, and bringing matters to the arbitration of the sword.   War accordingly ensued, and the new monarch of Jerusalem displayed all the great qualities of a statesman and a soldier, for which he was chosen ; and though his success did not entirely correspond to his hopes or wishes, yet he made a successful defence, and maintained for a time the Latin kingdom against the growing power of its enemies.   He foresaw, however, that its gradual decline and final ruin were approaching, as it was now reduced to two or three towns, and preserved only in a precarious existence by the divisions and civil wars that prevailed among its enemies.

2. This intelligence rekindled the dying zeal of the Christian world.   A new Crusade was commenced, and a large force, chiefly of Hungarians and Germans, landed at Acre. The sons of Saphadin, who now ruled in Syria, collected their armies to oppose this formidable attack.   But the Crusaders, rashly conducted, and weakened by divisions, advanced into the country without concert or prudence ; provisions failed them : they were wasted, as usual, by famine and disease ·

and at length their leader, the sovereign of Hungary, resolved to quit a country where he had been exposed to hardship and danger, without glory. The crusading armies, thus weakened and discouraged, had laid aside all further idea of offensive operations, when, in the spring of the following year, a fleet of 300 vessels, from the Rhine, appeared on the coast, and brought to their aid powerful reinforcements, which recruited their strength, and restored their ascendancy in the field For reasons which do not clearly appear, they now retired from Palestine, and carried the war into Egypt, where they obtained important successes, having taken Damietta by storm, and spread such consternation among the infidels, that the most favourable terms of peace were offered, and rejected by the Crusaders. Soon after, however, having wasted their strength on the banks of the Nile, they were reduced to the necessity of bargaining for permission to retire to Palestine, by the cession of all their conquests in Egypt.

3. The next Crusade was undertaken by Frederic II., the grandson of Barbarossa, according to a vow which had been long made, and the performance of which had been so long delayed, that he was excommunicated by Gregory IX. By his marriage with Violante, the daughter of John de Brienne, he was the more especially bound to vindicate his right to the kingdom of Jerusalem, which he had received as a dowry with his wife. After many delays, he set sail with a fleet of 200 ships and an army of 40,000 men, and arrived at Acre. This was the most successful and the most bloodless expedition that had yet been undertaken. Without the hazard of a battle Frederic entered Jerusalem in triumph. The Saracen power was at this time weakened by divisions; and, owing to suspected treachery among his kindred, Kamel, the son of Saphadin, held precarious possession of the throne. It was his policy, therefore, rather to disarm the hostility of these powerful armies by treating with them, than to encounter them in the field; and accordingly a treaty was concluded, by which Jerusalem, Jaffa, Bethlehem, Nazareth, and their dependencies, were restored to the Christians; religious toleration was established, and the contending parties of Christians and Mohammedans were allowed each to offer at their devotions, the first in the mosque El-Aksa, and the last in the

mosque of Omar.* But all these services were performed by
Frederic while under the stain of excommunication; and hence
the patriarch, when he made his entry into Jerusalem, refused to crown him, or to be present at the ceremonial; Frederic, therefore, himself took the crown from the holy sepulchre, and placed it on his own head. The stipulations of
this treaty were not faithfully observed by the Saracens, and
the Christians in Palestine still suffered under the oppression
of the infidels. New levies were raised in Europe for the
holy war, and a large force of French and English, led by the
chief nobility of both nations, landed in Syria. Numerous
battles were fought, which terminated in favour of the Saracens; and the French Crusaders, accordingly, after severe
losses, were glad to purchase peace by the cession of almost
all their conquests in Palestine. Next year, when the Earl
of Cornwall, with the English levy, arrived at the scene of
action, he found, to his surprise, that all the territories and
privileges which had been ceded to the emperor of Germany
were lost; and that a few fortresses, and a small strip of territory on the coast, comprised all that the Latins possessed in
Palestine. He immediately prepared for the vigorous prose-
cution of hostilities. But the Sultan, being involved in war
with his brother in Damascus, readily granted favourable
terms as the price of peace—namely, the cession to the Christian armies of Jerusalem, Beirut, Nazareth, Bethlehem, Mount
Tabor, and a large tract of the adjoining country. But the
kingdom of Jerusalem, thus so happily re-established, was sub-
verted by a calamity from a new and unexpected quarter. In
the interior of Asia the conquests of Ghenghis Khan had
brought about the most stupendous revolutions, and the barbarous hordes of the desert, flying before his conquering sword,
rushed like a torrent on other nations. The Kharismians,
unable to withstand this powerful invader, were driven upon
Syria, and the coalesced powers of Saracen and Christian were
unable to resist their powerful assault. The Christian host
was overthrown in a great battle, which lasted two days, and
in which the grand masters of two orders, and most of the

* Both these mosques stand on Mount Moriah; the Christians believed that the
mosque El-Aksa (which was originally a Christian church), and the Moslems that the
mosque of Omar, occupied the precise site of Solomon's Temple.

knights, were slain. The merciless invaders revelled in the sack and pillage of the holy city, sparing neither sex nor age; and it was not until the year 1247 that they were routed near Damascus, by the Syrians and Mamluks, and driven back to their former settlements on the Caspian Sea.

4. Each new disaster of the Christian arms served to rekindle the languishing zeal of the Europeans; and Louis IX. of France fitted out an immense armament for the Holy Land, consisting of 1800 sail, in which he embarked an army of 50,000 men. He landed in Egypt, and, after storming the town of Damietta, advanced along the sea-coast towards Cairo, when his troops were so wasted by sickness and famine, that they fell an easy prey to the enemy. The king, the most of his nobles, and the remnant of his army, were made prisoners; and it was owing to the clemency of the Sultan Moadhdham, who accepted a ransom for their lives, that Louis, with his few surviving followers, was permitted to embark for Palestine.

5. The power of the Christians in Palestine, weakened, among other causes, by internal dissensions, was now vigorously assailed by the Sultan Bibars, the Mamluk sovereign of Egypt. He invaded Palestine with a formidable army, advanced to the gates of Acre, and, reducing the towns of Sepphoris and Azotus, massacred or carried into captivity numbers of Christians. The important city of Antioch yielded to his powerful assault, when 40,000 of the inhabitants were put to the sword, and 100,000 carried into captivity. The report of these cruelties in Europe gave rise to the ninth and last Crusade against the infidels, which was undertaken by Louis, the French king, sixteen years after his return from captivity. In place of directing his arms immediately against Palestine, he landed in Africa, and laid siege to Carthage, which he reduced. But he perished miserably on the burning sands of Africa, of a pestilential disease, which proved fatal also to many of his troops; and thus ingloriously terminated this expedition, which was the last undertaken by the Europeans for the recovery of the Holy Land.

6. The Europeans in Palestine were now confined within the walls of Acre, their last stronghold, which was besieged by a Mamluk host of 200,000 troops, that issued from Egypt, and encamped on the adjacent plain. In this their last con-

flict with the infidels of the Holy Land, the Europeans fully
maintained the glory of their high name.   They displayed all
the devotion of martyrs in a holy cause, and performed prodigies of valour.   But, equalled as they were in discipline,
and fearfully overmatched in numbers, by their enemies, they
were overborne by the weight and violence of their attacks
and in the storm and sack of the city, all either perished or
were carried into captivity.   Thus terminated for ever all
those visions of glory and conquest by which so many adven-
turers were seduced from Europe to the Holy Land, there to
perish under the complicated perils of disease and the sword.
The other smaller towns which still remained in possession of
the Christians yielded without a struggle to the Moslem arms,
and, under the religious tyranny of the infidels which succeeded, the Christians in Palestine were everywhere reduced
to the lowest degree of debasement.   The pilgrims who still
visited Jerusalem were exposed to insult and danger; and
large contributions were exacted by their oppressors for a free
passage through the Holy Land.   The Mamluk Sultans of
Egypt continued to rule over Palestine till the year 1382,
when the country was overrun by a barbarous tribe from the
interior of Asia.   On their expulsion, the sovereignty of the
Egyptian Sultans was again acknowledged, until the country
yielded to the formidable irruption of the great Tamerlane.
At his death Jerusalem reverted to the kingdom of Egypt,
and was finally subdued by the Turks, under whose barbarous rule it has continued for more than 300 years.   The
country was partitioned into provinces, in each of which a
pasha ruled with a despotic authority equal to that of the
Sultan.

7. In this condition Palestine remained without any remarkable event in its history, except that for nearly three
centuries it was the scene of domestic broils, insurrections,
and massacres, until the memorable invasion of Egypt by the
French army.   Bonaparte, being apprised that preparations
were making in the pachalik of Acre for attacking him in
Egypt, resolved, according to his usual tactics, to anticipate
the movements of his enemies.   He accordingly marched
across the desert which divides Egypt from Palestine, and
invaded the country at the head of 10,000 troops.   El-Arish

surrendered, and the lives of the garrison were spared on condition that they should not serve against him during the war. Gaza also yielded without opposition; and Jaffa, stormed after a brave resistance, was given up to pillage. The French army then proceeded to form the siege of Acre; and this fortress, the last scene of conflict between the Christians and infidels of former days, became a modern field of battle, in which were exhibited prodigies of valour that rivalled the most renowned deeds of those chivalric times. The trenches were opened on the 10th of March; in ten days a breach was effected, and a desperate assault took place. At first the defenders were forced to give way; but Djezzar Pasha, who had shut himself within the walls, and who was aided by Sir Sidney Smith with a body of British sailors, rushed forward among the thickest of the combatants, and, animating the troops by his example, drove back the enemy with heavy loss. Bonaparte still persevered in a series of furious assaults against the fortress, which were all most gallantly repelled; and after a protracted siege of sixty days, a last assault was ordered, which being equally unsuccessful with all former attempts, and attended with the loss of some of his bravest warriors, dictated the necessity of an immediate retreat.

8. In the present century a new power arose in the East, namely, that of Mehemet Ali, pasha of Egypt, who, having collected large treasures and a well-disciplined army, openly renounced his allegiance to the Grand Signior. A war took place, in which the hasty levies of Turkey were broken and put to flight by the veteran troops of Egypt; and a series of brilliant successes added Syria, with Palestine, to the pasha's dominion. The people generally were disposed to hail the change of masters with pleasure; and by a well-advised and moderate system of government, Mehemet Ali might have bound them firmly to his person and his cause. But, although in some respects an enlightened man, his notions of government were still Oriental and despotic; and the sort of European discipline and order which he had introduced into his civil and military service, was chiefly valued by him as an instrument in giving the more general and certain effect to his extortions. The Syrians soon discovered that, instead

of being relieved from the exactions of the Turkish government, much heavier burdens were laid upon them. The
conscription, or forcible impressment of young men for the
army, and the disarming of the population, were, however,
the measures which created the most general discontent, and
led to such disturbances and revolts, as encouraged the Porte
in the design which it had always entertained, of reducing
the pasha and recovering the ceded provinces.   Eventually a
Turkish army appeared on the northern frontier of Syria,
and soon came into collision with the Egyptian army under
Ibrahim Pasha, eldest son of Mehemet Ali. The Turks were
completely routed by the Egyptians in the battle of Nezib ; and
the great powers of Europe then deemed it right to interfere,
to prevent Ibrahim from pursuing his victory, and to crush
the ambitious designs of his father.   This was accomplished
chiefly through the brilliant operations of an English fleet,
under Admiral Stopford and Commodore Napier, by which
Acre and other strongholds on the coast were taken for the
Sultan ; and the pasha was at length compelled to evacuate
Syria, and restore it to the dominion of the Porte, which has
since administered the government of the country with greater
mildness, and with less disregard of European influence, than
they formerly manifested.   Jerusalem, which had long been
overlooked in the policy of nations, has recently become of
importance in the eyes of the greatest states in the world.
The five great powers of Europe have established consuls in
the city, and two of them. England and Prussia, have joined
to found there an Anglican Episcopate, in connection with
which a Protestant church has been built upon Mount Zion.